HOMECOMING

The Tauber Institute Series for the Study of European Jewry

SERIES EDITORS: *ChaeRan Y. Freeze, Sylvia Fuks Fried, Jehuda Reinharz, Eugene R. Sheppard*

The Tauber Institute Series is dedicated to publishing compelling and innovative approaches to the study of modern European Jewish history, thought, culture, and society. The series features scholarly works related to the Enlightenment, modern Judaism and the struggle for emancipation, the rise of nationalism and the spread of antisemitism, the Holocaust and its aftermath, as well as the contemporary Jewish experience. The series is published under the auspices of the Tauber Institute for the Study of European Jewry—established by a gift to Brandeis University from Dr. Laszlo N. Tauber—and is supported, in part, by the Tauber Foundation and the Valya and Robert Shapiro Endowment.

For the complete list of books that are available in this series, please see https://brandeisuniversitypress.com/series/tauber

KATEŘINA KRÁLOVÁ, *Homecoming: Holocaust Survivors and Greece, 1941–1946*
AMIT LEVY, *A New Orient: From German Scholarship to Middle Eastern Studies in Israel*
JULIET CAREY and ABIGAIL GREEN, editors, *Jewish Country Houses*
BLANCHE BENDAHAN, YAËLLE AZAGURY and FRAN MALINO, editors, *Mazaltob: A Novel*
*SCOTT URY and GUY MIRON, editors, *Antisemitism and the Politics of History*
JEREMY FOGEL, *Jewish Universalisms: Mendelssohn, Cohen, and Humanity's Highest Good*
STEFAN VOGT, DEREK PENSLAR, and ARIEH SAPOSNIK, editors, *Unacknowledged Kinships: Postcolonial Studies and the Historiography of Zionism*
JOSEPH A. SKLOOT, *First Impressions: Sefer Hasidim and Early Modern Hebrew Printing*
*MARAT GRINBERG, *The Soviet Jewish Bookshelf: Jewish Culture and Identity Between the Lines*
SUSAN MARTHA KAHN, *Canine Pioneer: The Extraordinary Life of Rudolphina Menzel*
ARTHUR GREEN, *Defender of the Faithful: The Life and Thought of Rabbi Levi Yitshak of Berdychiv*
GILAD SHARVIT, *Dynamic Repetition: History and Messianism in Modern Jewish Thought*
CHARLES DELLHEIM, *Belonging and Betrayal: How Jews Made the Art World Modern*
YOSEF HAYIM YERUSHALMI in Conversation with SYLVIE ANNE GOLDBERG, *Transmitting Jewish History*
CEDRIC COHEN-SKALLI, *Don Isaac Abravanel: An Intellectual Biography*
CHAVA TURNIANSKY, *Glikl: Memoirs 1691–1719*
CHAERAN Y. FREEZE, *A Jewish Woman of Distinction: The Life and Diaries of Zinaida Poliakova*
DAN RABINOWITZ, *The Lost Library: The Legacy of Vilna's Strashun Library in the Aftermath of the Holocaust*   *A Sarnat Library Book

HOMECOMING

Holocaust Survivors and Greece, 1941–1946

KATEŘINA KRÁLOVÁ

BRANDEIS UNIVERSITY PRESS

WALTHAM, MASSACHUSETTS

Brandeis University Press
© 2025 by Kateřina Králová
All rights reserved
Manufactured in the United States of America
Designed and composed in Lexicon and Carter Sans
Maps by Philip A. Schwartzberg, Meridian Mapping, Minneapolis, Minnesota.

For permission to reproduce any of the material in this book,
contact Brandeis University Press, 415 South Street, Waltham MA 02453,
or visit brandeisuniversitypress.com

LIBRARY OF CONGRESS CATALOGING-IN-PUBLICATION DATA
available at https://catalog.loc.gov/

cloth ISBN 978-1-68458-252-5
trade paper ISBN 978-1-68458-257-0
e-book ISBN 978-1-68458-253-2

5 4 3 2 1

For my Grandma
1932–2022

Contents

Preface   ix

Abbreviations   xiii

Introduction: Greece, a Home to Return to?   1

CHAPTER ONE
Coming Out of Hiding in Greece   15

CHAPTER TWO
Demobilization and Its Aftermath   47

CHAPTER THREE
Returning from the Camps:
Treblinka, Auschwitz-Birkenau, and Bergen-Belsen   85

CHAPTER FOUR
Returning from Abroad   151

CHAPTER FIVE
After Homecoming   175

Conclusion   189

Acknowledgments   199

Notes   205

Bibliography   267

Index   297

Preface

What I want.
What I am.
What you force me to be is what you are.
For I am you, staring back from a mirror of poverty and despair,
Of revolt and freedom.

GORDON PARKS[1]

MY CHILDHOOD involved a lot of listening and talking about World War II, but whenever I asked about its aftermath, there was silence. My grandmother was a Jewish child survivor. Coming from a mixed marriage, she was seven years old when World War II started. Her mother had been persecuted for racial reasons, her father for political ones. But my grandmother's silence wasn't the only one: in Communist Czechoslovakia—where I grew up—there was another silence, both self-induced and imposed by the omnipresent state, which pressed down on us. The narrated past and the lived present became an integral part of my emotional education.[2]

Both of my grandmother's parents came back home in 1945, but countless others had been murdered. This meant that life for my family (as for so many others who had lost Jewish loved ones) was never anywhere near the same as before. Soon after returning from the camps, my great-grandparents divorced, making the aftermath of World War II the most challenging and simultaneously life-shaping period for my grandmother's "vital memories."[3] The rise to power of the Communist Party and its policies since 1946 were additional factors. In this way another family-history episode began, separate from the Holocaust and their return home.

Try as she might, my grandmother could never erase the painful memories of her family's homecoming. Even through her own marriage and the birth of her daughter (my mother), these events left a lasting imprint. Grandma would not talk much about this, until I showed her a set of old

X · PREFACE

photographs, asking about people and events. In that moment, she spontaneously started narrating her family history from a new perspective that she had carefully concealed from us and the outside world for years. In this sense, I understand "narrating" and "narration" not just as a story but as an infinite process of storytelling, sometimes in seemingly disconnected pieces, illogical chronologies, and broken spatialities, and as a recreation of a bygone world—a world full of fear and pain, but also full of hope and the struggle to survive.

My grandmother's narration was shaped by the Holocaust, which was yet to be called by that name. Still, she has always been with me to narrate her (hi)story, or at least parts of it. Only decades later, once I was equipped for an "honest introspection," did I realize how my grandmother triggered my interest in recovering and confronting those missing pieces. And here they are, narrations of expectations, hopes, and despair connected to survival and homecoming. Transmitted from one country to another—regardless of how they are culturally and historically conceptualized—these stories demonstrate personal ability to withstand and remake a sense of belonging.[4] In a process described by the anthropologist Carol Kidron, my grandmother's and my own universes have become merged, creating "shared understanding" and "overlapping fields of vision."[5]

In 2015, when politicians and the public worldwide started panicking about refugees coming from the war in Syria, xenophobic and hateful slogans pervaded Europe—evoking those widely heard about Jews on the eve of World War II—while policymakers and humanitarian organizations speculated about repatriation. At that point, these individuals and groups were not thinking much about past experiences related to post-conflict returns and migration. For me and many other people, the Syrian refugee crisis has profoundly shaped my *inner* world of research and compelled me to write, inspiring scholarship that translates personal histories and stories that endure through merged biographies. In a way, I had unconsciously transferred questions of my childhood that were reflected in the unsettling present(ness) into a different setting, and this made my questions more real.

To keep reasonable academic distance, I moved, at least mentally, to Greece, a country that in modern times had been part of a different empire than Czechia but which had also cultivated the myth of three hundred years of suffering under foreign domination. Although the postwar regimes established in 1946 were ideologically antipodal, their impact on the populations was in many ways comparable. Both in Greece and in the Czech Republic, 1946 sets a clear line for Holocaust survivors up to which it was still possible to talk about homecoming. From this point on, the decisions of Jewish returnees were no longer determined by the Holocaust, but by new political circumstances that were in some respects analogous: on the one hand, the civil war and anti-Communist repression in Greece, and on the other, the rise of Communism and the persecution of its opponents in Czechia. Both Greece and Czechia were places where Jews did not feel welcome. If we accept this lens of similarity, we create a new map of Europe, breaking out of the dominant Cold War delineation.

Moreover, much like Czechia, Greece is a country that expelled its inhabitants in order to homogenize its population—Greece in the interwar and Czechia in the postwar period. Greece also effectively abandoned marginal religious groups, not by making religion the "opium of the people" (as it was once called under Communism),[6] but by making the Christianity of the Greek Orthodox Church the one and only true faith of Greeks. What's more, both countries share in hegemonic narratives of the past. Greeks have their modern myths and their reputation of being the cradle of Europe (with Thessaloniki as the Jerusalem of the Balkans). Czechs too have "proof" of being the "heart" of Europe.[7] Both are theatres of great philosophy loaded with mythology and mysticism, where everything is holy but nothing is sacred and where history and memory intertwine in thrilling and dangerous ways. Both continue to provide me with great inspiration, bringing me back to childhood and who we are. This existence is enforced by our own choices, which are delineated by historical myths and by past, present, and future opportunities, though stigmatized by a painful past that we all in some way must contend with.

Abbreviations

AIVG — Aid to the Jewish Victims of the War (*Aide aux Israélites Victimes de la Guerre*)

EAM — National Liberation Front (*Ethniko apeleftherotiko metopo*)

EDES — National Republican Greek League (*Ethnikos dimokratikos ellinikos syndesmos*)

EEK — Greek National Socialist Party (*Elliniko ethniko sosialistiko komma*)

ELAS — Greek People's Liberation Army (*Ellinikos laikos apeleutherotikos stratos*)

EME — Jewish Museum of Greece (*Evraiko mousio tis Ellados*)

EPON — United Greek Youth Organization (*Eniea panelladiki organosi neon*)

ICRC — International Committee of the Red Cross

ITS — International Tracing Service

(A)JDC — (Archive of the) American Jewish Joint Distribution Committee

JFCS — Jewish Family and Children's Service Holocaust Center

KIS — Central Board of Jewish Communities (*Kentriko israilitiko symvoulio*)

KKE — Communist Party of Greece (*Kommounistiko komma Elladas*)

OKNE — Greek Communist Youth Federation (*Omospondia kommounistikon neoleon Elladas*)

OPAIE — Organization for the Relief and Rehabilitation of Greek Jews (*Organismos perithalpseos kai apokatastaseos Israiliton Ellados*)

SHAEF — Supreme Headquarters Allied Expeditionary Force

SMIAVE — Association for Jewish Leased Property of Northern Greece (*Syndesmos misthoton israilitikon akiniton voriou Ellados*)

SOE — Special Operations Executive

UNRRA — United Nations Relief and Rehabilitation Administration

USHMM — United States Holocaust Memorial Museum

VHA — Visual History Archive

YDIP — Office for the Disposal of Jewish Property (*Ypiresia diachirisis israilitikon periousion*)

INTRODUCTION
Greece, a Home to Return to?

We must beware.
Lightning strikes at random.
Disasters give no warning.
Be on your guard.

Isaac Matarasso[1]

When Isaac Matarasso (1894–1960), a Jewish physician from Thessaloniki, entitled his manuscript *And Yet Not All of Them Died*,[2] he conveyed two things. He was, on the one hand, indicating satisfaction of sorts that the Nazis had not succeeded in murdering all Jews and, on the other, suggesting fear of a new beginning under circumstances defined largely by the anti-Jewish policies and sentiments of the wartime years. This ambivalence—as with other matters discussed in this book—was by and large internalized by Jewish survivors in Europe who tried to return and reestablish themselves in their homelands after World War II.[3] Much like Matarasso, many Holocaust survivors whom I learnt of in my research expressed a sense of fulfillment that Jews survived as a collective entity despite all the evil. Through their narrations, however, it is clear that for most of them, survival was predominantly an individual rather than communal act.

This book tells the stories of survivors that rarely feature in our discussions of the Holocaust. I study the Jews of Greece who returned home from having been in hiding or living as combatants, deportees, and refugees during World War II.[4] I document how all of them wanted more than anything to survive and come back home. Yet their expectations of homecoming could not be met in the reality of postwar Greece. They faced isolation, anguish, deprivation, and hostility. With this realization, a new era began for them— the life *after* the Holocaust. To them, it was not the liberation of Auschwitz but the return home that marked the end of the Holocaust. It is

1

2 · HOMECOMING

the process and experience of homecoming that this book portrays through their voices. While escaping or avoiding death and then, usually, returning home, they thought less about being Jewish but more about their loved ones, their families, fickle fortune, and remembrance. Though often forced into making a "Sophie's choice," as portrayed in William Styron's 1979 novel about a Holocaust survivor,[5] keeping a sense of belonging and bonds was at moments still essential for personal survival. To survive terror, personal motivation is necessary; what anchors that motivation varies, however, from case to case, as we shall see on the following pages.

World War II, more so perhaps than all preceding wars, affected the lives of everyone who survived, regardless of how they survived. But while non-Jewish soldiers and partisans were hailed as heroes upon returning home, Jewish survivors were traumatized by their own direct experiences and by losing most of their families and friends.[6] As discussed in the groundbreaking volume by David Bankier on European Jews surviving the Holocaust who were returning to their countries of origin, they were rarely welcome.[7] Before the German occupation, there were twenty-four autonomous Jewish Communities of various composition in Greece and two in the Dodecanese. After the war, Greeks were counting the living; Jews all over Europe were counting the dead. For most of them, the next generation would grow up without grandparents, aunts, or uncles. Cheerful gatherings of a once traditionally big Jewish family, as was common in Greece and elsewhere, were no more.

When mapping trajectories of homecoming, it is important to note the factors that made Jewish survival and return to their homes in Greece different from those of many other occupied countries. They include the late start and early end of the occupation (from April 1941 to October 1944); occupation by three armies (Italian, German, and Bulgarian), of which only Germany and Bulgaria were applying the "Final Solution"; the existence of institutions that ostensibly represented the non-Communist Gentile Greeks even during the occupation (the Greek Orthodox Church, the police, and the government); a strong resistance movement controlling most of the Greek mainland in 1944; a strategic position in the historically connected parts of the Mediterranean, near neutral and allied countries (Turkey, Cyprus, Egypt, Palestine); and a high number of people who have been conferred the title the "Righteous among Nations" (357 as of January 2020, compared to, for example, 113 in similarly populated Austria and 119 in Czechia).[8] Despite all this, with no organized evacuation of the Jewish population, only 12 percent of Jews in Greece (12,726 out of 71,611) survived the war. A high percentage of Jewish survivors, though, returned (over 95 percent).[9]

Outlining these particular features helps us understand the character of Greece when considering the Holocaust there. While we may debate which aspects were particular to Greece and what Greece shared with other occupied countries, we cannot avoid the problem that arises whenever we particularize or generalize these phenomena. As we will see throughout the book, survival and return always occurred within a specific regional and cultural context, constituted by the broader web of politics, policies, and personal strategies.

The Hopes and Experiences of Coming Home

What clearly distinguished Jews from many other people living in German-occupied Europe was that they all had to face forced internal or external displacement. Staying put was not a feasible option as it meant deportation, ordered by the Nazi authorities. Consequently, once the war was over, the Jews who survived had to wrestle with the question of "returning" to a world that hardly resembled anything they had known before the war.[10] Physical return could only start when the oppressive regime was defeated and the racial laws, which had been a life-or-death factor up to that point, were abolished. Although personal strategies and return routes were many, spatial trajectories were primarily dictated by the victorious powers, who also provided subsistence for the journey, both at the place of liberation and along the way. But this would not have happened without the personal choices and actions of the survivors. While traveling and when arriving home, Holocaust survivors in Greece and elsewhere were seen as outsiders. Their own networks, if not totally ruined, were considerably narrowed, and their chances of a true return in a social, institutional, and spiritual sense were seriously limited.

Holocaust survivors, however, longed to return home, to the bygone imagined routines, because they sought to reverse the flow of time. This is also what makes this book markedly different from other accounts of the Greek Jewish experience, as my narrative analysis portrays returns by

4 · HOMECOMING

often imaginary routes, which distort chronology into anachronic temporality. Holocaust survivors were trying to return home both in a physical and emotional sense: they wanted to go home to Greece, to their houses, loved ones, friends, and comrades, home to their towns and communities, which at that moment were in fact lost to them socially, institutionally, and even spiritually. Without necessarily being aware of it, this fact irrevocably shaped their relationship to the past, present, and future.

The state of being a survivor, a complex phenomenon involving the ability to survive and recover, is best understood as a combination of one's personal nature and external, environmental factors of the past and present.[11] To cope with their ordeal, to overcome their trauma, and finally to rebuild their lives, strong personal resilience was imperative. Adaptive coping strategies of Holocaust survivors differ from person to person and thus reveal the diversity, indeed irreducibility, of the individual homecoming. Based on clinical observations in 1981, the psychotherapist Yael Danieli and her colleagues delineated three main types of Jewish survivors based on how they had coped with the Holocaust. At one end of the spectrum, they identified the first, least hopeful type as "victims"; at the other end, those with the most inner strength and a strong identity as "fighters." In between, they placed "those who [just] made it."[12] While I return to identity issues later, it is important to stress that "survivors" (or "victims") is used as a general category in much of the Holocaust literature, with "victim" given its ontological meaning of someone who was murdered. This is also why I use the more empowering term "survivor" for all those who returned and tried to reestablish their lives.[13]

Holocaust survivors tried to accommodate their society's various expectations and attitudes, such as patriotism and social stability.[14] Their ultimate aim, to return physically, was at the core of their coping strategies from the beginning of their displacement. This makes return an integral part of survival. For many, return was emotionally or materially impossible. Many had been murdered during the persecution and even after liberation or died before stepping onto Greek soil again. Others, their expectations severely disappointed, took their own lives. But the Jews of Greece who did not survive or decided not to return are not the focus of this book, though they are a subject that still merits comprehensive research.

Drawing on Koselleck's triality of hope, experience, and memory, I paint a picture of tortuous and hopeful returns. Each return, Reinhart Koselleck rightly remarks, ultimately comes with expectations that must be fulfilled in order for personal reconstruction to follow. In his pioneering *Futures Past*, he elaborated on how the "horizon of expectations" was constructed around three concepts, which jointly create our vision of a bright future. Such expectations provide us with a destination that deceptively seems to be within reach in the near future but is in fact fixed in the past. This vision, especially in the dynamic present, often remains unfulfilled.[15]

Jews of Greece: From the Jewish Community to Greek Identity

The historical experience of Jews in the Balkans and Jews of Greece provides to the stories presented in this book important context for their complex and fluid belonging. In the early nineteenth century, when the modern nation-state was in its infancy, the populations of the Ottoman Empire were essentially organized on religious grounds by the *millet* (community) system, within which non-Muslim inhabitants enjoyed near self-governance. This is where the understanding of community as a diverse association of distinctive religious groups within a particular space was established. In postwar Greece, once the rule of law was reintroduced and belonging to an institutionalized "Jewish Community" (with a capital C) was legally guaranteed, Jews and Greek citizens in general distinguished between the Jewish community (with a lowercase *c*) in the sense of interactions shaping their collective identity, and the Jewish Community in the sense of an institution (and thus capitalized).[16]

This brings us to an important point that stimulated the return of Holocaust survivors—namely, their longing for old bonds, inherent in the meaning of the word "community." A community in general, and a religious one in particular, with its established structures and institutional framework, provides meaning and facilitates perception and representation of collective and individual practices. It creates the basis for a collective identity, which tends to be continuously reconstructed by means of intercommunal encounters. These encounters and even confrontations nourished

6 · HOMECOMING

the sense of belonging to the friendly, supportive community survivors imagined.

Since the late nineteenth century, a small number of Jews in the Ottoman Empire had the legal status of foreign nationals, mainly Italian and Spanish. In 1916, based on a bilateral agreement between Greece and Spain, this status, enjoyed by several hundred Spanish subjects, was officially recognized by the Greek authorities.[17] Similarly, Jews of Italian citizenship remained Italian nationals and registered their children accordingly. Additionally, apart from the growing number of Jewish refugees from what became the Soviet Union, about three dozen Jewish citizens of Portugal, Hungary, Switzerland, Egypt, Iran, the United Kingdom, the United States, Argentina, and some from neighboring Turkey and Bulgaria settled in Greece before the outbreak of World War II.[18] Without ever living in the country of their citizenship, some of them were even appointed honorary consuls of their de jure homeland (e.g., of Italy and Spain).[19] Under the civil law, therefore, such Jews were not Greek citizens but foreign nationals.

Whereas Jews on the Ionian Islands and in the cities of Patras, Volos, Athens, and Ioannina mostly belonged to a small but ancient Romaniote community speaking Greek or Italian, an even smaller group consisted of the Ashkenazi Jews whose ancestors had fled to Ottoman territory as early as the end of the fourteenth century. They were escaping anti-Jewish policies and violence in central and eastern Europe. More Ashkenazim arrived in the late nineteenth and the early twentieth century in search of safety after the pogroms in Galicia (1898), Kishinev (1903), and Odessa (1905). Many of them lived temporarily in Ottoman Thessaloniki under the most precarious conditions. Their new life was not always peaceful or free of antisemitism but was nothing like the massacres in their hometowns of eastern Europe.[20]

In the Dodecanese yet to be integrated into the Greek state we know today, the Sephardi community, which had moved to the Ottoman Empire after being expelled from medieval Spain, found itself under Italian rule in 1912. Wherever the Sephardim constituted a majority among the Jewish population, as in Rhodes and Thessaloniki, they absorbed the Romaniote or Ashkenazi settlers. More than just a change in denomination, the shift brought about intensive revisions to their way of life, both in the embracing of Castilian Sephardic traditions and the Judeo-Spanish language, often referred to as Ladino.[21]

The Balkan Wars, World War I, and the Greco-Turkish War and their consequences, such as the population exchange between Greece and Turkey following the Lausanne Treaty of 1923, placed the Jews—especially those of Thessaloniki—in a completely new position within a practically homogeneous Greek Orthodox environment.[22] World War II drastically diminished the presence of non-Greek Orthodox minorities, completing the process of homogenization in Greece. For those Jews who survived, the experience of the Holocaust shaped their understanding of community in more abstract and transnational terms, such as of the Jewish community of Sephardim, or of Holocaust survivors, or of Jews in general.[23]

Although today's Greece often emphasizes its philosemitism, anti-Jewish stereotypes, prejudices, and even violence were not without historical precedent. In the late nineteenth century, anti-Jewish discourse and sentiments were widely present in the press, the church, the security forces, and the judiciary.[24] In Corfu, the disreputable case of an alleged blood libel in 1891 exacerbated longstanding tensions between local Jews and Orthodox Christians.[25] During the Holocaust, Jews of Corfu, Ioannina, and Rhodes and many of those seeking refuge in Athens were tracked down, misled, or betrayed by local Orthodox Greeks. The Jewish community was significantly shaken by this and carried the trauma even after surviving the Holocaust and returning home. Moreover, these circumstances made the Jews of Greece vulnerable to criticism and forced them to prove their Greekness to the majority society.[26] Repeatedly, the Greek citizenship of local Jews was questioned by the Greek Orthodox Church, the mass media, the state authorities, and society in general. The majority assumed that Jews were disloyal to the national struggle of Greeks but also mistrusted their religion.

Since the adoption of the Greek Constitution of 1844, when the idea of modern citizenship was gaining ground in Europe, Greek ethnicity was based on the principle of religious belonging. In addition to making a distinction between nationals and foreigners, the Greek citizenship law of 1927 made a distinction between Greek citizens of the Greek Orthodox Church sharing the Greek language, culture, and history (*homogenis*) and Greek citizens of non-Greek descent, that is, holding beliefs other than Greek Orthodox (*allogenis*). The terms, however, were not defined as strictly legal categories; rather, they are flexible ideological concepts sensitive to the changing political priorities of the time.[27]

8 · HOMECOMING

In 1929, with Greece still under the liberal Venizelos government, any activities or ideas which could have been classified as subversive to the existing political order were criminalized. Leftist workers' unions were officially dissolved, Communists persecuted, and proselytism (in Greece also ascribed to Jews) was prohibited by law.[28] In the 1930s, Jews increasingly sought to attend Greek schools, especially institutions of higher education (partly because of a lack of comparable Jewish institutions in Greece), fostering a Greek national identity, intercommunal mobility, and interreligious encounters. In any case, obligatory Greek-language instruction had been introduced by the state, even at private and religious schools generally teaching in French, German, Italian, English, or Hebrew.[29] Young Jews thus gradually acquired Greek national consciousness and Greek as their first language while the older generation, especially in the Sephardic communities, still adhered to French, Italian, and Judeo-Spanish and their local identities.[30] After the war, returning Jews wholeheartedly embraced Greek national identity. They also did not have a choice as Greece was consolidated as a nation-state that marginalized ethnic minorities and where the Greek Orthodox Church dominated.[31]

WHAT DO WE KNOW ABOUT RECOVERING VOICES OF THE PAST?

My analysis of the homecoming of Holocaust survivors in hiding, on the battlefield, in camps, or in exile follows them from their displacement from about April 1941, the beginning of the Axis occupation, to late February 1946, the moment when the Central Board of Jewish Communities declared the number of survivors in Greece as definite.[32] By bringing closer to the reader their multifold ways of return, I reveal the main impetus behind the return, that is, what constitutes the importance of home, which nurtured their survival.

To reconstruct the circumstances of survival and homecoming, existing research provides only limited insights. Although inspired by the survivor-oriented research of Bea Lewkowicz and Rika Benveniste, my methodology greatly differs from theirs. Lewkowicz, an anthropologist who recorded eyewitness accounts in Thessaloniki in the 1990s, mainly examined how the survivors' identities and memories were shaped over time. Benveniste centers her historical research on the microhistory of her own Thessaloniki Jewish family, not the differences among the Jewish communities of Greece.[33] Rather than focusing on the overemphasized example of Thessaloniki, my approach distinguishes itself by being equally concerned with Jewish survivors and the wider context of Greece, thus encompassing a much broader array of experiences and backgrounds in a seemingly small territory. The universal longing of Holocaust survivors for homecoming has blurred former differences in their local communities and given their Jewish identity a new meaning, which has been neglected in the influential earlier research of Katherine E. Fleming and, more recently, in that of Paris Papamichos Chronakis.[34] I also incorporate Jewish consciousness of the Holocaust into survivors' postwar identity in the years before the establishment of Israel.

My approach is cognizant of the unique role of the Civil War in Greece (1946–1949), which for Greeks created a new layer of memory, covering up the memory of occupation. This pseudo-amnesia in Greek society and most of academia, perhaps together with egotism, nationalism, and a lack of interest, also affected research on the Holocaust and its survivors.[35] Moreover, as Lagrou has suggested regarding other nations of postwar Europe,[36] Greece arguably belonged to those countries where the central discourse was nationalized, and the war experience was long presented (sometimes even up to today) as the collective suffering of Greeks, without differentiating between religious, ethnic, or gender groups. In such an account, the postwar fate of the Jewish communities remained on the margins.

Indeed, in the aftermath it took more than a decade until courtroom testimonies of Holocaust survivors attained a new, indeed groundbreaking, position in the reconstruction of history through the Eichmann trial in 1961. The trial was of little interest to Greeks but aroused unprecedented interest in other countries, along with condemnation of the Nazi perpetrators and compassion for their Jewish victims.[37] Among the more than one hundred witnesses at the trial was one Holocaust survivor from Thessaloniki: Itzchak Nachama, the sole representative of the Jewish community of Greece and the Sephardic Jews. The prosecution used his voice to add potency to the story of the destruction of the Jews, which nevertheless remained dominated by Ashkenazim.[38] Upon closer inspection, it becomes clear that the Eichmann trial largely disregarded the fate of the Jews of Greece and the diversity of the local Jewish communities.[39]

10 · HOMECOMING

Though the attitude of Thessaloniki's Jewish Council was questioned during the Eichmann trial, no light was shed on the Nazi perception of the Greek territories. A lack of understanding of the stance taken by the perpetrators toward Jews living in these areas has lingered to this day. Berlin did not perceive Greece—geographically remote and with no German minority—to be a possible *Lebensraum*, a place suitable for German colonization. At the same time, up to the early 1940s, Germany entertained the possibility of considering Sephardic Jews to be "Aryans of the Mosaic persuasion."[40] This notion was concocted without any reference to another, specific group: the Romaniotes, an ancient Jewish community living in Greece. But the Nazis soon abandoned these ideas, and most of the Jews of Greece, regardless of Sephardic or Romaniote origin, were deported to concentration camps and murdered.

There is a base of sources, though, on which I was able to draw. While excluded from the dominant narratives of the Holocaust and its aftermath— both the Jewish and the non-Jewish—the experiences of the Sephardim, the Romaniotes, and the Ashkenazim of Greece have been kept alive in the diaries, memoirs, autobiographies, document collections, and numerous recordings of audiovisual archives in Greece and beyond, all of which I draw upon here. These include the Visual History Archive (VHA) of the USC Shoah Foundation, the Fortunoff Video Archive for Holocaust Testimonies (HVT), the Yad Vashem Archives, Centropa, the United States Holocaust Memorial Museum (USHMM) Audio Collection, and also locally the Jewish Museum in Athens (EME). My research took advantage of about a thousand of these personal accounts related to Greece, particularly those in the VHA collection. I focus on the accounts reflecting on the act of return from the perspective of the four distinct survivor groups—people who survived in hiding or as combatants (including the demobilized), deportees, and refugees.

In over a decade of listening to survivors' interviews and conducting more than a dozen myself, I have grown close to the people behind these voices and have therefore decided to call them, throughout the book, by their first names. By contrast, when dealing with personal stories only on paper, which applies mostly to the older generation of survivors, I use their surnames. Particularly worthy of mention are the personal accounts of the representatives of the American Jewish Joint Distribution Committee (JDC or Joint, established in 1914 to aid Jews in Ottoman-ruled Palestine) in Greece during this period, especially those of Gaynor Jacobson and the unique interview conducted by a former *New York Times* foreign correspondent, Tad Szulc, who wrote a book on a JDC-organized intelligence network for illegal immigration to Palestine. On twenty-eight tapes (forty-two hours in all), the biographic interview with Jacobson proceeds strictly chronologically and details not only his actions taken in central east Europe to facilitate the survivors' repatriation *aliyah* to the Jewish state but also about four hours of his observations on Greece. When referring to official JDC representatives, I also use their surnames.[41]

The plurality of information in personal accounts (gradually collected by others before me), which I have combined with archival collections, primarily of the Jewish Communities' archives at the USHMM, the Joint Distribution Committee archives (JDCA), and the Arolsen Archives (known also as the International Tracing Service, ITS),[42] has allowed me to cross-check individual stories. I could deal with the selectiveness and contamination of memory but also compare the narratives of different people with similar Holocaust experiences. Much like Tim Cole, I understand eyewitness accounts as deeply personal experiences alluding to unwritten layers of history that are lacking in traditional sources. This lets us go beyond conventional macro-narratives. Written sources can likewise illuminate the unspoken, the forgotten, or the suppressed, providing us with a more accurate time span.[43] Since every source must of course be approached critically, the next, and final, section of my introduction will present the problems that I encountered.

Narrating Survival and Return: Methodological Challenges

The days when first-hand World War II experience was generally shared in Europe because of the many living witnesses to the atrocities are nearly over. But violent conflicts in Iraq, Afghanistan, Syria, and most recently in Ukraine, among others, keep the problems and experiences of surviving and homecoming very relevant. Yet these topics are often discussed by people without a first-hand experience of war who treat refugees as mere items on a list rather than people with their own will, hopes, and expectations. Today it seems as if Europeans have in general forgotten what it felt and looked

12 · HOMECOMING

like when millions of displaced people wandered the continent in 1945.[44] With new wars raging around us, poverty crippling many lives, and with increasingly more displaced people washing up on our shores and crossing our borders, we are forced to seriously reconsider how to share our space and occasionally how to assist in their successful return.

During my decade-long research, I went through about a thousand accounts of Holocaust survivors of different ages, genders, languages, wartime experiences, postwar trajectories of return, and communities to which they belonged, from all across Greece.[45] Within its extensive Holocaust-related collection of interviews, the Visual History Archive of the USC Shoah Foundation, with more than 54,000 unedited recordings, holds about 700 interviews with Holocaust survivors born in the territory of today's Greece and with those who settled there before World War II. Of this total, 396 were conducted with Jews born in Thessaloniki, that is, more than half of the VHA interviews from today's Greece.[46] The necessary limitation of the number of accounts ultimately means that many survival stories do not appear here, or indeed anywhere, in a personal account.

The VHA interviews themselves have some limitations. First, only the younger eyewitnesses lived until the 1990s, so the experiences of older generations are underrepresented, although parents' experiences are often reflected in the accounts.[47] Family members are easy to find since the VHA uses personal data and is equipped with indexing terms and a "people search" to single out those mentioned by the interviewee. This basic personal information then helps to perform a narrower search through the Arolsen Archives, which usually provides less narration but more specific dates and locations of Holocaust survivors' whereabouts at a given historical moment. Originating from World War II, the register has developed into an archive comprising about thirty million documents that finally became easily accessible to researchers through digitalization in 2007.[48]

Second, the time gap between today and the war plays a role in which the postwar experience may have been revised and potentially reshaped by many different circumstances and changing historical contexts.[49] The only solution here is corroboration. As Dalia Ofer, Christopher Browning, François Azouvi, and many others have shown, this is no impediment to its use as historical evidence if cognizant of this limitation.[50] While early collections of interviews with survivors exist (e.g., the Boder's Voices of the Holocaust in

1946), they are not useful for understanding the actual return. This is because of three factors: in the Boder's archive, for example, Jewish survivors from Greece had not yet completed their journey home at that time, the number of interviews was small and only with Thessaloniki residents, and most of the survivors interviewed did not actually return to Greece.[51]

Third, the interviewer's potential objectives had to be taken into consideration. The topic of return was often addressed in the interviews in the VHA collection, but it was sometimes marginalized by interviewers (or interviewees) in comparison to the prewar and wartime period.[52] The narrators entered the semi-public interviews with certain expectations and their own ideas about the process, and with accounts that their potential audience—still in the pre-digital age—might expect: the story of the Holocaust. The interviewers also affected the interviews in other ways. The narrators act differently depending on their personal ties with the person conducting the interview. They are usually more explanatory to foreign interviewers and the third generation of survivors than to the first and second ones, but they also may go into less detail once they talk to Holocaust researchers (like Rena Molho, Vasilis Ritzaleos, Yitzchak Kerem) or to direct Holocaust survivors (like Yvette Leon) unless asked. This creates one more obstacle to a fair assessment of the accounts—namely, a knowledge imposed on the narrator which would otherwise be absent from their thinking.

Fourth, language and regional limitations existed, although the VHA interviews cover thirty-two birthplaces, mostly identical with the prewar Jewish communities of Greece, plus the Diaspora and Israel. The overwhelming majority of the personal accounts, however, are from Jews born in Thessaloniki.[53] The accounts on Greece are in eleven languages, but most of them (273) are in Greek, and more than another hundred are in English (150) or Hebrew (112). Only a few interviews relating to Greece are in other languages (including Judeo-Spanish). Not only the language but also its translation of memory, by the interviewer or the narrator, is of utmost importance for shaping and transmitting experience.[54] Finally, the VHA interviews clearly show that to consider diverse languages is epistemologically important. Personal accounts given by survivors in other parts of the world are far more critical of Greece. Omitting them would most probably leave us with one-sided narratives reflecting well-established Greek national myths.

CHAPTER ONE

COMING OUT OF HIDING IN GREECE

"Nobody knew it," recounts Rachel Serror half a century later, visibly ill at ease with her experience of the liberation day after four years of war. "We found out when the people started screaming in the streets. 'The war, they're gone, the Germans, they are gone, they are gone....' And the Greek flags. And everything was just—I don't know, I cannot explain it—there was just going...the joy [...] I was just walking in the streets and I wanted to find out when my people would come, who wanted to come."[1]

Rachel, one of the few Jews who, on October 30, 1944, witnessed the liberation of Thessaloniki, was young, single, and with a good command of Greek (her mother tongue was Judeo-Spanish). She had only just returned from a nearby hiding place, which was provided to her by a Greek Orthodox family. Nostalgic for the past and dreaming of the future, she desperately expected the return of her loved ones, who had been deported to Auschwitz.

During the German occupation, the Jews who remained in Greece lived under assumed names, hiding in the cities or as resistance fighters in the mountains, changing locations, shelters, acquaintances, and protectors. They embraced the moment of regained freedom in autumn 1944 with mixed feelings. Many Jews had done forced labor or had been imprisoned, and all Jews had experienced extreme suffering, persecution, and deprivation. First, living through the famine of 1941–42, they again stared death in the eye during the deportations of 1943 and 1944. Their resilience was shattered and they could certainly not have envisioned the evil of the extermination camps. Still, those in hiding were unable to imagine or fully appreciate the fate of others who were deported or forced into slave labor.

16 · HOMECOMING

Some Jews were betrayed; some survived with the help of partisans and aid givers or joined the armed resistance.[2] Some Jewish children, often still babies, were entrusted to non-Jews after their families had decided, with heavy hearts but sensibly, to leave them behind rather than take them on the journey to what, before the war, used to be Poland.[3] What counted most was their adaptation—or adaptability—in Greek society. Unlike Rachel Serror, most Sephardic Jews of adult age in Thessaloniki and elsewhere had not mastered Greek, a language introduced into schools only in the interwar, after their territorial annexation by Greece. It is hardly surprising, then, that none of the forty-six VHA interviews of Jews born in Rhodes (acquired by Greece in 1947) is in Greek, not even the one recorded in Greece. Though internally displaced Jews decided to emigrate later in their lives, their longing for the Jewish community they had lost in Greece often went hand in hand with their nostalgia for Greece. Those few who had remained in the country witnessed the birth of a new and undeniably different postwar Jewish community.

In the autumn of 1944, as soon as the war in Greece had ended, the Jews displaced within Greece started coming out of hiding to return to their homes. This rudimentary statement, however, requires elaboration: Greeks may have been celebrating the end of the war as best as they could, but few of them considered the fact that practically all the Jews were still missing. At that point, the general public knew almost nothing about the vast suffering and systematic murder of the Jews. At best, the Greeks remained indifferent to Jewish returnees.[4] Accounts given by Holocaust survivors who had been internally displaced strongly suggest that they, too, were lacking information and unwilling to believe the magnitude of the Holocaust. In Zakynthos, the only Greek island with a Jewish community that was spared deportation, Erkanas Tzezanas and his family could not rejoice with their Greek compatriots, which was a reason for their othering. "I think a pastor knocked on the door and he said, 'Are you sad that the Germans left that you don't go out to celebrate with us?'" But Erkanas and others had felt "so tyrannized that [they] only wanted to sleep, nothing else."[5]

After lengthy physical and psychological deprivation, even for those in hiding, returning to normal could not be taken for granted. Lili Pardo's father, for example, became paralyzed when he suddenly started walking and moving around after a year in hiding in Thessaloniki. Paulette

Mourtzoukou points out that she lost the ability to play with other children after having been surrounded for nearly a year exclusively by adults in their Athens hiding place.[6] Overcoming mental and physical fatigue would become a lifelong quest for many Holocaust survivors, often with mixed results.

Once the occupation was over, internally displaced Jews were impatiently waiting for their loved ones, but the date of return depended on their whereabouts during the war and how they were able to return. No survivor had an easy journey getting home, even within Greece. Roads, bridges, and railways had essentially ceased to exist. Of the 220 prewar locomotives of the Greek state railways, only fifteen remained intact after the war. The number of private cars, taxis, and trucks decreased by more than half; 80 percent of all buses had been destroyed.[7]

When he took up the job of JDC country director in postwar Greece, Gaynor I. Jacobson remarked in spring 1945 that "it was quite a job to cover Greece because due to the war and the Civil War a good many of the bridges were out." Apart from Italy, Greece was at that point the only liberated country in which the JDC had relaunched its activities providing aid to the Holocaust survivors. But it was impossible, even for the JDC, to support all the Jewish Communities in Greece equally. Based in Athens, Jacobson described how transportation to outlying Communities looked at that time: "There were places it was very difficult to go to even with a Jeep. So at some of the places you got on a transport ship and you went from harbor to harbor, you got off and you got the next one because of the difficulties of transportation."[8] Needless to say, not all the Jewish Communities in Greece were in harbor towns.

The most reliable, affordable, and usually only way for Jewish returnees to get home from hiding was therefore a long and exhausting walk.[9] Traveling home in Greece itself could take about a month, as it did for the Tampach family, who had survived in the mountains of the Peloponnese.[10] Leon Batis, the first camp survivor to return from Auschwitz to Greece, made his self-guided return, traversing Europe, in about two months.[11] In general, the physical return and, if possible, pulling oneself together mentally usually took from about autumn 1944 to spring 1946.

After liberation most Jewish survivors in Europe considered the prewar idea of assimilation to have been misguided. Their previously tepid support for the Zionists, who had insisted that the only right way forward was to create a Jewish state, which would guarantee their fundamental rights and liberties, gained momentum. Still, many internally displaced survivors decided to try once more and rebuild their lives in their country of origin. The reasons for this were plain. First, after experiencing displacement, Holocaust survivors often idealized their home. If they had been aided by local non-Jews during the persecution, once being confronted with the extent of the genocide, their loyalties shifted to those helpers. They were hoping to return to a familiar environment, regain their property, and perhaps improve the prospects of other family members and help them put down roots after their return. Seeking a "return to normal" in a seemingly familiar place was for many a natural and rational act. They made the decision to return, either finding their way alone or assisted by liberation forces and international organizations. All returnees, however, soon realized that the home they had known no longer existed after liberation.[12]

The timing of return was crucial both in the formal and the informal reconstruction of the postwar Jewish community in Greece, but the state of the Community into which they were about to return greatly differed from what had been there before. Whereas in the former German and Bulgarian zones the destruction of the Jews had been nearly total, in places originally occupied by Italy it was not unusual that whole Jewish families had survived in hiding. To achieve this, their human, social, and material capital were of utmost importance in obtaining credible false identities, effective hiding places, and blending in with the local Greek population whenever necessary, until eventually returning home.

Jews hidden in their immediate surroundings mostly returned at the earliest opportunity, with those displaced elsewhere in Greece close behind. Obviously, with occupation units leaving Greece one after another and the country in ruins in autumn 1944, the actual homecoming was physically, socially, and emotionally almost impossible. Since the greatest number of Jews found refuge in the capital, I open the story with Athens. I then move on to Thessaloniki, which had by far the largest and most influential prewar Jewish community but failed to protect its members effectively. Before discussing the Jewish communities, however, we need to look at how Holocaust survivors in Greece understood their liberation.

LIBERATION

Although most German troops had already withdrawn from the Peloponnese in August, the liberation of Greece is commonly dated a full two months later, on October 12, 1944, when the last German soldiers took down the Nazi swastika flying over the Acropolis and left Athens.[13] That same day, British, American, and Greek flags were fluttering in the streets of the capital, stores were closed, and church bells rang. Schoolgirls, flowers in hand, stood along the main avenue to welcome the liberators. Virtually the entire city and most of the country was under the control of leftist resistance forces, who now celebrated together with Greek civilians, accompanied even by members of the national security forces. At noon, a parade of the Greek People's Liberation Army (ELAS) in British uniform was held, without them officially taking power in Greece. A week later, however, skirmishes between the very same units and the British forces raged throughout Athens.[14]

With a delay of only a few days, the Greek government-in-exile arrived in Athens on October 17, 1944, supported by about thirteen thousand British soldiers.[15] Regarding the Bulgarian zone in eastern Macedonia and Thrace, the occupation was over at the end of October 1944. In Northern Greece, German forces, accompanied by Greek collaborators who had joined the Wehrmacht on its retreat to Germany, crossed the borders in early November 1944, three weeks after the installation of the Greek government in Athens. The Government of National Unity, as the ruling coalition was called, brought together representatives of the political right and left, including the EAM-ELAS. Salonika, a Jewish city, had altogether disappeared; at the end of the war, it became Thessaloniki, Greek. From Crete, Rhodes, and other Aegean Islands, the last German garrisons were evacuated only after the unconditional surrender of Germany in May 1945. Thus, there was hardly a singular moment of liberation, nor was there one clearly identifiable liberator.

Apart from some common denominators of Holocaust survival in hiding, such as flexibility, a readiness to disobey, and a good deal of luck,[16] in Greece the factors generally differed depending on the zone of occupation (with particularly exceptional conditions in Thessaloniki and Athens), the attitudes of local leaders, and the timing of occupation and liberation. The Jews of Thessaloniki, feeling somehow protected by their great number and the influence they used to have in the city, had been taken by surprise by the anti-Jewish measures introduced in summer 1942. Their survival rate was woefully low, but the expulsion served as a warning to other Communities when, shortly afterwards, they too were confronted with similar measures. Nonetheless, this awareness could not prevent similarly timed deportations of Communities trapped in the territories annexed by Bulgaria or in most of the German zone. In prewar Athens, the Jews had been a small, well-integrated community. Moreover, the resistance movement was already well developed and effective locally and worked with several Jewish representatives when the German occupation started in autumn 1943. Once the Germans had left, the Jews hiding in Athens were the first to establish efficient Community leadership, communicate with the Greek state, and distribute international humanitarian aid.

Throughout the war, finding a hiding place in Greece was mostly achieved by individuals. It required sources of reliable information, a high degree of integration with the Greek population, personal or occupational networks, complex arrangements for assumed identities, fluency in Greek—at least for breadwinners—and sufficient funds. Citizenship of a neutral country or one friendly to Germany, like Spain and Portugal, was an indisputable advantage. Yet it could lead to a false sense of security with devastating consequences. In smaller Jewish Communities, especially in the Italian zone, informed at least a bit in advance of the imminent deportations, whole families and groups of dozens of Jews, often inspired by the Community leaders, could leave their vulnerable place and seek safety near their hometowns. By no means did this mean that the Community would continue to exist long after liberation.

For many Jews, who generally regarded their families as indivisible, it was an unwritten rule not to leave them. This rule, however, could be broken if it meant increasing one's chances of surviving in hiding. After months of being displaced, local Holocaust survivors were taken by surprise by the end of the war. Ironically, to this day, the survivors who witnessed the German withdrawal from Greece after coming out of hiding are unable to clearly identify the liberators. This applies in particular to the Jews who had hidden in big cities, and it signals their political leanings at the time, which, with the looming civil war, became crucial for rebuilding personal lives.

At the moment of liberation, many Jews felt overwhelmed, lost, confused, or unaware of what was going on. While some of them years later plainly stated that the Germans were simply gone, others provided elaborate details about the British or partisan liberation of Greece. Paulette Mourzoukou, the daughter of the most influential industrialist in Volos and the future wife of a partisan—whom she later joined in the United States, where he had been living since 1946—inaccurately ascribes the liberation she experienced in Athens to both the British and the Soviets: "The Germans left because the Russians were coming. I think it was the British and the Russians. I remember pictures on Russian posters, that there were Russians with the flag with an ax [*sic*] and sickle and the Russians were like a bear. Although we couldn't go out, I think outside our home there was a wall. What is this? It's the Russians coming and the Germans are afraid of that and we will soon be liberated."[17]

In Thessaloniki, Rudolf Amariglio, witnessing the events as a child survivor of a mixed marriage, describes with great enthusiasm the rule of the common people (*laokratia*) under the aegis of the left-wing resistance. Rachel Serror—who soon after the war met the love of her life, a British Army officer called George Curtis—is absolutely sure that it was the British who had come and liberated her.[18] While Soviet units never crossed the borders to liberate Greece, British troops and Greek resistance units (both of which included Jews) were rushing into Greek towns nearly at the same time as the German retreat.

Liberation can, generally speaking, hardly be reduced to the moment when the aggressors are retreating or being driven out. In contrast to a personal experience of liberation, it is the collective dimension of being liberated, of family members and friends in other places, like concentration camps or refugee camps, which plays the most essential role. What Dan Stone says about the liberation of camp prisoners applies equally to Greece, where liberation too was a process, sometimes exceedingly long.[19] The moment the occupiers withdrew from Greece thus represents only a fraction of homecoming—the full structural, social, and emotional return—in space and in time.

ATHENS

In the Greek capital, unlike in other parts of the country, the prewar Jewish community consisted predominantly of foreign and local newcomers seeking employment in an expanding city rather than hoping to find a flourishing

22 · HOMECOMING

Jewish culture.[20] Their transition to Athens was hardly smooth, since Greek society was certainly not immune to antisemitism. While the archetypal image of the Jew as the devil and the "Christ-killer" still prevailed in the countryside, where few Jews lived, in the cities a new antisemitism, based on class and race, appeared beside traditional religious discrimination.[21]

After five months of being at war with Italy, the German blitzkrieg launched on April 6, 1941, divided Greece into three zones and installed a Greek puppet government in Athens. The Germans initially administered only the most strategic regions, while Bulgaria received coveted southeast Macedonia and coastal Thrace, with Italy taking the rest. Only after the capitulation of Rome in early September 1943 did the former Italian zone with Athens and the Dodecanese come under the Reich control. By then, the Jewish population of Athens had doubled with the influx of refugees from the two other zones where the chances of hiding were almost nil.[22]

Already on Wednesday, October 11, 1944, a day before the German troops left Athens for good, the Zionist leader Asher Moissis (1899–1975), himself one of the Thessaloniki refugees to Athens, cautiously ventured out to explore the streets. His aim was to discuss the future of the community with Jewish friends, survivors hiding in the capital. Originally from Trikala and an Athens law school alumnus, Moissis was a native speaker of Greek and had extensive networks in the capital. After about a year of hiding on the outskirts of Athens with his family of five (including his elderly mother, Myriam), he was now savoring his first taste of regained freedom.[23]

The next day, a meeting was held at the synagogue on Melidoni Street, the same spot where the Jews had been lured to register in March 1944 for deportation to German camps. This gathering of Jews who had managed to survive hidden in the capital or nearby was headed by Asher Moissis, the ex-president of the Jewish Community in Thessaloniki, and Elias Barzilai (1891–1979), the Chief Rabbi of Athens.[24] Despite the festive mood, the sight of the crowd was by no means comforting. "We all looked like storm-tossed castaways," said Moissis, describing the pitiful assemblage. "Some were all skin and bones from hunger; others, on the contrary, were swollen from the lack of vitamins, but all were shabby and with an appearance that depicted our sadness and our anguish. We conducted the first religious ceremony and sounded the shofar to invite to join us those of our brethren who had been displaced by our ruthless persecutors and whose tragic fortune we did not yet know."[25]

To become the first postwar president of the Central Board of Jewish Communities (*Kentriko Israilitiko Symvoulio*: KIS) and later honorary consular official of Israel in Athens, Moissis had moved with his family to the capital at the end of the Greco-Italian War, in 1941, when the persecution of the Jews of Greece was no longer just an evil premonition but a real and imminent threat. Moissis certainly had little reason to trust the German invaders after his imprisonment and interrogation back in Thessaloniki.[26] Neither did the other 3,500 Jewish refugees from the German and Bulgarian occupation zones, when they left for Italian-controlled Athens. The Greek capital promised safe haven and for some provided a better opportunity for possible escape to the Middle East.

Still, during the German occupation about two hundred Jews in Athens were denounced, identified, and deported to camps. Among them Yomtov Yakoel (1899–1944), a member of the Jewish elite in Greece, an attorney, and a fervent Zionist. A longtime legal adviser to the Jewish Community in Thessaloniki, he was also originally from Trikala and had escaped to Athens only during the deportations in July 1943. After being betrayed, he was deported to Auschwitz together with his wife and children in April 1944. None of them survived. Moissis, his childhood friend, a fellow student, and business partner, later used the wartime diary that Yakoel had drafted in hiding as part of his written testimony against Eichmann in 1961.[27]

Throughout their time in hiding, Moissis and Yakoel maintained personal links not only with international Zionist organizations and Greek Jews in Palestine but also with the Greek Orthodox Archbishop and the partisan movement. Formed in September 1941, the National Liberation Front (EAM), pillar of the leftist resistance in Greece, which was soon operating all over the mainland, became a particularly annoying thorn in the side of the Germans.[28] In Athens, an active group of Jewish leaders in hiding was informally established and became involved in organizing operations to rescue the Jews of Greece. Since these operations were top secret and were in the gravest danger of being detected, the leaders naturally left little trace of their actions. In 1948, the Greek-Canadian historian Leften Stavrianos wrote, without mentioning any names, about the wartime efforts to rescue the Jews in Athens. These efforts were overseen by the "Jewish Sector," close to the EAM resistance, which, he said, had already assisted in providing Jewish relief in Thessaloniki.[29]

24 · HOMECOMING

According to other sources, an organization called the Jewish Secret Rescue Committee, consisting of five to nine members, was created in Athens and ceased its activities after rescuing the Chief Rabbi in Athens. Those involved in the mission were supposedly Moissis and Yakoel, plus one more lawyer and the active EAM member Daniel Alchanatis, the Sephardic scholar Josef Nehama, the prominent banker Pepo Benousigiio, and his associate Robert Raphael, all former representatives of the Jewish Community in Thessaloniki who found hiding places in Athens. The survivors of that group became leaders of the Jewish Community in postwar Greece. But whereas these efforts saved Moissis and the others, the very same actions led to Yakoel's denunciation and death.[30]

Not just political but also spiritual leaders of the Jews in Greece rightly felt protected in the capital and dared to act against German orders. Born in Thessaloniki and educated at the Hebrew University of Jerusalem, Elias Barzilai became the Chief Rabbi of Athens in 1936. He features here as another link between the prewar and postwar Jewish Community. After the capitulation of Italy in September 1943, when German forces proceeded with their deportation plans in the formerly Italian zone, Jürgen Stroop, the SS officer who led the suppression of the Warsaw Ghetto Uprising, took on the Jews of Athens. Rabbi Barzilai was ordered to present the Germans with a list of all Athen's Jews, including details about their property. Instead of obeying, he and his family were smuggled into EAM-held territory. Other Community members followed his example.[31] Rabbi Barzilai was quick to lead the Jewish spiritual recovery in Greece in the aftermath. As is clear from his postwar statements, he felt deeply indebted to the resistance for their wartime assistance. Nevertheless, this made him suspect in the eyes of the anti-Communist elites ruling Greece from December 1944 on. In Jerusalem in early 1945, the Sephardic chief rabbi, Ben-Zion Uziel, pleaded to the JDC in Greece to help Barzilai, who was "now without position, because of relations with partisans, and in dire hardship." According to Uziel, it was "most vital to help him to reach Palestine and to assist him meanwhile."[32]

Representatives of the public sphere, such as the prominent journalist Sam Modiano (1895–1979), who had worked for the Jewish daily *Le Progrès* in Thessaloniki and for Reuters since 1938, also made it to Athens during the occupation. He reacquired Italian citizenship in wartime Thessaloniki thanks to the Italian consulate. Although Modiano and his wife were from wealthy and influential Jewish families, most of their relatives had been deported to concentration camps. After the war, their social position deteriorated significantly. The only accommodations they could find in Athens when coming out of hiding were in shabby hotels lacking basic amenities. For returning survivors, reestablishing prewar living standards was often blocked by intruders who had occupied Jewish housing. Modiano was fortunate. He was soon offered a full-time position at Reuters in Athens and could thus look after his family unlike others without aiming to return to Thessaloniki. Documents of the JDC mention him as a Central Board member of the Location Committee in 1945.[33]

Another key figure of the postwar Jewish establishment who spent the war in Athens was Kanaris Konstantinis (1889–1977). Originally from Zakynthos, he was educated in Greek schools and employed by the state as Inspector General in the Greek Post, Telephone and Telegraph Service. During the war, he arranged a hiding place in Athens for his family. Konstantinis, a well-known personality, and his Sephardic wife, who spoke Greek with some difficulty, feared being denounced and hardly ever left their hiding place. Their son Moisis (1932–2018), less suspicious to the authorities at his age, was assigned the task of making arrangements outside, in normal circumstances no business for a child.[34] Their hiding places were revealed several times, and so the Konstantinis family had to move again and again, always paying a considerable sum. Once liberated, they were among the lucky few to immediately get back to their original house in Athens. Finding none of their belongings, with the furnishings long gone, they first had to sleep on the floor without blankets, which did not feel like homecoming.

Soon after the war, Kanaris Konstantinis returned to his prewar job and also served as the head of the Central Board of Jewish Communities, an umbrella organization established by law in mid-1945 in Athens,[35] somewhat to the disapproval of the Athens-based Thessalonican faction. It was the JDC country director for Greece, Gaynor Jacobson, who tried to reconcile the internal disputes over the "self-chosen representatives on the Central Board."[36] When Konstantinis's son Moisis repeatedly held the office until 2016, it made him the last Holocaust survivor worldwide to head a Central Board of Jewish Communities, speaking volumes about how this elite of survivors managed to monopolize key positions for seven decades after the war.

26 · HOMECOMING

Conditions in Athens were certainly quite different from those in the rest of Greece, and not only because Athens was the capital. Alfred Cohen, who was based in Egypt with the Greek government-in-exile and, according to Rabbi Molho, spoke in favor of the Jewish Committee,[37] reported that the number of Jews in Athens at the time of the Italian surrender (September 1943) was about eight thousand (half of whom were refugees from Macedonia, particularly Thessaloniki). Though the Jewish residents of Athens could find hiding places more easily thanks to their local network, they were justifiably more afraid than nonresidents of being blackmailed. The refugees who were not well known in the city could benefit from greater anonymity, but their networks were usually smaller. In addition, finding funds to live on was difficult since the Germans had already confiscated the property of most Jews in the German zone. By the summer of 1944, the number of Jews hiding in Athens dropped to five thousand. About two thousand had registered with the Gestapo and had been deported to concentration camps, about four hundred had managed to escape to Palestine and Egypt, and others found hideouts with the help of the EAM-ELAS outside Athens.[38]

Consequently, at the end of May 1945, before the return of most camp survivors, a list of Jews in Greece, published by the JDC in Athens, had only 3,300 names. After dropping their false identities, these internally displaced Jews registered with the Community and were ready to cooperate with the postwar authorities in the capital. As a JDC document states, considerable funds had been allocated to facilitate the return to their town, Community, and religious practices, but most of the money never left Athens: "During the first five months of 1945 [alone] the Joint Distribution Committee appropriated $500,000 for the relief and rehabilitation of the Greek Jewish community."[39] The list, in alphabetical order, is preserved only up to the letter O, making it impossible to identify all the originally listed survivors. Quite tellingly, the Moissis network of Community representatives, for example, is listed as residents of Athens, thus signaling a clear intention to remain in the capital. At the same time, perhaps to give the impression of aiming for regional balance, Moissis and Raphael appear on the Central Board as representatives of the Jewish Communities of Trikala and Thessaloniki respectively.[40]

At the end of the war, a handful of the Jews in Greece had not yet been released from the Chaidari (Haidari) concentration camp on the outskirts of Athens, the only camp in Greece still holding Jewish internees. Established as a military prison under the rule of the Greek authoritarian leader Ioannis Metaxas in late 1930s, with just one building, the camp resembled a construction site. During the German occupation, in addition to a number of Jewish prisoners, the camp held resistance fighters and Greeks accused of anti-German activities. After the capitulation of Rome in 1943, many Italian POWs ended up there.[41] Although the number of Jews who survived Chaidari is disputed, diverse camp accounts suggest these were foreign nationals of neutral countries. Though nearly all their kin had been deported from Chaidari to Auschwitz, or Bergen-Belsen (155 Spanish and 19 Portuguese citizens), in 1944, some were left behind, most probably thanks to the intervention of Sebastián de Romero Radigales (1882–1970), the Spanish consul in Greece. In 2014, while recognizing Radigales as one of the Righteous Among the Nations, the Holocaust remembrance center Yad Vashem stated that in his actions Radigales had gone beyond his diplomatic duties and had not hesitated to help Jews, even against his government's policies.[42]

Once the Germans had left Athens, Jewish prisoners were set free and, in some cases, met with other family members who had remained in hiding, as was the case of Erietti Molcho, the mother of Yvonni Molho Kapoyanno.[43] Being the citizen (even fictionally) of neutral countries or of countries friendly to Germany was an important factor for potential survival, especially if the diplomatic representatives of those countries were supportive in this regard.[44] Nevertheless, as long as these Holocaust survivors decided to retain their foreign citizenship, their struggle for an acceptable place in Greek society would continue for decades to come.

THESSALONIKI

In Thessaloniki and the rest of what had been the German zone from the beginning of the occupation, few Jews survived by hiding in the city or escaping to partisan-controlled territories. The process of deportations was swift, and these people could have had little inkling of what was going to happen to them in spring 1943.[45] Because most of the 56,500 Thessalonican Jews had been deported, the first Community gathering since the occupation in 1944 numbered only 173 people of the several hundred who had been internally displaced. While some of its prewar representatives were active in

28 · HOMECOMING

Athens, at that point with little prospect of returning to their hometowns, a new Community board started to take shape from the ranks of returnees mostly associated with the resistance. Their appearance and the immediate aftermath in the city is well illustrated by a remark made by Michael Molho, the only rabbi in the city at its liberation:

> On December 1, 1944, some young people broke open the rusty doors of the Monastir Synagogue. This synagogue [one of the thirty-five from before the war][46] was used by the International Red Cross as a base camp, and had therefore escaped the Nazis' fury of destruction. [...] The partisans had not broken themselves of old habits. Within the sacred precinct, a few machine guns reflected the faint rays of the sun that the dirty windows had let in.[47]

The implementation of anti-Jewish measures in Thessaloniki and the German-occupied zone of Greece as a whole began by mid-1942, when the German authorities, with the cooperation of locals, gradually began to confiscate Jewish property.[48] The only Jews spared were those married to non-Jews. Public action against Jewish Greeks started in Thessaloniki in June 1942, after the fear of famine in the winter of 1941–42, haunting even the German occupiers, had passed, with a directive on the forced labor of the male Jewish population. On July 11, 1942, more than 9,000 men signed up; 5,500 of them were subsequently deported to temporary forced labor camps nearby in order to be put to work for the Reich.[49] This brutal act, which the Greek anthropologist Pothiti Hantzaroula marks in her work as the milestone of traumatic Jewish memory in Greece,[50] motivated at least some Jews to search for hiding places.

Analogous to "Aryanization" elsewhere in Europe, the Office for the Disposal of Jewish Property (YDIP) was established in Thessaloniki on German orders on March 8, 1943. Headed by a Greek board of directors and backed by local elites, the YDIP was to deal with all Jewish property. Before being deported, the Jews of Thessaloniki were thus left empty-handed, with no financial means to counter the deportation orders. A similar maneuver was later used in the former Italian zone after Rome surrendered.[51] Be it merchants, intellectuals or university students, young or middle-aged individuals, or whole families, many of them hoped that Athens would be under a less racist regime and provide easier contact with Gentiles and greater anonymity. Due to impoverishment and anti-Jewish restrictions, however, Athens as a temporary safe haven was beyond their reach. Sometimes, as with Moise Saltiel's family, the rescue mission spiraled out of control. Though the father and the child were not captured, the mother's true identity was revealed, and she was arrested. Back in Thessaloniki, Olga Saltiel and her parents were made examples of and executed for disobeying the ordered measures. As they had intended, the Germans thus amplified the atmosphere of fear and deterred other Jews from escaping.[52] Throughout the occupation, fifty-eight Jews were put to death by firing squad in Thessaloniki; the last group execution of Jewish prisoners was in the Pavlos Melas prison courtyard on September 8, 1944, less than two months before the German withdrawal.[53]

The Jewish students who had escaped Thessaloniki to Athens, where they had attended university together with non-Jews, stood a good chance of survival in a familiar environment. During the occupation, Jewish youngsters often urged their families to join them on the journey to the Italian zone and in this way stand at least some chance of survival. For the rest of his life, Andreas Seficha (1929–2007), for example, was proud of having made his way to the capital alone and of the fact that his family had followed him. The family took several different routes to escape from Thessaloniki and reached Athens during the occupation. Andreas travelled by train. Mois Matalon, his grandfather, a Greek-speaking gynecologist who had graduated from university in Athens, travelled there by boat together with his wife and three adult daughters accompanied by their husbands and children. René Amaratzi, Matalon's youngest daughter, together with her son and husband, already awaited them in the capital. Soon the family members each went their own way to different hideouts. The four granddaughters of Mois Matalon survived the war in Athens without their parents. The Amaratzi family survived there hiding all together. Andreas Seficha and his parents went with his grandparents to the countryside. To hide a grandmother who spoke only broken Greek was a challenge, so she occasionally pretended to be deaf and unable to speak. But the hiding places of two of Matalon's daughters and their husbands were discovered, and all of them were deported to Auschwitz.[54]

The internally displaced Matalon family reunited in postwar Athens to set out for Thessaloniki after the events of December 1944 which

30 · HOMECOMING

unleashed the battle of Athens. The two adult daughters returned from the camps in 1945 after almost unimaginable hardship. Their lives would never be the same again. Struggling with trauma, fighting for the return of their stolen property, trying to reestablish the bond between deported mothers and daughters in hiding, and forever marked by irreplaceable loss in the Matalon family, the Amaratzis soon left Greece for good. Andreas Seficha, nevertheless, returning to his hometown after graduating from university in Switzerland, confirmed his dedication to the Jewish Community of Thessaloniki, and served as the Community president from 1993 to 2001.

Just one Jewish family managed to hide together right in Thessaloniki for the rest of the occupation. During the deportations, Haim Pardo, his wife, and three school-age daughters were offered a hiding place by Pardo's physician. Their escape from the ghetto after the roundups caused much trouble to the Community, since Pardo was listed as an influential member, among the first to be punished if a Jew tried to flee. Rozina, Pardo's middle daughter, who wrote her diary in hiding when she was eleven (published in Greek in 1999), is often referred to as the Greek Anne Frank. Unlike the Franks in the Netherlands, Rozina and her family were lucky not to be discovered. Until the liberation, the Pardos remained in the house of their rescuers, who in the aftermath were richly rewarded for their kindness and courage. From the hideout, they observed the Royal Air Force bombardment of Thessaloniki in 1944 and the German withdrawal. After that, they abruptly left with the same suitcases they had brought into hiding eighteen months before, to find temporary shelter at their neighbors, next to the Pardos' prewar apartment. Rozina recalls in her diary how the family ate their first meal just on a suitcase, the prewar elegance long gone. Given the poor health of Haim Pardo and, later, of his eldest daughter, Lili (fifteen), which had been the initial reason for moving to Athens after the war, their postwar recovery was in every sense a long process.[55]

Regardless of how hampered, family cohesion was a crucial factor for the Serrors, but in the opposite sense from how it was for the Pardos. Only one family member had seized the opportunity to escape the ghetto; all the others were resolute about staying together at the time of deportation to Auschwitz. Rachel Serror was twenty when she found shelter with the help of a non-Jewish friend and later moved to the family of a Greek Orthodox priest. After spending most of the war in Thessaloniki, she was liberated after returning from her hiding place in a village on its outskirts. The liberation took her by surprise, but most of all she was incapable of processing the terrible fate of her family. Only her younger sister, Lola, survived the camps and death marches, but she never returned to Greece. Rachel, who kept her cover name Maria, later joined her in Australia, where they both married and became mothers. The paintings of Thessaloniki in Maria's living room are daily reminders of her beloved hometown in Greece.[56]

In other instances, families made the difficult decision to split up and go into hiding separately before the deportations started. Loykia Koen, almost an adult, ended up in the nearby village of Aggelochori with a family acquaintance, Panagiotis Kazantzidis. He was connected to the National Republican Greek League (EDES), an anti-Communist resistance organization competing with the EAM resistance; EDES had been established in September 1941 and operated in Greece until the end of the war. Loykia's father left for the mountains while her mother and sister remained hidden in Naousa. Both women were denounced by Greeks collaborators and deported to Auschwitz.[57] The most infamous armed collaboration unites in Greece, Security Battalions, a voluntary corps nominally subordinate to the Greek Ministry of the Interior, were de facto under the command of the Sicherheitsdienst (SS and Nazi Party intelligence service). In summer 1944, the armed militias in Greece totaled seventeen thousand men, operating both against the Jews and the resistance.[58]

After Panagiotis's two brothers had been killed by the leftist partisans, he began to fear being next. At the end of the war, Panagiotis decided it would be safer to return to Thessaloniki. Loykia recalls how her guardian was the first to show her the face of fear:

> The only thing I remember is that he cried for his brothers and he kept telling me, "We will cry Eleni [Loykia's cover name during the war], we will cry, and you will cry and I will also cry." But it did not come to my mind that they killed my mother and my sister. [...] We went to the beach, at the White Tower [a central monument and symbol of the city at the waterfront promenade generally called *paralia*, "the beach"], and the partisans were passing by, having the captives with them, the Germans. This was the day to remember.[59]

32 · HOMECOMING

It usually took some time until internally displaced Jews returned to their former homes. Moris Leon, originally from Thessaloniki, managed to obtain false papers as a young teenager before the introduction of anti-Jewish measures. Together with other family members, he fled via Athens to the island of Skopelos, where they survived thanks to the protection of locals. When Skopelos was liberated, Moris was sixteen. His account brings us closer to the particular time and place: "The Germans had left the village. We met in the church and people were weeping. We didn't want to go back to Thessaloniki right away; it hadn't been liberated yet." After returning to his native town, Moris's fears proved well founded. His remaining hopes were dashed and his expectations disappointed. He clearly sensed the extent of the disaster that had struck the local community: "In Thessaloniki, they looked at us as if we were ghosts. Much had changed, empty city quarters, tombstones from the Jewish cemetery they had destroyed everywhere on the sidewalks."[60] The Jerusalem of the Balkans, as this prosperous port and metropolis of the former Ottoman Empire had been referred to even in the interwar period, was gone forever.[61]

In the sinister time of the occupation, only Jews in mixed marriages were spared the worst. Unlike in more secular parts of Europe, for Jews of prewar Greece, the only way to marry out of one's faith was to convert or to have the ceremony abroad in a country where civil marriage was available.[62] This often entailed social exclusion from one's original religious community and did not necessarily lead to full acceptance in the new one. Moreover, getting married abroad was costly. As a result, few Jews of Greece married non-Jews, compared to Jews in more liberal communities in other countries.

As of 1940, intermarriages were forbidden in Greece altogether. In given circumstances, the German authorities, when registering Jews for deportation, did not bother to include the few Jews in mixed marriages that predated the occupation. Isaac Matarasso, for instance, was married to a non-Jew and therefore was not deported, nor was he forced into hiding. After the war, he was energetically involved in the revitalization of the Jewish Community of Thessaloniki from very early on and could therefore have been regarded as an obvious choice for a post in its leadership after the war, but he was the Community vice-president only briefly, in 1944, before the return of Jewish deportees. His fellow-Jews were not yet ready to reconcile themselves to his having broken with tradition by marrying out of the faith.[63]

In the whole of Thessaloniki, when the occupation began in April 1941, there were only nineteen families of mixed marriage. Next to the Matarassos, there was the family of Salomon Amariglio. Neither Amariglio nor his three sons needed to hide since the boys' mother, Margarette, was a non-Jewish German. Amariglio was exempt from persecution, so he could take care of his non-Jewish wife and children.[64] The same applied to Isaac Matarasso, a dermatologist from Thessaloniki whose French wife was considered "Aryan" under the German racial laws. After the liberation, still waiting for his brother's family to return from the Middle East, only to learn too soon that they had lost their father in Auschwitz, Matarasso opened his house to all Jewish survivors who wanted to come in and talk. His postwar account, including testimonies of women who were victims of cruel "medical" experiments in Auschwitz, was the first to be published in Greek in 1948.[65]

Though some Jews married out of the faith before the war, others feverishly looked for ways to find non-Jewish partners or seal their interreligious bond during the persecution. If blessed by the church, with the date adjusted accordingly, such a step would ensure their survival in Greece regardless of sex. In Thessaloniki, even Sam Broudo, the son of a rabbi, transgressed the rules of his religion during the persecution when he went into hiding at his non-Jewish girlfriend's place.[66] David B., born in 1902, said to the anthropologist Bea Lewkowicz, who visited him at the Jewish home for elderly at the age of eighty-eight, how grateful he was to his non-Jewish wife, who had, after his arrest by the Germans, arranged for an antedated wedding certificate. By contrast, Sam Geni, who had been seeing a Greek Orthodox girl for quite a while, much to the displeasure of his family, was betrayed by her and deported to Auschwitz. He revealed this to his relatives upon his return, having survived the camps by sheer luck.[67] The wartime rescuers of Maidy Florentin and Graciella Benousiglio became their postwar husbands. Both men were Greek, and getting engaged to Jewish women, at considerable risk to themselves, saved not only their Jewish wives-to-be but also the closest relatives of their wives.[68]

The only spiritual leader of Thessalonican Jewry who survived the Holocaust in Greece, Rabbi Michael Molho, escaped with his family to the Italian zone and endured hiding in the mountains with the help of the EAM-ELAS. A descendant of prominent Sephardic rabbis, he played a considerable part in the Holocaust commemoration in his native Thessaloniki and the legacy

34 · HOMECOMING

of the Jewish community in Greece in general. Molho's historical and ethnographic scholarship on Sephardic Salonika is still highly regarded among scholars.[69] In his influential work on the Holocaust in Greece, *In Memoriam* (first published in French in 1948), he calculates how minimal the number of Jews in Thessaloniki was immediately after the German withdrawal in 1944: "On 30 October, the Jews of Thessaloniki appear. There are seventy couples in the city. Usually the wife is of the Aryan race. From the suburbs, another four hundred soon arrive. The number of those who had joined the resistance is much higher."[70]

The first postwar register of the Thessalonican Community, which started only on August 6, 1945, also shows that the first internally displaced Jews had returned in November 1944. Many of those who followed openly declared that they had been "rescued by the resistance movement," which was also true of Rabbi Molho's family of five. Others gradually headed back either from the countryside or their Athens hiding places. Among the latter, we find Chaim Saltiel and his two sons. A textile merchant, as he stated in the register while trying to get his house back, still destitute in summer 1945, Saltiel was calculating the material losses of his business and his home. For six months, he was also worried about his youngest son, at that time still a POW in Italy. All this may have motivated Saltiel to become, on December 6, 1944, the first interim president of the Thessaloniki Jewish Community, authorized to speak on behalf of the survivors. Initially, the restored Community had two main aims: to get bread cards for everyone and to get Jewish shops returned to their rightful owners.[71]

The Community lawyer, Samuel Nachmias, with his wife, also decided to return from Athens to Thessaloniki and to help in the restoration of Jewish life there. His postwar clientele consisted mainly of Holocaust survivors, who needed help with restitutions. According to his son, Fratelis, who after the liberation remained in Athens to attend university, many internally displaced Community representatives had lived close to each other in Athens throughout the war. Thus Nachmias, for example, had been regularly in touch with Yakoel, Moissis, and others. But in postwar Athens the atmosphere on the Central Board was tense. In Thessaloniki the Community even took the wartime elites to court. After they had returned from Bergen-Belsen, they were accused of having had privileged positions in the camp and been responsible for the suffering and deaths of the others. The main instigators of the lawsuit were Saltiel and Nachmias. In his account, Nachmias's son, Fratelis, stated, somewhat ambiguously, "one cannot say that the best part of the Community survived."[72] The former elites of the once most prosperous Jewish Community in Greece—discredited, at least for a while—were thus sidelined, kept out of power, and effectively replaced by those first in town, Jews in hiding.

COMMUNITIES DOOMED TO ERADICATION

While Thessaloniki was unable to provide protection to its Jewish population, by 1943 Athens had already become the new center for the Jews of Greece. However, there were also other towns in Greece with Jewish populations that were perhaps less numerous but sometimes more important than Athens. In the zones under German or Bulgarian rule, in the once large and eminent communities, it was next to impossible for the Jews to survive near their homes. Alexandroupoli, Drama, Kavala, Komotini, Serres, and Xanthi, towns in the Bulgarian zone, with the homes of more than 4,200 Jews in all, lost nearly their whole Jewish population in March 1943, with only 1–4 percent surviving. Almost all these Jews were deported and murdered in Treblinka.[73] On Greek territory and in Vardar Macedonia (part of prewar Yugoslavia), the Bulgarian occupiers were clearly less accommodating to local Jews than in Bulgaria proper.[74] But several distinguished communities formerly under Italian control were soon also destroyed: Corfu (where less than 10 percent survived), Arta (16 percent), Preveza (6 percent), Ioannina (9 percent), Kastoria (5 percent), and Rhodes and Kos (11 percent).[75]

Having knowledge of what was going on in Germany, some Jews, especially from the upper classes, hoped to avoid deportation under the Italian occupation, that is, by moving to Athens. Like some local Christian Greeks who feared Bulgarian persecution, once Greece was divided into zones in 1941, a few Jews escaped to the German sector, which they blindly expected to be more civilized. In the end, only a small number survived among those who had fled the area to find refuge in parts of Greece under Italian control; joined the resistance; escaped abroad; or were saved, almost miraculously, by being assigned to do forced labor in Bulgaria.

After liberation, these Jewish refugees in Greece, although they felt rooted in Thrace, typically did not return home to their original community,

36 · HOMECOMING

but to the last place where they had been living more or less freely during the occupation. And that was mostly Athens. Matilda and Alvertos Simcha had escaped from Kavala in the winter of 1940. Alvertos, an Ashkenazi of Polish origin, used to be the manager of a tobacco company in Kavala. He rented a house in Athens—which was the last safe place for himself, his wife, and his three sons—and obtained false identities for his whole family. During the German occupation of Athens, the family split up. Matilda and their three sons found hiding places in Athens; her husband escaped to Egypt in early 1943 to join the Greek army-in-exile and fight against the Axis powers. Alvertos, returning to Greece in early 1945, was ready to go back to Kavala but his job was gone. It took some time until he found gainful employment in the capital.[76]

Matilda was among the few Jews in the city who actually headed "home" on the same day as liberation, meaning the house her husband rented in Athens. Her youngest son, Alexandros, who was seven at the time, felt confused about the many parties proclaiming the end of war but he also felt strengthened by the new responsibility of helping his mother rebuild the family:

> We all went out in the streets and we celebrated. All the different organizations were talking into the megaphones: the KKE, which means the Communists, together with the EAM; the rightists, together with the EDES; the "X" organization [paramilitary collaborationists], but there were also many others. On every corner a megaphone. [...] People were celebrating in the streets and I celebrated of course at home. And my mom came and took me immediately [from the guardians]. And she took me to Plaka, where we had the home we were hiding in before. And we stayed there for some time, not too long. After that, we left little by little, we took our things, we loaded them onto a cart, we caught [hired] a porter; back then there were neither lorries nor horses; there was nothing.[77]

In a similar way, Eliezer Haim left behind in Kavala his thriving family business, Solomon Brothers & Co., selling textiles in Greece and beyond, and moved with his wife, a Jewish maid, and three daughters—Allegra, Sarah, and Laura—to Athens in 1940. Eliezer, liberal and not particularly religiously observant, was fluent in Greek and, thanks to his business, had some non-Jewish connections in the capital. Three years later, after the

Germans took over the Italian zone, the Haims went into hiding under false identities. But Allegra, Eliezer's eldest daughter, aged eighteen, was captured and deported to Auschwitz in 1944. She never returned. Despite having sufficient financial means to survive the famine without being able to work and sell (astonishingly, since at least 250,000 people in Greece died from deprivation between 1941 and 1943),[78] Eliezer became seriously ill. He died in September 1944 near the end of the occupation, unable to get proper care. Blackmailed and betrayed, with one family member deported and the others in Athens, robbed of the last of their valuables, and finally losing their breadwinner, Eliezer's wife and their two half-starved daughters lived in dire poverty.[79]

During the German withdrawal, Laura (twelve) and Sarah (sixteen) were all alone in a hiding place in Piraeus. Years later, Laura recalled the unsettling stillness marking the liberation: "And then the Germans weren't there anymore and then it was quiet, everything was so quiet. Couldn't understand what was going on... Nobody on the street. Nothing, nothing, so Sarah and I—oh, we were so hungry, so hungry—we decided to go to see what's going on, we opened the door, mind you, we were living in one room inside a house like [that of a] the royal family."

The next day, both sisters, who could not yet fully internalize that the war was over, walked six miles (ten kilometers) from Piraeus to their pre-hiding flat in the center of Athens, which they found locked but at least abandoned. While Laura stayed behind in Greece to care for her mother, who was mourning for her deceased daughter and husband as well as for the overall Jewish tragedy, Sarah, a self-confident teenager, decided to leave to help build a new Jewish homeland in Palestine. Her journey stretched, however, over five months. Sarah and her 545 traveling companions who boarded *Henrietta Szold* at the end of July 1946 were sent to British internment camps in Cyprus. Only after the immigration restrictions imposed by Britain were finally lifted did they reach Palestine at last, at the end of 1946.[80]

Sara eventually returned to Athens to help her mother and sister Laura recover from the deprivation. After the passage of the Refugee Relief Act in 1953, they moved to the United States, which became a frequent destination for resettlement of Holocaust survivors from Greece and elsewhere. Laura returned to Kavala only decades later to visit. It was Christmas break 2015–16 when I met Laura in her house in California. The recording was in English

38 · HOMECOMING

but our chat included interludes in Greek, hers accent free. In our interview, she recalled her ignorance of what was happening during the liberation: "Slowly people started coming here from all over. I could not understand where they were coming from. The whole street became like an ocean of people. And we couldn't understand, and the bells started to ring."[81]

In many cases, Jews from towns left for nearby villages, hamlets, farms, or simply to the woods in the mountains to hide. After the war, however, most of them returned as soon as possible to towns and cities to look for their social circles and work. The journey home could take weeks, during which one's sense of time became highly elastic. Nelli Tampach, for instance, left Komotini as a child and settled with her immediate family in Athens. From there, they escaped to the mountains. They returned to the capital right after the liberation. In her narration, what should have lasted only a few days instead became a protracted period: "It was already the 12th of October 1944, and on the 13th we left. [...] We left with pack animals again. We went down to Navpaktos, we stayed there for fifteen, no five, days, to find someone to guide us safely through to Aigio," Nelli described from the perspective of her childhood. The 149-mile (240-kilometer) journey to Athens, which even in peacetime would take a fit adult well over a week on foot, was supposed to follow, but it was not a straightforward process:

> There was no transportation from there to Athens, and we didn't have a place to stay. So we went to the partisans—it was the partisans in Aigio in those days—and we went to the committee to ask for some shelter. And they took us in, in a villa, amazing, of some very rich people from Aigio, who were not there. [...] And we played piano with my brother there. We stayed for fifteen days. Then we went down with a lorry and came to Athens. We needed some two days to do this trip of course.[82]

Jewish survivors in Greece generally recall encountering partisans during the liberation, whether on the streets, on the journey home, or at their place of residence. This was true of Gentille Koen of Xanthi. While her brothers joined the EAM-ELAS resistance, Gentille (thirty years old) moved with her non-Jewish fiancé and her sister to her fiancé's house in Psychiko, which in those days was on the outskirts of Athens. In an interview, Gentille described the atmosphere of fear in which she dreaded a last possible denunciation:

We were at home and it was late. That evening I was with Giorgos, who stayed over because there were rumors that the war was about to end and the Germans were withdrawing. And all the partisans, the Liberation Army, went down and one unit came to Psychiko. [...] "Open up! Open up!" I thought, huh, who betrayed us again? And they will catch us here. I open the shutter little by little. But it was wooden so it made noise. Once it opened, "Who are you?" I asked. "Hurry! Open up!" [...] And he said, "Who's inside?" Me and my sister! And who are you?" "The Liberation Army." As he said "the Liberation Army," I was so relieved and I said, "Welcome, come in!"[83]

Since the partisans were still fighting in the neighborhood, Gentille decided after that encounter that it was better to go with her sister to a nearby hiding place and wait until morning. They told the men at home about their brothers, that they were Jews and partisans. Gentille's fiancé, Giorgos, who had joined the royalists during the war, fled, since the EAM-ELAS might have considered him an enemy. Gentille continues her narration by describing her excitement despite the dire conditions, but one senses that the approaching civil war would cast a shadow over her joy:

What cannons, what pistols, what shouting, what cries we heard [...] and only around daybreak it was over and little by little we were coming out. And we went home to take a look ... [...] Blood everywhere. I went to the bedroom, on the sofas in the living room, on the white sheets, lice everywhere. In the kitchen they [the partisans] were roasting what they found. I told them, "Whatever you find in the kitchen, I know you are hungry, take it, cook, do whatever you want!" And so we understood that this is the liberation. And next day, really, there started a yelling, "Freedom, freedom!" and so on. [...] Until December, when the December events started and a shift in the other direction took place.[84]

Jews who had fled Crete to Athens and its surroundings at the beginning of the war, before the island fell into German hands, were basically the only ones to survive.[85] The Battle of Crete, in May 1941, resulted in many casualties and was followed by German atrocities against the civilian population. The Venturas family escaped by boat to Piraeus in 1942, that is,

40 · HOMECOMING

two years before the deportations, and went into hiding after the German takeover. Iossif Venturas, the youngest of the family, recalls that they never returned to their native Chania after the war, and they settled in Athens for good. Apart from the Venturas, only three Jews of Crete survived; all other Jewish community members, about 350 souls, drowned when the *Tanais*, the German merchant vessel deporting them from the island, was sunk by a Royal Navy submarine. More than half a century after the catastrophe, Iossif Venturas—today a distinguished Greek-Jewish poet—called one of his poem cycles "Tanais," commemorating the destruction of the Jews of Crete, thus perhaps facilitating the emotional return to his roots. The poem starts with a quotation from *The Odyssey*: "There do thou beach thy ship by the deep eddying Oceanus, but go thyself to the dark house of Hades." This refers not only explicitly to the Greek mythological underworld but also implicitly to the resurrection after a fulfilled prophesy and Venturas's lifelong Holocaust trauma.[86]

Though there were several places in Greece where the probability of survival and rescue was seen, at least by Jewish representatives abroad, as higher than elsewhere,[87] Jews were rarely as lucky as they hoped to be. This is especially true of the northwestern towns of Ioannina, Kastoria, and Preveza, communities in the Italian zone, from where most Jews were deported to Auschwitz in complicity with Greek and sometimes even Jewish collaborators. The Jews of the islands of Corfu, Kos, and Rhodes met a similar fate. On Corfu, where there were enough Greeks keen to assist the Germans, the family of Ilias Balasteras, the president of the local Jewish Community in the Holocaust aftermath, was probably the only one to find refuge on the island. A Greek Orthodox acquaintance of the Balasteras family there was the future husband of Ilias's niece, Elpida Soussi.[88]

While the names of Greek collaborators remain largely unspoken even within the Jewish community, names of the few collaborators coming from its own ranks were widely communicated, evoking the prejudice that the Jews themselves were to blame for their misfortunes. Moreover, the Jewish collaborators Daniel Cohen and the Rekanati cousins, who spent the rest of the occupation in Greece, were, unlike the Orthodox Greeks, put on trial by their own community and punished in 1947 for betrayal and enrichment at the expense of their fellow-Jews in the Italian zone of Greece.[89] Jews in Greece, ultimately vulnerable, were forced somehow to prove their true

Greekness, which influenced their Holocaust-survival narratives, narratives that only rarely allude to Greek complicity.[90]

COMMUNITIES WITH A HIGH PROBABILITY OF SURVIVAL

On other occasions, Jews managed to find hiding places close to their hometowns and were therefore able to return immediately after the occupation. These were generally but not always Jewish communities under Italian occupation, close to areas ruled by the leftist resistance or areas with only a few Jewish families. This is especially true of Patras, in the Peloponnese; Trikala, in the middle of partisan territory; Larissa, Volos, and Chalcis, on the east coast (again largely under resistance control); and Zakynthos, in the Ionian Sea, towns with between several hundred and two thousand Jewish inhabitants. In the German zone, there were also some exceptions to the brutal rule. All the Jews of the small community in Katerini and just under a third of the Jewish community in Veria, a few miles west of Thessaloniki, were saved by acting quickly and having a good deal of luck.[91]

Once news of the anti-Jewish measures in Thessaloniki had reached Veria (forty miles/sixty-four km away), worries and fears increased considerably within the local Sephardic community, since many of them had immediate family or other relations in the metropolis. Soon after the Germans introduced these measures in Veria, the Community president, Menachem Stroumza, telephoned the chief rabbi of Thessaloniki, Zvi Koretz, to learn what was coming next. After he warned him about the approaching deportations to Poland, Stroumza made the quick decision to flee with his family to the mountains, urging other community members to do the same. As a result, 135 Jews saved their lives. In March 1943, the Germans put another 660 people living or hiding in Veria and its surroundings on a train to Thessaloniki and then immediately on another to Auschwitz. Veria was liberated by the EAM-ELAS on October 27, 1944, and Jews hiding in the town or outside it returned almost right away. Some Greeks even welcomed them with joy, but those who coveted the Jews' abandoned property were filled with resentment. Stroumza resumed running his shops and performing his duties as the first postwar president of the Jewish Community in Veria, a fact never mentioned, oddly enough, by his sons in the VHA interviews.[92]

42 · HOMECOMING

Most of the Jews of Katerini, only thirty-three people, first found refuge in the nearby village of Kalavia-Charathra with the assistance of local Greeks and under the passive surveillance of the local German commander. Matthew Yosafat, a Jewish child survivor from Katerini, confirms in an interview the words of Michael Matsas, that his family had received a warning from an acquaintance who worked at the Katerini post office. This acquaintance postponed the delivery of the arrest order for all local Jews, a courageous act that proved decisive for their rescue. Matthew's father took up his office as president of the Jewish Community in 1944, but the family decided to leave about a year later, as the Civil War was about to break out, first for Thessaloniki and then for the United States. Situated in the foothills of Olympus, Katerini was a stronghold of the Communist resistance, prompting many Jews to leave. Consequently, the Jewish Community in Katerini ceased to exist not long after.[93]

In some communities in the former Italian zone, such as those of Larissa, Volos, Chalcis, Patras, and Trikala, hundreds of Jews, for various reasons (including help from partisans and simply the fact of being in this zone), were able to escape deportation. In the small Jewish settlements of Agrinio (with 40 people) and Karditsa (with 150), everyone was saved. The Matsas family, originally from Ioannina, ended up in Agrinio in 1940. Leon Matsas, an employee of the National Bank of Greece, was drafted into the army during the Greco-Italian War. Because of his job, he had to move from town to town in the late 1930s, first to Arta, then to Preveza, and finally to the small town of Agrinio. Only by good fortune did he and his family avoid the German registration in three cities from which almost all the other Jews were deported to Auschwitz and murdered. Just as they were supposed to register with the Germans in Agrinio, the forty Jews of the tiny community went into hiding. When they complained about their food having been stolen during their rescue attempt in the nearby hills, Michael Matsas recalls, the local Greeks threatened to hand them over to the Germans. Once denunciations really started, they had to flee again. All this, naturally, left the Matsas family and others with painful memories.[94]

Based on her own recollections and on a written account by her mother, Ninetta Matsas (who was eight years younger than her brother Michael) says, in what is surely an understatement, that after the war the family "really had a hard time" finding housing. Since the EAM resistance was in control of Western Greece, its local bureau then provided the Matsases with suitable accommodation, despite the anti-Jewish sentiments expressed by the owner of the house they were sent to. As in Michael's account, in Ninetta's story her affection for the leftist resistance is conspicuous when she compares their white-collar father to the resistance fighters, clearly distinguishing him from his middle-class background: "And my mother in her memoirs describes their first night in the city. There we really did not look like city people anymore. My father had a long beard and he looked more like a partisan than a bank employee."[95] In the aftermath, Leon Matsas offered his services as a teacher of Judaism in a room rented out to the local Jewish Community for all social and religious purposes. Together with Savvas Mizan, the son of a chief rabbi, Matsas helped out in the Community and assisted at religious services. And for a while, he served as the president of the postwar Community in Agrinio.[96]

The most important industrialist of Volos, and director of the Leviathan company, Anselmos Mourtzoukos was well integrated into Greek society. With the Italian surrender approaching and anti-Jewish measures to follow in Volos, his representative in Athens, Minos Konstantinis, offered to help. Given his importance in the region, Mourtzoukos, unlike many other Volos Jews, decided to leave for Athens in the hope of blending in with the crowd. Well informed about the deportations from Thessaloniki, he set off in spring 1943, in a little cargo boat, together with his daughters (Yola and Paulette), his wife, his mother-in-law, his sister-in-law Julia with her husband and son, and a maid. The journey lasted roughly a week. In Athens, they moved about under false identities, forced to change their hiding place three times until they were finally liberated. "We listened to the radio, and I think some people also came to announce the freedom, that we were free now. They didn't know we were Jewish, but they came to say the Germans have left, or are leaving. And it was going to be a big celebration downtown in Athens," said Paulette years later, adding her regret at having missed the collective jubilation: "I stayed home with my parents, but Yola, my sister, and Maria [the maid] went, and they came home about 12 o'clock [at night], and they were telling us it was such a frenzy, it was wonderful, everybody was jumping and laughing, and it was great." The Mourtzoukos family could afford to rent an apartment and settled in Athens for good, but they had no possessions except some folding chairs and a table. Still opposed to

44 · HOMECOMING

Communist ideas and lukewarm about religion, though keen on Zionism, Mourtzoukos became a member of the Central Relief Committee and the new Central Board of Jewish Communities as a representative of Volos. He also started a new business in Athens but, as Paulette puts it, "It took us years to go back to normal—to recover."[97]

At the end of the war, even before learning about Auschwitz, many Jews suffered the traumatic loss of their loved ones. Rachil Barouch, then six years old, was born in Volos as the only child in the family of Isodor Barouch, the head of the Barouch-Levis Bank. In December 1942, Isodor Barouch changed the name of his bank to the "less Jewish-sounding" Universal Bank. But the new name did not help for long, and the family was soon looking for a safe haven outside the city, leaving everything behind in the process.[98] They survived the war in the mountains thanks to the help of family friends and the partisans. Her recollections of the return to Volos are mostly intertwined with the memory of death and a lost childhood:

> We came back to Volos in November-December 1944. Back then, the conditions were so tragic that there was no chance to celebrate a birthday again. There were other priorities. The priorities of survival. [...] But when we came back, and we took the way back and arrived to Trikala, we were all together: father, mother, grandfather. [...] My grandfather, due to his age and all the hardship he had suffered, was of very poor health. [...] He stayed in Trikala in the state hospital to get care and food. [...] Unfortunately, shortly after we returned to Volos, we received information that he died ... That was in 1944, he was another victim of the war.[99]

In Chalcis and the surrounding areas in Euboea (EAM-ELAS-controlled territory on a gulf of the Aegean Sea), some Jews joined the partisans, others left for the Middle East. Among those in hiding was the president of the Chalcis Jewish Community, Solomon Maisis, and Chief Rabbi David Matsas. The leaders of Chalcis were not the only people to disobey the German orders to register the members of their community. The president of the Jewish Community in Larissa, Abraam Negris; the chief rabbi of Larissa, Isaac Cassouto; and the chief rabbi of Trikala, Abraham Sasson all found refuge in the mountains.[100] Esdra Moissis (twenty years old) from Larissa turned to an acquaintance in Stomio, a mountain village only twenty miles (thirty-two

COMING OUT OF HIDING IN GREECE · 45

km) from his home. Involved in the youth movement of the wartime leftist resistance (EPON), poor but well adapted to the non-Jewish environment, Esdra was able to bring his parents and five siblings to safety. While in hiding under a false identity, they earned a living as fishermen. Esdra was in a position to make good use of his literacy. Since he was probably the only young person there who could read and write good Greek, he was employed in an office of the Stomio town hall. On their first postwar visit to Larissa, the Moissis family succeeded in recovering all of their few belongings, but their house was occupied, so they had to stay in Stomio until May 1945. After that, Esdra, together with Isaac Cassouto (a Larissa Community representative and one of the few rabbis of Greece who survived the war), applied himself to rebuilding the Community. Esdra, who eventually became a long-serving president of the Jewish Community of Larissa, later recalled that the battle for survival really started only after he had returned.[101]

One story of heroism, connected with the dubious honor of Greek dignitaries, tells of the "miraculous rescue" of the Jews of Zakynthos. Conventionally, the credit for the survival of 275 local Jews is given to Bishop Chrysostomos and Mayor Loukas Karrer, who were later declared Righteous among the Nations for their deeds. As the story goes, the bishop and the mayor presented the German authorities with their own names instead of the names of the Jewish residents Gentiles.[102] Regardless of how fortunate the Jews were to have been rescued, and regardless of how the rescue was achieved, these Holocaust survivors were also traumatized by the war in general and anti-Jewish persecution in particular. Erkanas Tsezanas, born on Zakynthos in 1930, was hiding with his family in the mountains during the war. His memories of everyday life in those years are far from happy. And he recalls the end of the war with some cynicism:

> We were in a village in the mountains. There was a big explosion. While leaving, the Germans blew up a large ammunition dump, and this left a hole perhaps a kilometer [0.62 miles] around, a terribly big hole. And we heard a horrible noise when we were in the mountains, and then partisans told us (because then we had the partisan resistance ELAS there) that the Germans left. And it was ironic that after the Germans left the English came a few days later, but they didn't know that the Germans had left and so they were throwing bombs on us again.[103]

46 · HOMECOMING

The postwar reconstruction of the Zakynthos Jewish Community was short-lived. Because of migration and especially the devastating earthquake experience in 1953, this was yet another Jewish community that ceased to exist.[104] Like Erkanas, most local Jews eventually moved to the capital, ensuring that Athens would now hold the prominent position among the Jewish Communities of Greece.

The narrative of heroic and selfless assistance provided by local Greek officials, the municipality, and the church, which is not uncommon also in other European countries occupied by the Nazis, has regularly been supported by representatives of the Central Board of Jewish Communities, specifically Mois Konstantinis, its former president whose ancestors were from Zakynthos. The list of only two Greek names has never been found and several accounts plainly state that the Jews of Zakynthos survived.[105] However, promoting the myth of Zakynthos against the backdrop of the overall number of Jewish victims in Greece only underscores the Community's desperate need to side with the hegemonic narrative of Greek hospitality, heroism, and, eventually, martyrdom.

CHAPTER TWO

DEMOBILIZATION AND ITS AFTERMATH

With the arms, with the arms,
forward in the fight
for priceless freedom.

Partisan song "In the Arms"[1]

DATED SEPTEMBER 12, 1945, almost a year after the German withdrawal, the report *The Jews and the Liberation Struggle*, issued by the leftist Greek resistance in English translation, reached the New York office of the JDC. "The Jews of Greece are Greeks," the document said bluntly of their Jewish compatriots, "they have a strong national sentiment and a Greek consciousness."[2] Among Holocaust survivors, such words, which come across as sad irony, certainly raised hopes that they would finally be respected as loyal citizens of Greece.

The original EAM pamphlet was first brought to my attention by the staff of the Contemporary Social History Archives (ASKI) in Athens in March 2004, immediately after I showed interest in holdings on Greek-German relations. It was undated and uncategorized, but the main message was clear: Greek partisans had helped the Jews during the war and both were suffering in its aftermath. My research at the ASKI back then was inconclusive; in fact, it had not produced a single additional record, and I had half-forgotten about this document until I rediscovered it in the JDC collection. But the narrative presented in the pamphlet, which touches upon the heroic role of the Greek leftist resistance in fighting fascism and being the ultimate rescuer of the Jews of Greece, appears in contemporary history writing published in Greece and elsewhere. Only the problem of Jewish strong national

48 · HOMECOMING

feelings for Greece as their homeland is often somehow overlooked. And, like in this document, the credit for bringing about the rescue is given to the Greek Christians, not to the Jews who went to great pains and devoted considerable resources to reach EAM-controlled territories.

The European-wide discussion about Jewish participation in the armed resistance groups had already started in the 1950s when Holocaust survivors opened the debate on psychological-moral resistance and armed struggle.[3] This was in connection with creating the first official Holocaust memorial sites and attempts to dismiss accusations of the Jews going "like sheep to the slaughter" and allegations of passivity. Perhaps the most significant effort was made during the Yad Vashem ceremonies and a conference in 1968, marking the twenty-fifth anniversary of the Warsaw Ghetto Uprising and honoring the Jews who had risen against their oppressors.[4] The first Conference Committee meeting was held in Israel in 1966. Only a year earlier, the head of the Central Board of Jewish Communities in Athens, Asher Moissis, had written his article on the continuous armed struggle of Jews in Greece. In "Jews in the Greek Armed Forces: A Short History," published in *Makhberet* (a periodical of the Israeli Defense Ministry), Moissis looks at the years from the outbreak of the Greek War of Independence, in 1821, to the end of World War II, in order to highlight the Greek patriotism of the Jews.[5] Jewish determination to fight for their home country, Greece, is usually emphasized in connection with the outbreak of the Greco-Italian War (1940–41), when the Jews stood behind Metaxas, with 12,898 of them fighting and Colonel Mordechai Frizis losing his life, side by side with their non-Jewish compatriots in the struggle for an independent Greece.[6]

One question that has been raised many times is why in the 1940s more Jews had not joined the partisans, especially in countries like Greece where the resistance was rapidly gaining momentum. While many factors, such as geography and the timing of the deportations, played a part, it is important to understand the thinking of the Jews before anybody in Greece knew of places like Auschwitz and Treblinka at all or as anything other than remote and cold settlements in Poland. Since openly disobeying wartime measures would most likely have met with the death penalty, individual decisions about going into hiding, let alone taking up arms in resistance against Nazi rule, seemed to pose a much higher risk for the Jews than remaining in their

50 · HOMECOMING

communities and following orders that were strict and odd, but ostensibly not life-threatening.[7]

Yet some of the families that were most severely affected by persecution before the deportations, not only for racial but also for political reasons, felt provoked into fighting back. One was the family of Avraam Carasso, a Thessalonican Communist who was among the twenty-eight Jews executed on December 30, 1942.[8] As Evgeny Finkel points out in his work comparing behavior patterns of the Jews in three ghettos of occupied Poland,[9] Jews whose political activities had been curbed even before the German takeover possessed the necessary skills to organize most effectively under the occupation. The existence of a non-Jewish Communist resistance was known among the Jews but was still either not well developed or had simply yet to be called upon. For all these reasons, those Jews—once selectively repressed—acted individually, or as a family unit, rather than collectively. This corresponds to the situation faced by Jewish Communists in Greece. Moreover, the deportations in Thessaloniki were quick: the Jews were only briefly in separate ghettos, which gave them little time for clandestine action.

According to Steven Bowman, who pioneered the research on Jewish partisans in Greece, the Jews who joined the resistance were predominantly men who had either served in the Greek army on the Albanian front during the Greco-Italian War, or Communist Party members, or those who had been smuggled into partisan-held territory and effectively recruited by EAM, and eventually all of the above.[10] Formed in September 1941, several months after the collapse of the Molotov-Ribbentrop Pact, when Operation Barbarossa was in full swing and the Soviet Union under attack, EAM emerged as a catch-all leftist resistance movement. Six months later, units of its Greek People's Liberation Army (ELAS) were already fighting in Greece against the occupiers. During the occupation, these turned out to be the main, though by far not the only, opposition forces in Greece.[11]

After the emergence of Greek resistance organizations, some men and women of Jewish origin joined the EAM-ELAS to escape the cities ruled by the occupiers. Several hundred Jews actively enlisted in the leftist resistance during the war. But Jewish armed resistance in Greece did not develop independently of EAM-ELAS.[12] Though boundaries existed among young Greek-speaking Jews and, on the other hand, non-Jewish members and sympathizers of the Communist Party of Greece (KKE) before the war, some trust

DEMOBILIZATION AND ITS AFTERMATH · 51

was established between them to escape the deportations. In contrast to the common perception of what constitutes a warrior, Jewish armed resistance was not motivated by the "crucial test of manhood,"[13] but by the feeling of urgency. Although their parents and the Jewish community in general tried to dissuade them, some young men and women willingly joined the resistance.

Besides becoming a partisan, enlisting in the Greek armed forces would have been a logical choice for able-bodied men and women eager to escape German tyranny and to fight the Axis powers. However, there were several obstacles. First, the Greek military units were dissolved in April 1941, after Athens had surrendered, which ultimately led to occupation by Germany, Italy, and Bulgaria; the Greek army as such ceased to exist, but a number of Greek troops, together with the Greek government, were evacuated to Egypt. Afterwards, the only reasonable option was to risk crossing the sea and signing up for the British Middle East Forces.

Another obstacle, as Rae Dalven, the Jewish-American scholar originally from Epirus, observed about Ioannina, after visiting the hometown of her youth in 1947, Jewish spiritual leaders and their followers were facing the dilemma of whether or not to oppose the moral code of their religion and take up arms in order to kill. As written in Exodus (14:14), "The Lord shall fight for you and ye shall hold your Peace."[14] This certainly applied to pious Jews not only in Ioannina or Greece, but in general. A third obstacle was that many Jews were doing all they could not to be associated with Communist ideology, which, for them, the EAM resistance embodied, either because of their own non-Communist view of the world or simply in reaction to the anti-Communist measures introduced in Greece.[15]

Although in the past thirty years much has been published about the Jewish resistance, particularly in post-Communist Europe,[16] little was said before Bowman about the armed struggle of Jews in occupied Greece. To this day, not much has been written on Jewish partisans and next to nothing on Jews in the Greek armed forces abroad. The silence has to be seen in the framework of the Greek Civil War and the Cold War, during which, until 1974, Athens fiercely fostered anti-Communist sentiments, thus suppressing the narrative of a mainly leftist resistance.[17] Only after the fall of the Greek junta, which ruled from 1967 to 1974, and with the Greek socialists coming to power in 1981, was Asher Moissis's article on the history of Jewish

52 · HOMECOMING

armed struggle translated into Greek and published in the Central Board monthly *Chronika*.[18] Four years later, in a speech agitating for recognition, Joseph Matsas, a former ELAS fighter from Ioannina, stated in defense of the Jewish Communist partisans, "it is an imperative that those Jews who gave their life for the freedom of their country be honored, and we express our gratitude to the organizations of national resistance for the efforts they made to save as many Jews as they could."[19]

Apart from those in hiding, the only internally displaced Jews were partisans, and thus they were the only other Jews who experienced the end of the occupation in Greece. What is more important, unlike Jews in hiding, partisans in EAM-ELAS-controlled territories may have been able to move more freely than other Jews during the anti-Jewish persecution. Surprisingly, some Jews in the Middle East Forces were also to witness the return to more normal life in Greece shortly after the German withdrawal. While others were still in internment, concentration camps, or exile, the homecoming of Jewish officers from the Middle East almost coincided with the Battle of Athens in December 1944.

With the ultimate withdrawal of the Wehrmacht in the autumn of 1944, the situation in Greece favored the left-wing partisans, who controlled about two-thirds of Greek territory at the end of the occupation. By the end of the war, the EAM had perhaps as much as half of the seven-million Greeks on its side.[20] This encouraged the leaders of the EAM to think that they could legitimately take power in the country. In this climate of "dual power," the leftist resistance in Greece and the Greek government returning from exile, some of the Communist Party's radicals aspired to seize power in Athens immediately by force. Since the geopolitical setting of Greece soon took a different turn, internally because of the Civil War and internationally because of the Cold War, the fact that Jews had fought against the occupiers was rarely mentioned.

The changing political climate of 1944 kept not only the political elite busy, but also members of the Greek armed forces abroad, the partisans, and everybody else in Greece. For decades, however, historians rarely wrote about the Jews in the Greek resistance and their homecoming. Once they started, the non-Greek history writing has tended to romanticize Jewish partisans, and the non-Jewish to nationalize or ideologize Jewish involvement, too often inserting Jews into the established Greek (Gentile) resistance narrative rather than using the experiences of Jews to particularize and challenge it.[21] But Jews who joined the resistance did so less out of ideological conviction or Greek nationalism than out of an all-consuming desire to avoid being deported. In postwar Greece, however, this fact was not necessarily acknowledged, nor did it mitigate their not being fully accepted as Greek.

Despite victory over the occupiers in Greece, the autumn of 1944 soon turned out to be less cheerful than one would expect of a country that had recently broken the grip of a triple occupation. Before long, hopes for a peaceful life were gone, as another conflict was unleashed that would have a lasting impact on Greek society in its entirety. The Civil War (1946–1949) created irreparable cleavages in Greece, which have outlived the combatants, as was clear, for example, from the heated debate sparked in 2004, beyond academia, over the post-revisionist approach of Stathis Kalyvas and Nikos Marantzidis, two social scientists arguing against the ideological hegemony of the left in Greek historiography.[22] The same certainly applies to the Jewish community, to which has been attributed ideological conservatism. Unlike the historian Nikos Tzafleris, I see no uniform Jewish conformity to the "conservative ideological hegemony" of their elites.[23] Rather, I accept the idea of the Jews' tacit agreement to keep a low profile in order to maintain their position in an ethnically homogeneous country that acknowledges only indigenous religious minorities (Jews and Muslims), not ethnic ones. The privilege to exist as an officially recognized outgroup was fragile and easy to contest, not only in everyday encounters but also in Greek law.

Heading toward the Battle of Athens

While war was still raging and it was clear that the map of Europe would be redrawn by the victors, few people knew that Churchill and Stalin had already agreed in early October 1944 upon spheres of Soviet and British influence in what has become known as the Percentages Agreement. At that time, all Greece would be obliged to decide which end to take hold of. That meant not only Holocaust survivors but also Greeks who had stood up to the enemy but were still keeping their powder dry, be it at home or abroad, and regardless of the ideologies dictated by the various authorities. Such a decision naturally came with consequences: while some World War II resistance fighters were decorated, others were jailed. Many tried to avoid these

54 · HOMECOMING

undesired outcomes by simply keeping a low profile and quietly demon-
strating their loyalty to Greece more than ever before.

During the Cold War, Athens continued its prewar policy, and Greece
soon became a stronghold of the anti-Communist camp. But this was hardly
the case during World War II. When viewed from Egypt at the beginning
of 1944, where the Greek government-in-exile was based, even Great Britain still seemed sympathetic to the Greek leftist resistance. Nonetheless, in
autumn 1944, based on the Caserta Agreement signed by the official Greek
government in exile and the Greek resistance leaders of both the leftist EAM
and the royalist EDES, domestic resistance units were to disband as soon
as the national liberation struggle against the occupiers came to an end.
The agreement, however, was not fully respected, and tensions quickly escalated.[24] Realistically, one could hardly expect the unease in Greece during
the terror campaigns against the civilian population by the Germans in
1944, with considerable assistance from local collaborators, simply to be
relaxed following the retreat of the occupying forces and with political
agreements.

The Greek Communists, the nationalist right, and the postwar government, together with the Royal Palace, all sought a monopoly on power
during the transition. Three blocs also persisted among the Jews—Zionists,
non-Zionists, and leftists. While the first, numerous group found little support in non-Jewish milieus, the second opted to embrace the Greek nation as
much as it could, and most of the latter group tried to make the story of their
resistance fit exclusively within the national liberation narrative. Moreover,
almost everybody who spent the war in Greece started to have serious doubts
about the future. Malfunctioning institutions, the absence of the rule of law
backed by unbiased security forces, and social and economic hardship drove
the country into a crisis within weeks of liberation.[25]

After the withdrawal of the Wehrmacht, the ELAS followed the German
troops and seized vacant rural areas that were not yet under its control. The
Greek government in Athens, in fear of losing power over Greece, did not
hesitate to openly use its security forces, right-wing radicals, and former
collaborators against the resistance.[26] Given their political orientation and
Nazi indoctrination, these groups had not been resistant to antisemitic propaganda. The circumstances and polarization of power triggered a chain of
violence that broke out in the December Events. This led not only to many

DEMOBILIZATION AND ITS AFTERMATH · 55

retaliatory actions from both political camps but also to many Holocaust survivors' ultimately choosing to emigrate from Greece, this time for internal political reasons, not because of the German persecution of Jews.

On December 2, 1944, when Prime Minister Georgios Papandreou Sr. ordered the demobilization of partisan groups, he made the members of the EAM-ELAS step back from the fragile coalition, leaving them vulnerable. On the eve of the general strike called for December 4, 1944, a consequence of the brutal suppression of a previous mass pro-EAM demonstration, fighting spread throughout the center of Athens, and martial law was eventually imposed in several provinces. From December 6, 1944, on, barricades were erected during the thirty-three-day Battle of Athens, and the city was bombed by the Royal Air Force. This was the first and only bombardment of the Greek capital in World War II. But the bombardments were not limited to Athens: the Allies also targeted the ports of Piraeus, Volos, and Thessaloniki.[27]

At the time of liberation, at least among the liberated and the liberators, spirits were still high, with many partisans making it from the mountains to Athens. Salvator Bakolas and Salomon Koen, whose family members had been deported from Ioannina to Auschwitz-Birkenau in 1942, were among them. Even decades later while already living in Israel, Salomon proudly stated that at the liberation parade marching toward Syntagma Square in the center of Athens, he had been the one carrying the banner with a *K*, representing part of the acronym of the Greek Communist Party, KKE. Yet his link to Communism remains only implicit in his narration.[28]

For Salomon, festive feelings were soon overtaken by sorrow. His wife, Toula Dolma, a non-Jew whom he had recently married and who was the mother of their infant son, Samis, was killed in front of his eyes during a funeral procession for those shot dead on the eve of the general strike. Placing his now motherless baby in the Jewish orphanage in Athens, Salomon started to plan Aliyah for himself and his child. Samis was one of the child passengers on the first and only official voyage to Palestine, which set sail on August 4, 1945. Salmon joined the Hachsharah, a vocational training camp for adults, before leaving for the Holy Land together with 213 other Jews about a year later on board the overcrowded *Haviva Reik*.[29]

During the December Events, Athens became a battlefield. With bloody fighting in the city, tanks in the streets, night bombings, and a harsh winter

56 · HOMECOMING

under way, there was no hope that anyone in Greece would receive food and medical supplies. Prime Minister Churchill's visit to the Greek capital on Christmas Day 1944 did little to calm the population, nor did it settle the peace for Salomon or his fellow fighters. As fate would have it, the strikers were fired upon by Greek squads led by the police officer Angelos Evert. During the war, this man had been close to Archbishop Damaskinos, who was now the Greek regent appointed in place of King George II. Both Evert and Damaskinos had spoken out against the deportations in 1943 and helped with the issuing of false papers for Jews in Athens. After the war, Evert was accused of having collaborated with the Germans but was soon acquitted since he had assisted Jews as well as British and Greek military officers to escape to the Middle East.[30]

By that time, the Holocaust survivors in Athens were facing all kinds of shortages, and their lives were in danger as fighting raged around them. The non-Jewish population were no better off, but they at least had the church, their families, friends, and acquaintances. Nelli Tampach, who was sixteen during the December Events, later recalled the atmosphere of fear when she returned from the countryside:

> They started to distribute rations at the synagogue, but from Syntagma Square to there, the area was already in the hands of partisans. [...] I remember one day I went with my father to get food because we had heard they were giving it out at the synagogue. And starting from Klafthmonos Square, the bullets were flying over us. And we heard a bzzz and just went down. It popped some hundred meters from us. We arrived at the synagogue. Though they weren't letting anybody through, when we said we were Jewish, the partisans let us pass. I remember Aiolou Street where the bullets were coming from both sides, on the one side the "nonleft," and on the other the partisans. And a war was going on, guerrilla warfare, civil war... And we reached the synagogue, got food and went back. But we never tried again because it was far too dangerous.[31]

From Nelli's account, we observe her siding with the left but also notice how the fear of continuous fighting paralyzed her family life. A similar experience is expressed by Andreas Seficha, whose family was under British protection. Moreover, in Andreas's account, he also brings out the many-layered dilemma of returning and the lack of information passing between Thessaloniki and Athens:

> When we arrived on a British Army truck from Argos in Athens, it was the time of the December clashes. My father saw us safely installed in the Europa Hotel on Omonia Square. Should we stay in Athens or go back to Thessaloniki, to our home? Home? What home? [...] We had hardly settled in when the Battle of Athens broke out at various points in the city. [...] The British commandeered the Hotel Europa and set up their machine guns on balconies overlooking Omonia Square, where the first pitched battles had already begun. The hotel management found a place for us in the basement with the central heating boiler and brought us mattresses to sleep on. What were we to do? Outside bullets rained in all directions and stocks of food were dwindling. It was very dangerous to venture out, but [aunt René] approached two of the British officers and explained [to] them our situation. One of them was, I think, Jewish, and was most sympathetic. He gave us tinned food and milk. We also had some chickpeas and currants that we had brought with us from Argos. We stayed in the basement for a long time, right until the December clashes were over.[32]

In those days, Thessaloniki represented the stronghold of the opposition that was trying to introduce a *laocratia*, rule of the common people. Much like during World War I, Greece was for a moment yet again divided into North and South. The clashes in Athens and elsewhere, as well as the overall destruction, resulted in the EAM-ELAS partisans, including Jews, remaining in the field while other Holocaust survivors in Greece found themselves trapped on the way to their prewar homes and afraid to be accused of pro-Communist sympathies. Only after the EAM-ELAS had been defeated in Athens in early January 1945 could the Greek government restore order somewhat. At that point, the Ministry of Justice initiated steps toward the reconstruction of the judiciary.[33]

The situation in Greece deteriorated not just politically but also socio-economically. Out of the nearly eight thousand Jews in Greece, about 85 percent were totally unprovided for. During the exceptionally harsh winter of 1944–45, the average daily caloric intake in some provinces dropped to

58 · HOMECOMING

under one thousand, equivalent to the levels of wartime famine, due to the lack of job opportunities, extreme inflation, and continuous fighting. People in Greece began yet again to starve to death.[34] Shortly after the armistice, in January 1945, the Central Board of Jewish Communities in Athens sent letters describing the critical situation to the Jewish Agency for Palestine in Jerusalem, the American Jewish Joint Distribution Committee in New York, and the Union of Jews from Greece in Tel Aviv, which represented the Jews of Greece in Palestine. It stated, in somewhat broken English:

> The last troubles came. It has made our situation completely tragical and desperate. Those possessing few belongings, have lost them. Those living in some miserable dwellings, have seen their houses being destroyed in the middle of winter, which makes the situation still worse. Jews were already morally deprimated, and physically very weak from hunger because of lack of food. For this reason there is a great percentage of T.B. cases. After the latest troubles, the mortality and suicide cases augment daily. [...] numerous families possess only one dress in order to go out into the street: the members of the family, who can use it, wear it in turn. [...] several members of the same family go to sleep into the same bed at fixed hours and in turn etc.[35]

The mission of the United Nations Relief and Rehabilitation Administration (UNRRA), with its Welfare Division and Glen Leet as its director, was the most important relief provider operating in Greece from October 1944 to June 1947. The UNRRA was to assist all people in need regardless of ethnicity or religion and therefore was not in a position to give special aid to Holocaust survivors.[36] But there were other problems as well. For example, the JDC complained that half a year after the December events, "rations and clothing are distributed on the basis of old identity cards." The practice of issuing identity cards during or immediately after the occupation discriminated against Jews who were forced to live under false identities, both those in hiding and those in the resistance, "making them automatically ineligible for rations and clothing."[37] In addition, the UNRRA had a limited number of staff and rations, which, according to an agreement with the Greek government, were distributed not by the UNRRA itself but by officials of the Greek Ministry of Social Welfare. Due to Greece's pervasive instability and constantly changing governments, communication breakdowns and logistical problems were a regular occurrence.

The JDC, which had been present in Greece before the war but ceased its mission because the persecution of the Jews had put its staff in great danger, had previously requested formal permission to enter Greece at the end of 1944. The British, at Allied Forces Headquarters, at first refused, since the security situation was still unpredictable. Only in March 1945, after being repeatedly called upon by the Jewish community representatives, did the JDC renew its ground activities here. By offering financial support and assistance in rebuilding institutions exclusively to Holocaust survivors, the JDC, unlike the UNRRA or the Red Cross, focused solely on the Jewish community. Since the JDC maintained and cultivated the reputation of an apolitical supra-national Jewish network, it was able to act efficiently even in an extremely polarized Greece.[38]

On February 12, 1945, the Varkiza Agreement was signed, bringing about a short-lived armistice between the Greek government and the leftists. But it did not bring social peace along ethnic lines.[39] By early February 1945, most Jewish partisans were discharged and disarmed, which they often accepted with mixed feelings. Their return was frequently accompanied by nostalgia and fear. Dick Benveniste, the sole survivor of his family, who escaped being sent to the ghetto by fleeing to the mountains, was lucky enough eventually to move back to Thessaloniki and start rebuilding his life in peace. Moise Eskaloni, also from Thessaloniki and in his mid-twenties at the end of the war, felt that his gun, after being carried so long, had become part of him.[40] Raphail Sampetai, born in the EAM stronghold of Trikala, surrendered control of a partisan infirmary at the foot of Mount Pelion and went to study in Athens, though worried that his political profile would be considered unacceptable to the university. It took him more than twenty years to admit, at least to his grown-up children, that he had been a member of the leftist resistance.[41]

Several prominent personalities of the prewar and postwar Jewish community in Greece paid tribute to the leftist resistance during the occupation and its immediate aftermath. Two such figures were Rabbi Barzilai of Athens and Rabbi Pesah of Volos. Elias Barzilai was obviously grateful to the leftist resistance, for his family had survived the occupation thanks to EAM support.[42] As is clear from his letter sent to Captain Dimitrios Dimitriou (alias

60 · HOMECOMING

Nikiforos) of ELAS, a man whose achievements and pro-Jewish attitudes were mentioned after the war by several Jewish partisans, Rabbi Barzilai felt indebted to the EAM for their assistance: "May God always be with you and let us hope to see freedom quickly and me being happy to fulfill my duties, letting all the world know about your great patriotic work and the one [*sic*] of all EAM–ELAS fighters."[43] The chief rabbi of Volos, Moshe Pesach (1869–1955), who had encouraged his Community members to take refuge in the countryside without any registration, also felt obliged to the EAM-ELAS. Two of his six children, Allegra and David, joined the partisans. His eldest sons, Iosif and Simeon, both graduates of a Hebrew teachers' college in Jerusalem, were deported in 1943 together with their families from Thessaloniki and never returned from the camps. Obviously deeply affected by this loss, Rabbi Pesach's wife died in 1944 from wartime hardships. Despite all these misfortunes, Pesach resumed his post in the Jewish community immediately after the occupation.[44]

It was in early January 1945, about the time the Red Army was closing in on Auschwitz and about a month before the Varkiza Agreement, that a letter from Rabbi Pesach was made public. In it, he warmly thanks the EAM-ELAS for their wartime assistance to the Jews: "The universal history of Judaism will devote a special chapter to the noteworthy event of the salvation of the Hebrews of Greece who took refuge with the ELAS and from them received adequate assistance and protection from the hard persecution of the barbarous Germans. We Israelites of Greece will never forget the great kindness and the warm reception which we all received without discrimination at the hands of the heroic national army of ELAS, and of other groups of the liberating organization of the EAM."

Rabbi Pesach closed his letter with a flowery phrase underscoring the equivalence of leftist partisan forces and Greece as a whole with the proclamation "Long live the ELAS! Long live Hellas!"[45]

In the immediate aftermath of the December Events, with more semantic battles over politically controversial terms to follow, the Central Board of Jewish Communities repeatedly described the Battle of Athens as the "latest troubles." Though they continued to recall the resistance, Holocaust survivors of Greece rarely spoke about their experience. With the political attitudes of the ruling parties oscillating between more or less criminalizing the left until the fall of the junta (1974) and, at the other extreme, want-

DEMOBILIZATION AND ITS AFTERMATH · 61

ing its full rehabilitation or even glorification in the 1980s, and with the uncertainty of where Communist ideology would stand in post-Cold War Europe, the Jews as an outgroup continued to keep a low profile. Though Jewish representatives, such as Barzilai and Pesach, were the first to speak out about their connection with the resistance, they were not subjected to harsh anti-Communist persecution. Despite all speculations, Rabbi Barzilai remained in office, and Rabbi Pesach was promoted and honored by the Greek state, which awarded him the Royal Order of George I. The Jewish leaders' noninterfering attitude to the Greek political setback, along with the day-to-day impartial routine of the JDC and UNRRA on the ground, perhaps encouraged the community to accept the established narratives as the only reasonable choice and to concentrate instead on rebuilding their private lives.

BACK FROM EGYPT

At the end of September 1944, when the leaders of the Greek resistance met in Italy with the Greek government-in-exile and the representatives of the Middle East Command of the British Army to sign the Caserta Agreement, Allied troops were already marching toward Bologna. From that point on, all resistance forces in Greece were to be placed under British command. Already by summer 1944, some high-ranking officers tried to support a rescue plan for Jews in Greece, to be orchestrated by the leftist resistance. Among them was a former captain of the Royal Hellenic Air Force, Alfred Cohen, the prominent son of a reputable Jewish family from Trikala. He had escaped from Athens to Cairo through Turkey in 1944 and was closely attached to the Greek Ministry of Justice and the Ministry of Foreign Affairs in exile.[46]

Alfred Cohen, a lawyer by education, prepared his memorandum on the rescue of Jews in Greece in connection with the Lebanon conference of Greek resistance representatives in May 1944 at the request of the JDC.[47] He was fully aware that together with its youth organization EPON, to which most young Jewish partisans belonged by then, the EAM-ELAS comprised about fifty thousand fighters. Of the at least 650 Jewish partisans, only 63 had been killed in action.[48] Given the proportionally low mortality rate of Jews in the armed resistance in the face of their otherwise almost certain death, Cohen's rescue plan, organized from Cairo in cooperation with the resistance in 1944,

62 · HOMECOMING

suggested that all unmarried able-bodied Jews still living in Greece should immediately join the EAM-ELAS partisans.[49]

Alfred's father, Chaimaki Cohen, who was close to King Constantine of Greece and had even served as an MP under Venizelos's party before the war, died during the occupation. His wife, Rachel, and their two children, Tilde and Michel, were provided with a hiding place by Princess Alice in Athens. Meanwhile, two other sons of this renowned family, namely, Elie and Jacques, managed to escape with false papers and join the Greek forces in Egypt.[50] Two months after the German withdrawal, Alfred returned to Greece, in December 1944, during the fierce Battle of Athens. He soon started to serve on the Central Board, working closely with the JDC (in Greece since March 1945) and its local director Gaynor Jacobson, and he oversaw the restoration of Jewish institutions and survivors' reintegration in society in Thessaloniki. Immediately becoming Jacobson's most trusted assistant, Alfred initially helped him from the headquarters in Athens but later also locally, especially in Thessaloniki. His brother Elie returned to Greece to continue his university studies in physics while earning his living with the JDC. Alfred, a leading KIS member and a founding member of the JDC-run Kassa (providing small start-up loans to Holocaust survivors), was deeply involved in the efforts to achieve the restitution of Jewish property, a difficult task for which he had to use all his organizational skills and connections.[51]

After the German invasion of Greece, it was not only the Greek government and army officials who escaped to Egypt. The Greek political elite also invited several prominent figures of the Jewish community to flee with them to Cairo as early as May 1941, when the Battle of Crete was lost. Among them were the chief rabbi of Thessaloniki, Zvi Koretz, and the director of the Bank of Greece, Minos Levis, who was involved in the transfer of Greek gold reserves to safety.[52] Whereas Koretz—according to his wife's postwar testimony—refused to abandon his congregation, Levis was lobbying on behalf of Jewish compatriots from the other side of the Mediterranean, helping them, for example, to get by once they were in the Middle East. Moreover, Jews who were regular members of the armed forces, or were only pretending to be, joined the land, sea, and air forces of the Middle East, ready to put their lives on the line to fight against the Wehrmacht in North Africa.[53] For Levis, it was quite logical to come back to Greece after the government returned and help rebuild what was left of the Jewish community.

DEMOBILIZATION AND ITS AFTERMATH · 63

Most of the men intending to serve in the Middle East units left Greece between late 1943 and early 1944, after the Germans had deported the Jews of Thessaloniki and before they started to deport them from Athens. These men were not as close to the Greek government as Minos Levis or Alfred Cohen, but all of them were young, single males, able and willing to fight. The usual route was risky, from Athens to the Greek island of Euboea north of the capital, which was separated from the mainland by only a narrow strait. From there, they crossed the Aegean Sea to Çeşme in Turkey and headed to Cairo over land, through Aleppo in Syria, and then to Palestine. This was the route the Alvo brothers took, each of them separately so as to increase the life chances of at least one of them surviving if captured by the Germans on the way to neutral Turkey. Though both were almost the same age and both attended university in Athens, their memory of the departure differs: the elder brother, Miko, managed to return to Thessaloniki and leave again for Athens with the blessing of his parents; Danny did not have the privilege of meeting his family, a missed opportunity that traumatized him for the rest of his life. Not even the prominent position of their father, a successful entrepreneur and distributer of hardware and bathroom fixtures, protected their parents from deportation. Both of them and their little daughter, Rosa, as well as an array of other extended family members, as the brothers learned upon return, were murdered in Auschwitz.[54]

After a few months in Athens, Miko, in August 1943, and then Danny succeeded in crossing the sea. Accompanied by several Greek officers and civilians, the two Alvo brothers volunteered for air force training in Gaza, though Danny was not old enough for military service at the time. Transfers from Euboea to Çeşme were clandestine but had been overseen and coordinated by the British Army since at least mid-1943. Nevertheless, the priority was transferring British soldiers and other British subjects and obtaining valuable, classified information. As a British officer, Edmund Myers, who then headed the military mission in Greece controlled by the Special Operations Executive (SOE), wrote years later, it was a deal between the British and the resistance forces without much involvement of the Greek government-in-exile.[55] Regarding Jews, negotiations between the Jewish Agency, British Army officials, Greek political elites in exile, and EAM representatives started in Cairo only in April 1944. Nonetheless, the Jewish men to be recruited by the Middle East Command of the British Army had already

64 · HOMECOMING

left several months earlier. The main aim of the Jewish Agency was essentially to bring Jews from Bulgaria, Hungary, Romania, and Greece over to the Middle East, and they were heading to the Turkish coast by the hundreds.[56]

After passing through the Greek consulate in Izmir, women were generally sent to refugee camps, whereas able-bodied men, like the Alvo brothers, were first interrogated by British intelligence and then eventually drafted for basic military training in Palestine. Later, they were typically directed to Cairo, where they went through medical testing. If capable of military service, they had to undergo further training. Miko and Danny were both sent to the RAF in the British colony of Southern Rhodesia, today Zimbabwe. Arriving earlier, Miko continued his training in air navigation in South Africa along with, for instance, Elie Modiano, a well-established architect of Italian citizenship who had also left Greece to fight the Axis powers. Danny eventually became a pilot. Both brothers met again in Cairo in autumn 1944, just before the German withdrawal from Greece. At the end of 1944, Miko had managed to arrange his return to Athens with the assistance of the Ministry of Aviation, only to learn about the deportation of his family.[57]

Not all the Jews who had enlisted made it to Egypt. According to David Konis of Thessaloniki, who had been promoted to the rank of sergeant, two Greek divisions, including his own, were sent to the Italian port of Bari after military training in British Palestine in 1944 and reached Greece by boat in early 1945.[58] By contrast, Jackos Arouch, also from Thessaloniki, arrived in Italy in 1941, after being taken prisoner by the Italians on the Albanian front. When Italy surrendered in September 1943, he was put into a British displaced persons (DPs) camp and then transferred to a transit camp of the Greek armed forces in Egypt. The boat from Cairo that brought him back to Piraeus at the beginning of 1945 sailed for nine days over a heavily mined Mediterranean. About a month later, back in Greece, Jackos was captured by the guerillas, who threatened to kill him simply for being in the Greek army. In an interview years later, he said that several Jews had been among his captors and that they had orchestrated Rabbi Barzilai's clandestine escape to the mountains.[59]

Solomon Saltiel, a Jewish soldier taken prisoner in Albania in 1941, also eventually returned to Greece in late 1945, but his path was quite different from that of most Jewish combatants in Greece. He passed through several POW camps, first in Italy and then Germany, all the while concealing that

DEMOBILIZATION AND ITS AFTERMATH · 65

he was Jewish, only to be liberated together with seventy thousand prisoners in STALAG VII-A by the Americans in April 1945. Before coming back to Greece, he was taken to Britain for a few weeks to recover. In Athens, he met his future wife, Dora Levi, who had survived the occupation as a child in hiding. In his hometown of Thessaloniki, however, Saltiel did not find any of his close Jewish friends. Like many other Jews, he decided to leave the country with his new family and give life another chance in the United States.[60]

Jewish men who stayed alive by serving in the Greek armed forces or being captured by the Italians during the Albanian campaign did not really know what was happening in Greece. Only those in the Greek forces in Egypt were well-informed about the developments. Closely following the negotiations and frictions between the government-in-exile and the EAM delegation in Egypt, they too were about to take sides.[61] At a meeting with EAM representatives in Cairo in 1943, Churchill supported the return of the king against the will of the EAM self-administration in the Greek highlands, but Britain maintained its delivery of material aid to the EAM nonetheless. The attitude of both the British and especially the Greek government-in-exile changed in March 1944 after the leftist resistance started to rule independently in Greece and thus to challenge their legitimacy. In only a month, this culminated both in the pro-ELAS mutiny of the Greeks in the armed forces, including several high officers, and later, at the Lebanon Conference, in an agreement to create a new Greek government. Once the mutiny was suppressed, nearly half of the twenty thousand men in the Greek armed forces in the Middle East were arrested and sent to detention camps in Libya and Eritrea, from which they returned home only after the Battle of Athens in 1945.[62]

Gavriil Gavriilidis, a Jew from Athens with leftist leanings and a strong loyalty to the EAM (which he says he mentioned to the Brits during the enlistment screening test) served in the RAF in the Middle East. In his VHA interview, Gavriilidis describes his escape from Greece together with a group of Greek officers in July 1943 over the Aegean Sea to join the British armed forces in Cairo. After several weeks, he found himself serving with another Jewish refugee, Edgar Allalouf, under Greek command at RAF Station Kabrit, north of Suez. In March 1944, having sided with the Mountain Government, Gavriil was arrested and ended up in the British internment

66 · HOMECOMING

camp Dekemhare in what was then Ethiopia, which he describes as a "concentration camp," postponing his homecoming until 1945.[63]

In postwar Greece, the fortunes of Jews returning from the Middle East and Africa varied considerably. Some arrived in late 1944, before Auschwitz had been liberated; others did not reach home until the summer of 1945, when the terrible magnitude of the Holocaust became widely known. Some crossed the Mediterranean directly; others first travelled through different European countries. Years later some of them published memoirs; others gave interviews; other fragments of information can be found in archives, but many of their experiences remain unexpressed. In Thessaloniki, for example, several Jewish men between July and August 1945 registered with their Jewish communities as former soldiers in the Middle East. One of them, Samouil Nissim, was without work. His brother Albertos, who had survived as a wounded resistance fighter, lived in Greece in the immediate postwar years before emigrating to Argentina. Samouil Beza had been a merchant before the war, when he was recruited by the Royal Hellenic Army and sent to the Albanian front. He married in 1945 and continued his service in the army. Mois Kamchi, a mechanic with a secondary-school education, also stayed in the Greek army after the war.[64]

Miko Alvo, after being discharged from the army in 1946, stepped into his late father's position and reestablished the family business.[65] Edgar Allalouf, also originally from Thessaloniki, stayed in the Greek army until his retirement. Since his death in 2003, Allalouf's gravestone in Athens— unlike many others that are written in Hebrew, Judeo-Spanish, French, or English, sometimes combined with Greek—proudly states, and only in Greek, that the "Brigadier of the Hellenic Air Force faithfully served his country and the Jewish people."[66] The gravestones deliver the final testimony about where the dead belonged, felt they belonged, or where their families wished them to belong.

RETURNING FROM THE MOUNTAINS

Once the occupation was over, the Jewish partisans were desperate to know what had happened to other family members with whom they had lost all contact. Word soon spread that few of those deported would be returning from the concentration camps. To whom would these partisans return? And

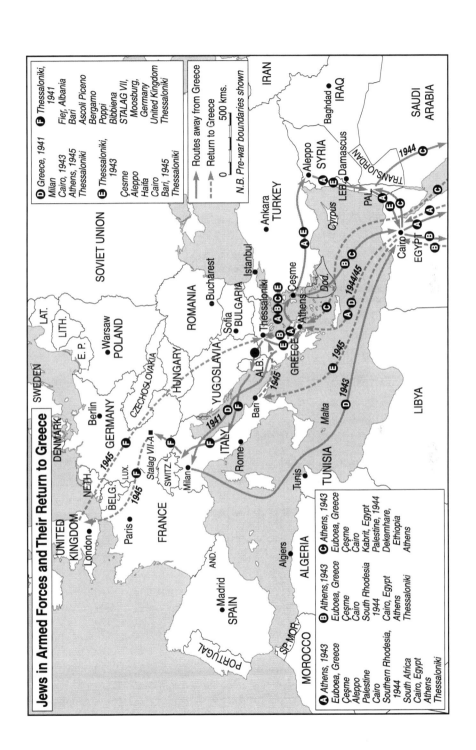

68 · HOMECOMING

how would they adjust to the postwar environment? Rika Benveniste, in her historical research on the Jews of Thessaloniki, states that most Jewish partisans were between the ages of fifteen and twenty when they joined the resistance. Closer inspection of the postwar registers of the Jewish Community in Thessaloniki, however, shows that the Jews who joined the resistance were often in their twenties or thirties. Some of the men had already gained combat experience in the Greco-Italian war.[67]

Benveniste also emphasizes the difficulty in ascertaining the complete number of Jewish resistance fighters in Greece. To distinguish between Jewish and Gentile combatants, Jews who were protected by the resistance or resistance networks, and Jews who were arrested or killed under a false identity during the war is indeed difficult. No strict criteria exist for doing so, and records are often inconclusive. Like others, Jewish partisans (for instance, Ido Shimshi, alias Makkabaios)[68] used *noms de guerre*, which rarely related to their Jewish background, as in Shimshi's case. Moreover, most of them had already gone to the mountains with false Christian identities, which they usually dropped only upon returning home after the war. Given the politics of Greece, even decades after World War II, these Jews largely edited their memories of resistance because of their fear of persecution.[69]

During the German withdrawal, most partisans remained with their ELAS regiments. One exception is Dick Benveniste, who, at the age of twenty-three, first returned to Thessaloniki on October 31, 1944. One day earlier, after the Germans had left the city, the ELAS forces celebrated the liberation of Thessaloniki with a military parade. The period from this parade to the beginning of 1945 is widely called the "Eamocracy," a postwar pun on the democracy of the EAM. The second largest city of Greece was under EAM-ELAS control, but with the discreet presence of British troops and Papandreou government officials. On January 11, 1945, once the ELAS and British representatives had agreed on a ceasefire, the resistance forces lost power over Thessaloniki. All remaining partisan units withdrew from the city within a week, and, little by little, reprisals against EAM followers were carried out by the new regime.[70]

Benveniste had already rejoined his regiment on its way to the mountains on November 2, 1944, to fight in the final battle of Kilkis. After some back and forth, he was dismissed as a result of the Varkiza Agreement. In his diary, Benveniste accurately depicts the difficulties he and other partisans faced after demobilization: "The thought that tortures me now is the question of my re-settlement in Thessaloniki. So far, so bad: you went everywhere with your mess kit, and you somehow got something to eat. But now we need to struggle to eat. Every night before I fall asleep, I make a bunch of plans for how to get by."[71] Regardless of his prior EAM-ELAS engagement, the idea of again joining the rebels did not cross his mind; he immediately chipped in to help the local Jewish Community Council at its first meeting on March 11, 1945, and soon became its accountant and, years later, president.[72]

Dick Benveniste was not the only one heading to Kilkis. Many others remained with their units. One of them was Isaac Moissis, who used the name "Kitsos," the diminutive of his assumed Greek name, Kyriakos, as an alias. Isaac served in the Greek army during the Greco-Italian War. Upon returning to Thessaloniki, however, he became one of the roughly 8,500 Jewish forced laborers working for the Reich on construction projects in Greece in 1942.[73] Stationed in the Vale of Tempe, south of Thessaloniki, on the east coast of Greece, he had to work under terrible conditions: no place to sleep, no food, and at permanent risk of malaria. Surrounded by mountains, he escaped and joined the EAM resistance active in the area.[74]

At first, Isaac Moissis was the only Jewish partisan in his group. Later, with the deportations from the German zone in spring 1943, more Jews joined the partisans. At that point, the resistance movement was strong enough and Isaac got involved in sabotage and other operations against the Germans and their collaborators.[75] On November 4, 1944, three weeks after the reinstallation of the Greek government, Isaac fought in Northern Greece with the ELAS against Greek collaborators. Even in the aftermath of this armed clash, which Isaac called an "orgy of killing," the bloodshed continued. Fighters from the ranks of the collaborators were shooting local villagers suspected of being sympathetic to the ELAS, whereas the ELAS was slaughtering its alleged opponents by the thousands.[76] While more formal and informal means of violence followed, the Battle of Kilkis became one of the most devastating events signaling what the Civil War might be like.

Though he claimed to be the only Jewish escapee from the Tempe labor camp to fight together with the EAM-ELAS,[77] Isaac Moissis was certainly not the only one to do so while being forcefully displaced within Greece. David Broudo, another young Jewish man from Thessaloniki, escaped from forced labor in Karia. Some Jews from Thessaloniki dared to walk away from the

70 · HOMECOMING

ghetto to join the partisans. Once Italy had surrendered, Jews from Corfu and Ioannina ran away during the transfer to Auschwitz before being loaded onto cattle cars. For many, the transit camp in Larissa was the last stop on Greek soil, but few of the people on board made use of it to set themselves free and take part in the resistance. Within the crucial nine days assigned to them in this facility in the spring of 1944, about a dozen single young men from Ioannina left the camp one by one after secretly erasing their Jewish identity from their ID cards, which were still in their possession. On the Plain of Thessaly, they met resistance fighters, an encounter that defined their lives not only during the occupation but also in its aftermath.[78]

After the war, some Jewish partisans were persecuted or imprisoned, or they left the country regardless of their patriotic feelings; some of them experienced all three. Few of them managed the transition without directly facing discrimination. Several resistance fighters left the ELAS army to start their lives anew. For instance, Leon Idas-Gavrilidis (originally from Athens) abandoned his unit near Thebes when he was nineteen years old. He recalls that at a time when it already looked like civil war, many people headed north and sought refuge in Communist countries because they feared political persecution at home.[79] This included a few Jewish fighters, but the number was insignificant compared to the tens of thousands of non-Jewish adults and children. Due to the absence of any documentation of their Jewish identity, a blurry spot in history remains as to how many, if any, Jewish orphans who had been hidden in rebel-controlled territories were later relocated to these countries as part of the KKE plan to evacuate children in 1948–49.[80]

Leon Idas-Gavrilidis nonetheless recalls, "I had no reason to go down there [to the neighboring countries sympathetic to Moscow], so I deserted. I threw away my gun some place, I hid it in the river and I went up to the bell of a church in the night to hide myself, hoping there would soon be the British there." Still wearing what was perceived as a partisan uniform, he was considered a spy by the Greek authorities, beaten up, and imprisoned in the Chaidari, where only a few months earlier many Jews had spent their last days before being deported to other Nazi camps. Leon was eventually freed thanks to the Varkiza Agreement, whereby he was pardoned for his alleged political crimes.[81] Later, he learned that both his parents and his brother had been murdered in Auschwitz. In October 1947, amidst the Civil War, he started his mandatory three-year military service, fighting against leftist

DEMOBILIZATION AND ITS AFTERMATH · 71

guerrillas like many other Greek men of his age, including Holocaust survivors, with the sole exception of former soldiers in the Middle East Forces. After this experience, although migration restrictions were imposed on Jews and non-Jews alike who had fought with the partisans during World War II, Leon Idas left for the United States and settled in Baltimore in 1951.[82]

Avraam Svolis of Ioannina, who was in his early twenties when he escaped from the Larissa transit camp, expressed in an interview much later that the Civil War did not actually end until the last days of his long life. Once disarmed after the Varkiza Agreement, he was tried and then banished to a political prisoners' camp on the island of Makronisos. Avraam was not a member of the Communist Party before or during the war, at least, as he claims, one would find no evidence of his having been a member, but he was denounced as a Communist after the war. This alone became his incentive to join the party. Recruited by the Greek army to fight against his comrades, he went on the run for three years.[83]

After the Civil War, in 1949, Avraam claims to have returned to Ioannina, but neither he nor any of the few men who had escaped from the Larissa transit camp made it through the aftermath to become representatives of the local Jewish Community. In fact, a handful of young Jews, including Ioannina partisans who had lost most of their families, decided to make Aliyah as soon as possible.[84] What lasted was a strong connection within the male partisan community, based not only on the discipline and camaraderie experienced during World War II but also on traditionally gendered Greek society.[85]

JEWISH WOMEN IN THE RESISTANCE

Though Isaac Moissis started off his partisan involvement as a lone wolf, he ended up marrying a comrade in arms, Daisy Carasso. She and Isaac had met before he was sent to do forced labor. After the war, in 1948, they wed when she turned twenty-two, and subsequently they decided to leave for Israel.[86] On December 30, 1942, the Germans executed twenty-eight Jews, including her father, who was a Communist. In the spring of 1943, they began to send the Jews of Thessaloniki to the ghetto. Daisy, together with her mother and little sister, escaped with false identities provided by a Greek acquaintance, an EAM member named Dimitris Chalkidis. Daisy took her elder brother,

72 · HOMECOMING

Mordochai, as an example. He had entered the ELAS together with friends from university, and this influenced her to join the resistance youth movement EPON and the partisans. While registering with the Jewish Community in Thessaloniki in summer 1945, almost simultaneously with the camp returnees, the Carassos still believed Mordochai would return home. The opposite was true. Mordochai had been killed in combat the previous summer. In the Community register, Daisy concealed her membership in the EAM but was not afraid to declare that the resistance movement had protected her and her relations and had provided for them.[87]

Fanny Matalon, neé Florentin, was another young Jewish woman who escaped from the Thessaloniki ghetto during the early days of the 1943 deportations. She did not do so with her parents (who were sent to Auschwitz and murdered), but with her husband, Leon Matalon. The couple had married out of love just a few days earlier, on March 21, and rushed to join the resistance. Fanny served as a nurse in a small hospital in Epirus. When the Germans seized the village in July 1944, she was detained in the Pavlos Melas camp, in Thessaloniki. Fortunately, her Jewish identity was not revealed, and her sister, Maidy, hiding with her non-Jewish fiancé, managed to arrange her release with the help of a Greek Red Cross representative. Fanny, a tiny girl in her early twenties, then joined her sister and continued serving as a volunteer nurse. She reunited with her husband only after the occupation. While already in Thessaloniki, her childhood friend Dick Benveniste, by then an ELAS partisan, visited her at home in November 1944. At that point, they were two of the roughly one hundred Jews in this formerly Jewish metropolis. In the aftermath, Fanny was decorated for her nursing services by the Queen of Greece, but with the Civil War, Greece no longer felt like home. In 1951, she and her husband, Leon Matalon, succeeded in leaving Greece with visas for the United States together with their little daughter, who was born during the Civil War. The baby was named Rena after Fanny's late mother, but the name was modified to its Greek form, Irene, meaning "peace."[88]

Women in hiding were mostly subordinated to their fathers or husbands; those who joined the resistance were clearly taking matters into their own hands. They frequently did so despite their young age, like the Jewish nurses Bouena Sarfati of Thessaloniki, Sara Yesoua of Chalcis, and Elli Siakki-Decastro and Rozita Koen of Volos. They often first volunteered for medical service, then became members of the resistance youth movement EPON and occasionally even carried a weapon.[89] Though both Jewish men and women sometimes joined the resistance mainly to gain independence from mostly traditional families, for girls this step also offered a unique opportunity to achieve emancipation in the extremely conservative Greek society. Jewish women in the leftist resistance, however, were generally not promoted to the upper ranks in combat or politics, and, unlike Greek women, were thus mostly spared anti-Communist persecution, particularly imprisonment, after the war.[90]

At the age of twenty-five, Bouena Sarfati joined the International Red Cross, and then, with false papers, escaped to Athens and made her way back and forth across the Mediterranean, accompanying Jewish refugees. Sara Yesoua, at the age of only seventeen, headed for the mountains of Euboea with the blessing of her widowed mother. There, dressed in trousers, she became a teacher, since she was the only person in the village who knew how to read and write. Popular for her singing but ready to take harsh steps when necessary, Sara did not hesitate to kill a Greek who had participated in the torture and killing of a Jewish girl. After the war, once the mood against the leftist resistance escalated, Sara too left for Palestine, together with her mother and sister.[91]

In prewar Thessaloniki, the Bourlas family, with six children, had lived in abject poverty. Dora was the youngest, only about fifteen on the eve of the deportations. Before the war, Dora's father, a Communist Party supporter, tried to make a living in his hometown of Volos and also in Cairo and Naousa, where Dora was later born. Unlike most Jewish Community members in Thessaloniki, the family did not speak Judeo-Spanish, and the children were sent to local Greek schools. Once the anti-Jewish measures began, the Bourlases quickly took steps to escape persecution. Their Greek connections, political leanings, and fluency in Greek helped decisively. While the mother and two unmarried daughters went into hiding with prewar acquaintances in Naousa, the father and both sons joined the EAM-ELAS right away. Still, the women kept in touch with Dora's father, who, as head of the family, had the last word in decisive matters. When Dora decided to join the resistance, she had to get his approval first: "I saw the partisans and said to my mother: 'Mom, I'll go with them.' She said, 'That is out of the question. I can't let you go, not like this, without telling Dad.'"[92]

74 · HOMECOMING

Not without hesitation, Dora's father gave his blessing to both Dora and her elder sister Yolanda to join the EAM. Arriving in the mountains, dressed in rags with no proper shoes, it was hard for the girls to get by. Dora found her way in the wild, and even liked it. Yolanda left the mountains and hid under a false identity in Thessaloniki. Dora soon started to disseminate leftist propaganda amongst the villagers, whose support was vital to the resistance. As she explains in a 2020 interview recorded in Israel, in Greece back then everything, food and clothing, had been donated by or requisitioned from towns and villages, voluntarily or involuntarily. It was her job to win them over with optimistic words. And the peasants listened to her. Dora was able to keep their spirits up, as she describes, and the older women, who were often illiterate, especially appreciated the comfort. Being migrants themselves who spoke a heavy dialect, few could understand them. Moreover, they had no access to information except from church and chatting with Dora:

> "With time, with advice, everything will go well. You will see how we'll live, what we'll do, how life will be, very different from how things have been so far," I said. I don't know where I had all this from. [...] We told a story about how they would no longer have the thing [the plow] that the oxen pull, that machines would do this and that. I don't know what. And the women would bring their husbands, too, so they could hear what exactly was going to happen. [We also said] that the villages would not stay as they were, that they would develop and one would do this and that. [...] I had my doubts about it and thought we were telling them this to boost their morale, to make them stronger. But that didn't mean that the story boosted my morale; it wasn't like that for me.[93]

Dora expresses her observations and emotions quite differently from her male counterparts. She gives little space to heroism and more to pondering the absurdity of war. When her younger brother Solomon died in battle during the retreat of the Wehrmacht in late September 1944, she did not stop wondering what happened to him and his comrades:

> They died in Veria. When they went there, we were already free in Naousa, but the ones in Veria were not yet; they [the partisans] were still after them, pursuing them. The Germans. [...] While we were already liber-

ated. It had been a couple of days, so not long, but we were free. So we thought it was over. Now there is a monument in Veria. It bears the names of everyone, including Kolokotronis's [war name] and my brother's. His name was Shlomoh, Sarlo, but they didn't manage [to get it right]. But it says "Israelite." I took a picture of it, when we were there; I took a picture and it says that he was an "Israelite." [. . .] He wasn't the only one who had fallen there. But they chased the whatsit [the Germans]. Why did they want to hunt them if they were just about to leave? [She is clearly moved by the pointless killing.] Why did they have to chase them? When retreating. Yes. They withdrew; they saw that things were as they were, and withdrew. It was our turn to do a victory dance. Of course, we were [celebrating]. "The war is over!" We had dreams, we were dreaming. [. . .] On the one hand we celebrated because we were free but he had died. Imagine! Awful.[94]

Allegra Felous-Kapeta, originally from Trikala, tells a different story. From a strongly Communist family, she joined the party before the war. This was possible only once she had resettled, in her twenties, in a larger, less traditional environment in the port town of Volos. To the rest of society, indeed even to the Communist Youth Organization (OKNE), "a woman was a parasite." Before the war, Allegra was imprisoned for her Communist activities and sent to the prison camp on the small island of Folegandros. Allegra was not religious; she believed "something new can be created," and, in her eyes, the KKE "was God." As a Communist, a Jew, and a woman (socially confined by Greek tradition), her decision to join the leftist resistance was straightforward. Nevertheless, her own beliefs, spiritual and ideological, left her wondering why EAM-controlled territory was the first and, until 1982, the last place in Greece where civil marriages were possible. Many partisan couples, however, would never abandon their religious affiliation and family traditions and therefore would not marry out of the faith.[95]

During the occupation, Allegra joined the resistance with both of her siblings and some other family members, for which many of them were subsequently persecuted. Climbing the party ladder during the war by participating in underground KKE meetings and serving as a secretary to National Solidarity, the Communist aid organization, she was elected a deputy member of the Central Committee at the Seventh Congress of the

76 · HOMECOMING

KKE in October 1945. She was thus one of four women and the only Jew in this post.[96] Soon after the Varkiza Agreement, the new regime launched a terror campaign against the partisans. Jacobson, the local JDC director, was immediately "aware of the civil war starting to take place."[97] Especially for a Communist partisan, everything was illegal. Mass persecution, including hostage-taking on the one side, numerous imprisonments on the other, and executions on both sides, achieved the regime's aim of intimidating the public.[98]

In Larissa, where Allegra was based on the eve of the Civil War, youngsters marked as rebels were killed by the locals, and their heads were displayed in the square as a warning. Most of the locals were afraid to help the partisans, and after the partisans disarmed, they had no means to protect themselves. As soon as it became clear in 1949 that the Communists would be defeated, Allegra and her non-Jewish husband took refuge in East Germany. She knew perfectly well that state violence against Communists had not been restricted to her male Greek Orthodox compatriots. Her cousin, Chryssoula Fellous, had been sentenced to death by the military court in Volos in August 1949, together with another Jewish partisan, and executed only a few days later.[99] Allegra returned to Athens after the fall of the military junta in 1974, when the anti-Communist hysteria had somewhat subsided and she was able to feel at home and safe in Greece again; she died in 2011, her story almost forgotten.

Between the Mountains and Imprisonment

Unlike Allegra, Jewish partisans generally did not unquestioningly accept Communist ideology and did not feel committed enough to fight beside their Greek comrades during the Civil War. Rather, joining the resistance was part of their survival strategy. When Isaac Nehama, originally from Athens, joined the EAM-ELAS in Thessaly in autumn 1943, he was seventeen. Travelling to Karditsa with a Greek friend who helped him obtain false papers, Isaac did not much care in which partisan group he enlisted, but his friend subscribed to the nationalist Republicans:

> Thanassis, who had a specific destination in mind, asked the teacher [a local in Karditsa]: "We're going to go and join Zervas, so where do we

go to do that?" And the teacher said, "Zervas was around this area, but that's a few months ago, and there's been some fighting with ELAS," so that was the other side, "and I'm afraid that the nearest place that you can find Zervas was [the region of] Epirus," which is near the Albanian border, which was very far away, and totally beyond our means, even if we could find transport to go there.[100]

Whereas Thanassis decided to return, Isaac continued up the mountains with the blessing of his friend. Both of them knew that for Isaac this was the only option. In Athens, Isaac had left behind his father, his mother, and his two younger brothers, all hiding in separate households. Still, Isaac was not the only partisan in his wider family; his cousins Jamila Kolonomos and Isaac Kamchi of Bitola also joined the resistance, Jamila in Macedonia and Isaac in Croatia.[101] When the war ended, an acquaintance of his father's came to ask Isaac to return to Athens. At that point, he was stationed in Larissa doing administrative work and did not know that only his father, lame since childhood as a consequence of polio, had stayed safe in hiding. In mid-November 1944, Isaac was given three-week medical leave from EAM-ELAS service. He had no idea that his mother, a former teacher of French, once full of energy, as well as his younger brothers, Sam and Meko, schoolboys just four years apart, had all been deported to Auschwitz in August 1944, from which only Sam would return.[102]

Since Isaac was not demobilized, he planned to depart from Athens and rejoin his unit. Having sworn an oath, ELAS fighters were not supposed to leave their units without formal permission. From summer 1943 onward, the ELAS was more-or-less organized like a regular army. The structure was based on a tripartite leadership: each unit had an EAM political representative, a military specialist, and an elected leader (*kapetanios*). The smallest body was a squadron of fifteen; these further combined to form platoons, companies, battalions, and regiments. The whole of the ELAS comprised about seven divisions and some specialized brigades, mainly carrying out ambushes and sabotage.[103]

In addition to the formal obligation, there was also another reason to return to the ELAS: partisans developed strong bonds with one another. Indeed, for some EAM-ELAS partisans, choosing between comrades and possibly being reunited with their families was difficult. Different combatants

78 · HOMECOMING

of course had different reasons for remaining in active service. Some believed in their cause; others thought that the EAM would soon rule the country and they might be rewarded; but others remained in service out of fear. Moise Eskaloni, for example, belonged to the last group. As he explained in an interview many years later, his family was staunchly Communist, and he became a party member while serving in the ELAS. After the Varkiza Agreement, he began to fear being bullied or even attacked by people in his own ranks as frictions in Greece increased.[104]

Isaac Nehama's father, however, kept dissuading his son from returning to the resistance. While waiting for the repatriation of other family members from Nazi camps, Isaac and his father found themselves in the middle of a new armed conflict. Once the December Events erupted, Isaac, like many partisans, made his way to the center of Athens to support the demonstrations. Soon afterwards, he was detained by the police. Years later he described the rapid sequence of events and the conditions in Athens at the time:

> Everything had been closed, there would have been no food, other than what one had kept in [store] before the trouble started. So the following day, I went and stood in line at the grocery store two blocks from our apartment, waiting to get whatever was available. And five minutes later, after I started standing in line, a number of police officers, gendarmerie, came and they're going down the line: "Who is Isaac Nehama?" So, me. Well they took me, and first they took me to the apartment and I saw my father. There were other policemen and gendarmes around, some of them in plain clothes, some of them in uniform.[105]

The policemen were not hunting for valuables, contrary to what Isaac suspected, but for ELAS fighters. They immediately took him to the police station for interrogation, and without kid gloves:

> They began to pummel me with the butt of the rifles because they wanted me to reveal names of EAM-ELAS people in the neighborhood. I told them I hadn't been in the neighborhood for over a year. I was not a part of that before I left. Yes, I was in ELAS, but I went to survive, not for political reasons, and certainly I did not know anyone in the neighborhood [...]. Well, I was beaten for quite a time, but at the end I was put

DEMOBILIZATION AND ITS AFTERMATH · 79

in a car, and taken to the place in the center of Athens, which was ironically the place where the Gestapo used to round up their prisoners in the basement.[106]

The December 1944 Report of the EAM Central Committee, which opened this chapter, also states that thousands of people associated with the leftist resistance, including Jews, were imprisoned and persecuted. Some of them were tortured and then transferred by Allied forces to camps in North Africa, yet the Greek authorities took no measures at that point for their rehabilitation.[107] Isaac Nehama was among the deportees and recalls how it happened:

> They had been rounding up people, and the following day they put us in trucks. They took us to a minicamp, a detention camp with barbed wire, near the shore, Glyfada, which is a suburb of Athens. [...] I was kept there for a day and a half, and then we were taken to Piraeus and put on ships. We didn't know where we were going, and after a traverse of I think three or four days and nights, then also it happens in darkness we will disembark. And we found ourselves in the middle of a desert.[108]

In late 1944 and early 1945, British forces assisted by the Greek police identified eight thousand left-wing suspects, imprisoned them in Athens, and then deported them to an exterritorial internment camp. The El-Daba camp, a former RAF base encircled by barbed wire, was located on the Egyptian coast near the Libyan border. The prisoners were not fully aware of where they were heading, and once in the camp they could not determine its location, nor did they know its name. Looking back, Isaac Nehama, for example, thinks he was detained in Libya. During the December Events, more Jewish partisans were locked up in Goudi prison in Athens, and many of them found it difficult until later in life to admit openly how dreadful their situation truly had been in the aftermath of the war.[109]

After returning from Africa, Isaac was lucky enough to start university in Athens. By October 1946, thanks to his father's persistence, he moved to the United States. His father remarried after the war, but this part of their family history is kept silent, probably out of respect for Isaac's mother, who was murdered in Auschwitz. Much later, while visiting Greece, Isaac met Paulette

80 · HOMECOMING

Mourtzoukou, a Jew who as a child had survived in hiding. Her father gave up his war-damaged factory in Volos and resettled with his family in Athens. There, Paulette and her sister befriended a group of young Holocaust survivors, including Sam Nehama, an Auschwitz returnee and a younger brother of Isaac's. These networks, though badly damaged, still provided a chance for young Jews to marry in the faith, as their families would have expected and Greek law still stipulated. Paulette and Isaac fell in love and left together for the United States but never gave up their Greek identity, which had been fostered by Isaac's partisan experience in the mountains.[110]

The immediate postwar persecution of Jews (and others) who had been partisans was naturally not limited only to those from the main cities, that is, Thessaloniki and Athens. Louis Koen, another Jew who gained military experience in the Greco-Italian War, was one of the few Holocaust survivors from the Northern Greek town of Xanthi in Bulgarian-occupied Thrace, whose Jews, deported to the Treblinka death camp, never returned. Louis was among the lucky ones, and his family, thanks to his father's connections in the tobacco business, had obtained false IDs and been able to walk all the way down to Athens at the time of the occupation. While he and his sixteen-year-old brother, Isaac, both of whom were energetic and without commitments, fled to the hills around Mount Parnassus, the rest of his family found a safe haven in the capital thanks to local non-Jews. In the account of his sister, Gentille Koen, we have already heard what she encountered in Athens after the liberation. But she did not finish discussing her eldest brother Louis's sudden reversals of fortune after the war.[111]

Louis was arrested four times soon after the German withdrawal. It was a period when, on the one hand, many of his fellow partisans were in Communist Bulgaria preparing for yet more fighting on Greek soil, and, on the other hand, numerous Holocaust survivors were preparing to leave for Palestine. But Louis never intended to choose any of these options. After the December Events, he was imprisoned in Goudi to await deportation to the El-Daba camp. Louis recalls that in the Athenian prison, which was not the last detention he would experience, he was stigmatized for being Jewish, which reflected the profound xenophobia and socioeconomic prejudices against Jews in Greece: "The commissioner says: 'What's your name?' 'Louis Koen.' 'Jew?' 'Yes.' 'So, a Communist.' I didn't say anything. After fifteen days, another committee: 'What's your name?' 'Louis Koen.' 'Capitalist. Jew,' he says to me. 'Yes.' 'Capitalist. So, a Communist.' [...] Third committee: 'What's your name?' 'Louis Koen.' 'Are you Jewish?' 'Yes.' 'Where are you from?' I say, 'From Xanthi.' They say, 'A Bulgarian.' Go figure!"[112]

Among former ELAS fighters, few Jews remained organized as Communists after the December Events. They were aware of the risk of being imprisoned or even executed for their political orientation. Dimitrios Dimitriou, the ELAS captain to whom Rabbi Barzilai addressed his letter in April 1944, considers the war's aftermath to have been the most critical period of his life. As one of the main ELAS representatives, he was renowned for his view that the EAM should seize power by overthrowing the Greek government. For this, he was hunted down and imprisoned in 1946. While on the run, he was assisted by a couple of former Jewish partisans: the high-spirited David Broudo, who used to serve at EAM headquarters, and Albertos Cohen, a doctor from Kastoria. Having lost his entire family in Auschwitz, Cohen moved to Thessaloniki after the war, but he did not hesitate to provide his former commanding officer with medical and financial assistance. Perhaps because he was a member of a much-needed profession, Cohen managed to avoid severe persecution. By contrast, David was caught on a mission to Athens, which he had agreed to accept with Dimitriou, and was put in jail. Not only did he never come to terms with the death of his thirteen family members in Auschwitz, but he remained bitter about his ten-year imprisonment by the Greek state and his subsequent forced departure to Israel.[113]

The Bourlas family returned to Thessaloniki two days before the Varkiza Agreement was signed. At the age of seventeen, while earning his bread as a lathe operator, Dora's brother Moisis joined the Communist Youth Organization (OKNE) in 1935. His precarious living, among other things, made him radical and political. As a veteran of the Albanian front in 1941, he decided to join the leftist resistance at the first opportunity.[114] Upon his return, Moisis was first arrested during the V-Day celebrations in May 1945. At that moment, his family was about to find out that the two daughters and their husbands had not survived Auschwitz.[115] Soon afterwards, Moisis was sent to several detention camps on Greek islands, where only his sister Dora dared to visit him.[116] For Moisis and other Jewish prisoners in Greece, the sole way to regain their freedom after the Civil War was to leave for the State of Israel. In order to be transferred, however, they had officially to express remorse, renounce their Greek citizenship, and give up the right ever to return to

82 · HOMECOMING

Greece, since the government feared they might join the Communist insurgents.[117] In this way, first Moisis Bourlas and later David Broudo came out of Greek detention during the 1950s. Whereas Moisis returned to Greece in 1987 after many years of intermittent stays in Israel, Bulgaria, and the Soviet Union, David stayed in Israel for good.[118]

In 1950, the JDC representative Herbert Katzki wrote from Athens to headquarters in New York that Greek discrimination against the Jews was well known. In his letter, Katzki demonstrated how in Greece, as elsewhere in Europe, Jews were suspected and stigmatized for alleged "Judeo-Communism":[119] "There have been cases of Jews being imprisoned without charge—for security reasons. It does not seem, however, that this was a particular discrimination against Jews, for a far greater number of non-Jewish Greeks were in the same unhappy situation. It is true, however, that [the] Courts had a predisposition to believe that Jews who were charged were likely to have had leftist sympathies and to have in one way or another collaborated with the guerillas. Documented cases of such discrimination, however, have not been brought to our attention."[120]

As a nonpartisan Western aid-giver, the JDC had no way to intervene officially and effectively on behalf of former Jewish partisans, who were considered a leftist threat to what should be the established order in Greece, especially when it was a matter of young men and women who wanted to stay in the country. But more often than not, the JDC staff in Greece did not toe the apolitical line of their organization and instead sided with former Jewish partisans.

The JDC representatives' friendly attitude to sympathizers of the "rebels" was, however, perceived by JDC headquarters as interfering in Greek internal affairs and thus a violation of the apolitical humanitarian mission.[121] Marguerite Glicksman, a trained British secretary of Jewish origin in her early thirties, who had been a JDC representative in Greece for five years, since the spring of 1945, admitted to having secretly helped Jews with leftist leanings once the turmoil of the Civil War began to spread. In an interview years later, Glicksman describes the situation in Athens, where she went beyond her mandate by assisting Jewish partisans and thus risked losing her job:

> Every half an hour or so, soldiers would march by. They were in a long line, five of them, and they'd have the guns, and they would march by,

DEMOBILIZATION AND ITS AFTERMATH · 83

and it was very ominous. But we kept very quiet and we had no lights on and they would just pass [...] and fortunately nobody was ever caught and nobody was ever in danger, really. I was in danger because if I'd been—if I'd been found out the Joint would have sent me home too. [...] You mustn't interfere and you mustn't do anything that's politically unsound.[122]

For a long time, Moisis Bourlas was the only Jewish fighter to deliver multiple accounts of his ordeals after returning back home to Greece. He even published a memoir elaborating on his wartime experience, homecoming, and postwar life. The audiovisual recordings and scarce archival sources of partisan men and women alike differ somewhat from the Jewish survivors in hiding. They contain far more discussion of personal achievements than of the family fate. Given their complex experience beyond the Holocaust and the critical turn in Greek history writing toward the endorsement of a national resistance after the fall of the junta in 1974, Jewish partisans never became part of the Greek historical narrative.[123] Thus, while the history of Greek women is slowly but surely being integrated into the historiography about the leftist resistance in Greece, the intertwined story of Jewish partisans has not yet made its way into these works.[124] What is more, the stories of the Jews who joined the Middle East Forces are basically absent from both the Greek and the Jewish collective memory.[125]

Even after the 1970s, historians looking at the Greek resistance remained utterly divided in their viewpoints, and there was little desire to include the resistance experience of Jews in Greece into the narrative of the national struggle. In 1998, for example, the long-time director of the Service of Diplomatic and Historical Archives of the Greek Ministry of Foreign Affairs, and thus one of the official arbiters of the Greek historical narrative, Photini Tomai-Constantopoulou, launched the collection *Documents on the History of the Greek Jews* with the following personal anecdote. The former prime minister of Israel, Shimon Peres, shared with her the story of his father, Yitzhak Peres, a volunteer paratrooper in the Royal Pioneer Corps of the British Army, who, on a mission in Greece in 1941, was "rescued by Greek rebels and protected by Orthodox monks at a monastery in Attica." More than half a century after the events, once the Cold War in Europe was well over, Tomai-Constantopoulou—ignoring the fact that Greek resistance had

84 · HOMECOMING

yet to come into existence—still used the loaded term "Greek rebels," which had been established by the German occupiers in the 1940s and was prevalent in Greek discourse until the 1970s. Far more than that, by including the anecdote in the introduction to her book, she again strengthened the exclusivist perception of what it means to be Greek and at the same time supported several hegemonic narratives, one about a Greek national resistance, another about Greek Christianity, and another about Greek hospitality.[126]

The Civil War opened a new chapter in the lives of Holocaust survivors in Greece. After the occupation, a turning point in the lives of all Jews in Greece, as Moris Leon recalls from his then-teenage perspective, first "everyone was looking for what they left behind, valuables, etc. And then the Civil War started."[127] For Jews who survived the Holocaust, in the course of which they were exposed to mortal danger, the new war put an end to all their hopes and expectations associated with homecoming. It was again unjust, fraught with fear and mistrust, comparable to how many Jews in Eastern Europe perceived the rise of Communist regimes. The new circumstances of the Greek Civil War motivated not only Isaac Nehama and other Jewish EAM partisans discussed in this chapter to emigrate but also families who feared that their children would either be conscripted into the army, relocated to Eastern Bloc countries, or victimized in their own country.

CHAPTER THREE

RETURNING FROM THE CAMPS

Treblinka, Auschwitz-Birkenau, and Bergen-Belsen

I am searching for all of them,
And wasting my time in emptiness.

MOSHÉ BECHAR[1]

CROSSING SEVERAL BORDERS before finally entering Thessaloniki, the first deportee to share his experiences in the concentration camps upon homecoming was Leon Batis. After the heavy bombardment of Ioannina in 1941, during which his house had been hit, Leon and his family moved to Athens, where he ran a textile shop. In April 1944, he was deported from Athens to Auschwitz after registering with the Jewish Community, which he did in order to receive ration tickets for his family. His wife Sofia and two children remained in hiding, anonymous. Following the evacuation of Auschwitz-Birkenau in mid-January 1945, Leon managed to escape, and he reached Thessaloniki on February 28, 1945, before meeting his wife and daughter in Athens.[2]

The first one to write down Leon's observations and to describe the mood of the aftermath was Isaac Matarasso. According to his medical assessment, Batis—somehow "neurasthenic"—seemed quite cynical as he began relating his story, in which his audience—Jews who had survived in hiding and now gathered at Matarasso's home—would hear about the existence of gas chambers for the first time: "I went through many countries, and in every

86 · HOMECOMING

place I was taken for mad at the beginning. Oh, what have I seen, what have I suffered! What you are about to hear will one day be known to everyone, it will be published, will even be turned into a film. Then you will remember Batis, whom you considered mad!"[3] Only at that moment did Matarasso realize the true fate of his father and tens of thousands of Jewish deportees from Greece.

Back in Athens, Leon Batis was confronted yet again with general disbelief and, worse, bitterness from those who were futilely awaiting their loved ones: "Various women now without their husbands were coming to him," recalls his daughter Astro. "Leon, have you seen my husband? Where is he? Did he return? Will he return? Is he on his way? Were they liberated? What are they doing now?" Batis initially hesitated to give an answer to the relatives. But once the journalists came in, he was precise about the true nature of Auschwitz. Yet they would not trust him either, commenting: "This is impossible, he is crazy, he must be mad. He has taken leave of his senses; he has lost his mind." Consequently, the account of the first Jewish returnee from Auschwitz was not made public until more camp survivors returned and the gravity of what had really happened started to be mentally processed.[4] Still, decades later, many Holocaust survivors from all over Greece refer to Batis's account of his time in the camp and his return as the one they could not, or did not want to, believe.[5]

For internally displaced Jews, the occupation was a thing of the distant past and most of them returned to their communities, professions, and dwellings to try to rebuild from the ashes the place they used to call home.[6] The mass deportations and genocide meant that the once strong Jewish voice in Thessaloniki had been marginalized beyond anything imaginable, and the Jews' encounter with the city meant further trauma for them. By the time of the liberation, the Jewish population of Thessaloniki had dropped to a number far below that of Athens, roughly to the level of Larissa and Volos, towns with proportionally far fewer inhabitants than Athens.[7] Statistics should of course be approached critically, particularly if they have been compiled in a climate of political terror and chaos. Yet the figures in table 3.1 give us some idea of just how hard the Jewish communities were hit. Whereas the Jewish population in the EAM-held Trikala dropped significantly after the Varkiza Agreement, which enabled many Jews to leave the mountainous areas for the big cities, the Jewish Community of Zakynthos—untouched by the deportations—ceased to exist after the 1953 earthquake. Whether in Thessaloniki, Ioannina, or Corfu, the severely reduced Jewish communities there began to grow slightly only after the return of the camp survivors, as can be seen in table 3.1. In Ioannina and Corfu, camp survivors would make up more or less the entire community. Their return and integration was, however, anything but smooth.[8]

The deportations from occupied Greece, which started in early 1943, ended in the summer of 1944, about two months before its liberation. It was generally known that Jews were being deported for forced labor, mainly to Poland, but only in the aftermath did the names of the three camps become disturbingly familiar: Treblinka (northeast of Warsaw), Auschwitz-Birkenau (in Lesser Poland, close to Cracow), and Bergen-Belsen (in the Province of Hanover, Northern Germany). Whereas the former two were death camps, Bergen-Belsen was originally a POW camp, gradually expanded with subcamps for Jewish inmates. It was there that the "exchange Jews" (*Austauschjuden*) of Greece were detained but kept alive, particularly if they were citizens

TABLE 3.1 Postwar populations of Jewish Communities in Greece (of at least 100 people)

Community	1940	Mar. 1945	Aug. 1945	Mar. 1946	Aug. 1967
Athens	3,500	4,500	4,100	4,930	2,802
Thessaloniki	56,500	800	1,300	1,950	1,122
Larissa	1,175	750	750	726	438
Volos	882	700	700	646	209
Trikala	520	600	350	360	105
Chalcis	350	175	200	170	98
Patras	337	175	150	152	23
Zakynthos	275	250	175	275	N/A
Veria	850	150	N/A	131	29
Corfu	2,000	N/A	N/A	185	51

Compiled from Molho (1981) and JDC and KIS reports.

88 · HOMECOMING

of neutral countries, to be eventually used in negotiations with the Allies.[9] By contrast, none of the roughly 4,200 Treblinka deportees who left Greece in early March 1943 survived to return.[10]

Like so many countries at the time, postwar Greece was politically and economically unstable. In Thessaloniki only a handful of soup kitchens, operated by the UNRRA, provided basic nourishment for about 561,000 hungry souls in January 1945.[11] Once the ex-deportees, both politically and racially persecuted, began to return en masse in the summer of 1945, it became clear that the UNRRA was incapable of providing effective assistance. Although the amount of supplies that the UNRRA brought to Greece was extensive, their distribution (entirely in the hands of the Greek government) was totally inadequate. The Reception Center for Deportees from German Concentration Camps at Larissa train station in Athens had no recovery facilities, not even beds, so that, as Jacobson noted, survivors numb by their camp experience "lie on the floor singly or in family units all day long."[12] All that was available to them was food twice a day. Jacobson further observed that even Greeks who had volunteered to work in the Reich were treated the same as the pitiful Jewish camp returnees. What is more, the ban imposed on imported goods had long made it impossible for Jews overseas to provide food or clothing to Holocaust survivors in Greece.[13]

Greece also lacked natural resources, fuel, and other raw materials. Typhoid fever, tuberculosis, dysentery, and malaria once again spread widely among the local population, while there was a shortage of medical supplies, food, clothing, and blankets.[14] For a while, once Kyriakos Varvaressos—the governor of the Bank of Greece who advocated strict market control—was appointed Deputy Prime Minister in early June 1945, the economy improved slightly. Varvaressos always lent an ear to Gaynor Jacobson in discussions of matters related to the Jewish community. By temporarily holding down inflation with a rationing system, price controls, and using special police forces to curtail the omnipotent black market, he also indirectly helped the JDC and survivors by making staples like sugar, butter, soap, and medical supplies (all of which were being sold at prices far beyond what they cost, say, in the United States at the time) more affordable. Despite his efforts, the crisis reached yet another low point in only a few months. Just as camp returnees were about to register with their communities, inflation began spinning out of control again.[15]

Under these circumstances, the return of a handful of Jewish deportees was of little significance in the bigger picture, but for the Jewish community it was of course the primary concern. In cooperation with the JDC, Jewish Community councils established special committees to facilitate contact with camp survivors and their return and readaptation. The Jewish relief committees, which were helping all the truly needy Jews who had survived internal displacement, were preparing for the returning deportees while other committees were taking care of specific vulnerable groups, such as children, elderly Jews, and young women. And rightly so, because some Jewish girls who survived the extermination camps suffered such a "disintegration of morals," as observed by the Union of Greek Jewish Deportees of Poland (Union des Juifs Grecs deportés en Pologne; in Greek, Enosi Omiron Israiliton Polonias) in Thessaloniki, that it led them into prostitution.[16] The location committee was responsible for inquiries into the whereabouts of displaced Jews in general and deportees in particular. Lists of camp survivors still outside Greece were regularly updated and posted on the noticeboards of the Communities.[17]

The waiting was tense, filled with restless hope for family reunification. In his account published in Athens in 1948, Isaac Matarasso described the "total ignorance of the tragedy" common to all the Jews who had survived in hiding or in the resistance in Greece before the repatriation of deportees: "We could imagine, of course, that from among the deportees some children, or old or sick people would have died because of the cold, or the hunger, or the diseases. But we could never imagine the horrible fate that awaited the 46,000 Jews of Salonika in 1943."[18] The total disregard for professional ethics, which he was soon to be confronted with when medically examining Jewish returnees who had been subjected to pseudo-experiments, finally brought home to him the previously inconceivable dimension of the vicious inhumanity.

For reasons all too understandable, not even former inmates were able to emotionally process the terrible reality of the Nazi concentration and death camps, in which extreme savagery had been combined with chilling rationality. As Dan Stone explains, Jews had been incarcerated under the pretext of their being put into protective custody. Their only offense under Nazi law, that they were Jewish, left them no course of appeal or redress. They were deeply traumatized by their experience, regularly confronted

90 · HOMECOMING

for months with the killing of their loved ones and fellow deportees, and, if lucky enough to survive, they were in a state of wretchedness by the time of liberation. They had to struggle for the bare necessities with means that would have been absolutely unacceptable, even unimaginable, in their past lives. At the moment of liberation, all they hoped for was a return to normality. But liberation alone could not put an end to the deaths nor suddenly restore trust or resolve confusion. Jewish survivors and even their liberators were all asking themselves if these lives could be restored at all. Yet, formerly deprived of their individuality, which had changed their behavior in many ways upon homecoming, Jews were now seizing the opportunity to resume normal life.[19]

Much like the internally displaced Jews, camp survivors were brimming with unfounded expectations. As the JDC director for Greece Gaynor Jacobson observed: "Once on their way to Greece, the deportee was filled with hopes glamorizing his return home to friends, some relatives, a place in which to live, a job, and the future. These hopes are shattered on arrival as in most cases none of the foregoing exists. This causes a terrific let-down with aggression manifested against themselves and against their luckless brethren who lived in hiding and who are, only in some cases, slightly better off."[20]

Leaving the United States for Europe in autumn 1944, Jacobson's first posting as a JDC country representative was Italy, but he left Rome for Athens in March 1945 before the Nazi camps were liberated and ended his mission there in January 1946 as the last Holocaust survivors were arriving in Greece. In regular correspondence with his wife, he made clear to her that Greece at that moment was no place for their family.[21]

Immediately after their liberation, the optimistic projections of camp survivors were nourished by Allied broadcasts, which seemed to promise them a better tomorrow.[22] But while members of the armed forces were generally hailed as heroes upon their return, Jewish returnees were confronted with widespread resentment.[23] Hope gave way to despair and was followed by further deprivation, displacement, and widespread death. Many deportees died at the moment of liberation or shortly afterwards, from exhaustion, disease, or malnutrition, while others, unable to cope mentally with the reality of the Holocaust, committed suicide.[24] Back home, a considerable number of the formerly internally displaced Jews were ashamed of having survived without being directly exposed to mass murder. This was later exploited by legislators in West Germany and a number of other countries in the legal definition of Holocaust survivor, drawing a division line within the shattered Jewish communities. When applied to compensation payments, only those who had been deported to a death camp were eligible, which considerably reduced the budget for this expenditure. It was not until recent decades that the definition expanded to include other survivors as well.[25]

Once some Jews, a small proportion of those who had been deported, but a large proportion of those who had survived the camps, had returned to Greece in the course of spring and summer 1945, a sense of distress that most of the deportees had not survived began to spread among the formerly internally displaced. At home, both Jews and Gentiles often ignored camp returnees or, worse, criticized them for having survived allegedly at the expense of fellow prisoners.[26] Jacobson's observation in December 1945 confirms these sentiments: "The question is almost asked: why are you alive and not my relatives—my mother, father, sister, and so forth? This led to the untrue generalization on the part of leading members of the community, that only the worst elements of the Jews survived the concentration camps."[27] Jacobson also makes it clear that at a time, when the community was still predominantly represented by non-deportees, the earlier ideological divisions were largely in place. With the return of the camp survivors, however, the division on ideological, political, or religious grounds faded, and the distinction was mainly between deportees and others. To meet their needs, the camp survivors organized in the Association of Jewish Hostages of Greece (Enosi Omiron Israiliton Ellados), not as deportees or victims but as "hostages" (*omiri*).[28]

Like Leon Batis, many of the camp returnees were looking for a chance to speak up and share their traumatic memories, which would enable them not only to give testimony but also to start again with a clean slate.[29] Yet most Greeks, and even most Jews who had not been in a concentration camp, were reluctant to listen to descriptions of the horrors of internment and, consciously or subconsciously, avoided the deportees.[30] Until recently, little has been written about their return, and given the nature of archival sources, personal accounts are mostly the only way to begin to trace their arduous journeys. Though by far most deported Jews did not live to relate what they had experienced, their ordeal is retained in the narratives of those who did survive. Like Batis in Greece, camp returnees in general and Auschwitz

92 · HOMECOMING

survivors in particular have in recent years become the symbolic voice of the Holocaust.

Consequently, the accounts of camp survivors far outnumber those of internally displaced Jews or those who managed to leave the country by their own means. The accounts of Auschwitz, the death marches, and the camps after liberation, which I quote from in the following, are drawn from memoirs, interviews, and archival records providing a cross-generational perspective. At the same time, they epitomize a single analytical category of survivors, that is, returnees from concentration camps. Apart from being of a certain age, having a remarkable tenacity, and a great deal of good luck, these young single survivors with little fear of death, siblings sticking together during the worst, and mothers and fathers who hoped to be reunited with their children all had one thing in common: an unceasing desire and determination to survive based on how they perceived interpersonal ties at that moment. Family bonds, if they had a chance to exist after homecoming, largely determined whether survivors decided to go home.

The voices of Jews deported from Greece to Treblinka are completely absent. All were murdered without leaving us any personal account of their hopes for return. What is more, their homecoming—much expected by the handful of Jewish survivors from Kavala, Serres, Drama, Xanthi, and elsewhere in the Bulgarian zone who had gone into hiding in Athens, joined the resistance, or succeeded in crossing borders—did not materialize even symbolically. The only cemetery monument in Greek Thrace, erected in Kavala by the remnants of the Community in 1952 in memory of the Jewish victims, remains out of sight to the Greek public, a silent memorial for the Jewish community itself, the only people who cared.[31] Fragmented perceptions of the fate of the Treblinka deportees can, however, be reconstructed from accounts about Jewish encounters along the way and upon arrival at the camp as well as about disappointed expectations and the lack of return.

For the Bergen-Belsen survivors, how they had been categorized in the camps upon arrival became decisive both while imprisoned and when they got home. Whereas those Jews who had originally been "privileged" experienced the end of war under the conditions of deadly deprivation in Germany, the early deportees who had been citizens of neutral countries cheered the liberation as free people but far from home, as refugees in Palestine, where they had been transferred after Spanish diplomatic intervention. Thus,

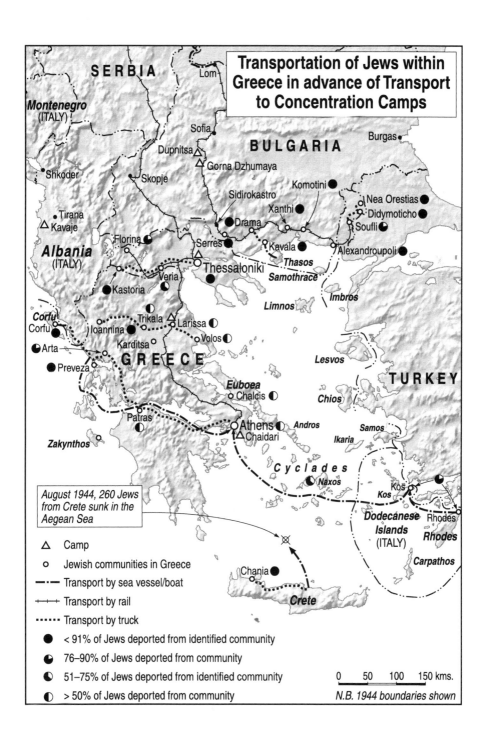

94 · HOMECOMING

paradoxically, those eventually liberated in Germany were to enter Greece earlier than those moved from Bergen-Belsen to the Middle East.

TREBLINKA, NO RETURN

Bulgaria, which had sided with the Axis powers in the spring of 1941 and thus made possible the German invasion of Greece in April, did not deport the Jews of Bulgaria proper to concentration camps outside the country. But one cannot legitimately claim that the same attitude applied to Jews from the newly acquired territories of prewar Greece and Yugoslavia. Simultaneously with the de facto annexation of Thrace and eastern Macedonia (called Belomorie under the Bulgarian occupation), the anti-Jewish measures of the Bulgarian Law on the Protection of the Nation and the high taxation of Jewish property came into force. Radios were confiscated, and valuables had to be deposited in the Bulgarian National Bank.[32] After the Wannsee Conference in January 1942, more restrictions on Jews were enforced. In June, the Bulgarian parliament passed a new decree under which Jews in the Bulgarian-occupied territories were prohibited from obtaining Bulgarian citizenship. Soon, they were issued "yellow passports" and plastic Star of David buttons by the Bulgarian authorities. Their shops and homes were labeled as Jewish, and they were prohibited from entering public spaces (including main streets and parks), restaurants, hotels, and nightclubs.[33]

In February 1943, Sofia and Berlin signed the infamous agreement on the deportation of 20,000 Jews from the new territories. Lists with the names of about 4,200 Jews were drawn up in Belomorie, including each person's occupation and address. Less than two weeks later, Jews from Kavala (1,678), Eleftheroupoli (5), the island of Thassos (16), Serres (471) and its nearby village of Nea Zichni (19), Komotini (904), Alexandroupoli (48), Drama (592), Xanthi (537), and Chrysoupoli (12) were deported.[34] Jolted out of their sleep and expelled from their homes in the middle of a freezing winter night, many Jews were only able to take what they had on them at the time. In small places, the roundups were carried out by the local police. Escape was impossible from the towns encircled by the Bulgarian Army. In these regions, generally rich in tobacco production, large, often multi-story tobacco warehouses proved to be big enough to squeeze in all the detainees until their transfer. Immediately upon entering, Jews were required to hand over their money and valuables to local officials and wait until given further instructions a day or more later.[35]

Because the railway track in Greece was a different gauge from that in Bulgaria, at Sidirokastro Jewish deportees were loaded onto another train for the journey through Bulgaria. Other transfers were later carried out by the Bulgarian police, ultimately for boats to Vienna (from where the Jews were sent by train to Treblinka), but this particular stop at Sidirokastro was probably the last chance to escape. Yet, as Sampetai Tsimino of Kavala recalls, nobody on board could have known this. He was one of forty-eight comparably lucky Jewish young men from Bulgarian-occupied Greece who had been the only ones recruited by the Bulgarians for forced labor and were, at the moment of the deportations, working on the railway next to the Bulgarian village of Belitsa.[36]

About fifty years after the events, a tearful Sampetai describes how, for a moment, Jewish slave laborers had an opportunity to glimpse their relatives being sent to Treblinka. Sampetai saw his mother, two sisters, and two brothers first, but what was most unexpected and traumatizing for him was bumping into his brother Jacques:

> Each train had to go slowly through the curve where we were working next to the track. While we were working I suddenly heard, out of the blue: "Sampi, look, it's me, Jacques!" [. . .] [Sampetai hopped aboard.] We sat together, the train was moving, and I was inside: "Look, Jacques," I told him, "I get nothing for my work." I took off my pullover and gave it to him. "Look, Sampi," he said, "May it serve you well! I have one leg in a plaster cast, so I have one spare shoe. Take it to remember me by!" At that moment, I don't know, I'm taking the shoe and the guard is coming and shouts at me, "Get off, and don't talk!" We were two meters from the guard. "Get off, I will find my way," Jacques said, "[. . .] Go, otherwise they will find out!" I summoned the courage. The train was now going between ten and fifteen kilometers [six and nine miles] per hour. I jumped out into the sand. I made it and the train went on.[37]

Clearly, at that moment, neither brother considered this sudden chance encounter as their last goodbye. Sampetai and Jacques both thought, on the

96 · HOMECOMING

one hand, that it would be far more dangerous for Jacques to escape from the train than to make the journey to what used to be Poland and, on the other hand, Sampetai was afraid of punishment for sabotaging forced labor.

The next stop was Gorna Dzhumaya (today, Blagoevgrad), where the deportees from Kavala (including Sampetai's family), Alexandroupoli, Elefteroupoli, Serres, Thasos, and Nea Zichni were placed in a tobacco warehouse and two school buildings, and the deportees from Xanthi, Chrysoupoli, and Komotini were put in tobacco warehouses in Dupnitsa, just twenty-five miles away. During more than a week of detention, while deportees were falling sick and several had died on the way or in the facilities, women who had been deported at the peak of their pregnancy gave birth. In Gorna Dzhumaya, seven Bulgarian Jewish doctors were allowed to assist the inmates. Thanks to them, the People's Court in Sofia in March 1945 would learn of the deportees' misery. Dr. Iosif Confino portrayed the dark picture of Gorna Dzhumaya:

> There was an area of only sixty square centimeters [nine square inches] per person together with the luggage. The deportees were randomly placed in rooms until they got filled. [...] In the school there was only one tap for about a thousand people to wash themselves in the morning (without soap, which was taken from them earlier). They had to stand in a queue for hours. [...] The situation was the same regarding the restrooms. There was one for three to five hundred people. [...] As a result, after one [or] two days they overflowed so people started using part of the yard, the only place where they were allowed to go to during the day.[38]

Shortly before leaving Dupnitsa, the Jews of Chrysoupoli and a few more with Bulgarian citizenship were released on Bulgarian soil. For everybody else, the last part of the journey across Bulgaria began on March 18 and 19, when Jews from both camps were moved to the border town of Lom on the Danube River, where they then boarded four ships. After about a week, they reached Vienna only to be transferred by rail to the Treblinka death camp. In this way, the Jewish Communities of Belomorie lost almost all their members.[39]

Though it was the last extermination camp built under Nazi rule, Treblinka received the Bulgarian transports of Jews from Greece at roughly the same time as the deportations from Thessaloniki to Auschwitz-Birkenau in early April 1943. From a platform long enough to get rid of all new arrivals from Belomorie at once, twenty wagons could be unloaded simultaneously. It is hard to say what exactly happened after the trains were emptied, but the entrance to Treblinka, lined with corpses and severed limbs, more a horror scene than a "sanitized death factory," clearly signaled what was to come.

According to Yankel Wiernik, a Jewish slave laborer from Warsaw who spent a year in Treblinka but managed to escape during the desperate camp rebellion by its last Jewish inmates against certain death in early August 1943, all deportees from Bulgarian-occupied Greece were sent directly to the gas chambers without the usual prior selection. His recollections of what he anticipated upon the arrival of the deportees from Bulgarian-occupied territories, at least when compared to his previous experience with the Jews of Warsaw, Radom, Lublin, and elsewhere, is probably the last eyewitness account of this murder:

> The new transports were handled in a simplified manner; the cremation followed directly after the gassing. Transports were now arriving from Bulgaria, comprising well-to-do people who brought with them large supplies of food: white bread, smoked mutton, cheese, etc. They were killed off just like all the others, but we benefited from the supplies they had brought. As a result, our diet improved considerably. The Bulgarian Jews were strong and husky specimens. Looking at them, it was hard to believe that in twenty minutes they would all be dead in the gas chambers. These handsome Jews were not permitted an easy death. Only small quantities of gas were let into the chambers, so that their agony lasted through the night. They also had to endure severe tortures before entering the gas chambers. Envy of their well-fed appearance prompted the hangmen to torment them all the more.[40]

Few Jews from Belomorie managed to save their lives through internal displacement or in neighboring countries. Though some of them returned to their hometowns, many turned away after being confronted with the haunting absence of their murdered families. While many disappeared, the once large Jewish communities of Drama, Kavala, and Komotini were so marginalized that the representative of the Central Board of Jewish Communities, Kanaris Konstantinis, who over four years, beginning in December 1945,

98 · HOMECOMING

issued reports on each Jewish community of Greece, did not even bother to write about these.[41]

Not so Jacobson, who visited Kavala in summer 1945, attracted by its ancient history and Jewish presence, which goes back to the days when Saint Paul first set foot on European soil. Symptomatically, however, not even the JDC representative, who in his private correspondence was otherwise always outspoken about Jewish affairs in Greece, remarks more than cursorily on the Jewish community that had once been there. Instead, Jacobson, a passionate pipe smoker, recorded his observations of the Kavala tobacco industry in a letter: "Kavala is a center of the Macedonian Tobacco industry," he remarks. "The leaf is stored in the large warehouses which lie close to the Harbor. Some of the best tobacco still known as Turkish is grown in the district and for a long time the tobacco workers were the only electors in Greece who sent Communist members to Parliament."[42] Though he did not mention it, the many tobacco workers used to be Jews and these were the same warehouses in which the Jews of Kavala had been assembled before deportation.

According to archival sources and other written accounts, Jewish flats and houses in Belomorie were auctioned off almost immediately after the transports had departed. Few Jews survived to sue for their property in the aftermath. Community buildings and synagogues were looted, tombstones and cemetery walls were demolished or otherwise dismantled. Jewish schools were made into Greek Orthodox schools. After lengthy negotiations, fifteen sacks of remaining items from the safety deposit boxes of the Bank of Bulgaria were finally returned to Greece in the late 1970s to become a cornerstone of the Jewish Museum established in Athens, the carrier of displaced Jewish memories, which has now been open to the public for nearly five decades.[43]

AUSCHWITZ-BIRKENAU

By the time the Jews of Greece started to arrive after a journey of between seven and ten days in overcrowded cattle cars, Auschwitz-Birkenau had already been converted into an extermination camp with four fully functioning gas chambers. On average, 80 percent of the new arrivals were immediately murdered in the gas chambers. Since the extermination installations were designed to hold about 2,000 people at a time, it was usually possible to

RETURNING FROM THE CAMPS · 99

murder all the victims selected from the Greece deportations as soon as they arrived. Danuta Czech, a Polish Holocaust historian who has been working in the Auschwitz-Birkenau State Museum since 1955, has calculated that 41,032 of these deportees from Greece did not make it through the selection process upon arrival or simply did not survive the train journey.[44]

Scholars have provided enough data on the three quarters of the inmates destined to die to be able to show decisively that children under the age of fourteen, visibly pregnant women, women and men accompanying children or carrying babies, individuals found to be sick or disabled, and elderly Jews had little chance of ever being selected for work. All that awaited them in Auschwitz was a gruesome, certain death. Only those who were healthy and strong or skilled and gifted (who, according to the standards of their oppressors, could claim to be doctors, nurses, dentists, pharmacists, barbers, electricians, artisans or musicians, etc., or those having extraordinary knowledge of languages, including German of course) were selected for slave labor and then tattooed with a registration number. Only 30 percent of them were women.[45]

At Auschwitz, only a few days after initially receiving reassurance that they would be reunited with their relatives who had been deported with them, the prisoners became fully aware of the dreadful reality. Moreover, since many young Jewish women had left Thessaloniki as newlyweds, it is reasonable to suppose that several of the brides were also at an early stage of pregnancy and were either unaware of the fact or, most likely, concealing it. Giving birth in Auschwitz-Birkenau inevitably put them in a terrible dilemma: either they and their babies would end up in a gas chamber about a week after birth or the mothers would find a way to terminate the pregnancy and spend the rest of their lives—however short—consumed by the feeling that they were responsible for the deaths of their babies.[46]

The new arrivals at Auschwitz who were assigned to slave labor survived day-by-day under the constant threat of having to go through another selection process. According to many accounts, it was probably the Jews of Greece who first brought louse-borne typhus to Auschwitz.[47] The epidemic led first to quarantine in the summer of 1943 and then, around the Jewish holiday of Yom Kippur in September, to a vast selection process, for which more prisoners fell victim than ever before. Under this constant psychological pressure and physical exhaustion, many prisoners committed suicide by throwing

100 · HOMECOMING

themselves against the electrified barbed wire fence of Auschwitz-Birkenau. Stella Massarano, a former prisoner deported from Thessaloniki, remarked that some prisoners had attempted to escape in order to get killed.[48]

Of the 12,757 selectees from the twenty-two transports from Greece, only 2,496 (70 percent of whom were men) were still alive in September 1944.[49] At that point, Jews were already being transferred out of Auschwitz. In 1945, the daily death rate in liberated camps with the highest number of survivors—Buchenwald (20,000), Bergen-Belsen (60,000), and Dachau (30,000)—saw deaths that exceeded one-fifth of the surviving populations in the weeks after they were liberated. Though Jews made up a far smaller proportion of camp internees than did political prisoners and POWs, their deplorable state made them the most likely to die.[50] About 200 Auschwitz survivors originally from Greece decided to restart their lives in other countries; the rest, which dropped to about half in the course of death marches and subsequent suffering, returned to Greece. Among the two thousand overall camp returnees, about 80 percent had been through Auschwitz, and most of them now headed for their hometown of Thessaloniki.[51]

Initially they were encouraged to return by general Allied policy, in which repatriation was the priority. Thus, agreeing to be repatriated increased one's chances of getting out of the camp and returning to normal life more quickly than those categorized as displaced persons and located in DP camps who wished to go, say, to Palestine or the United States.[52] Lacking a clear idea of the political and economic conditions in Greece, Jews were hoping that new career opportunities would open up for them at home. Soon, however, all prospects of Greek state care evaporated as local governments proved unable to meet their expectations.[53] Survivors who wished to return longed for the Mediterranean climate, but above all they imagined Greece as the central place for family reunions. Yet most of these returnees soon realized that few of their hopes would be met upon homecoming.

Minors

In a December 1945 report for JDC Headquarters in New York, Gaynor Jacobson made clear that most of the survivors were men rather than women. He also summed up from their perspective how in Greece from early on, the expectations of the Jewish camp returnees were disappointed by the

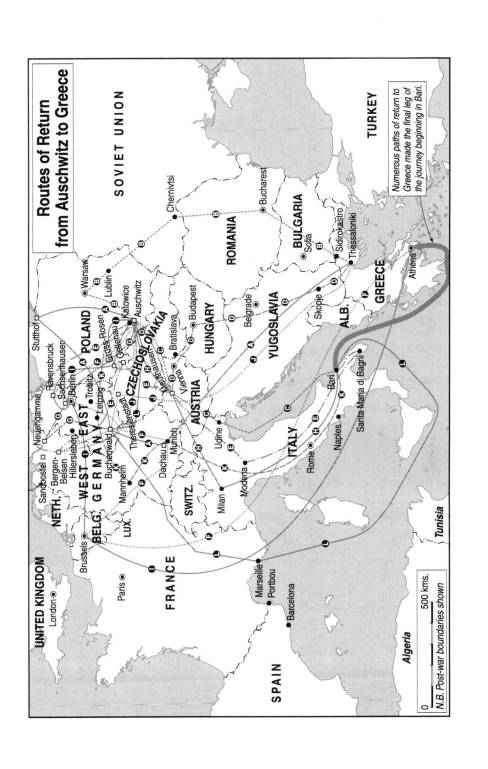

102 · HOMECOMING

insensitivity they met with from the authorities: "When at first deportees began returning to Greece, almost all of them were men and boys but after two or three months, girls began to appear. The UNRRA, through the Greek government, had arranged a Reception Center at a storehouse at Larissa Station in Athens where Jewish and political deportees were housed together with Greeks who had volunteered, during the occupation, for work in Germany. It was a great set-back for the unfortunate Greek Jews who had visualized on their return the occupation of their former homes, and good treatment from the government."[54]

The lists of Auschwitz survivors reveal that many of those who had survived long enough to be liberated were teenagers or minors, that is, under Greek law at the time, someone younger than twenty-one. Girls of this age usually had the clear advantage of still being childless, while boys had not yet been recruited to fight in the Greek-Italian war and become war invalids and therefore did not contribute to the macabre collection of prosthetic limbs that are now on display in the Auschwitz Museum.[55] Behind the fence of the camp in remote, occupied Poland, they suffered the shock of losing their other family members, mostly parents, grandparents, and younger siblings, who were taken immediately from the ramp to the gas chambers. Again, none of this applies only to the Jews of Greece. Rudolf Vrba (born Rosenberg), for instance, was deported to Auschwitz from the Slovak town of Topoľčany at the age of eighteen. He has since become famous for having successfully escaped from Auschwitz-Birkenau and, together with his fellow prisoner Alfréd Welzer, delivering a report on the inconceivably huge scale of the murder of the Jews. In his memoirs, Vrba remarks that the reason why death never became a reality for him was most likely because of his youth: "Probably because I was young and healthy, I built a carefree philosophy of a soldier who believes that they can kill the men next to him, but he will remain intact."[56] This axiom of youth is present in all the narrations of prisoners who were minors. Not a reflection of selfish egoism but rather of ingenuous solidarity and the pursuit of belonging somewhere, as Vrba longed for, allowed them to defy reality.[57]

According to the Database of Greek-Jewish Holocaust Survivors' Testimonies, which lists personal accounts recorded from 1959 up to the present day, 177 out of the 391 Jews from Greece who survived Auschwitz-Birkenau were teenagers. This includes 98 people who had been born in Thessaloniki and 7 who had been deported at the age of fourteen or younger.[58] Though one could plausibly argue that the database predominantly includes those still able to contribute to the large collections of interviews conducted in the 1980s and 1990s, like the Fortunoff or Visual History Archive, a similar picture is offered by postwar lists of survivors. The first list, from the summer of 1945, comprises 61 Auschwitz deportees, out of which over a third (24) were minors, and only 1 was older than forty when sent to the camp.

The first female survivor in Greece to write down her memoirs was Berry Nachmia, née Buena Cassouto. In the aftermath, she became a confident representative of the Association of Jewish Hostages of Greece. She had been deported from her native Kastoria on March 26, 1944; though she had had ample opportunity to flee the deportations, Berry was determined to remain with her family. Shortly after her arrival in Auschwitz-Birkenau, she turned twenty. Being from a Zionist family, Berry studied Hebrew while her father, Israel Cassouto, was arranging for a permit to leave for Palestine. The family, however, focused first and foremost on helping poorer relatives get to Palestine, where they hoped to start a better life. Before it was her family's turn to emigrate, it was already too late. In Auschwitz-Birkenau, Berry's stepmother, with a baby in arms, and five other siblings were sent straight to the gas chambers. By comparison, Berry was the only lucky one, being among the women selected to work in the Kanada Kommando sorting food, clothing, and valuables taken from newly arrived prisoners. In this way, she was not only able to improve her diet but also to help herself and other women get good shoes, which were essential for the long journey to come. Always being an outsider to her stepmother, she was, unusually for a girl in Greece of her times, accustomed to seeking close friendship outside her family circle. For Berry, as for many other people, women and men alike, sociability and solidarity were crucial components of survival, as is evident from her memoirs and from numerous interview recordings with her and others.[59]

Berry was sent on the death march from Auschwitz on January 18, 1945. At that time, the most important person in her company was her cousin, who was not only someone to count on in difficulties but also represented home and family. For the roughly ten-day journey, they stuck together all the way, covering about 1,000 kilometers (621 miles) to Ravensbrück, from where they were relocated a few days later to Retzow for two or three months and then to their final internment in Malchow. Though a Greek national identity was

104 · HOMECOMING

typically assigned to them by the authorities along the way and generally aimed at repatriation, most of these survivors seem to have acted of their own accord. They were able to surmount national boundaries, particularly thanks to their ability to communicate in languages that people outside Greece could understand. Earlier, in Kastoria, Berry had become friendly with a Jewish refugee from Bitola who would later share her bread rations with Berry in the camp. Berry regularly recalled this as an unforgettable act of solidarity.[60]

On the morning of May 1, 1945, Berry realized that the guards had fled, abandoning the camp. At that moment, she and her cousin set off, with no particular destination in mind, just to get out. The girls soon met other camp survivors, POWs, and German refugees marching ahead of the Soviet front, which was approaching fast. All of them were determined to reach the American zone. For Berry, the logic was simple and again related to family bonds. She recalls saying to her cousin, "If the Americans liberate us, there's a chance they will quickly send us to America. And you know we have relatives there, and we can stay close to them, but if it's the Russians who liberate us, maybe they will send us to Russia, and we have no one there."[61]

Wandering along motorways and through the woods, while constantly at risk of being shot, struck by bombs, or raped, they deliberately spent the third night in the Malchow camp. Much to their surprise, the camp was again under German supervision the next morning, but this did not last long. Soon all the internees—Jewish prisoners and POWs—were emptying previously locked warehouses full of Red Cross food provisions. After getting hold of these, they would dart off into the woods. It was a French POW who led the group of between eighty and a hundred people and separated them by sex in an abandoned two-story house while waiting for liberators. Once the Red Army was on the doorstep, Berry suddenly lost all her strength. She was separated from her cousin and hospitalized with typhus. During her recovery, she befriended two Jewish girl patients from Thessaloniki who would accompany her to Greece.[62]

At a provisional sanatorium in Germany, in some comfort but still covered in lice, Berry was able to regain at least a bit of her dignity by eating normal meals, sewing, and even dancing. She was also able to make use of her Italian when communicating with the POWs. This interaction resulted in a group decision not to wait for their home countries to organize their return, but to set out for home on their own instead. Equipped with cover letters from the Soviet authorities, three Greeks, three Yugoslavs, and three Italians left the camp determined to reach their diplomatic missions in Berlin, where they would ask to be repatriated. During their journey, the cover letter served not only as a *laissez-passer* but also as a ticket for free travel on trains and buses, for food vouchers, and occasionally for accommodation. The group finally reached an internment facility run by the Red Army in Berlin, where the nine friends were separated into groups according to nationality.

Along the way, Berry communicated in basic German, which she had learned in the camps, and occasionally, to her great surprise, used Greek when talking to educated Germans, who were likely to have had Ancient Greek at school. In Berlin, the Greek component of the DP camp, composed solely of former forced laborers, was ready to help the newcomers as compatriots. It is reasonable to suppose that for the girls, who both came from Thessaloniki, Judeo-Spanish was either the language of everyday communication or a coded language that others in the DP camp could not understand. Berry does not elaborate on this, but she makes clear that the dividing line between the Jewish and the non-Jewish internees was always present: "We told them that we were three Jewish Greek women who had survived the crematoria. [...] Their jaws dropped: they had never heard of anything like that."[63]

For the three girls, Berlin was just another stop on their return. In due time, the Greek group moved clandestinely from the Soviet to the American DP camp, hoping in that way to reach their homeland faster. Nevertheless, the transfer from Berlin to the US zone in Bavaria only happened in August 1945, when the Allies provided some trucks that brought them to Munich. From there, they were taken by buses to a transition facility in Brussels for the Location and Repatriation Section of Aide aux Israélites Victimes de la Guerre (AIVG), an office specifically serving Jewish survivors. Berry was determined to repatriate to Greece so that she could see with her own eyes who remained of her family and perhaps meet her cousin again. In early September 1945, she finally left on a military airplane for Athens. In her recollections, they were greeted "with a lokum [traditional Greek confection of starch and sugar] and a hello," which could hardly meet the needs of the Jewish camp returnees.[64]

106 · HOMECOMING

In Athens, Berry and her friends were taken to the reception center in the Eighth Gymnasium, only a few blocks from the synagogue. They were given identity cards and allowed to rest for a couple of days but, as the JDC reported, the state of the returnees was most unsatisfactory with regard to the overall "cleanliness and hygiene" of the facility.[65] Berry was also met with skepticism when relating her experience of the death camps. For the listeners, the reality of Auschwitz seemed to be apocalyptic fiction. Since her whole immediate family had perished in the camp, she considered joining the Hachsharah, the vocational training facilities to prepare Jews to emigrate to Palestine, but, according to Berry, her friend Polina Altcheh from the camp had insisted that they go to Thessaloniki instead. These three girls were among the 985 Jewish camp survivors who returned to Greece in September 1945.[66]

The next month, another eighty-one deportees—including three POWs—were to follow the Athens-Thessaloniki path. Later in life, Berry appreciated the decision to stay in Greece. Looking back, she realized that she would have been unable to cope with yet another internment, such as one of the British detention camps in Cyprus, which were the fate of many illegal immigrants to Palestine. Whereas her friend Polina—by then married—seized the first opportunity to leave for the United States in 1951, emigration was no longer an option for Berry and her husband, Mentes Nachmias, who had survived with his parents and siblings by hiding in the mountains of the Peloponnese. At this point, she rebuilt her life solely in the environment of her new family. With her newborn son and, not long afterwards, two baby daughters, the family became her main concern again. Nevertheless, it took her years to overcome the distinctive claustrophobia characteristic of all death camp survivors, which was coupled with an equally strong devotion to fellow inmates.[67]

Nata Gattegnio, a Corfiot Jew born in 1923, whose birth name was Eftychia (Mazal) Osmo, was another young Auschwitz survivor who returned to Greece. When the Germans occupied Corfu in 1943, Eftychia, as the eldest of four sisters, had decided to take matters into her own hands. Thanks to her involvement with the Red Cross and her membership in EPON, the leftist resistance youth movement, she was well connected with non-Jews, which enabled her to arrange hiding places under false identities for two of her sisters. Only the youngest one and Eftychia, who had been planning on taking good care of the family once they were relocated, were deported together with the parents. Because she had been unable to achieve her aims, her decision ceaselessly haunted her after the war. Eftychia's two sisters who had survived in hiding would later also have emotional difficulties in coming to terms with having married their non-Jewish saviors. More than that, although Eftychia married another Auschwitz survivor, she was, unlike Berry, infertile as a result of brutal beatings in the camp.[68]

Eftychia was yet another Jewish girl among the many who were unwilling to break close family bonds, consciously or subconsciously, in the dramatic moment of a journey into the unknown. Still, there was also local sociability and solidarity, which, as she remarked, made it possible to survive despite the certain death of her family. After some initial back-and-forth and under heavy Allied bombardment, the *Judenaktion* on Corfu was completed on June 9, 1944, when 1,800 Jews were rounded up, stripped of all valuables, and deprived of their homes. In this, as in Kastoria about two months earlier, the Germans were actively assisted by the local authorities. Over the next two weeks, the Jewish captives continued by boat via Lefkada to the port-city of Patras in the Peloponnese. From there, they reached the Chaidari transit camp. On June 29, 1944, an eight-day transport by rail brought them, together with more than two hundred Athenian Jews, to Auschwitz-Birkenau. There, Eftychia became closely attached to a group of Jewish girls from Corfu who provided for her during the persecution as much as circumstances allowed, despite the risk of severe punishment.[69]

From Auschwitz-Birkenau, Eftychia was moved to Bergen-Belsen in October 1944 and then to Gellenau before finally ending up in Mauthausen in February 1945, where she was liberated on May 5, 1945. At that point, her health had seriously deteriorated. She was suffering from malnutrition and her legs were so swollen she was unable to walk, but by May 21 she was found fit enough to be released from the Mauthausen Evacuation Hospital. According to her, the Jewish Brigade arrived together with the US Army, clandestinely sending some of the Jewish survivors who knew Hebrew, accompanied by Magen David Adom staff (the Jewish equivalent of the Red Cross), to Treviso, Italy, for Hachsharah. Still only in provisional clothing, they continued undercover to Modena. Eftychia's fluent Italian (a language commonly used on Corfu back then) must have come in handy while wandering around Milan, Rome, and Modena. Her Hebrew helped

108 · HOMECOMING

her connect with the Jewish organization Sochnut and join the DP camp in Santa Maria di Bagni, the largest in southern Italy, near Lecce in Apulia, under the supervision of the Allied Commission.[70]

After a few months of teaching Hebrew in the Santa Maria DP camp, which had a strong presence of Jews from Thessaloniki preparing for Aliyah, Eftychia received a telegram from her sister Rina through the International Committee of the Red Cross (ICRC). Both sisters in Greece had survived the war, but Ika was suffering from tuberculosis. They wanted Eftychia to return. At that very moment, she made up her mind not to move to Palestine immediately—which had been her initial plan—but instead to return to Corfu, at least for a while. Passing through the DP camp in Carbonara di Bari, she learned that the Italians of Corfu had been expelled from the island as enemy aliens, which (along with the deportations of Jews) had completely changed its demographics. Another obstacle appeared on her way home. Whereas most of the sixty-nine Jewish former deportees arrived in Corfu in September 1945, Eftychia only got back in early 1946. On boarding the boat to Patras, priority among people returning home to Greece from German camps was given to non-Jews. But Eftychia would not be deterred. It was not long before she left for Corfu.[71]

The locals on Corfu, both Greek and Jewish, offered Eftychia employment in Greece. They sought to discourage her from moving to the Middle East. Though they predicted a dark future for her if she emigrated, she remained firm in her decision: "They told me, 'Look, Eftychia, dear girl, we do not want you to leave. You have your two sisters here, we will give you a job at the business school, you will go to Athens twice a year, we will take care of everything. Why should you go there to get killed by the Arabs? You were spared from the Germans, you have people who love you here, is it not a pity [to leave]?'"[72]

But for Eftychia, who had been persecuted only because she was Jewish, Palestine became the place to live as a Jew.

At that moment, Samouil Mizrachi was already organizing the Aliyah of some hundred Corfu Jews eager to resettle in Palestine. Eftychia was soon on the boat to Patras again, in order to reach the Hachsharah in Athens. After about a week there, on June 8, 1946, she illegally boarded the overcrowded *Haviva Raik* on the beach of Sounio along with another 462 young Jews mainly from Greece, heading to the new Jewish homeland. At that moment, the Civil War was already raging in Greece. Eftychia's future husband, Israel Gatenio, was eligible for conscription to fight the insurgents for another two years despite his being a Holocaust survivor. An effective way to avoid the draft was to take up training in Hachsharah, where he met Eftychia. Her poor health, on the other hand, prevented Eftychia from serving in the army in Palestine, which for the Jews of their age, including Israel, was otherwise obligatory.[73] Throughout her life, Eftychia stayed in close touch with former camp inmates. Regardless of their ascribed nationality, the Jews of Corfu were always prominent in her network. It seems that, for her, Greekness was a category assigned from above, whereas her Corfu identity, a colorful Greek-Jewish-Italian fabric, was the one she internalized but did not find anymore in Greece.

All able-bodied male Jews in Greece were required by law to serve in the military. Isaak Mizan, one of twenty-five deportees from Arta who had survived the camps, was enlisted when he reached the age of twenty-one in 1948. After his interview in 1998, he became one of the most heard Holocaust survivors in Greece: "I tell my story everywhere, at schools, universities, memorial events, in the mass media because I feel it is my mission," he explains, "a debt to the good fortune I had to survive."[74] By articulating his motivation, Isaak is communicating the message that any disrespect for humanity can have dreadful consequences. Nevertheless, whereas Isaak's oral account mostly leaves the impression that he has learned to cope well with the terrible events which deprived him of his parents and three siblings, the biographical novel, based on his narrations, brings us closer to reality. Isaak's nostalgia for his native Arta, for the Jewish school of his childhood, for the old cemetery of which no tombstone was spared, and for the two synagogues, which suffered heavily from Allied bombardment, leaks through his story.[75]

Isaak and his relatives—except for one brother who managed to go into hiding in Athens—were deported together with the other Jews of Arta and nearby Preveza. The Germans, in collaboration with the Greek security forces, sent them via Patras to the Chaidari camp on March 26, 1944. First joined by the Jews of Patras and Athens and, on the way, by the Jews of Chalcis, Volos, Trikala, Larissa, Ioannina, Florina, and Kastoria, none of them could any longer enjoy Italian protection. During the deportation, Isaak may have glimpsed Berry Cassouto for a moment when she was put on the same train in Thessaloniki. In Birkenau, he at first occasionally managed to keep

110 · HOMECOMING

in touch with his cousins who had been assigned to the *Sonderkommando*, the unit of inmates working in the crematoria, and with his older sisters. They tried to provide him with an extra piece of bread whenever they could. Even under these perverted circumstances, the family bonds remained as strong as possible, but other than that, Isaak claims, everybody was on their own. As soon as he was transferred via Oranienburg and the nearby camp of Sachsenhausen to the Neuengamme subcamp in Hamburg, Isaak no longer knew where his family was. Being together with Soviet POWs cleaning the rubble of a city constantly under Allied bombardment felt less life-threatening to him than the selections in Birkenau or the internment that followed.[76]

As is symptomatic of people persecuted for their identity, Isaak, too, internalized the false Greek name Takis Mizanis, consciously trying to shake off his Jewishness. This would later lead to much confusion when his brother in Athens tried to track him down with the help of the Red Cross. If his identity concealment was indeed effective, this might also be the reason why, after Hamburg and then Ohrdruf (a subcamp of Buchenwald), he was transferred to the POW camp in Sandbostel. Isaak ended up in Bergen-Belsen, where he was finally liberated by the British Army on April 15, 1945.[77]

In the days leading up to his liberation, Isaak was suffering from dysentery, with no food and housed in a hut holding deceased bodies: "Imagine, to sleep there we used corpses, plain corpses, instead of pillows," he recalls. The liberators initially shuddered but immediately provided the inmates with medical care, which saved Isaak's life and got him back on his feet within ten days.[78] After he had more or less recovered and put on some weight, Isaak decided to join some Serbian POWs on their way home. Going through Soviet-liberated territory with a stopover in Belgrade, he and a former fellow prisoner, another Jewish boy from Greece, felt that this journey was more straightforward than awaiting repatriation in a DP camp. Crossing the Greek border in Koula, north of Florina, Isaak was able to celebrate his eighteenth birthday in his native land.[79]

Looking for what was left of Jewish life in Athens, Isaak was informed that his brother had survived and was eagerly awaiting his siblings' return. After a short stay with his aunt in Athens, Isaak went back to Arta to join the other fifty-eight Holocaust survivors of the town and to start the family business all over again. But the Mizan brothers first had to expel the local intruders and get some money together. Isaak could have never imagined how much his town had deviated from what had once been normal and how many cleavages had grown among the Greeks, not only due to the occupation but most prominently to the climate in society just before the Civil War. In Arta, in 1945, Isaak had experienced some difficult moments trying to deal with the trauma in his own teenage way, but he generalized it to apply to most camp survivors: "We threw those who were there out of the house. I did not go to school. Psychologically, we were a bit unwell, and I could not think about starting school again, so I started my own life instead. Nor was I at the shop that my brother ran. I started with ouzo, drinking and getting drunk every night, and in bed I remembered my family."[80]

From the Red Cross, the Mizan brothers learned that at Auschwitz-Birkenau two of their sisters had been liberated by the Red Army, but one had died on the way home, and the other did not get back to Greece until December 1945. For their sister, the brothers arranged a marriage with a bereaved brother-in-law, an Auschwitz returnee. These remnants of family, which were so dear to Isaak, stayed in Greece for his lifetime, but he never fully swept away the feeling of solitude caused by the dehumanization he had experienced in the camps or a constant fear for his loved ones.[81]

One of the youngest Jewish internees from Greece in Auschwitz-Birkenau was Sam Nehama, whose family of five had split up in Athens to have better prospects of survival. Whereas his elder brother, Isaac, had joined the partisans, and his half-lame father had hid alone in the city, his mother and his grandmother, together with two younger boys—Sam being one of them—ended up in a poor neighborhood on the outskirts. What Sam first perceived as a thrilling game of cops and robbers soon became deadly serious, even in the eyes of a fourteen-year-old. At the end of June 1944, they were sniffed out by Germans and their collaborators. After brutal interrogations at the SS headquarters in Merlin Street, Athens, they were transferred to the Chaidari camp, where Sam's grandmother died of hardship. A month later, they were deported with the Jews of the Dodecanese on the final transport from Greece to Auschwitz-Birkenau. There on the platform after an eleven-day journey, he saw his mother and brother for the last time, having been separated from them during the internment at Chaidari. As Sam remembers, what little Meko asked before getting on board the cattle car was: "Will they kill us?"[82] In Auschwitz-Birkenau, a ten-year-old did not stand a chance of being selected for work, nor did his mother.

112 · HOMECOMING

Sam was assigned to the male group of forced laborers, enduring five months in Birkenau and at a farm complex of the Budy subcamp, which luckily provided him with more food than usual. Looking back, he thinks that the summer internment in Chaidari made him stronger and pushed him to survive: "If you combine the good air of Chaidari, because we were outdoors, the hard work, very hard work, and the good food [sic]—I know myself that I grew at least this much [showing with his hands about one foot], this is maybe the secret. Because when we later arrived in Auschwitz and they made the selection I looked like a man."[83]

Already in the male section of the Chaidari camp, Sam developed strong personal ties with adult prisoners who helped him to hold on to life in Birkenau. Sam describes the boys of his own age as extremely cruel. Although he initially had almost no knowledge of Judeo-Spanish, Sam often refers to the Jews of Thessaloniki and Rhodes as the people who made up his closest social environment. He even learned some of their language in Birkenau. In January 1945, while marching with another ten thousand prisoners in the frigid cold to Buchenwald, where he would spend another four months until being liberated by the US Army, Sam was at first indifferent to life.[84] By then, his weight had dropped to seventy pounds (thirty-two kg), about a third of what he should have weighed at that age. Dressed in two blankets and a pair of clogs, the most common footwear in the camps, he was brought to a makeshift ward for former prisoners with infectious diseases. After a three-week recovery, during which patients were grouped by nationality (a usual practice in facilities for DPs), Sam started to refer to himself as Greek and feel like one. In mid-June, believing that there was a good chance that his brother and father had survived, Sam was repatriated, through France and Italy, to Athens, the destination he stated in the questionnaire of the Office of Military Government, United States (OMGUS) in occupied Germany two months earlier.[85]

In Athens, Sam's name was already being read out on the radio and listed in the newspapers as being among the living, much to the joy of his brother and father, who had harbored little hope that a fourteen-year-old boy would have survived the Auschwitz inferno. A ferry operated by UNRRA brought him from Bari to Korinthos in early August 1945, at which point he telephoned his family.[86] Some hours later and to his brother's obvious surprise—since what he saw was contrary to his expectation of camp survivors in striped pajamas, which he had seen in the local cinema's newsreels—Sam stepped off the train in Athens dressed in "brown corduroy pants, in the manner of lederhosen [looking] very, very healthy and well fed." Afraid of causing him only more pain, his family did not ask much. Their father tried to restore normal life for both sons by encouraging them to go to school and to work. Even to Isaac, who remained very close to Sam, many traumatic moments of the displacement were mediated only much later through Sam's recorded accounts.[87]

When Sam Nehama was asked about his destination of repatriation, he, unlike many DPs, clearly stated Athens, to reunite with his family. He was probably also thinking about his mother, whose thoughts throughout the internment had always been with his brother Isaac. Sam's homecoming was thus a symbolic fulfillment of the mother's hope that the family would be reunited.

Siblings

Love of family and the expectation of reuniting with family members seem to have been the strongest motivation of many camp survivors who otherwise had no reason to return. A similar motivation is evident in the narrations of brothers and sisters.[88] While the four youngsters, Berry, Eftychia, Isaak, and Sam, were all deported from the former Italian zone of occupation and thus had to endure a maximum of fourteen months in captivity, some Jews from Greece managed to overcome two years of internment to see the liberation. Among them, there were several siblings, including the brothers Alberto and Dario Levi of Thessaloniki.[89]

Alberto, five years older than Dario, was born in 1918, when the Jews of Thessaloniki were still trying to get used to the fact of no longer being part of the Ottoman Empire but part of the Kingdom of Greece instead. Although the Jews of Thessaloniki were used to extreme hardship caused by recent wars, that was nothing compared to the general persecution they would have to face during the German occupation. In the summer of 1942, Alberto was sent, together with other Jewish men of Thessaloniki, to do forced labor for the Reich in Greece. The next shock came when the Jews were enclosed in ghettos, separated from the rest of the city's population. Since their father had died years before, only Alberto, Dario, their little brother, and their

114 · HOMECOMING

mother were sent to the transit camp called the Baron Hirsch ghetto. As with other couples, Alberto entered into a last-minute marriage with Allegra, a girl he had barely known, whom he would provide for in a foreign country. On April 3, 1943, they were all deported to Auschwitz. On the freight train of 2,800 passengers, several died during the one-week journey. His mother and little brother (about ten years old) were sent directly to the gas chambers.[90]

Dario and Alberto never parted ways during their captivity, and they were able to provide each other with moral and sometimes material support. They occasionally established contact with Allegra using Greek as a code while in Birkenau. Afraid they might be separated if anyone found out they were related, they told no one. After eight months in Birkenau, Alberto was sent to Auschwitz; Dario was sent soon after. They were assigned to clear the rubble after the Warsaw Uprising in August 1944 and the German destruction of the city that followed in reprisal in the autumn. During the preparations for the Auschwitz evacuation, they managed to run away, prompted by the decision to take revenge for the ordeal they had suffered while in captivity. Alberto was well received by the Polish resistance and was armed to fight the Germans. There, he started a romance with a Jewish woman from Poland who was also in the resistance. The Levi brothers spent about a month in Warsaw, but, aware of the possible atrocities to follow, they were eager to leave as soon as possible.[91]

Leaving Warsaw on foot, the brothers wandered through the Polish countryside, not understanding a word of the locals and still fearing German attacks. They were prevented from continuing their journey at the Vistula River once the Germans clashed with the advancing Red Army in January 1945. They returned to Warsaw only to continue on to Lublin after learning about a group of camp survivors being looked after by the Soviets there. Although Alberto was hoping to reunite with his wife, he received the false information that Allegra had died in the camp. In the company of other Jews from Greece whom they encountered in Lublin, they continued south, reaching Chernivtsi, in Western Ukraine, around Passover. The Soviet-run reception facility in Chernivtsi, divided according to nationality, marked the actual beginning of their return to Greece. Traveling by train for more than a month with stopovers in Bukovina and Bucharest, the Levi brothers finally reached the Greek border at Sidirokastro. At the crossing, they sensed for the first time that their expectations of family reunification were unrealistic. As Alberto says, "The goal was to return first to Thessaloniki, to look for my family. I knew I had nothing to look for. And now, after all the suffering, I suddenly wept."[92]

From the reception camp in Sidirokastro, which was run by Palestinian staff of the Magen David Adom, the survivors were escorted to Pavlos Melas, the former prison and detention center in Thessaloniki, for quarantine. Since they had entered Soviet territory, they were thoroughly vetted to find out whether they were open to Communist indoctrination and work for Soviet intelligence.[93] It was there that they found Alberto's wife, Allegra. Alberto started to earn his living in the Thessaloniki office of the JDC, the only job he could find, and Dario went to Athens to join the Hachsharah. In Sounio, in June 1946, he clandestinely boarded the *Haviva Raik* for Palestine, sailing, unknown to him, together with Eftychia Osmo and her husband-to-be. After the Civil War ended in 1949, Alberto and Allegra followed him to the new Jewish state.[94]

Two other Thessalonican brothers, Jacob and Dario Gabbai, were first able to avoid forced labor in Greece in 1942 and the deportations from Thessaloniki in 1943 thanks to their Italian citizenship. In March 1943, 281 Jews were registered as Italian citizens in the whole district of Thessaloniki.[95] Besides the Gabbais, the two sons of the Venezia family, Mois and Shlomo, who were distant cousins of Jacob and Dario, also had Italian citizenship. But, as was the case for many other Jews and non-Jews with Italian papers at the beginning of the Greco-Italian War, in autumn 1940, the men were detained as enemies of Greece. Mois Venezia, Dario Gabbai, and his father, Victor, were among them. Paradoxically, it was the German authorities who set them free as allied nationals in April 1941 and brought them back to Thessaloniki.[96]

Soon after the seventeenth transport left Thessaloniki, in June 1943, the Italian authorities, still friendly to Jews, decided not to try the luck of Italian citizens of the Jewish faith any longer but to transfer them to Athens instead.[97] In the capital, under Italian auspices, they were offered lodgings in temporary collective housing and obliged to register with the authorities every week. But in September 1943, Rome signed an armistice with the Allies and its protection of Italian citizens in Greece was over. On March 24, 1944, the Gabbais and the Venezias, together with about 800 other Jews, including

116 · HOMECOMING

some 180 Italian nationals, were taken hostage by the Germans and deported to Chaidari. Their newly established contact with the EAM resistance was not strong enough to set them free as they hoped.[98] On April 2, thirty cattle cars were loaded with Jews from Athens and other Jewish communities that until recently had been under Italian control and rolled north. On the way through the Greek mainland, more cars were added to the train in Larissa and Thessaloniki, all heading to Auschwitz-Birkenau. Treating Jews like freight, this twentieth transport with 5,026 people on board was by far the largest in Greece. Upon arrival, 4,212 of the newcomers were sent directly to the gas chambers; among them was the mother of the Venezia family, her two daughters, and the Gabbai parents with their little son.[99]

Together with about 800 Jewish and non-Jewish prisoners from most of the German-occupied territory in Europe, the two young Gabbai brothers and the two Venezia brothers were selected to work for the *Sonderkommando* in the "death zone," a strictly isolated killing area. Of the four, only Jacob Gabbai, aged thirty-one upon arrival—which made him about ten years older than his brother and two cousins—was married. His wife, together with the eldest of the Venezia sisters, was also selected for work, but separated from their male relatives in the female section of the camp. Because of the work they were required to do, the four young men no longer harbored any illusions about the whereabouts of their parents: being on the *Sonderkommando* meant continuous direct confrontation with mass murder. Since May 1944, they were among the 150 to 200 Jews from Greece who watched people being sent into the gas chambers and then disposed of the corpses, "afraid that one would encounter a family member." Unlike their older fellow prisoners who were already fathers, they at least did not have to face the distressing task of burying their own children. Shortly after the murder of Jews from Hungary early in the summer of 1944, they witnessed the *Sonderkommando* revolt, narrowly escaping German retaliation. Though alcohol provided by the guards to the *Sonderkommando* inmates, solidarity, and even friendship, kept them together, it was above all the family bond that allowed the Gabbai and Venezia brothers to live on, because prisoners often competed with one another, at times physically fighting, in this arbitrary system full of suspicion.[100]

After January 18, 1945, as the evacuation of Auschwitz was underway, the Gabbais and Venezias crossed Bohemia and Austria, first on foot and then in freight trains, covering a total of almost 620 miles (1,000 km). The locals along the route watched them with both curiosity and disgust at their wretchedness. In one week they arrived, exhausted and severely frostbitten, at the Mauthausen camp in Upper Austria, where the Gabbai brothers were then separated. It is hard to assess the extent to which they were in charge of their own lives at that moment; nevertheless, it is clear that they strategized. Whereas the Venezia brothers, for example, changed the spelling of their names when volunteering for work (which at this late stage was more desired than obligatory in the camps), the Gabbai brothers calculated that Jacob should leave to increase the chances that either he or Dario would survive.[101]

After five days in Mauthausen, on January 29, 1945, the Venezia brothers and Dario, the younger of the Gabbais, were selected for work in the Melk subcamp. Two and half months later, they were transferred to Ebensee. This Mauthausen subcamp in a beautiful Alpine landscape next to the Traunsee was established as a concentration camp in November 1943. The area came under systematic Allied bombing from mid-1944 onward. At that time, thirty-two barracks in Ebensee housed about nine thousand prisoners. The number of dead had reached seven thousand by the time of its liberation; many sick prisoners had been killed by Nazi doctors by means of heart injections.[102]

From April 17, 1945, at the very end of their incarceration, prisoners were forced to build tunnels for A9 rockets, but by this point they did so without food and proper clothing. Dressed in rags and sleeping mostly on the bare ground in the barracks, tunnels, or outdoors, the inmates began to fade away. On May 5, 1945, two days before Germany signed the unconditional surrender, Ebensee was abandoned by the guards, and the prisoners started to look for food and to plunder the surrounding areas. Their unregulated consumption of anything they could find led to serious intestinal ailments and the deaths of many. This is one of the reasons why Mois Venezia probably fell into a coma. Under these conditions, being placed in a hastily set up field hospital, there was no way for him to leave Austria within the next few months. In Mauthausen and its subcamps, only about eighty-five former *Sonderkommando* prisoners lived to witness the liberation.[103]

Once freed, all the former inmates had to remain in Ebensee. The camp was adapted as a DP facility, but staying in the former place of so much

118 · HOMECOMING

suffering in order to recuperate was difficult. Furthermore, the US super-vision of the Ebensee tent camp was chaotic at first. Survivors, including Shlomo Venezia, were taking revenge on former kapos (prisoners chosen to oversee other prisoners on labor details) with a sense of satisfaction and without the liberators intervening. Logistics were also lagging; this encour-aged survivors to loot outside the DP facility, much to the fear of the locals. Finally, repatriation was to be organized as usual on the basis of ascribed nationality. Shlomo remembers that attitudes differed considerably from one country representative to the next: "We were liberated on May 6, 1945, and I stayed until the end of June. Nearly two months, as we didn't know where to go. The French who came with the Red Cross were well organized and with great urgency took away the sickest of the French deportees. The others were repatriated to France in trucks. They were [the] first to organize anything. The Italians did nothing. As for the Greeks, they didn't even think about doing anything."[104]

After they disinfected him with DDT, X-rayed him, and gave him a gen-eral checkup, Shlomo was diagnosed with tuberculosis by Allied doctors and nurses, who found that his lungs were no longer working efficiently. Against medical advice to remain in the hospital, he decided to join Jewish survivors from Greece and to repatriate at the earliest opportunity. Initially, the group toyed with the idea of moving to Palestine; but upon reaching Udine, in northeastern Italy, Shlomo proved unable to continue and had to remain in medical care for a full seven years after the liberation. Of the four men, Dario was the first to reach Athens, in July 1945. After his recovery in Ebensee, Mois also repatriated to Athens via Bari at the end of the summer of 1945. Although their expectations were high, upon returning, the reality of the situation was much different: "Before leaving they said: 'Don't forget, once you go back you will have a good life, lots of money will be given to you and everything,'" Dario recalls. "Didn't happen. The Greek government took us and said 'go.'"[105]

The oldest of the group, Jacob Gabbai, had been held in Mauthausen for a month until the Germans transferred him to yet another subcamp, in Gusen, where he established contact with Italian and French Jewish pris-oners. After about two months of slave labor in a munitions factory, he was liberated by the US Army on May 2, 1945, but he was then handed over to the Soviets, who had taken over this territory. By way of Vienna, Budapest, and Skopje, he finally reached the Greek border in November 1945 and reunited with his brother Dario in Athens. His wife, Laura, also survived but returned in the poorest health at the end of 1945. Jacob succeeded in transferring her from Thessaloniki to a hospital in Athens, and he started to work for the JDC, the sole paid job available. In 1949, after the Civil War, the couple decided to migrate to the newly formed Israel. Two years later, Jacob's brother, Dario, left for the United States, and so did Mois Venezia. Shlomo Venezia underwent lung surgery, got married, and he and his wife settled for good in Italy, of which he was still a citizen. Late in her life, while describing her feelings to Shlomo, his wife claimed that "something of him stayed forever in the camp."[106]

In general, migration from Greece, resulting from unmet expectations upon homecoming, was something many siblings sought to do together. Suzanne and Stella, two Tchemino sisters originally from the town of Serres in Bulgarian-occupied Eastern Macedonia, were living with their mother in Thessaloniki at the outbreak of World War II. This spared them from Treblinka but did not prevent their deportation to Auschwitz on April 5, 1943. Suzanne was twenty-two and already married, so after passing the selection, she registered under her husband's surname, Hanoh. Five years younger than her sister, Stella was also selected for work in the camp, and she quickly decided to change the spelling of her surname and register as Hemino, an alphabetically closer listing to her sister. She was afraid that she and Suzanne would be separated and was too scared to disclose that they were sisters.[107] Concealing family relationships in camps seems to have been a common practice, given the Jews' overall suspicion of the Nazi policy of separating families. Obviously, the perpetrators considered family ties and their dynamics as a source of resilience. Ágnes László of Hungary, who was deported to Auschwitz and selected for work with her sister and her mother in mid-June 1944, explains, for example, that they "were warned not to refer to one another as mom or sister. Rosalia [her mother] saw the way families were separated when they had used the terms 'mom,' 'grandma,' or 'daughter.'"[108]

The Tchemino sisters were literate, but they were only homemakers, without real occupations. Yet they registered as pharmacists in the hope that the Nazis would find their skills useful and spare their lives. Regardless of the reason, they were indeed fortunate to have stayed together, whether

120 · HOMECOMING

it was because of their alleged professions, having changed their names, or just sheer luck. Their mother, however, was sent straight to the gas chambers. In Birkenau, Suzanne learned that her husband had also been gassed, which of their immediate family left only the two of them alive. During the camp evacuation, on January 19, 1945, they set out on open-topped rail cars for Bergen-Belsen, a journey that lasted two weeks. With no gas chambers in sight, they initially felt great relief. Soon, however, they experienced the horrors of slowly dying of hunger and thirst, which forced the inmates to eat the flesh of the corpses around them in the final days before the liberation. The Tchemino sisters believe that ultimately what enabled them to survive was sticking close together and caring for each other.[109]

Even after being liberated, until the International Red Cross brought them food, medicine, and things to entertain them, they feared more atrocities. Much like the men and boys, they too felt satisfaction when the German guards became the victims. With the metamorphosis of Bergen-Belsen from a concentration camp to a DP facility, the Tchemino sisters started to find comfort within the camp circle despite what they had been through. Too aware of their own losses, Suzanne refers to the survivors of Belsen as a "big family," and Stella adds to this by describing how they were "like a village, girls [together], [watching] American movies." To be part of a family was what they longed for. But, since the liberators, international organizations, and the governments of the home countries were making their decisions about what to do with survivors based on their citizenship, Greece was imposed on them as their homeland and the destination of return. Once repatriation could be carried out, they were sent by train to the AIVG transition center in Brussels, where they were grouped with another 387 Jews from Greece out of the 3,300 international Holocaust survivors around them. After being taken care of for about a month, they were brought by military aircraft to Athens in early September 1945.[110]

Only a few weeks after arriving in the capital, Suzanne and Stella decided to go and see what was left of Thessaloniki and perhaps find fellow Jews from Serres. They were put up by the local Jewish Community in provisional collective housing, but they soon moved into a private home. Unable to reconcile herself to the death of her husband, Suzanne entered a new marriage with their Jewish benefactor three years later, quite late for the times. What they experienced in Thessaloniki was deeply upsetting. They had lost not just their loved ones but also all their property; only some family pictures were given back to them by their non-Jewish neighbors. "Why did you come back?" was the question they were confronted with far too often while trying to regain their belongings. After all this, the Tchemino sisters and their husbands migrated to the United States in 1951.[111]

Profound disappointment is largely what both the Sephardim and the Romaniotes felt shortly after the liberation. Renee Gani was born in Preveza, in the region of Epirus, northwestern Greece, in 1919. She was deported to Auschwitz with six of her family members on March 25, 1944. She recalls that since her family was Romaniote, they used Greek as their language of everyday communication. In addition, she knew some French and Hebrew from the Jewish school. None of the inhabitants of Preveza, however, had any real knowledge of German. Without anybody to explain to them what was actually happening, Renee's parents were gassed upon arrival while the rest of the family was selected for labor; only Renee and her younger sister, Rachel, survived. Her three brothers were assigned to the *Sonderkommando* and occasionally smuggled food to them until September 1944, when they too were murdered. Staying close together during their internment in Birkenau as well as during the death marches helped Renee and her sister endure the further suffering they encountered at Ravensbrück, as well as in Malchow, one of its subcamps, in Mecklenburg. The last transfer left them abandoned in an unknown location after a long march. In her account, recalling the past as if it were today, Renee refers to solidarity among the Jews of Greece as "Greek," which nonetheless seems to relate more to the common language than to their national identity:[112]

> So we got ready, we start to walk again, day and night time. May, but it was real cold over there, believe it or not, and we [had been] walking for two days. We stopped just for a while to get a rest and walk again. Food, forget [it]. All of a sudden, after two days walking, the guards disappeared. We start to talk about how the Greeks were together, the only bit of us. Where we [were] going now, where we [are] going, don't know nothing, where to go here? Nobody, nobody to tell us what to do. So we [are] just a group of a couple of girls together. [...] We decide together to go here or there until we find a place. Finally one agent [officer] came and tried to concentrate all the Greeks in one place and we went with him.[113]

122 · HOMECOMING

Placed in collective housing while being fed and nursed by the UNRRA, Renee and Rachel Gani's repatriation to Athens finally took place in September 1945 by air. Upon their return, there was nobody to welcome them back, so they went to the reception center in Athens, located in a gymnasium building already overfilled with camp returnees. Therefore, they were forced to spend the first night back in their home country sleeping on the pavement. For some time, Renee kept hoping that at least one of her brothers was still alive. Perhaps liberated at Auschwitz, a brother might be coming back through the Soviet Union. But none of them was to return. Altogether, out of the 172 deportees from Preveza, only about 10 survived the camps, all young women, in addition to 11 Jews who had gone into hiding. Besides the Civil War raging in the mountains of Epirus along the Albanian and Yugoslav borders, it was the lack of community that eventually led Renee and her sister to emigrate with their new husbands to the United States.[114]

The Auschwitz survivors who were natives of Rhodes, mostly liberated at Bergen-Belsen, include a high proportion of sisters. Some of them had kept going only to die of poor health and exhaustion immediately upon liberation. This was a devastating experience for those who were still alive since their relationships, because of the suffering they had endured together, exceeded the usual emotional ties of siblings in peacetime. Lucia Capelutto, who was just eighteen when her sister died, explains their transformative relationship in her memoir: "With my elder sister Rachel it was different. We quarreled often, she and I, because she would forego her own ration, so that I, the younger one, should eat. For her, I was a daughter rather than a sister."[115] The guilt of having survived at the expense of a sibling tormented Lucia and others throughout their lives, making it impossible for them to be reconciled to their homecoming.

Parents

Though many of the young camp returnees, disillusioned with homecoming, sought the first opportunity to go where the sun shines as brightly as in Greece, like Palestine, Africa, South America, and the southern United States, and where one's life prospects would be less hampered by war, this was not nearly so true of the parents who had returned in the hope of reuniting with their children in hiding. Often absent in interviews with child survivors, this hope is expressed in memoirs written by their surviving fathers shortly after the war. By contrast, for mothers, similar accounts most often appear in the form of interviews. Firstly, they were usually younger than the fathers and therefore more likely to have lived to the era of recording, and secondly, they were given a hearing as storytellers rather than as memoirists. This might be related, among other things, to the traditional social structure in Greece, where women as authors were rare, and, more broadly, because there was little interest in gender aspects of the Holocaust.[116]

Once the parents' generation of camp survivors decided to write down their experiences, it still took a long time for their writing to gain wide circulation. For various reasons, whether it was the language or possible doubts that autobiographical writing by Jewish survivors would meet with interest and approval among readers, Greek editions of early eyewitness accounts usually appeared long after those in French, English, or Hebrew. Still, regardless of when a memoir was written, we need to highlight yet another difference related to gender. Whereas men mostly end their narrative abruptly after the liberation, or at most with some information about arriving back in Greece, women elaborate on personal reconstruction, especially resuming family life or starting a new family, both in written and oral accounts.

A good example of a man who wrote about his experience of the camps is Marco Nahon. He was born in 1896 in the town of Didymoticho, in the Evros region, next to the Turkish border. His entire family was deported on May 5, 1943, and they arrived at Auschwitz-Birkenau eleven days later, after having covered about 1,250 miles (2,000 km) with a three-day stopover at the Baron Hirsch ghetto in Thessaloniki. His wife and daughter (who was not considered old enough to do forced labor) were sent to the crematoria. Marco and his sixteen-year-old son, Chaim, were selected for slave labor. Although Marco's being a physician by training was an advantage, it also meant that father and son were separated. While otherwise using notably stark, unsentimental language throughout the manuscript, written in Dachau in the summer of 1945 just after liberation, Marco dedicates the book with obvious emotion to all those who had been murdered, explicitly mentioning his wife and daughter. His son is mentioned only twice and not by name in the description of Auschwitz, at the selection and early on at roll calls. Then he disappears into the anonymous crowd of Birkenau inmates

124 · HOMECOMING

and reemerges only in the postscript account, when he is reunited with his father back in Greece.[117]

Marco's excruciating journey from Auschwitz back to Didymoticho started in October 1944, when he was transferred to the Stutthof camp, east of Danzig. After that, he was among the six hundred Jewish prisoners at the Echterdingen camp, south of Stuttgart. When typhus broke out in January 1945, Marco was transferred again, this time aboard one of the twelve train cars heading to Ohrdruf, a subcamp of Buchenwald. Anyone able to march was evacuated from the advancing Allied troops on April 2, 1945. Those who survived travelled for four days to get to Buchenwald, about thirty miles (forty-eight kilometers) away. From there, they continued by way of Weimar to the Dachau camp, which they reached on April 27. Only two days later, they were liberated by the US Army. At this point, expressing satisfaction that his German persecutors were being taken prisoner and with a prayer for the victims, Marco closes his memoir.[118]

At the end of September 1945, Marco Nahon was back in Didymoticho. In a letter addressed to Israel Djivre, a native of Didymoticho living in New York City, who was trying to find out where his relatives were, Marco attached a list of Holocaust survivors from all three municipalities of Evros (Didymoticho, Nea Orestias, and Soufli). His list of 32 was close to the total number of Jews who, of the 1,150 deportees, had survived and returned to the region. According to Marco, the deportees also included Jews of Spanish citizenship, deported to Auschwitz. At that moment, as we learn from his letter (written in French—the usual language of communication among educated Jews in post-Ottoman Greece), Marco was already reunited with his son, Chaim, intimately addressing him as "my boy."[119]

Marco Nahon became the chief representative of the Jews in postwar Didymoticho, but given the low number of survivors, there was no way of reestablishing the Jewish Community.[120] In his letter from October 1945, Marco asks American Jews originally from Didymoticho to provide financial and material support, and he complains about the local situation: "Most of our houses here are in very bad condition, and, since we are bankrupt, we are in no position to undertake even the smallest repairs. Even the houses, minimally damaged, threaten to fall into ruin during winter, which is approaching. Naturally, everything was pillaged; not a single chair, stove, plate, spoon or glass is left. As to clothing, including underwear, our situation is truly pitiful. The help we receive is nominal. I do not wish to say it is almost nothing."[121]

Given the desperate state of affairs, those Jewish survivors who had either survived the camps or returned after having fled persecution soon decided to leave their hometowns in search of a better life elsewhere in Greece or abroad. Nahon, who had married his sister-in-law and fellow Auschwitz survivor in the aftermath, moved with her and his son to the United States in 1956. His son, Chaim, nineteen years old at the liberation, never had his own story recorded but later sought financial compensation from the Federal Republic of Germany for the time he spent in Auschwitz-Birkenau, Melk, and Ebensee and for the mental and physical injury he had suffered from pseudo-medical experiments at the SS Hygiene-Institut in Auschwitz.[122]

Marco Nahon was certainly not the only Jewish doctor from Greece providing medical services in Auschwitz-Birkenau, nor was he the only one to survive and bear witness. Errikos Levis from Ioannina in Epirus, Greece, which was formerly the center of the Romaniote Jews, became a medic and second lieutenant in the Greek Army in 1935 at the age of twenty-two. During the Greco-Italian War, he served as a medical doctor on the Albanian front. By then, his wife and newborn son were living in Thessaloniki, but once the German occupation started, Errikos decided to move them back to Ioannina for their safety. From then on, he served as a doctor in Athens, which, like Ioannina, was under Italian occupation. When he accepted a wedding invitation to Vlorë, where relatives were living, an opportunity arose to move his family to Albania. Errikos was about to join the EDES resistance operating in and around Ioannina. In his oral accounts, he hardly ever mentions them, but the pictures he shows in the VHA video and the correspondence he had with Michael Matsas reveal deep feelings for his family.[123]

On March 25, 1944, a few months after the Germans took over the former Italian zone, Errikos was among the 1,180 Jews rounded up in Ioannina and deported first to a transit camp in Larissa and then to Auschwitz. Soon after his arrival in Auschwitz, he was transferred to Wolfsberg, part of the Projekt Riese of the Gross-Rosen subcamp, in Lower Silesia, which was established in May 1944. There, he provided medical assistance to fellow prisoners while building the camp facility and later working as a slave laborer on construction projects for the Reich. In February 1945, Errikos

126 · HOMECOMING

was loaded onto the open bed of a truck headed for Bergen-Belsen. From there, he was relocated to Barth, a Ravensbrück subcamp on the Baltic Sea. At the end of these ordeals, with all his strength depleted, he was unable to march anymore, and thus became one of the three hundred seriously ill male prisoners left behind. He was liberated by the Red Army on April 30, 1945. In his account of the liberation, his recollections of the Soviet soldiers are contradictory; on the one hand, he refers to looting and raping of women, young and old; on the other hand, he greatly appreciates that they nursed him back to health. After getting better, Errikos Levi and five other Jewish survivors reached the British zone in Berlin, from where they were sent to Brussels. And on August 23, 1945, he arrived by air in Athens. Yet, despite his good position in the Greek Army—which he rejoined as a medical officer—it took him until December 1945 to bring his family back from Albania.[124]

Another early account is by Errikos Sevillias, which he began writing in 1951, in the aftermath of the Greek Civil War. After serving for three years in the army before World War II, he established himself well enough to get married in 1936, at the age of thirty-five, and became a father. As a leatherworker, he had his own workshop and was able to rent a small house near Athens to keep his wife and daughter out of sight when the Germans took over. Consequently, when he was arrested during the registration on March 24, 1944, and then interned in Chaidari, the women remained in their hiding place. On April 11, 1944, after nine days on a freight train, Errikos Sevillias arrived at Auschwitz-Birkenau and, despite his age, was selected for work. On many occasions—and especially with every new transport coming from Greece—Sevillias's thoughts were with his wife and daughter:

> On 10 August they brought a shipment from Athens. When I heard about it I waited in agony for them to be brought to the camp in order to discover what might have happened to my loved ones. On the following day they were brought and put into Block 26 and when I returned from work I ran over to see them. Most of them were friends; when I saw that none of my family was among them I was greatly relieved. I asked about my family and learned that my wife and child, as well as the rest of my family, were safe in Christian homes. The thought that all my family in Athens, especially my wife and daughter, were safe gave me great comfort.[125]

This emotional relief probably helped Sevillias endure the deadly conditions of Auschwitz-Birkenau for several more months. By October 1944, the Germans had withdrawn from Athens, but Sevillias's odyssey continued to the Gross-Rosen subcamp in Breslau. Hard labor throughout the winter left him with severe frostbite; with open wounds on his hands and feet, he survived by mere luck until May 8, 1945, when he was liberated by the Red Army. Compared to Errikos Levi, Errikos Sevillias paints a remarkably positive picture of the Soviet soldiers. Again, from the diet of normal food, which the liberators served them, many camp survivors died. Witnessing this, Sevillias became afraid that if he were not careful, he would never reach his family in Athens. It took until June for him to recover somewhat. Much to the dismay of the medical staff, he left the reception facility after forty days in the company of other Jews from Greece, led by the great desire to reunite with his wife and daughter back home. They were traveling with the *laissez-passer* issued by the Soviets and with food for three days, but they got lost. Their inability to speak the regional languages and the hostility of locals caused them to end up in Poland instead of Hungary. From there, the group—being taken care of by the Red Cross—caught a train to Gliwice. For five days, they were provided with lodging, clothing, and food; after that, they continued to a Soviet reception camp in Katowice, where they stayed for another twelve days.[126]

As Sevillias recalls, the next stop was Leipzig, where thousands of liberated prisoners were staying. It was here that the Soviets and the Americans exchanged them for Russian inmates. Again by railway, they got to Sponheim in the Rhineland, where Sevillias became particularly impatient about homecoming, but ill health prevented him from continuing his journey. His family still did not know that he had survived; only in the hospital in Sponheim was it possible to send the first card home. After forty days of travelling and forty more of recovery, Sevillias finally set out for Athens, a journey much longer than that of the Breslau subcamp survivors who had been put directly on aircraft. From Mannheim he went to Munich, where his departure by air was repeatedly postponed. Finally, at the end of the summer of 1945, he left by train via Rome for Bari. After arriving in Piraeus on August 22, 1945, and registering in Athens, he was to meet his wife and daughter back at his house. Too old to be recruited by the army during the Civil War and lucky enough to have his property returned (in Athens, Jewish assets

128 · HOMECOMING

seized under the German occupation were much more readily and under different terms and conditions handed over to the original Jewish owners than in other parts of Greece), Sevillias gradually regained his physical and mental strength.[127]

In contrast to the previous examples we have seen, which involved either a father and his son who survived the camps or fathers yearning to meet their closest relatives in hiding, the four-member Kounio family, all of whom had been deported from Thessaloniki together, returned as a whole. Again, the parents' efforts were central to survival. Before the persecution, the head of the family, Salvator Kounio, was a photographic supplies wholesaler and owned a camera shop in his hometown. Traveling regularly to Germany for business, he became romantically involved with and married Hella Löwy, a university student in Leipzig, who originated from Carlsbad, Bohemia. At home they spoke German, Hella's mother tongue, but in Thessaloniki she also learned Greek, in addition to being fluent in French, Spanish, and English, with some Czech too. When the Germans occupied Greece, their language skills enabled them to effectively communicate with the occupying forces, an advantage most other residents of Thessaloniki did not possess. Their position, however, drastically changed when local informers disclosed to the German authorities that the Kounios were circumventing anti-Jewish measures by nominally putting their business under the name of an "Aryan" associate.[128]

As a result of their disobedience, the Kounios were put onto the first transport to Auschwitz-Birkenau, on March 15, 1943. Reaching the death camp in five days, they arrived comparably faster than later convoys disrupted by resistance-led railway sabotage and general bomb damage to the railways. It was unlikely that the forty-three-year-old Salvator, who had walked with a limp ever since a childhood accident, would be selected for work. Nevertheless, because the Kounios were fluent in German and Greek, they seemed to be a useful acquisition. As the men and women were separated, Salvator and his fourteen-year-old son, Heinz, who followed his father's advice to present himself as older, were assigned to comparably advantageous forced labor in the tailoring section. With the evacuation of Auschwitz—as happened to Chaim Nahon, the Venezia brothers, and Dario Gabbai—Salvator and Heinz were sent along the slave route, with all its hardships, to Mauthausen, Melk, and finally Ebensee, where they were liberated by the US Army on May 6, 1945. Throughout his memoir, combined with a diary from the Austrian camps written right after liberation, Heinz expresses gratitude to his father and states that their support for each other was the main reason he survived: "I had spent almost two years here and somehow had survived. I have often reflected back on this, as have so many of the other survivors. Why did I live when so many others died? Was it fate? Was it luck? One true advantage I had was to have my father constantly by my side. He advised me on what to do in every circumstance. Without him, I doubt that I could have ever withstood the severe conditions I was subjected to."[129]

After liberation, Salvator took care of his son, who, suffering from dysentery and hunger edema, was unable even to stand up. Salvator was again a language mediator, but this time it was for the liberators when supervising the deployment of Austrian workers.[130] Well versed in photography, Salvator was able to obtain a camera from the Allies to document the magnitude of the Ebensee hell. Among the photographs depicting the camp and its inmates, there is one of Heinz's naked skeletal body, which took two months to recover enough to be able to travel home. From Ebensee, they went to Milan to join a group of 3,000 international deportees, Jewish and political, of whom about 250 were originally from Greece. In his report for the JDC and the Jews of Greece, Salvator highlights how, while being taken to the reception facility in Bari, he and his fellow prisoners were shown compassion by the local Italians, which gave the former prisoners great moral support. From Bari, they continued on to Athens and then to Thessaloniki, finally arriving in mid-June 1945.[131]

Upon arrival, Salvator not only started to see to private matters but also got involved in the Jewish Community of Thessaloniki. While looking for his wife and daughter, who had yet to return, and trying to get back as many of his family possessions as he could in order to reestablish their lives, he became the vice-president of an independent body outside the Community structure, called the Union of Greek Jewish Deportees of Poland, representing about 1,100 deportees who had returned to Thessaloniki in the second half of 1945. Only a few days after his return, Salvator delivered an impassioned speech at a meeting of sixty Jewish Community leaders in Athens, called by the JDC envoy Gaynor Jacobson. In his address, Salvator offered a unique, emotional account in which he harshly criticized the inaction of the Jewish survivors in Greece and the discord among them, stating:

130 · HOMECOMING

Do you think that anybody I have met here until now showed the smallest regret for our terrible suffering in the Nazis concentration camps? Not at all. These people, instead of helping me morally, look at me just as though they would reproach me for not bringing with me also the others they were waiting for, and who died there. They forget that it is not my fault if these comrades are not returning; Nazis stole them from us and our hearts break when making the balance and seeing the final result. [...] You must understand that the inmates of Nazi concentration camps who have been lucky enough to escape death there, suffered so much that most of them are not only physically but also morally ill. They still feel themselves persecuted, don't yet believe that Nazi terror is abolished.[132]

Salvator was among the comparably lucky ones not only to find his house undamaged but also to be able to reclaim some of his belongings, like books, a supply of photographic paper, some furniture, and even equipment from his store, carefully protected by non-Jewish friends who had accepted them for safekeeping. Being one of the early camp returnees to Thessaloniki, he was able to move back in to at least one room of his house and eventually evict the squatters. But this only happened after his family had been reunited; his daughter, Erika, did not return until November 1945 and his wife, Hella, did not get back until February 1946. After the evacuation of Auschwitz, where they had been working in the administrative section (*Politische Abteilung*), they were taken to the Ravensbrück women's camp north of Berlin and, subsequently, to Malchow.

From there, they were evacuated on May 1, 1945, marching in columns that reminded them of their terrible experience when leaving Auschwitz. Seeing other prisoners escape and hide in the forest, they decided to do the same. After four days of provisional shelter, the group of Jewish deportees and POWs was found by the Soviets, who provided them with the bare necessities, like food and clothing. Joining other ex-prisoners, camp deportees, POWs, and foreign slave laborers, together with German refugees on the run, they tried to reach the Americans. Encountering some Yugoslavs, Hella finally decided that they, unlike their Jewish companions from Greece who had lost all their loved ones, would return to their hometown via Belgrade, where Hella's aunt was living. By then, Hella contacted her cousin in Switzerland by mail, which took several weeks to arrive, in order to get a message to her husband that they were both alive. While preparing for departure, Hella, who always seemed to maintain an attitude of someone able to take action, rather than being a passive victim, became feverish with typhus. After a month in Belgrade, her daughter Erika travelled to Greece alone. By train, she reached the Greek-Yugoslav border at Koula and continued south to Thessaloniki. Hella returned in poor health about two months later.[133]

In private letters written immediately upon her return, Hella confessed to her friend in Britain, "when I came home I found a lot of things to do and now I am very nervous and restless and I want to work. I do not like to sit and to think." The following lines reflect her inner conflict as a camp survivor: "we have seen so much misery that we are now so happy that we are still alive. You do know quite well the French proverb *'Laissez les morts aux morts.'* You see, our best comrade during 3 years has been death. Often we said it would be better to die than to see all this." About three months later, Hella replied to her friends' urging her to open up: "I cannot write it. It is too dreadful and nobody will believe us," thus confirming the camp survivors' emotional difficulty in returning.[134]

Among the survivors who returned to Thessaloniki, the four Kounio family members, though they had lost about two dozen relatives, including Hella's father, are a rare but not unique exception, as is apparent from the narration of the Hassid sisters. Originally from Thessaloniki, they were deported to Auschwitz from Belgium in summer 1944. They too survived this death camp and then internment after the evacuation. By sheer luck, their mother ended up on the same transport, and they were liberated together in Theresienstadt, Bohemia. They were reunited with their father and brother (also Auschwitz survivors) in Brussels, which they considered a miracle. Nevertheless, Belgium, not Greece, remained their ultimate homeland, and so it happened that in the collective memory of Thessaloniki, the Kounio family represents the only Auschwitz survivors who, for better or worse, returned as a family.[135]

These examples should certainly not give us the false impression that all fathers or mothers who survived Auschwitz-Birkenau would see their children grow up. Most parents suffered terrible loss in the death camps if their child did not make it through the selection process, because they were too young or no longer strong enough. For example, Lillian was the

132 · HOMECOMING

teenage daughter of Albert Menasche, a well-established Thessalonican physician. After being selected for slave labor and worked to exhaustion, she was murdered in the gas chamber.[136] Some fathers did not return even though their children were safely hidden with Gentiles in Greece. Leon Franko was a young man when he married in Kastoria less than a year before being deported. His child was born in Thessaloniki during the deportations, but his wife was betrayed and shot dead together with other Jewish captives shortly before the liberation of Greece, when the transports to concentration camps and killing centers had already stopped. Leon was murdered in Auschwitz, leaving his child an orphan in the hands of non-Jewish guardians.[137]

Even under the most abnormal of circumstances, however, it seems that a child hidden safely in Greece was an important incentive to a concentration-camp parent to survive and return. Germaine Koen, née Matalon in Thessaloniki in 1914, plainly states in her oral account that her main motivation to survive the camps was the hope of meeting her three daughters again. The girls were being protected as pupils at a Roman Catholic school in Athens while living with a non-Jewish acquaintance. As early as 1943, Germaine and her Matalon family escaped under false identities from Thessaloniki to Athens, but a traitor, a former neighbor, denounced her husband to the German authorities after Italy surrendered. Tortured during interrogation, he revealed his wife's hiding place. Germaine's sister Claire, her husband, and their nine-year-old son were denounced by their non-Jewish acquaintance at about the same time. They only secured a safe haven for their elder daughter; the rest of them were deported to Auschwitz on the same freight train as Germaine and her husband on June 21, 1944.[138]

As other women survivors who had been mothers in Auschwitz-Birkenau have testified, Claire too, upon arrival, was encouraged by a fellow Jewish prisoner from Greece to entrust her child to what was said to be the "Red Cross," since it allegedly provided transportation by truck to the camp.[139] It was an act of desperation on behalf of more experienced Auschwitz inmates aimed at rescuing the mothers at the very least. The truth was devastating and haunted Claire for the rest of her life. Nevertheless, the knowledge that one had another child hidden back home was a strong stimulus to invest as much as possible into one's own survival. This agonizingly sorrowful predicament takes center place in Claire's narration:

He told us we need to entrust our children to older women because the Red Cross would take care of them. We followed his advice because it sounded reasonable. Parting with our children was cruel, but we had to save the children. [The next day] I sighted a prisoner digging a trench. He was French. When I asked him, did he know where the children were and how we could see them, he turned around imperturbable and cynically said: "Madam, do you see that flame which comes out of the smokestack? He has come out of there already, I am sure." A worse, more cynical man I've never seen in my life. That moment I suffered my first death. [...] Other women who followed their children went straight to the crematoriums. But is it not better to die, mother and son together, than to survive and live with the memory of your child? If I decided to live on, this was because what sustained me was a thought that, in Athens, my other child awaited me.[140]

After the Auschwitz evacuation, Claire and Germaine, passing through Bergen-Belsen and doing forced labor in Raguhn, a subcamp of Buchenwald, were transferred to Theresienstadt, which was taken over by the Red Cross on May 4, 1945. When the Red Army entered it five days later, the camp held about thirty thousand prisoners. Because they had to recover from typhus, it took the sisters until autumn 1945 to reach Greece.[141] Even though other Matalon family members, including the sisters' parents, had survived in hiding, their girls were being taken care of in a Jewish orphanage, established in 1945 with the assistance of the JDC. For the interim in the spring of 1945, the orphanage was improvised in a rented single-family house in Kifissia, a suburb of Athens. It was also used as a temporary shelter and a convalescent home for children.[142] In 1945, it officially looked after up to sixty children, boys and girls, and was the only existing Jewish institution of its kind in Greece. Many of these kids were soon among the 175 Jewish child migrants from Greece, accompanied by twenty-five adults, who were sent to Palestine on August 4, 1945. One of the children on board was Ester Altcheh, Claire's teenage daughter. This too made Claire feel that her daughter had been stolen from her. They reunited only years later, after Ester had returned from Israel as a young adult. Upon arrival in Greece, Germaine was still in poor health and ended up in the hospital but, unlike Claire, was able to collect her daughters once she had physically recovered. To her great disappointment,

134 · HOMECOMING

the girls had already started to call their guardian "mother." While Germaine rebuilt her life around her parents and daughters, Claire remarried but never had another child.[143]

As Primo Levi put it, before committing suicide more than four decades after the liberation, unable to cope with the Auschwitz burden, none but these "true" survivors had faced the full loss of humanity and withstood it.[144] With much understanding for their ordeal, Jacobson has described the moral effect that the experience of a concentration camp had on those returning to society and normal life in Thessaloniki, about 1,100 camp survivors by December 1945: "Distrust and lack of basic co-operation are omnipresent, even in areas that mean survival on a physical basis. In the past few months a group of deportees not only wrecked the restaurant which we and the Salonika community provided, but when an attempt was made to get it to function again, the dishes and cutlery disappeared." Jacobson continues his report with a discussion of how camp deportees learned to live as if for the moment: "On my visit to the shelters I found most of the beds and some of the blankets gone. Sold, was the explanation and now the persons who did the selling are without them and the temporary advantage of the few drachma thus gained does not compensate for the long discomfiture."[145]

Auschwitz survivors had a long hard way to go to adapt socially and emotionally, which had to do mostly with the core of their own being and their personal reconstruction. Many of them had witnessed their parents, spouses, and children being taken away to certain death; many had seen them suffering till the end; yet those who survived came back to what had been home, hoping for a safe haven and to meet at least some family members. Only upon homecoming did they realize that their ties with the past had been irrevocably put asunder, their faith in God badly shaken. Many death camp returnees felt the shame of surviving while millions had been murdered; they were also confronted with the hurtful anger of others who accused them of surviving at the expense of their loved ones. The majority society and Jews who had not experienced the camps were reluctant to listen to the descriptions of the horrors experienced there, and, consciously or subconsciously, avoided those who had returned from Auschwitz. But the returnees themselves were also trying to find an explanation for the death of so many and to find the perpetrators, both among the Germans and within their own ranks, specifically among the wartime community representatives, the *Judenrat*, who had been deported from Thessaloniki to Bergen-Belsen instead of Auschwitz.

BERGEN-BELSEN

Though Bergen-Belsen was the concentration camp to which the fewest number of Jews from Greece were sent, the deportees who lived to see liberation became an important component of the post-war Jewish community in Greece not only because of their high survival rate but also because of their special status at the time of deportation and among Jewish deportees in general. While in most camps the prisoners were separated by sex, in Bergen-Belsen—at least in the daytime—Jewish inmates remained together as a family and close to their fellow Jews from Greece. Family structures and local bonds therefore played a central role, shaping the essence of community. The dynamics, however, differed considerably from those that existed among Auschwitz deportees. Family was important as a unit that was allowed to stay together and care for its members, but in the limited accounts of the Bergen-Belsen deportees, it appears more as a self-evident relationship than as something special.

For a few Jews at Bergen-Belsen, their citizenship also mattered a great deal since only the citizens of neutral countries were exempt from forced labor. More than that, they could hope for repatriation to Spain, a country most of them had never even visited.[146] For married couples in Greece, citizenship was not a matter of choice but the subordination of wife to husband, and of children to their father. In practice, this meant that if a woman was a Spanish citizen and married a man who was a Greek citizen, she lost her Spanish citizenship and their children became Greeks. By contrast, if such a woman divorced (not an easy step in a country like Greece, which lacked civil institutions to handle matters of family law), she could regain her original citizenship and so could her children.[147]

In the Nazi camp system, Bergen-Belsen had originally been established for POWs, but in 1943 it was transformed into an "internment camp" (*Aufenthaltslager*) destined for the exchange of about ten thousand Jews for German POWs. It initially comprised the barracks of a former military training area in the isolated woods of Northern Saxony. They were essentially vacant after most of the recently captured Soviet prisoners had been killed. The

136 · HOMECOMING

first group, 441 Jews, was deported from Thessaloniki in summer 1943; the second, 174 Jews, left Athens in spring 1944. Both were first loaded on to railway cars marked for Auschwitz-Birkenau but were detached in Vienna to continue further west. The first Bergen-Belsen transport consisted of 74 Jews, Thessaloniki Community representatives and their family members, plus 367 Jews of all ages who were registered as Spanish citizens but had failed to escape to the Italian zone in time.[148]

In Greece, Jews of Spanish citizenship typically lived in Thessaloniki and belonged to the upper social strata. Many of them were afraid of the possible shift in German policy with regard to Spanish citizens, and this led dozens of these Jews to escape to Athens. Consequently, the 1944 transport to Bergen-Belsen included far more Jews of Spanish citizenship than had ever been registered in the capital of prewar Greece. Additionally, the group of 174 deportees from Athens included nineteen Jews who were citizens of neutral Portugal but no "exchange Jews" who were not citizens of neutral countries. Whereas Spanish citizens who had been sent to Bergen-Belsen in 1943 were handed over to Spain after drawn-out negotiations between Madrid and Berlin, no Jew who arrived a year later was ever transferred.

At the beginning of a conference volume commemorating fifty years since the liberation of Bergen-Belsen, its editor, the British historian David Cesarani, expresses regret that the Jewish eyewitnesses from Greece who could have delivered personal accounts of their imprisonment in Bergen-Belsen were now deceased.[149] Indeed, the narrations of those incarcerated there are far fewer than those about Auschwitz-Birkenau. Nonetheless, they are not completely absent, and the archival sources on the Jews of Greece and other countries help to bring these stories to light. Most prominent amongst them are the accounts of "exchange" Jewish deportees from the Netherlands, such as Josef Weiss and Rudolf Levy, who started arriving in Bergen-Belsen in early 1944.[150]

Consequently, one has to follow the homecoming not of one but of two fully separate groups of Jewish inmates who had been deported to Bergen-Belsen and kept in two of the several different camps of the complex: the Community representatives in the Star Camp (*Sternlager*) from 1943 and the Spanish and Portuguese citizens in the Neutrals Camp (*Neutralenlager*) from 1944. Returning home from geographically and politically opposite sides in the emerging Cold War, these two groups stepped onto Greek soil in September 1945, adding considerable tension to the community of Jewish survivors in Greece. For they were perceived as prominent people who had undeservedly received special treatment before and during their incarceration. We must here leave aside those transferred to Spain and beyond, since they were more often considered refugees than returnees from the camps.

The Star Camp

On September 11, 1945, only two days after the former inmates of the Star Camp returned to Thessaloniki, a special meeting of the Board of the Jewish Community was held. The minutes of the meeting constitute a collective accusation of all fifty-three Jews who had finally made it back to Greece. Not even death along the way prevented the chief rabbi of Thessaloniki, Zvi Koretz, from appearing on the list, in first place no less. They were accused of the following:

> In remuneration for their services to the Germans, [they] were spared the suffering experienced by other Jews by having the privilege of being transported to the Bergen-Belsen Concentration Camp, where only those who had offered important services to the Germans could stay. There, their lives were not threatened, and they had everything in abundance, while their co-religionists and the victims of their criminal acts were being gassed and burned in the crematoria. [...] They had all kinds of pleasures at their disposal, even sexual enjoyment, as is evident by the fact that children were born in that camp. [...] They were evidently given this privilege in exchange for services rendered to the occupier during the deportation of the Jews; it is known, after all, that Germans never give anything to anyone, and especially to Jews, without something in return.[151]

The notorious images of Bergen-Belsen as an inferno, which appeared in postwar photographs and film footage made by the British liberators, did not prevent other Holocaust survivors in Thessaloniki from clearly identifying the culprits of the catastrophe in their own ranks. Controversies over the chief rabbi, however, had appeared in Thessaloniki much earlier. Prewar frictions within the Jewish community in Thessaloniki had been an incentive

138 · HOMECOMING

to look for a progressive new chief rabbi, who was eventually found: Zvi Koretz was a Polish-born scholar of Judaism trained in Austria and Germany. This background, once so widely appreciated, was later, in the aftermath of the Holocaust, used against him and his family. Having Greek citizenship, which he had been granted in 1937, did not protect Koretz from accusations of having been a traitorous foreigner. His wife and children were accused of the same.[152]

Though incarceration in Bergen-Belsen may not have been as hellish as Auschwitz, it was hardly what former Jewish deportees now back in Greece would imagine to be a comfortable life. Seventy-four individuals, former officials and their close family members, soon created the core of the emerging Star Camp in Bergen-Belsen, a section in which Jews still wore civilian clothes, though marked with the Star of David (hence the name of the camp). At some point, eighteen barracks were built for the Jewish inmates who were held for possible exchange, but the Jews of Thessaloniki were not among the lucky ones to leave the camp before liberation, that is, the Spanish and Portuguese Jews who were sent to Spain as DPs.[153]

Though the conditions they had to endure were excruciating, their being the first inmates of the Star Camp put these Jews in a somewhat privileged position. Despite their low number, they held the key roles in the Council of Elders (*Ältestenrat*), part of the Jewish self-administration that was nominally in charge of the prisoners. Yet this provided no relief from the long roll calls in all kinds of weather at least twice a day, forced labor, separate accommodations for men and women in separate parts of the camp, meagre food rations, and SS sadism. From the very beginning, sanitary facilities and health care were severely wanting, and, as time went by, Bergen-Belsen became dangerously overcrowded. But the worst was yet to come—disease and even less space and food than before. From the perspective of its inmates, the Star Camp was a torment far beyond anything they had ever imagined; to Auschwitz inmates, however, this ill-treatment seemed tolerable. Upon the latter's arrival in Bergen-Belsen after the evacuation of Auschwitz, when they saw their compatriots in the Star Camp with self-administration, social activities, normal clothes, and even cigarette rations, they became resentful.[154]

For his corrupt, mediocre character, the forty-year-old Jacques Albala, who became the Jewish elder of the Star Camp, was particularly criticized, even by his fellow prisoners. Albala was born in Vienna (the birth register has

RETURNING FROM THE CAMPS · 139

his given name as Johann), and he lived there long enough to become fluent in German. His career in Thessaloniki took off during the occupation, first as a German interpreter, then as the head of the Jewish Police, and finally as chairman of the Jewish Council just before the deportations. This made Albala perfectly qualified to become the head of transports (*Transportführer*) for the convoy to Bergen-Belsen. In the camp, walking around in a suit and tie and living in a separate section of the men's barracks with his young wife and toddler son, Albala only earned more contempt. The prisoners of all nationalities soon nicknamed the Star Camp the Albala-Lager.[155]

In the camp hierarchy, another person held in low esteem by his fellow prisoners was a German-speaking, Aleppo-born Jew from Thessaloniki, Edgar Kounio. Indeed, he became as infamous as Jacques Albala. In the Star Camp, he was given the job of work dispatcher (*Arbeitsanleiter*), responsible for assigning prisoners to certain tasks, and he thus remains present in the narrations, with a clearly unsavory reputation. After the war he was sentenced to eight years imprisonment in Greece, which he served.[156] Kounio's ill fame was never forgotten by the Thessalonican Jews. When interviewing him (in French) in Thessaloniki in 1998, only two years before his death, Rena Molho, a distinguished historian and second-generation Holocaust survivor from Greece, made clear her contempt for him.[157] Perhaps because of the scarcity of memoirs written by the Star Camp inmates from Thessaloniki and the difficulty they had communicating with the Jews of other countries, no other members of the pre-deportation Jewish Council in Thessaloniki are mentioned in the personal accounts of former prisoners from the Netherlands.[158]

By contrast, Rabbi Zvi Koretz, who in Bergen-Belsen was responsible for looking after the elderly, is remembered with kindness and sympathy by his fellow inmates of Dutch, German, and Polish nationality. The Galician-born psychologist Alfred Garwood, whose family was deported from Poland to Bergen-Belsen together with another 2,400 Jews in June 1943—even some weeks before the Thessalonicans—depicts Koretz in a positive light: "In Belsen, he maintained his compassion and integrity, comforting and supporting those that came to him in need and despair. My mother describes many occasions when he listened patiently to her and found words with which to comfort her."[159] In the aftermath, however, Rabbi Koretz received a lot of negative attention from scholars in Greece and outside the country.[160]

140 · HOMECOMING

The story of the ultimate guilt, compliance, or at least delusional naivety of Rabbi Koretz and the Jewish Council in Thessaloniki during the German occupation, from April 1941 to his deportation in August 1943, was already spreading at the end of World War II. The great prevalence of the accusations even led some Jews of Greece in Palestine, associated in the Hitachduth Oley Yavan, to set the record straight, pleading to the World Jewish Congress to clear the names of the members of the Jewish Council in Thessaloniki, except for Koretz, whom they hesitated to offer a clear opinion on. The fact that the chief rabbi was unable to act on behalf of the Thessalonican Jews because he had been imprisoned from mid-May 1941 to January 1942, and then again at the crucial moment of recruitment for forced labor, from June 3 to August 3, 1942, before finally, right after his personal appeal to the Greek prime minister, being separated with his family in the ghetto until their deportation, is hardly ever taken into consideration.[161]

With the arrival of Auschwitz guards and inmates in December 1944, Bergen-Belsen, including the Star Camp, gradually deteriorated into a typical concentration camp. On December 22, 1944, the self-administration was abolished, and Jacques Albala was removed from his symbolic office. The Bergen-Belsen crematorium was working at full capacity to eliminate the decomposing corpses of inmates who had died of exhaustion and sickness. But it soon proved unable to get rid of them all. At the end of March, Rabbi Koretz's sixteen-year-old son, Leo, noted down in his diary (written in Greek) that the new inmates were constantly "standing outside at the wire fence and screaming for food." The next day, when he first observed the typhoid fever breaking out in the Star Camp, which was immediately isolated with no one allowed to work outside, he matter-of-factly commented: "No wonder. The dirt, the filth, the total impossibility of maintaining a minimum of cleanliness, the lack of sanitary facilities, including toilets and functioning taps, all led to the outbreak of the epidemics. It's a miracle it did not happen sooner."[162]

With the British Army approaching, the Nazi commandants of Bergen-Belsen proceeded to evacuate themselves and the inmates to cover the traces of their crimes, including those of the Star Camp. The 6,800 of those still able to move, infected or not, were pushed onto three trains for Theresienstadt, Bohemia, which was still under German control. A train carrying 2,400 Star Camp inmates left Bergen-Belsen only five days before the camp

RETURNING FROM THE CAMPS · 141

was liberated.[163] With white flags flying to give the impression of it being a humanitarian convoy, the train was not bombed (as all the passengers had feared it would be) but continued its two-week journey of more than 310 miles (500 km). Given the conditions of the railways, Soviet troops discovered the lost train near Tröbitz, in Brandenburg, on April 23, 1945. Of the inmate-passengers, about 2,200 were still alive, though starving and dehydrated, many struggling in agony with typhus. Put up in the nearby villages, the survivors soon created a committee to see to burials, food, and housing, grouping themselves according to country of origin. The epidemic petered out only after eight weeks, but not before taking the lives of another 350 people, including the wife of the last elder, Joseph Weiss, together with several deportees from Thessaloniki and some local German civilians. The son of Jacques Albala died on the train, and Zvi Koretz, who had carried his unconscious typhus-infected son, Leo, in his arms 5 miles (8 km) to the train at Bergen-Belsen while he himself was struggling with typhus, died in Tröbitz on June 2, 1945, just two weeks before repatriations started.[164]

Many survivors planned to leave for Palestine, including the remnants of the Koretz family, but repatriation was possible only to the countries they had previously been residents of. In that respect, the Thessalonicans on the lost train were less fortunate than their fellow passengers from Western Europe. Bella Barzilai, for example, was the daughter of Solomon Uziel, who had been a representative of the Thessaloniki Jewish Council. Together with her parents, husband, and younger brother, Marcel, she waited and waited for repatriation. Decades later, she reflected on the failure of Greece to take care of its Jewish citizens: "The Dutch were picked up by UNRRA, by planes, they took them in planes... The Red Cross came for the French... For us, no one. [...] Then the Russians said they'd take us to Greece. [...] They loaded us again into the same wagons. They gave us dry chickpeas to eat. Every day, we made a fire at a train station to boil them. It went like that for maybe forty days. I can't say for sure."[165]

Had it not been for the unique account of the Saltiel family, compiled by the Greek historian Rika Benveniste, whose grandfather Beniko Saltiel also perished in Tröbitz, the memory of their arduous return to Greece starting in August 1945 would probably have been lost forever. With *laissez-passers* issued by the head of the Jewish Committee, Joseph Weiss, and some extra clothing, these Thessalonican Jews set out on their journey toward Katowice.

142 · HOMECOMING

On the way from Poland—sometimes ignored by the locals, sometimes met with sympathy—they crossed the border to Czechoslovakia. Down through the country, via Bratislava, occasionally assisted by the local JDC staff, they arrived in Budapest on August 20, 1945, and, two days later, continued via Bucharest and Sofia to the northern border of Greece.[166]

Grieving for the dead but relieved to be finally back in Greece, the Star Camp returnees were immediately disabused of their expectation of being welcomed home. On September 7, their Soviet escorts handed them over to the British at Sidirokastro; they were naturally shocked by the scorn they were already receiving from Magen David Adom at the border. The chief rabbi's widow, Gita Koretz, together with Salomon Uziel and other senior representatives of the Community before the deportations, was taken into custody and interrogated, but the group was released a few days later. The new Community leadership, however, was unwilling to issue them a document confirming that they had been interned, which they needed to receive any assistance. And the leadership also banished them from the Community. In September 1945 they were put on trial at the Special Court on Collaborators, which ran for ten months. Uziel was not subpoenaed, but his name remained tarnished. Facing verbal and physical attacks, he continued trying to restore his reputation until 1949. Four years later, his personal account, which he wrote in Judeo-Spanish, began to circulate in typescript. He died embittered, with broken feelings toward his fellow Jews, in 1957.[167]

At that point, many members of Uziel's family and other Star Camp survivors left Greece for good and drew a thick line through their bitter homecoming. In Thessaloniki, Laura Albala, who had returned from the camp pregnant, gave birth to another son of Jacques Albala. But she divorced her husband, who was sentenced in 1946 to eighteen years in prison, and she emigrated with her parents and the boy toddler to the United States. Gita Koretz clandestinely moved with her children from Greece to Palestine. Gaynor Jacobson, the JDC country representative in Greece, even recounts a "very dramatic story" of a Jewish assault against the lives of the last of the Koretz family in Thessaloniki: "It happens that the Grand [sic] Rabbi caught an illness in there and he died [in Tröbitz]. His widow and two children, younger children, came back to Salonica. I was tipped off that the people who had arrived from Auschwitz were about to execute the Grand Rabbi's wife and children. I could not talk them out of it so I put [forward] that arguments [had been] made and [I] had the Grand Rabbi's wife and children shipped out of Salonica."[168]

This was the only time the JDC panicked about the proceedings of the Central Board, which put the deceased rabbi on public trial for blasphemy (*chillul hashem*). A cable from the JDC representative in Paris, Arthur Greenleigh, urged Headquarters to get in touch with international Jewish organizations to remove the rabbi's name from the traitors list.[169] But no matter what, in the memory of the Jews of Thessaloniki, Chief Rabbi Koretz and the rest of the Star Camp inmates were the primary villains.

Leo Koretz later became a lawyer in Israel and remained close to his Bergen-Belsen friend Klaus-Albert Weiss, the son of the much-appreciated last Star Camp leader, Joseph Weiss. The Koretz family members never gave up their efforts to clear the name of Rabbi Koretz but ultimately had little success. What remains of their story is a disturbingly intrusive Greek narrative of externalized guilt presented in articles widely published in Greek newspapers in connection with the "Trial of the Jews" in the summer of 1946, arguing that it was traitors in their own senior ranks who were primarily responsible for the immense death toll paid by the Jews of Greece.[170]

The Neutrals Camp

Only a few days before the Star Camp inmates left Bergen-Belsen for good, 155 Spanish and 19 Portuguese Jewish nationals originally from Greece had been put on a train to Theresienstadt. After a year in the Neutrals Camp and a one-week journey, they were liberated by the Americans. Back in April 1944, as part of a much larger transport heading to Auschwitz, their cattle cars too were detached at Vienna and then sent on to Bergen-Belsen. As soon as Spanish nationals in Athens were required to register in October 1943, the Spanish ambassador stepped up his efforts to get them transferred to Spain. Although, unlike other Jews, they did not need to appear every week for roll call, for the German occupying authorities, who knew their identities and address, they could be easily tracked down. On the evening of March 24, 1944, they were rounded up and sent to the Reich a week later. Upon their arrival in Bergen-Belsen, they no longer encountered their fellow Spanish nationals who had been deported from Thessaloniki. At that point, the first group of 367 had already been repatriated to Spain. Madrid made it a condition,

144 · HOMECOMING

however, that the group from Athens could be repatriated only if the Thessaloniki group were sent out of Spain, to North Africa or elsewhere. This eventually happened, three months later. But after the Normandy landings on June 6, 1944, it was too late to implement any further repatriation across half of Europe toward the Iberian Peninsula.[171]

In this small camp section of between 250 and 366 souls—the Neutrals Camp—Jews were indisputably living under more favorable conditions than the rest of the camp's inmates, as they were exempt from forced labor. But the men and the women still had to separate every night, to line up for roll calls, and to be exposed to SS cruelty. In their self-governed barracks and the immediate surroundings within the barbed wire compound, they lived far below any of the standards they had before imprisonment. Initially, their barracks included rooms where men and women slept on bunk beds with straw, a common eating area with tables, chairs and closets, a washroom, and an in-door latrine. After being moved to another part of the camp, however, there were fewer beds and several inmates had to sleep on the floor. Exposed to the severe cold, some of them died. Though the conditions were primitive and the dirty barracks, reminiscent of a stable, were full of mice, to prisoners who had experienced other camps, it all seemed to be unfair luxury.[172]

In a book that quickly became the universally accepted account on the Holocaust of the Jews of Greece, Joseph Nehama, one of the Neutrals Camp inmates, later wrote: "they were locked in a separate barrack. They became acquainted with all the horrors of the concentration camps: hunger, vermin, epidemics, humiliation by the [Nazi] beasts."[173] Still, their food included soup made with vegetables (instead of just turnip), regular rations of bread, cheese, milk, meat, butter or margarine, marmalade, artificial honey, and hot ersatz coffee, and they had detergent for washing their clothes, all making their internment resemble life under war austerity more than a Nazi concentration camp. This allowed the Neutrals Camp inmates to barter goods among themselves, especially food and clothing. Cigarettes, rationed to two to three a day per prisoner, became the internal currency. In his report delivered after liberation, Rudolf Levy, an Amsterdam deportee who had arrived in the Neutrals Camp in June 1944, systematically and symptomatically called himself and his fellow internees "camp residents" living in a *Zwangsgesellschaft*, a society kept together by force.[174]

In the diverse Neutrals Camp community of Sephardic and Ashkenazi Jews of mostly neutral nationalities from all over German-occupied Europe, with Spanish nationals of Greece (155) and Turkish nationals of Italy and the Netherlands (105) at the top of the hierarchy, communication was often difficult. Whereas some Dutch inmates in the Star Camp considered the Thessalonicans to be interesting, peculiar, and very different from themselves not only in appearance but also in their being loud and extremely expressive, everyday life in the Neutrals Camp was, in the words of Rudolf Levy, a Berlin attorney with Turkish citizenship who had fled from Germany to the Netherlands in 1940, determined by "the mentality and temperament of these Sephardic Jews. Some of the leading clique tended to be manipulative, but the others soon recognized this. Then, one of these Greek Jews, his coat casually thrown round his shoulders, yelled at the offenders in strong language. The other then shouted back just as loud, and soon the whole room was filled with a violent dispute. Men insulted or even beat each other, while women sobbed convulsively. Finally, the noise ebbed away, and everything stayed the same as before."[175]

In such an environment, family became one of the most important sources of security and safety. Women took care of their families and did work to which they had not been accustomed in their upper-middle-class milieu before deportation; for men, used to a daily business routine, being productive in camp conditions without that routine was difficult,[176] even though the career backgrounds of the men (in general, few women had jobs back then) varied greatly; business, commerce, and banking were common occupations among the Neutrals Camp deportees from Greece. No wonder they favored flourishing barter to housekeeping. The exceptions among the Spanish and Portuguese nationals from Greece seem to have been David Benadon and Joseph Nehama. Benadon, who became the Head of the Council of Elders because of his fluent German, had served as a dentist to the royal family in Athens before the war. David Benadon, just entering his fifties, was interned in Bergen-Belsen with his wife and twelve-year-old son. By contrast, Nehama, in his mid-sixties, had arrived with his wife and married daughter, whose husband had managed to escape at the moment of deportation.[177]

Unlike in the "Albala Camp," no one in the "Benadon Camp" seems to have complained about its leader, but there is actually little documentation related to Benadon except for his death from typhus at the liberation.[178]

146 · HOMECOMING

In her account, Flora Benveniste, a young married deportee originally from Thessaloniki, merely remarks that Benadon had served as spokesman, a mediator in conflicts for the Thessaloniki group, earning his elder position precisely because of his language skills: "We had a person, Mr. Benadon from Athens, he spoke German fluently. He was the only one that could talk to the German people."[179] In contrast to him, Joseph Nehama, who had left for Athens during the occupation only to be captured with the group of Spanish nationals and sent to Bergen-Belsen, appears in many sources. Before the occupation, he was a well-known and respected director of the prestigious Jewish school Alliance Israélite Universelle, in Thessaloniki.[180] Aside from this, Nehama, educated at the Sorbonne, was the founder and prewar president of Union Bank, and he strived for cross-cultural collaboration and solidarity rather than adhering to Zionist ideas. As a journalist, writer, and scholar, he was genuinely interested in all aspects of the Judeo-Spanish language and the history of the Jews of Thessaloniki. By the camp inmates from Greece (and then in stories passed down), he is remembered as a gifted orator and the driving force of social activities (like singing and storytelling) while incarcerated, as well as the central voice of the opposition to the Jewish leaders of the Neutrals Camp.[181]

Anecdotally, in a childhood recollection of Flora Carasso's, Joseph Nehama also appears as the just, male stranger in lively social interaction with the women inmates of the Neutrals Camp and then as a source of moral support when things became more arduous in Bergen-Belsen, even for the Spanish nationals: "I remember there was only one man living in our barrack. He was a philosopher. His name was Joseph Nehama. He has written a lot of books. [...] he used to write down recipes and the women would pass by and he would say to my mother: 'Alina, can you tell me a recipe?' Then [he'd] write down a recipe even though we were so hungry we wouldn't even listen to that."[182]

Remarkably, the deportation both of Nehama's and of Benadon's closest family is never mentioned in eyewitness accounts. In the afterword of the German translation of *In Memoriam*, which was published in only two hundred copies ten years after Nehama's death, Peter Gerhard Katzung, a Greek-German translator and an *Iliad* specialist, thanks among other people "Mrs. Mary Nehama and Mrs. Nehama-Saporta," Nehama's wife and daughter, for their kind support, but he never mentions that they too had been through Bergen-Belsen.[183] Only in passing does Ketty Levi of Thessaloniki, who was sent to the Neutrals Camp as a Portuguese national together with her husband and two little sons, refer in her testimony to a young woman, the daughter of a "professor in Salonika," who made an effort to teach children in their camp section. Nora Saporta, née Nehama, later followed the path of a schoolteacher not only in Greece but also after emigrating to the United States. An admirer, like her father, of French culture, she became an initiator of the Ecole de l'Alliance Française in Atlanta, Georgia.[184]

While in Bergen-Belsen, exposed to air raids and aware that the Western Allies had finally invaded Europe, Spanish nationals gradually lost hope that they would be repatriated to Franco's Spain. The situation looked even grimmer for them when dysentery, smallpox, meningitis, mastoiditis, typhus, and other diseases started to spread even in their camp section. Transport lists were drawn up by the Jewish Council of Elders, set up in the Neutrals Camp on German orders, immediately followed by a rumor that the inmates would be deported to a killing center. On April 8, 1945, the Neutrals Camp inmates left Bergen-Belsen with Theresienstadt as their final destination, the camp in Bohemia that was still under German command. For another week, they were slowly zigzagging toward Berlin, but the train came to a dead end near Magdeburg, where the Jews were finally liberated.[185]

Though the deportees were still in a panic about being murdered, one of the liberators, Corporal Frank Gartner, in a letter from April 15, 1945, describes the scene outside the train: "Our advances were so swift, that the SS guards left this particular train where it was and took off." Once the box cars were unsealed, the liberators were struck by the dreadful state of the passengers: "those who still had the strength were almost dangerously ravenous, some swarming into the local bakery to lick up the raw flour."[186]

The Spanish and Portuguese nationals from Greece, among the roughly 2,200 deportees who had survived the journey, were accommodated in houses and barracks in Hillersleben and nearby villages. Local sources could not provide enough meat and bread to satisfy the basic needs of these wretched people. On top of that, many in the group of Jews from Greece were seriously ill, and seven of them, mostly elderly, died there of typhus. David Benadon, the Jewish Elder of the Neutrals Camp, was one of them. Nevertheless, the convoy of Neutrals Camp prisoners was the only instance of Jewish child deportees being liberated by the US Army. That particular train had 559 boys

148 · HOMECOMING

and girls, thirty-three of whom were from Greece, including twelve-year-old Elie, Benadon's son, who was about to return to Athens with his mother.[187]

The liberated Neutrals Camp prisoners had to wait a while longer in Hillersleben, a former Luftwaffe airbase with vacated barracks. Meanwhile, with the assistance of the local population, often pressed by US soldiers, the former prisoners were fed, deloused, and put into clean beds. But, as Wilson Rice of the 30th Division Medical Detachment put it, after having suffered severely for so long, they badly needed personal help to remind them how to live in normal conditions.[188] Decades later, Flora Carasso, a little girl at the time, the only child of a once-well-off Thessalonican businessman, described postwar looting by ex-deportees, which was done with a sense of satisfaction and the pleasure of revenge: "We were out stealing, I mean stealing. It was the first time in my life that I saw my mother steal. She did not steal things that she needed. She would take a plate, she would take anything she could find, and my father, holding a small hammer in his hand, going down to the cellar where he found a lot of china, all stolen from different countries of the world and he would tap them with the hammer and break everything."[189]

When combining personal accounts, in which time flows in the rhythm of each individual's perceptions, with different archival sources, it is fair to deduce that it was more than a month before most of the Neutrals Camp deportees of Greece, accompanied by medical personnel, boarded trains for the Low Countries, reaching Brussels in June 1945.[190] Again, after about a month, they were moved to France and accommodated in a reception center in Courbevoie, a Paris suburb, which had been badly damaged by Allied bombing. Provided with temporary ID cards and some pocket money, they were free to move around. Ketty Levi recalls how she, her husband, and their sons were received in France and how the journey continued: "In Courbevoie is the Vélodrome, a sports arena. It was empty and they put cots in the covered part. That's where we stayed for a while before they prepared something for us in Paris. We stayed for a long time in Paris, four months, until August. Then we went to Marseille for a couple of weeks. On the day that we were leaving from Toulon, August 17th [sic], Japan surrendered. The British were transferring soldiers through Italy, so they dropped us in Bari."[191]

This was the route that most former Neutrals Camp deportees from Greece followed, though other descriptions of the events are even less detailed than Ketty Levi's. From Italy, many Jews were heading to Palestine, but these survivors were waiting for repatriation to Greece. At last, in September 1945, a ship took them from Bari to Piraeus. For most of them, however, the long-awaited homecoming only brought yet another existential struggle and a lot of disappointment. Once they reached their hometown of Thessaloniki at the end of September, they faced the usual disadvantages of being among the last returnees to arrive. On top of that, they were even more obstructed than others from regaining their assets because they were not Greek citizens, and their movable property was long gone. Joseph Nehama immediately tried to get his Union Bank operating again. Before the war, its capital had amounted to US$800,000, but now the bank was ruined. Jacobson, with whom Nehama regularly communicated about Community matters, had his personal sympathies for Nehama, but could of course not use JDC resources to compensate him for his losses.[192]

Whereas about two-thirds of these Neutrals Camp survivors later emigrated overseas, even in 1961 there were still two hundred Spanish nationals left in Greece, though one third of them had moved from Thessaloniki to Athens.[193] But for Star Camp and Neutrals Camp returnees, their being survivors was long questioned in Greece and beyond. Bella Barzilai, a Star Camp survivor, recalls her brother being targeted in Israel for having survived "only" Bergen-Belsen.[194] The Spanish nationals and their offspring struggled with their identity, not only with regard to having their status confirmed in law but also emotionally.

Young Flora Carasso often felt distressed to hear her mother speaking Judeo-Spanish in public and saw her as selfish in this respect. Flora ceased to be a Spanish citizen only when she married her Jewish husband, who had Greek citizenship. By choosing a Greek-sounding name for her son, Flora hoped to avoid possible anti-Jewish sentiments. Much later, in her VHA interview, she refers to the rivalry between Jewish and Greek Orthodox identities by embracing the myth of a continuous Jewish presence in Thessaloniki since the Middle Ages and pitting it against the Greeks: "When you least expect it they intimidate you. I have to defend myself. They ask me if I am Greek. I had come here in 1492, you did much later and by how many years. They should distinguish that even if you have another religion, you are [a] hundred percent Greek."[195]

In postwar Greece, with some help from the JDC, these Bergen-Belsen returnees made great efforts before they were accepted into the association

150 · HOMECOMING

of deportees, whose very name, the Union of Jewish Deportees of Poland, is a declaration of who belongs there. As time went by, the Neutrals Camp deportees managed to establish a more accurate narrative of their having gone through a severe struggle at the camp. This was particularly thanks to the writing of Joseph Nehama and Michael Molho, the chief rabbi of Thessaloniki after the war. Alternatively, some of them, such as Flora Carassso, simply presented themselves as camp survivors without elaborating on a particular location or experience once back home.[196]

CHAPTER FOUR
RETURNING FROM ABROAD

As for us, let's journey into the wilderness.

NINA KOKKALIDOU NAHMIA[1]

HAIM PISANTE left his native Rhodes as a teenager. Encouraged by his relatives, the Alhadeff family, he went overseas, first to Argentina and later to Rhodesia, to make a living and to support his family back home after his father died. When Solomon Alhadeff had established the Britannia factory in Athens, Haim Pisante came to Greece to be its managing director. It was at Britannia during the 1930s, after Hitler had come to power, that he learnt more about the situation in Germany from Jewish refugees looking for work and eager to leave Europe. Haim became alarmed at what he heard and made up his mind to avoid the threat by leaving Greece. As soon as the Greco-Italian War started, Haim packed up and moved his family to Crete, which he considered a safe enough transit place. With the German airborne invasion, the Pisantes set on a long walk to the south of the island until finally evacuating to Egypt in May 1941, together with British troops. According to Haim's daughter Matilda, the five Pisantes were the only civilians on board the ship. It took them until summer 1945 to get back to Athens, where Haim reestablished his business, though for the rest of his life he remained wary of yet another war to come.[2]

Few Jews of Greece escaped deportation as Haim Pisante did by finding a safe haven outside Greece and changing their country of residence before—or, at most, at the very beginning of—the German occupation. True, there had been signs that things were going to get worse for the Jews, such as the appearance in Greece, as in the rest of the world, of that virulently antisemitic fabrication called *The Protocols of the Elders of Zion* (1903; first published in Greek in 1928, with a reprint in 1932). Yet few people, if anybody, could

151

152 · HOMECOMING

imagine the ultimate magnitude of what would become the Holocaust.[3] In Germany, the application of the 1935 Nuremberg Laws discriminating against Jews in every aspect of their lives caught the attention of some Jews in Greece, but it seemed too remote from the reality of most of them.

By the eve of World War II, anti-Jewish policies throughout Europe had radicalized. Just across Greece's northern border, Bulgaria hurried to expel Jews of German, Italian, Spanish, and Greek nationality who had been living there for decades. At the same time, Greek consulates were quickly instructed by their government not to issue tourist or transit visas to Jews (although, it seems, these instructions were ultimately ignored).[4] Nevertheless, none of this, not even the increasing number of refugees from central Europe heading to the Aegean coast and delivering first-hand accounts of *Kristallnacht* pogroms and the anti-Jewish measures, initially made many Jews of Greece question their own future. In their eyes, Nazi Germany remained far away, and it was almost inconceivable to them that such anti-Jewish measures would ever be implemented in Greece. Only some Jews, usually those who, like Haim Pisante, had transnational ties and some experience of the world beyond Greece, felt alarmed enough by Nazis' clearly articulated hatred to do something.

Before World War II, Jewish emigration from Greece was usually motivated by the desire to get away from socioeconomic hardship rather than persecution. By contrast, according to the *American Jewish Year Book*, compiled annually since 1906 by the advocate group the American Jewish Committee, the scores of Jews dying in Greece due to starvation rose after the harsh winter of 1942 to some 7,300. About half of them were children under fourteen. This was certainly not the case in Belgium, Italy, France, or even Spain, where several Jewish families from Greece had decided to resettle despite the effects of the Spanish Civil War (1936–1939) and of the authoritarian Franco regime.[5] But nobody could really predict how international affairs would develop and how they would affect Jews and refugees in general both inside and outside Greece in the next few years.

Although demanding in initial costs and paperwork, emigrating to Spain, the Americas, Africa, or Palestine proved to offer the Jews reliable protection against famine and the Nazi persecution raging in Greece. By contrast, migrating to other European countries might have seemed a good solution at first but soon proved to be as much of a trap as Greece. Despite all diplomatic efforts by Sebastián de Romero Radigales, the Spanish consul in Greece, Madrid refused to accept its Jewish citizens from Greece at the crucial time of deportation, and Italy, after Rome capitulated, could no longer protect its Jewish citizens in German-occupied countries from deportation. Rome even put foreign Jews on Italian territory under house arrest or into internment camps. Jews of Greece who were living in Belgium and France avoided the transports only by illegal acts, such as going into hiding. In Paris in the autumn of 1942, over one thousand Jews from Greece were caught in mass arrests. Most of them were deported to German concentration camps, where, with few exceptions, they were murdered.[6]

One's decision to live outside Greece potentially also had a crucial impact on one's national identity after the war. The law on Greek nationality has been based on the principle of *jus sanguinis* (in Greece, one's nationality was, at the time, determined by the nationality of one's father) supported by the ideology of Helleno-Christianity (by which one is really Greek only if one is a member of the Greek Orthodox Church).

The distinction between *homogenis* and *allogenis* Greeks made it next to impossible for Greek citizens of non-Greek descent to migrate without forfeiting their citizenship. In essence, this categorization already made the Jews second-class citizens in prewar Greece. The question of revoking the Jews' citizenship was seriously raised in postwar Greece in connection with their external displacement and homecoming. The Jews of Greece therefore rarely considered repatriation from new countries of residence, much like the Hassid family deported from Brussels to Auschwitz. Thus, when other Jewish refugees were returning to Greece from neighboring countries, or from Egypt and Palestine, only to have their hopes soon fade and their expectations unmet, Jews who had decided to move out of Greece before the war witnessed from a distance how the problems unfolded.[7]

Neighboring and Other Countries

The centuries in which Jews' lived throughout the Ottoman Empire, which had ceased to exist as a geopolitical entity only a couple of decades before World War II, created strong commercial and family ties across the Balkans. When the Germans invaded Northern Greece, these connections would naturally still be intact. Today, it should seem natural that the Jews searched for

154 · HOMECOMING

ways to find refuge in one of the neighboring countries, where persecution, though present in various degrees, at least did not mean murder. Given the government policies of those countries, however, finding refuge was far more difficult than the small geographic distances required to get there, the need for at least one language in common with the majority population, and the presence of socioeconomic bonds would suggest. Since Jews in the German and Bulgarian zones of occupied Greece had been forced to leave their homes about a year earlier than those in the zone initially occupied by the Italians, rescue attempts were made at different times and in different conditions.

Apart from citizenship, the main factor that Jews took into account when looking for a safe haven outside Greece was extended family abroad. Sometimes, however, the trajectories away from Greece were completely random because family rescue schemes proved to be absolutely out of the question. That was true for Jews living in Vardar Macedonia (today's Republic of North Macedonia), particularly in cities with large Jewish populations— Bitola (Monastir), Skopje, and Štip. Part of the Kingdom of Yugoslavia, it was occupied by Bulgaria, and most of its Jews were deported to Treblinka in early 1943, about the same time as the Jews were deported from the Bulgarian zone of Greece.[8]

Thus it was that, for the extended family of Dario Nehama, who in the interwar period had settled in Athens with his wife, Sarah (née Kolonomos), rather than in their birthplace of Monastir, Greece (despite the danger) and Albania became safe havens. The Nehamas, along with the related Kamhis, Kolonomoses, and Francos, were among the respected families of Monastir. Dario's brother, Solomon, was the local JDC secretary, and his grandfather had been president of the Jewish Community of Monastir before the war. Neither his transnational ties nor strong local background prevented Solomon's deportation to Treblinka in 1943, where he, together with his wife and two children, were murdered on arrival.[9] Whereas two young family members survived as resistance fighters, some parents and children, like Dario and his cousin Allegra Franco, together with her husband and daughter from Monastir, successfully hid in Athens.[10]

The chances of surviving as a Jew in the territories newly acquired by Bulgaria were close to nil and so was refuge in old Bulgaria. Considering the initial expulsion, the legal protection enjoyed only by Jews inhabiting Bulgaria proper, the experience of the Balkan Wars, and the fear of "deep-rooted

Bulgarian brutality," a tiny number of Jews chose this country as their place of refuge.[11] Apparently, very few were able to follow the path of Raphael Kamhi. He was originally from a secular Zionist family of Monastir, which later lived in Greece and then went to Bulgaria of their own accord. Kamhi managed to get to Sofia after escaping the deportations in Thessaloniki in 1943. Like most Jewish survivors in postwar Bulgaria, he settled in Israel after the war. So did the 39 Jewish DPs from Bulgaria who were sent to Palestine on a UNRRA Greece transport along with 175 Jewish children from Greece and their adult escort of 25 as early as August 1945.[12]

Only a small group of young Jewish men, between the ages of eighteen and twenty-two, from formerly Greek Eastern Macedonia and Thrace, survived because the Bulgarian authorities had sent them to do forced labor. In this way, according to the summary by Natan Grinberg, the head of the Commission for Jewish Affairs in postwar Bulgaria, forty-eight men were transferred from Belomorie to Gara Belitsa, a Bulgarian labor camp, to build an international railway line, to be used, among other things, for deportations.[13] One of them was Sampetai Tsimino, from the family of a tobacco manufacturer in Kavala. The work gang he was on consisted of young Jewish men from Kavala and Drama. Because of the work assigned to them, it was Sampetai's misfortune to see his mother and all his siblings for the last time in Bulgaria as they passed by in trains in March 1943 on their way to be murdered in Treblinka soon after.[14]

The experience of witnessing deportations eventually drove two of Sampetai's fellow forced laborers—Benjamin Mevorach and his cousin Leon Varon—to escape. Varon, who was originally from Gallipoli, settled in Greece after the Greco-Turkish population exchange in 1923. Mevorach and Varon then escaped back to Kavala. Wandering through all of Greece to the south, Leon reached Athens and soon joined ELAS, the Greek resistance army, in Arcadia, in the mountains of the Peloponnese. He disarmed after the Varkiza Agreement in February 1945 and returned to Kavala to start his own business, but he could not avoid being seen as a Communist.[15]

Sampetai Tsimino was held in Belitsa until November 1943 and then moved to Plovdiv, where he met Bella Benvasat, a young Sephardi from Bulgaria, whom he married in May 1945. By the time he wed, he had already gotten in touch with his father, who had been the only Tsimino to survive by hiding in Athens, seeking to reestablish the family tobacco business. In

156 · HOMECOMING

the political chaos ruling postwar Bulgaria, Sampetai had waited too long to obtain official papers for repatriation. So he fled illegally from Plovdiv to Thessaloniki, together with Bella and her father, who feared possible prosecution in Bulgaria. They arrived on April 1, 1946, after the hardship of interrogation at the transit camp in Sidirokastro and several days of routine refugee admissions in the reception center at the former Pavlos Melas prison. On the day of his release, Sampetai, who later became the head of the Jewish Community in Kavala, started to work again with his father. The Tsiminos were able to regain their apartment in Kavala, but they had to sue for the rest of their property. The overall situation upon homecoming was desperate economically and politically: "The flat was empty. [...] I had no money. The only thing I had was a suitcase full of crackers. Various inspectors were coming all the time. We filled our mattresses with straw. We had to live. We had to survive somehow."[16]

The trajectory of Markos Botton was quite the opposite to that of the Tsminos. In the summer of 1942, he made contact with EAM-ELAS after witnessing the roundup of Jews in Elefteria Square, in Thessaloniki, where he had been an agriculture student at Aristotle University. He later left the ghetto under a false identity, took up arms, and gradually went from fighting the occupiers to fighting Greek government forces during the Civil War. When the ELAS had withdrawn from the cities and was in fact dissolved with the Varkiza Agreement, Markos laid down his weapons and settled briefly in Thessaloniki. He soon became aware of the anti-Communist persecution. Newspapers started to spread panic, and former partisans tried to hide in the homes of friends. But this was not an option for Markos. According to his account, after several weeks, the group of about five hundred persecuted partisans which he belonged to was sent to the "Greek Commune" in the formerly German-inhabited village of Buljkes in Vojvodina. He was probably among the first Greeks in May 1945 to replace the local German inhabitants expulsed from Yugoslavia.[17]

Markos spent two years in Yugoslavia before going back to fight the Greek armed forces. After the Civil War battles in Grammos and Vitsi, in August 1949, the defeated guerillas entered Bulgaria, where the combatants surrendered their weapons. But Markos was one of a group of twenty men and women who were soon armed again and sent back to Greece "to keep up the morale" of the locals in the spirit of the Communist struggle. Only in

RETURNING FROM ABROAD · 157

August 1950 did he end his mission and return to headquarters in Bulgaria. In his account, Markos recalls the last days before leaving Greece for the next sixteen years: "We reached Chalkidiki at night. What do we see the next day at dawn? The mountains are full: coalmen, shepherds, beekeepers. People started to live as they had lived before the war."[18] At that time he had not yet realized that it was the end of the war.

Although there was much talk about possible or actual escapes from the transports, few examples and even less evidence of these dangerous escapades can be provided. Anry Botton, Markos' older brother, may be the only one who has ever told his story. He assisted the Greek partisan networks in Athens together with his close friend Marios Benaroya. Marios's father, Abraham Benaroya, was a prominent Jewish Communist who was held as a political prisoner in the Laufen Camp, in Bavaria, during the war and was liberated in May 1945.[19] In other words, not even friendship with the son of a prominent Communist leader made it easy to reach the partisans. Nor, on the other hand, did being a prominent Communist leader and a Jew, like Abraham Benaroya, necessarily mean being murdered in a camp.

Originally from Thessaloniki, Anry Botton was a student of chemical engineering not in his hometown, like his younger brother, Markos, but in Athens. Perhaps it was the capital and Anry's EAM connection that had given him false hope of security until the deportation in July 1944. But he did not give up easily. Escaping from the train a day before it arrived in Auschwitz, he found himself alone in the unfamiliar environment of northwest Slovakia, unable to communicate effectively with the locals. In 1943 and 1944, all the Greek transports and many Hungarian ones went through this hub on the strategic railway line on the outskirts of Žilina. The town was under the control of the Germans and the collaborationist Hlinka Guards. Indeed, it was the very place Jozef Tiso had announced Slovak autonomy in October 1938,[20] effectively making Slovakia a satellite state of Nazi Germany.

So Anry left the train in the mountainous lands at the borders of the Slovak state and the Reich, where Nazi Germany had created a security zone, and he wandered south from there toward Bratislava. By that point, the Vrba-Wetzler report on the Auschwitz extermination camp, first handed over to a Jewish resistance group in the same town two months earlier, was already in the possession of the underground Slovak Jewish Council, and the Slovak National Uprising was well under way. Unlike three other escapees from

158 · HOMECOMING

the same transport, Anry never reached Slovak partisan territory. Instead, he invented a story about his being an Italian deserter on his way through Slovakia and stuck with that cover till the liberation. Had he not escaped the transport, Anry would probably have been murdered in Auschwitz like his father, mother, and both of his elder siblings. Moving through the Soviet-controlled territory of eastern Europe, he finally arrived at the Greek-Bulgarian border in August 1945, where the Greek authorities suspected him of being a Communist spy. Upon arriving in Thessaloniki, he learned that his brother Markos had already left for Buljkes. A year later, his new life started with compulsory military service in the Greek army, where Anry was fighting against the partisan troops his younger brother had joined.[21]

One more country, Turkey, the large eastern neighbor of Greece, certainly needs to be mentioned at least briefly. Whereas Bulgaria and Slovakia had been allies of Nazi Germany and in the aftermath became part of the Soviet Bloc, Turkey had remained neutral until after the war. Like Greece, it then sided with the West and in 1952 even joined NATO military structures. But regarding Jewish refugees from Greece, only Turkish nationals, assisted by the JDC, were accepted by wartime Ankara. Shortly after the roundups in the former Italian zone of Greece in spring 1944, a group of 850 refugees arrived in Istanbul. Most of them were Jews from France, but, as the JDC representative Reuben Resnik telegraphed to headquarters in Lisbon, 36 Jews were from Greece.[22]

Since the geographical distances between the Jewish communities of Eastern Macedonia, Thrace, and Turkey were short, one would probably assume that more refugees would have fled to Turkish territory. The authorities of officially neutral Turkey, however, were not inclined to open their borders in Thrace to Greece, since Germany could have perceived such a move as hostile and a violation of territorial integrity, counter to the provisions of the German-Turkish Treaty of Friendship from June 1941.[23] Besides, rightly or not, the JDC claimed that these refugees found it difficult to earn a living there without knowledge of the language and the local environment, and that made them dependent on external humanitarian aid.[24]

Since autumn 1943, Jewish refugees from the former Italian zone of Greece had been heading for the Turkish coast by the hundreds. In Turkey, which in this case served only for rapid transit, these people were received by the Jewish Agency and Allied authorities and taken to the Middle East.[25]

As German pressure mounted on Ankara to seal its western borders against the mass escape of Jews from Romania and Bulgaria, the refugees' chances of crossing into Turkey by land were close to nil.

In a few cases, Jewish refugees did spend the war in Turkey and returned to their homelands later on. Among these exceptions were several Jewish inhabitants of Rhodes who had Turkish citizenship. An even smaller number managed to cross the sea to Cyprus. While Cyprus was in British hands, the Dodecanese islands would become a part of Greece only after the Treaty of Peace with Italy in 1947, and so during the Nazi persecution the Jews of Rhodes were not Greek citizens. After the Italian surrender, the Germans were in charge of Rhodes until May 1945, and then the island remained under British control until 1947.[26]

Whereas most Jews of Rhodes had been deported through Athens to Auschwitz in August 1944, forty-two stayed behind as Turkish subjects, but the Germans insisted on their "repatriation" to Turkey. In early January 1945, they finally crossed a rough sea to Marmaris in just a fishing boat. Maurice Soriano, the postwar head of the Rhodes Jewish Community, who succeeded in escaping to Athens, stated that "at the time of liberation, no Jews were left in Rhodes."[27] By the time Rhodes was incorporated into the Greek state, only three or four Jewish families resided on the island.[28] Being Turkish or Italian subjects during the war, originally Rhodian Jews were not eligible either to claim their immovable property in Greece or later to receive compensation based on the Greek-German Treaty of 1960.[29] According to the Greek legal interpretation, compensation and property restitution was intended solely for people who had been Greek citizens during the war. The property of Rhodians was considered abandoned,[30] making its appropriation by Greek nationals feasible.

Thus, Jews of Rhodes who had retained their Turkish citizenship usually sought their future abroad. The personal account of the Turiel family, who emigrated to the United States, has lately become an integral part of the German educational material on National Socialism, as an example of entangled transnational identities and trajectories.[31] Others, Lina Amato's family among them, first tried their luck back in Rhodes.[32] As a child survivor born in 1936, Lina describes how her family, once they were in Turkey, moved from Marmaris to the home of some acquaintances in Izmir. After the Germans evacuated Rhodes, the Amatos were about to return. From

160 · HOMECOMING

her childhood perspective, Lina recalls the abrupt postwar transformation of the cultural composition of Rhodes before her family moved to Africa and joined the Jewish Community of Rhodesia in 1948: "Now I am learning Greek. First, I studied in Italian, I had French lessons at home, spoke [Judeo-] Spanish with my granny, Greek with the maid. I knew [Greek] but I didn't know how to write. It was very difficult but I went to school for three years and it was nice being at school after all these years."[33]

The question of language preoccupied other survivors as well, especially if their temporary refuge turned into a long stay, as happened to several of them in Albania. Michael Matsas, a child survivor and the author of *Illusion of Safety* (1997), writes that his closest family, which moved to the United States after the war, was originally from Ioannina.[34] In the early 1990s, they relocated thirty-three relatives on the mother's side, Cohens, from Albania overseas. Nina and Leon Cohen, who had found refuge with Leon's sister in Vlorë, Albania, in January 1941, succeeded in returning to Greece only after twenty-six years. Nina recalls how it took her years after the war to master Albanian. She longed to go back to Greece, but the problematic Greek-Albanian relations and the Cold War prevented the homecoming of the young couple after the occupation.[35]

Ever since the Italian forces attacked Greece on October 28, 1940, from Albanian territory, Athens was at war with Tirana. In fact even today, when both countries are NATO members, they are still technically at war. In circumstances inherited from the onset of the Greek Civil War and the Cold War, the Cohens as de facto refugees did not receive a *laissez-passer* from the French consulate in Tirana until the 1960s. Only then, via Italy, did they end up in Athens, where they reunited with other family members. Even this protracted homecoming was followed by great disappointment. Greece did not welcome the Cohens with open arms but suspected them of being Communist informants. After all these unpleasant experiences, they decided to make a new start in the United States.[36]

The Central Board of Jewish Communities (Athens) and the Greek branch of the JDC were eager to assist the Jews in Albania; however, relief had to be provided by way of Communist Yugoslavia. As of September 1947, there were nine families of "Epirus Jews" (as Athens referred to them) registered to receive humanitarian aid. The same list also includes five Jews imprisoned in Albania "for political and other reasons."[37] The only option for returning to

Greece from Albania was to act quickly and not to be lulled into a false sense of security since what at first appeared to be a convenient refuge during the war became a threat in its aftermath. Two strategies were possible there: one was to try to return to Greece immediately after the German withdrawal, the other to use Albania as a transit country. The first required less physical effort but a strong authority, that is, someone with very good connections.

A fine example is the Kounne family of Thessaloniki. Once the deportations from Thessaloniki started, Mari and Elias Kounne were smuggled into Albania with their daughter, Frida, by an Albanian merchant. This happened thanks to the intervention of their non-Jewish son-in-law, Konstantinos Megas, an influential businessman. After the Italians had signed an armistice with the Allies in early September 1943, Germany got the upper hand over Albania as well. The Kounnes found refuge in Korçë with a family called Panariti. For safety, the women later moved to a remote mountain village while the father clandestinely returned to Greece.[38] Once the Germans left for good, in November 1944, Elias Kounne used all his influence to arrange their return to Thessaloniki, which they reached in mid-December 1944. In the years to follow, Frida would keep up a correspondence with the Panariti family members and in 2014 nominated them for the Righteous Among the Nations award, but personal contact was impossible during the Cold War.[39]

As for Errikos Levis, after he returned from the concentration camps, he used every connection he had as a military doctor to get his wife Jeannette, his son Alexander, and his parents in Albania back to Greece. Unlike Errikos, deported to Auschwitz in 1944, the rest of his family had changed their residence to Albania right after the Italian surrender in 1943 and spent the rest of the war in Vlorë, where Jeannette's sister lived married into the Matathia family. Since the Hoxha régime banned its operations in Albania, it was not until December 1945 that the JDC successfully arranged for UNRRA to finally get the Levises out of the country and back to Greece.[40]

Errikos also regularly sought to help other relatives and Epirus Jews in Albania, including the prewar Vlorë Community representatives, but all without success. While Mateo Matathia and Joseph Levis, part of the pre-Hoxha bureaucracy, negotiated the protection of Jews in Albania proper from deportations during the war, Hoxha's Communist regime was merciless to them. In October 1945, a military court in Vlorë found Levis, and in June 1946 Matathia, guilty of subversion and sentenced them to five years in

162 · HOMECOMING

prison and forced labor. Their rights were withdrawn and all their property confiscated. By the time of the Cold War, due to political developments, more Jews of Greece found themselves in Albanian prisons—among them forty Greek conscripts, including Michael Matsas's cousin, Albertos Negrin, who would return to Ioannina only eight years later, following de-Stalinization.[41]

For other Jews during the war, Albania served as a transit country to Italy and beyond. One person who took this route was Vital Chasson, a Jewish collaborator, the head of the Jewish police, the "Civil Guard," and right-hand man of SS-Hauptsturmführer Dieter Wisliceny and Alois Brunner in occupied Thessaloniki. Together with his family and lover, Chasson crossed the Greek-Albanian border using false IDs issued by the Italian consulate in Thessaloniki during the deportations. Michael Molho writes that the Italians offered help because Chasson had promised to accept the safe passage of thirty-four Jews of Italian citizenship to Athens in return for his own safety when the time came. Under the given conditions, it was a good enough deal for the Italians. In Albania, Chasson and his entourage ended up in the Kavajë internment camp near Korçë, which was also holding other Jewish refugees from Greece. Considering him to be a British informant, the Albanians were going to keep Chasson there for good. But when Italy surrendered, the situation in Albania became chaotic. Chasson was released and soon crossed the Adriatic. After reaching the port of Bari and remaining several days in custody in Italy, he and his suite were set free.

The Chasson group later continued on to Egypt. In Alexandria, after being identified by Jewish refugees from Thessaloniki, Chasson was arrested by the British and extradited to Athens, but he was eventually released again. In November 1945, Chasson returned to Thessaloniki. There he was handed over to the police after camp returnees beat him up in the street for what he had done during the war. Chasson was imprisoned in Pavlos Melas and tried together with Jacques Albala and Edgar Kounio in June 1946. He was sentenced to death and executed by firing squad in Thessaloniki.[42]

No Greek who was not of Jewish background was ever sent to prison for having persecuted Jews. The only German perpetrator tried in Greece for having orchestrated the persecution and deportation of the Jews was Max Merten (1911–1971), the military administration counselor in Thessaloniki. In 1959 a Greek court sentenced him to twenty-five years in prison, but he was soon extradited to West Germany, where he was released.[43] Dieter Wisliceny

(1911–1948), who besides his activity in Thessaloniki was actively and avidly involved in the destruction of Jews in Slovakia, was extradited to Bratislava and executed for war crimes. Infamous for overseeing deportations from both Thessaloniki and the Drancy transit camp in France, Alois Brunner (1912–2010?) disappeared without facing punishment. He was later located in Syria after many years.[44]

Another Jewish refugee who followed the route to Italy via Albania was Albertos Nachmias. Though living in Thessaloniki when the deportations started, Albertos was originally from Bitola, Yugoslavia. He left with two friends, both Jews in their late twenties. Soon after, the family of Mois Beza, a factory owner from Thessaloniki, followed the same route. They all escaped from the ghetto to the Italian zone and then further north until they reached Korçë, meeting in September 1943 on the Albanian coast near Corfu for the first time. An overcrowded boat carrying thirty-six Jewish refugees and about a hundred disarmed Italian soldiers set sail for Bari. Were it not for a British Army rescue mission, they would probably have drowned in the Adriatic. While Albertos remained in Southern Italy, liberated by the Allies shortly afterwards, the Beza family continued to Egypt. Albertos stayed in Italy, living in vacant houses in what became the Foggia Airfield Complex of the Allies and earning money as an interpreter in the port of Bari, a transit place for Jews and Greeks returning home as well as for Jewish survivors hoping to make Aliyah in Palestine. He repatriated to Greece in November 1945, about two months after the Allies abandoned Bari Airfield and returned the land to its original owners.[45]

The Bezas who crossed the Mediterranean were first placed in a refugee camp on Sinai and then transferred to Cairo. When their daughter Yvet, about nine years old, was to attend school, they briefly thought about resettling in Egypt for good. At that point of time, Bezas could not know that their resettlement in Egypt would have doubtless led to yet another expulsion during the Suez Crisis in 1956. Plus Mois Beza could not help but returning to see what remained of his business in Thessaloniki. And so the family sailed for three days before reaching Piraeus in May 1945. After a few weeks, they set out for Thessaloniki, where everything of theirs turned out to have been stolen or occupied. Back in her hometown, Yvet, by now in a Greek school, was confronted with antisemitic remarks, indifference, and ignorance. She vividly recalls being confused by a non-Jewish friend's

164 · HOMECOMING

jealous remark: "Look how lucky you are to have made such a trip!" When the Civil War broke out, the family left for Argentina so that Yvet's elder brother would not be drafted. Soon after the war, however, they returned to Greece for good.[46]

Though Yvet Beza and Albertos Nachmias had Thessaloniki in common, their homecoming diverged, and so did their views about the possible chances of the Jews of Greece being rescued. Whereas in his account Albertos states that the Thessalonican Jews' obedience to their leadership was mostly to blame for the disaster that followed the occupation, Yvet, in her account, says it was the Jews' insufficient integration in Greek society and the nonexistence of the Jewish state at the time. By pointing to their own ranks, as well as to the Nazis of course, and seeking greater integration in Greece, together with a Jewish state as a safety net, both Yvet and Albertos embody the most prevalent aspects of Holocaust survivors' self-representation in Greece.[47]

PALESTINE

During the interwar period, which by the mid-1940s seemed like the distant past, the impact of the Zionist movement had increased the numbers migrating from Greece to Palestine. The Jews of Greece mostly settled in the Sephardic communities of Jaffa, Tel Aviv, Akko, and Haifa, which quickly developed into modern Middle Eastern ports. The Greek Zionist club Kadima, in Tel Aviv, and the Moshav Tsur Moshe agricultural cooperative established by Jews from Thessaloniki and Kastoria near Netanya were responsible, among others, for taking care of Jewish refugees from Greece during the occupation.[48]

Having remained at the head of the Jewish Agency's political department throughout World War II, Moshe Sharett, a top representative of the Yishuv, the Jewish residents of Palestine, organized the Aliyah.[49] Thus, both the Jewish Agency's connection with the Jews of Greece and the network created by the Zionists who had left Greece before the Nazi persecution—most prominently Leon Recanati, the founder of the Palestine Discount Bank—were already established by the time the persecution started.[50]

The path from Greece to the Middle East was paved by British soldiers, and older networks were facilitating escape. By the time of the liberation, between 1,500 and 3,000 Jews (depending on the source) had crossed the

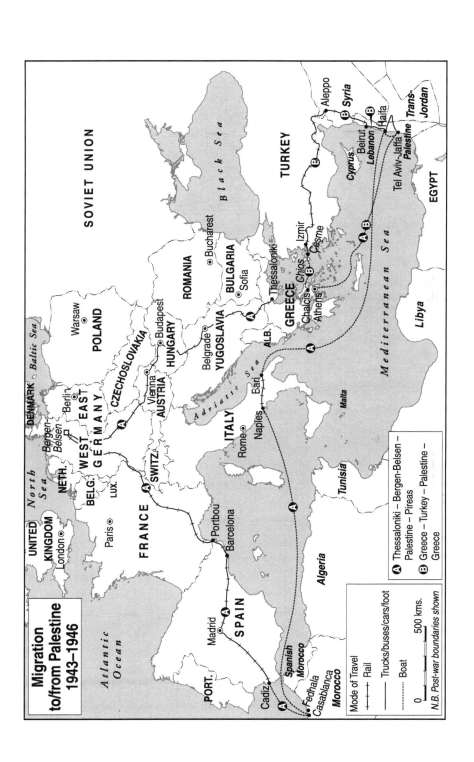

166 · HOMECOMING

Eastern Mediterranean from occupied Greece.[51] But only after September 1943, when the German administration took over the former Italian zone, ordering Jews to wear a cockade in the form of the Star of David, did Palestine become a possible destination. Until then, because of the war and the restrictions imposed on the Jews, crossing the Aegean was usually deemed far too dangerous.

Migration to the Middle East was no less complicated than migration to the countries neighboring Greece. Palestine, under British mandate, was not a sovereign state, let alone Jewish. The thought that the territory could soon be flooded by Jewish refugees concerned not only London and Berlin but also, above all, the local Arab leaders whose loyalty and alliance were considered by both the Allies and the Axis powers to be of utmost importance. Up until December 1942, already well informed about the scale of the persecution of the Jews, British political elites did not have the slightest intention of changing their position on Jewish immigration and increasing the Jewish quota. With the influx of illegal migrants to Mandatory Palestine, they carefully blocked all possible routes by land and sea. Rescue missions, primarily to save British soldiers and loyal political leaders trapped in Greece, were negotiated only at the end of summer 1943, after most of the Jews from the German and Bulgarian zones had ended up in extermination camps. At that time, as illegal Jewish migration continued, British and American intelligence services became keen to get more soldiers, even from among the Jewish refugees.[52]

For postwar Palestine, it was the British and their wartime Allies under the umbrella of the Supreme Headquarters Allied Expeditionary Force (SHAEF) who were dictating the terms and conditions of repatriation. For them, the unconditional return of refugees to their countries of origin was the priority, though they did not sufficiently understand what was in store for those returnees. Most Greek DPs in Palestine—Jewish and non-Jewish—were eager to leave the refugee camps in the Middle East and repatriate. The Greek consulate in Jerusalem encouraged them to do so and helped them obtain the necessary documents. The UNRRA, which operated under the command of SHAEF, took care of their travel. For several hundred Jews of Greek and Spanish nationality at the end of 1945, returning to Greece was, at least for a while, facilitated en masse regardless of citizenship.[53]

During the occupation, the more than seven hundred Jewish refugees from Greece who had reached Palestine by the summer of 1944 had, typically, arranged their escape in Athens. They were using a channel established by the Jewish Agency and the Jewish Community in Izmir in cooperation with the Special Operations Executive (SOE), the British secret service. The Union of Jews from Greece in Palestine (Hitachduth Oley Yavan), based in Tel Aviv, which assisted the Jewish refugees of Greece in Palestine, noted that the Jews originally from Thessaloniki were mostly of the upper social strata, among them, for example, the brother of a prominent Thessalonican banker, David Benousiglio, and the local JDC representative (of Hungarian citizenship) Joseph Lovinger and his wife. According to the Union, only rich Thessalonicans could afford to pay for their rescue given "the cost of the escape to Athens under tremendous difficulties." By contrast, as the document states, young independent Jewish refugees from other parts of Greece constituted a fairly mixed group, including members of the working class and unaccompanied housewives. Surely, if they dared to undertake the journey on their own, then the cost of travelling from Athens to Palestine was "within everybody's reach."[54]

The main contact in Greece soon became Solomon Barki. His brother, Rafael, had moved to Anatolia before the war, and he became closely associated with the Jewish Community leaders in Izmir. Because of his business, Rafael Barki was on good terms with the sailors, who had no qualms about crossing the Aegean. From Athens, Jewish refugees first travelled over land to the partisan-controlled shores of Euboea, where they were provided for by the locals, mostly to the benefit of everyone involved. But, according to a Hellenic Information Service report, based on the questioning of about sixty Jewish refugees from Greece, "Many Jews were shamelessly exploited [...] by people who offered to arrange their escape, extracted money from them, and then, in many cases, let them down."[55]

More often than not, the strategy Jewish families took was to send only their younger members to Palestine or to try their luck by travelling separately in smaller groups, similar to the precaution taken by people who went into hiding instead of fleeing. It could sometimes take months for the fugitives to find a capable mediator, a task impossible without a Greek connection, usually someone in the resistance. For the ferry, Jews had to pay up to twenty-five gold sovereigns per person, a high price considering that one gold sovereign was enough to live off for a month.

168 · HOMECOMING

The Negris family was originally from Ioannina but had already settled in Athens before the war. The father was the first to leave Athens, followed by the mother with their teenage daughter. As Eftyhia recalls, they first hid, under false identities, in a Greek house in Kifissia from where they left by bus for Chalcis in October 1943, taking only two travel sacks (following her father's directions). On mules, they continued to the villages in the mountainous area held by the EAM. The family reunited in Steni, the heart of Free Greece, where, together with other Jews, they stayed with the locals or in accommodations assigned to them by the partisans or simply where the locals put them. Waiting to be carried over the Aegean, they were vulnerable to random German patrols and local betrayals. About the time of the Purim festival in March 1944, they walked halfway across the island to the shore by the village of Tsakei to board fishing boats for Turkey.[56]

For most wartime refugees from Greece, their longing for a new Jewish homeland was not what brought them to Palestine. The Negrises and others longed to return home ever since they decided to leave Greece. The goal was simply to get out of a German-occupied country. Acher Benroubi, who escaped from Thessaloniki to Athens, soundly comments on the overall situation and resilience of Jewish refugees: "Would the Turks want us? No, they would not. They kicked all of the refugees out. They sent them down to the Brits. The Brits were in Syria, Lebanon, Palestine, and Egypt, so they [the Turks] took us to the Brits. We wanted to leave from here [occupied Greece]. To escape. If they would take us to the Chinese, we would have gone in order to escape the Germans since we knew what was in store for us."[57]

From Euboea, it was only about 100 miles (160 km) to the coastal town of Çeşme on the western end of Turkey, where the vessels were heading. Having reached the Turkish coast, the illegal migrants were put on trucks in groups of twenty to fifty and were taken to the Greek consulate in Izmir. Jewish civilians were separated from army recruits and were further provided for by the British officials and the Jewish Agency, who covered the transfers. After months of internal displacement within Greece and an exhausting journey, many refugees needed medical treatment and general hygiene care.[58]

Travelling further south from Izmir, the trains usually took them not directly to Palestine but to the British refugee camp in Aleppo. After about two days on the train and another short ride on trucks, the refugees were first registered and disinfected at a reception center and then admitted to the refugee camp, where they were required to remain until issued papers for Palestine. All Greek subjects were housed together, and, as the Jewish Agency noted, there were several episodes of maltreatment by non-Jewish refugees. Admittedly, the British in Aleppo were not acquainted with the real motives for the escape of the Jews, who repeatedly demanded to be set free. Instead, British officials subjected them to thorough interrogation by the British Security Mission before their journey continued via Beirut to Palestine.[59]

When finally arriving in Haifa and, later, Tel Aviv, Eftyhia Negris, who was eighteen at the time, saw the escape as an adventure. On the one hand, her family provided her with a safe haven; on the other, though she did not feel endangered, Eftyhia simply "did not understand the whole tragedy of the situation, seeing her parents terrified." As a young woman from a traditional Jewish family, Eftyhia was, as she observed, taken by surprise by cultural differences. She was not accustomed to traveling on Shabbat or seeing girls in shorts, which attracted her attention and, indirectly, introduced her to liberal Judaism and women's emancipation, ultimately changing the course of her life.[60]

According to British sources, the Greek government-in-exile, eager to draft men eligible for military service to the army, provided all the refugees with a small per diem. After March 1944, when the unrest of Greek recruits in Egypt escalated into a mutiny, government policy changed.[61] From that point on, Jewish men waiting in Palestine, and itching for action in the war, were left in limbo in Gaza, in the Nuseirat refugee camp for Greek nationals, suspect and with no way of joining any military forces. It was their relatives, the Jewish migrants from interwar Greece and the Oley Yavan, who often assisted them in finding accommodation and making a living outside the facility. Though they were under no restraint, it was next to impossible to have basic needs like clothing and footwear met, let alone find a job and suitable housing. The conditions were very simple, lacking almost everything of what they had been used to in their previous lives. Moreover, without knowing Hebrew, it was difficult to get by. In these circumstances, it was young men in particular who opted for life in kibbutzim. According to the Oley Yavan report, as many as fifty youngsters had already left to live in kibbutzim at the beginning of August 1944, and more would join them. Life there consisted not only of agricultural work and leisure but also included

170 · HOMECOMING

at least some military training, which would, it turned out, come in handy in the conflicts taking place in the aftermath of World War II, whether in Greece or in Palestine.[62]

For the 367 Thessalonican deportees from the Bergen-Belsen Neutrals Camp, many of whom had turned up in Palestine at the end of the war, nominal repatriation to Spain was transformed into a tangled voyage across the Mediterranean. At best, it took nearly two years until their homecoming. After negotiations between the Spanish and the Germans dragged on, obstructed by Madrid's unwillingness to host yet more refugees, the Spanish nationals from Greece were finally released from Bergen-Belsen, where they had spent six months under conditions quite like the ones described by Spanish nationals deported from Athens. Put on southbound trains in two groups, they crossed the Spanish border after more than a week's journey in early 1944; the first train, carrying 182 persons, left on February 10, and the second on February 13.[63] Whereas most of these refugees remember precisely how long they had been in the camp, the journey felt never-ending, and their time in Spain seemed like a "long holiday."[64]

Traveling on an old run-down passenger train with basic food provisions for three days and drinking only water distributed during occasional short stops, they reached the French-Spanish border. During the journey, they became aware of the overall destruction of Europe and the desperate situation of civilians. Isaac Gattegnio recalls that their attempts to obtain some additional food while passing through French towns, even in exchange for the last of their valuables, were in vain. At Portbou, after some delays because of the official transfer protocol, the German escort handed them over to members of the Falangist Militia and JDC representatives providing relief. A day later, after their first good meal in a long time, the ex-deportees boarded another passenger train, which took them to a reception facility in Barcelona for a medical checkup and delousing.[65]

Their taste of freedom was further intensified by the favorable conditions that the JDC, which took full responsibility for these convoys, had prepared for them in Barcelona. Based on lists of names provided by the Germans, the JDC officials took the refugees by family to local hotels and housing facilities. Izi Revah cannot forget how he "slept for the first time in many months in a bed with clean white sheets." With free accommodation, being well fed, and even given weekly pocket money, the ex-deportees were able to attend cultural events, buy newspapers to find out about developments in the war, and travel around freely. Some of them found relatives who had left for Spain either from Greece or France. Counter to the myth of the Spanish rescue of the Jews, however, almost none of these refugees was allowed to stay behind; that would have been against the transit agreement reached by the JDC and Madrid, which accepted repatriation only exceptionally, for instance, in the case of the family of the Spanish consular official to Thessaloniki, Salomon Ezratty.[66]

About three months later, in the early summer of 1944, the Jews of Spanish citizenship boarded trains for the port of Cadiz. Again, as Lili-Nina Revah recalls, it felt, especially to the children, "more like a holiday trip." After they reached the Atlantic coast, they were shipped from Cadiz to Morocco (in two groups, on May 12 and June 22, 1944) where they waited for permission to enter Palestine.[67] Altogether, 338 ex-internees of the Bergen-Belsen Neutrals Camp from Thessaloniki crossed the Strait of Gibraltar, arriving in Casablanca. From there, they were taken by trucks about ten miles (sixteen km) north to the Marshal Lyautey transit camp for refugees in the port town Fédala, run by the UNRRA and the North African Red Cross.[68]

Living in what was basically a tent camp, with only two separate barracks for single men and women, they were far less comfortable than in the accommodations they had quickly become used to in Barcelona. Nevertheless, each of the survivors who gave an account of that part of the journey emphasized that the camp administration took good care of them. There was a common room where they played cards and gathered for concerts and social dances. A wide choice of work activities, such as woodworking and writing for camp newspapers, were organized to keep them busy. A Jewish military chaplain was in charge of religious services, including bar mitzvahs. The refugees could regularly take day trips to the seaside and to Casablanca. Some of them even visited the French-speaking community of the Sephardim of Casablanca, who seemed to them "poor and forgotten about by the whole world."[69]

After several months spent on the west coast of Morocco, the Thessalonican Jews of the Fédala camp boarded ships yet again. A large group of 348 passengers (314 of them Thessalonican) left for the UNRRA refugee camp in Nuseirat. Another group of 234, including four Jewish families with Spanish citizenship, headed for the Jeanne d'Arc refugee camp in Philippeville,

172 · HOMECOMING

Algeria. The first group left on October 13, the second on November 15, 1944, with the family of Adolfo Benveniste on board. Raymonde, the younger of Adolfo's two daughters, recalls that their small group of only seventeen Jews from Thessaloniki did not plan to return. Given the antisemitism they had experienced in Thessaloniki before the deportations and the fact that the mother was a French citizen, the Benveniste family decided to "repatriate" to France. Five Thessalonicans remained in Morocco, and two died in the Fédala camp. In this way, the Nuseirat group of Spanish nationals from Greece had twenty-four fewer people than the group of those who had left Spain. Since other trajectories were fragmented and since none of those twenty-four refugees returned to Greece, they had no influence on the collective identity of this Nuseirat group and are completely absent from the generally accepted narrative of these events.[70]

Several of the Nuseirat refugees have elaborated on the difficulties encountered when crossing a mined sea full of shipwrecks in an ocean liner all the way to Palestine. They particularly remember an escort zigzagging the Mediterranean with them on the way to liberated Naples before sailing toward the Suez Canal and finally reaching Gaza. In Nuseirat, a UNRRA refugee camp organized by country of origin brought the Sephardim together with Greek recruits in the British Middle East Forces stuck in Palestine and civilian refugees from the Dodecanese. Accommodated in tents but free to visit their relatives in nearby Tel Aviv, some of them finally decided to take up the challenge of moving out of the camp and trying to settle down in Palestine. Others stayed behind, waiting to be moved to Greece, which was liberated in autumn 1944.[71]

Political developments, however, shifted things in a different direction. Rachel Saporta, a refugee about twenty years old at the time, travelling with her parents, explains: "we were getting ready to return [to Greece], but the December events started and many were still saying they would come while others said we saved ourselves after so many hardships, so why enter another war [...]?"[72] Under the circumstances, repatriation from Palestine was, for most of the refugees, postponed until late summer or even autumn 1945. Meanwhile, some chose to build the new State of Israel or to wait there for emigration permits overseas.[73] Even members of the same family were waving goodbye to each other for the first time since the war had started. Sailing from Haifa, they headed for Piraeus. In Athens, they were first accommodated in the school reception center before continuing on to Thessaloniki without further provisions. Their expectations of homecoming, based on their social status before the deportations, turned out to be completely unfounded.

They were now perceived to be foreigners in Greece, impoverished intruders, and, above all, unwanted Jews pouncing on property already appropriated by others. While planning to return, some of them, like the Saporta and the Revah families, had already been warned about the situation in Greece. But they were reluctant to believe what they saw as rumors. In an interview years later, Izi Revah shares a message a relative sent to Palestine: "Before we arrived, we had received a letter from my uncle, who had gone before us, Elias Revah, who then went to Mexico. And he says: 'I came from your house and saw a little donkey on the third floor. They are all refugees; the house is fully occupied.'"[74]

The Jews found their Thessaloniki houses looted, damaged, or completely seized when coming home; they were lucky if they could negotiate accommodations in one unfurnished room. Their businesses were gone too. Some of the returnees later went through years of lawsuits to get their property back; others simply started from scratch, setting out on a new journey of seemingly infinite toil. In Thessaloniki, it was only the Jewish organizations and a handful of fellow Jews to whom they could really turn. This led them either to emigrate or pushed them into a vicious circle of solidarity in an extremely limited group of people with no set rules to rely on. Like any other Holocaust survivors, they had idealized their hometowns. However, unlike those in hiding or in combat or who had been deported, they were also aware of the postwar situation in other countries and the troubled life of refugees there. When her Jewish fiancé, a former resistance fighter, tried to dissuade Lili-Nina Revah from homecoming, she insisted that life in Greece could not be that unbearable: "Greece is a paradise. I also saw the problems of life in Palestine, which wasn't easy. No work! I thought I would find the life I had left behind, the easy one, the beautiful one."[75]

Greek reality hit the Jewish refugees harder than they expected and more than any other group of Holocaust survivors in Greece. The economic and political decisions they had to take were just the opposite of easy and beautiful. Though all of them had been damaged by the loss of their possessions, and thus lost considerable social standing, the Jewish refugees

174 · HOMECOMING

who had escaped from Greece—more than the ex-DPs who were Spanish nationals—usually had to abandon the hope of reuniting with their closest relatives, which caused deep trauma. Albert Marcos had gone to Palestine with his sister and stretched his stay until 1953. After three years in Greece, he emigrated to the United States to join his uncle, though not without mourning his home: "I still believe that tomorrow my parents will return, that tomorrow my siblings will be back."[76]

Similarly to the accounts of internally displaced Holocaust survivors, the personal stories of the Jewish refugees in Palestine also highlight the narrative of Greek-Jewish solidarity, which typically unfolds in connection with domestic Greek assistance. Apart from the leftist resistance, in their case, the main positive actors mentioned at home were the Orthodox Church and the police, who provided them with false identities. These categories suggest a black-and-white picture of universal Greek solidarity between the returnees and institutions of power, a picture that has been largely exploited by Greek politicians, educators, and historians in the dominant national narratives, fully omitting the geopolitical constellations in which Greece found itself during and after the war.

CHAPTER FIVE

AFTER HOMECOMING

In my one hand I hold resurrection,
in my other eternal remembrance.

NINA KOKKALIDOU NAHMIA,
"After Twenty Years in Auschwitz"[1]

IN MID-NOVEMBER 1944, the first Community meeting of Holocaust survivors took place in Athens. In Thessaloniki, Jews coming out of hiding assembled on December 4, the day the December Events began. Local Jewish Communities, however, were not officially reestablished till the summer of 1945.[2] At that moment, internally displaced Jews who were already at home, especially if they adhered to the partisans, started to fear possible persecution for their real or alleged leftist leanings. Many decided to keep their heads down. While the repatriation of Auschwitz survivors was already in full swing, the camp returnees were also about to keep the "enforced consensus of silence," which Dan Stone ascribes as typical for Eastern Europe.[3] Since in Greece religion had an important role for social structures, not the Jewish belonging but the Jewish experience of war remained concealed or adjusted to the hegemonic narrative of Greek national victimhood.

Gaynor Jacobson finished his JDC mission in Greece in early 1946. In the 1988 interview, he summarized the achievements of his work and provided a telling account of the time: "By the end of the year [1945], you have functioning institutions for those who want to stay in Salonika, in Athens, as well as a number of the small communities and you have the assistance going out and you have, to a certain extent, a Jewish community who has revived itself even though it is only 11 or 12 per cent of the original size it was."[4]

On February 28, 1946, when Jacobson had already started his mission in Czechoslovakia, the Central Board of Jewish Communities declared the

175

176 · HOMECOMING

number of returnees in Greece as the final count. Next to ideological clashes and prevailing social differences, chaos, fear, insecurity, and violence would spread across Europe. Although only a month was left before the Greek parliamentary elections and the terror against any political or civil opposition was public knowledge, most people in Greece could not fully imagine the armed conflict that would break out and the level of violence it would bring in the next two and a half years.[5] Soon, the already-bittersweet taste of return for the ten thousand returnees (see table 5.1) was soon further soured by another war, this time Greeks against Greeks. Greece, on the eastern periphery of Europe in a buffer zone between East and West, became a blood land. Greek postwar elites quickly and skillfully appropriated the Communist strategy of the cross-party "national front," which Stalin introduced already during the war;[6] only Jews did not fully fit into this conceptualization of the Greek nation.

At that point, the main Jewish organizations in Greece, such as the Central Board of Jewish Communities, the Central Relief Committee, the Zionist Federation of Greece, the Institution of Professional Rehabilitation, and the Union of Jewish Deportees of Poland, were operating more or less independently. The dominant position that Thessaloniki held before the war in Jewish life was no more. All other Jewish organs were based in Athens with the exception of the Union, which had been officially established in March 1946 in Thessaloniki. To this end, membership in the Union was exclusively for camp survivors, about one-fifth of the Jews remaining in Greece, who in the aftermath of the Holocaust largely dominated the Jewish Community of Thessaloniki. This created further tensions, especially regarding the image of Jewish victimhood in the Holocaust. In all the other central organizations, offices were held predominantly by internally displaced Jews who had survived in hiding and were thus able to lay the foundations for the renewal of institutions before the return of deportees. Given the overall political situation, former resistance fighters encountered particularly hard obstacles. Out of the roughly thousand Jewish refugees repatriated to Greece, only two prominent names appeared among the central officials, Alfred Cohen and Minos Levis, both protégés of the wartime Greek government-in-exile in Egypt.[7]

Unlike in the interwar Jewish community in Greece, for the majority of whom Judeo-Spanish and French were the dominant languages of

TABLE 5.1 Number of Holocaust survivors in Jewish Communities of Greece that had existed before the war.

Thessaly	Survivors	Epirus	Survivors	Macedonia	Survivors	Thrace	Survivors
Trikala	360	Ioannina	163	Kavala	42	Didymoticho	33
Larissa	726	Preveza	15	Drama	39	Nea Orestias	3
Volos	646	Arta	60	Serres	3	Alexandroupoli	4
Continental Greece and Peloponnese	Survivors	Islands	Survivors	Thessaloniki	1,950	Komotini	28
Chalcis	170	Corfu	185	Veria	131	Xanthi	7
Athens	4,930	Zakynthos	275	Kastoria	35		
Patras – Agrinio	152	Crete	7	Florina	64	**TOTAL**	10,027

Compiled by the Central Board of Jewish Communities, Athens, April 1946 (USHMM, RG-45.010, KIS 096 – Report (9 April 1946).

178 · HOMECOMING

communication, English gradually became the language of international communication in the war's aftermath. Whereas the Judeo-Spanish-speaking Sephardic survivors were marginalized, English was convenient for communicating with the American and British aid-providers.[8] The regularly published Jewish newspapers, two in Athens and two in Thessaloniki, were exclusively in Greek. The publishers lacked Hebrew typefaces for their presses and perhaps also the commitment to write in another language. As Leon Saki wrote in a 1946 article (in English), Judeo-Spanish, "in which had spoken, written, dreamed and lived tens of thousands of Jews for many generations [...], had been exterminated."[9]

Once the Civil War started in the spring of 1946, men twenty-one years of age and older, including Holocaust survivors and even camp returnees, were called up to fight the Communist resistance in the mountains. Aware of what lay ahead of them, they mostly viewed the problem pragmatically, either complying with the draft or finding a legal way to avoid serving.[10] In the Civil War, the government in Athens, first with British and then American backing, finally managed to get the upper hand in the summer of 1949 by a massive use of coercion and structural violence similar to the dictatorships in Spain, Portugal, and especially its Cold War enemies in the East.[11] Nonetheless, a great number of Jews—many of whom had been saved by the EAM resistance during the occupation or supported them anyway—still sympathized with the Communists and were therefore either sent to Greek prisons or branded as regime enemies.[12]

In the midst of the postwar conflict, most Greeks, including Holocaust survivors and their Communities, inevitably had to keep a low profile, remain silent, or side with the Greek government to avoid being stigmatized as a fifth column. They were not given any alternative in their home country, just like in Eastern Europe.[13] Once it became unavoidable, many Jews accepted this state of affairs, adapted to social rules that were being bent by war, and modified their identities according to the situation. Even if they had strong patriotic feelings about Greece, that would not necessarily compensate for their foreign citizenship or views that were in conflict with those proclaimed, or at best were tolerated, by the regime in Athens. Any dissent could result in the Jewish community expelling alleged traitors and in the Greek society ostracizing those seen as leftist renegades, Italian collaborators, or simply Jews of foreign citizenship.[14]

Thanks to the fact that Greece was among the first European countries to be liberated, and because of lobbying and pressure from outside, the courts of Greece were nominally the first in any postwar European state to consider the problem of heirless Jewish property. Yet the matter was far more complicated. Most Jewish returnees were without finances and were exposed to increasing antisemitism, which was often ignited by their efforts to reclaim confiscated or stolen property.[15] Caretakers and tenants who had moved into and appropriated Jewish homes were reluctant to vacate them when the original inhabitants returned.[16]

In the 1988 interview we looked at, Jacobson describes the housing situation in the two main Jewish communities in Greece with the highest number of returnees: "I had [information about] for example the big synagogue in Athens. And the big synagogue in Salonika was the place where the surviving Greek Jews, whether they came back from Auschwitz or hiding, partisans, you know, where they had to sleep. Because they could not get back their apartments. They could not get their houses.[17] Breaking trust, in many cases, former friends, colleagues and neighbors denied that Jewish property had ever been left with them for safekeeping.[18] However, occasional, mostly individual attacks on Jews did not take the form of pogroms like in Kunmadaras (Hungary), Veľké Topoľčany (Slovakia), and Kielce (Poland) in 1945 to 1946.[19]

In the aftermath, it was the legal settlement of property ownership that became the biggest problem of the new Greek regime when it came to Jews, since several relevant pieces of legislation had been passed during the occupation, and not all were annulled at once.[20] Instead, they were gradually superseded by individual regulations. For quite some time, these regulations applied only in the former Italian zone but not in the former German-controlled part of the province of Macedonia, including Thessaloniki, where a vast number of Jewish assets had been confiscated early on and were not returned to Jewish survivors for a long time. In late December 1945, Act 808 at least did bring some order into this legal chaos and enable the restitution of property, not only to the original owners but also to their agents, guardians, and relatives.[21]

One of its important provisions stipulates that real estate was to be returned to the owners together with all the movable property listed by the Office for the Disposal of Jewish Property (YDIP) during the war. Whenever items specified on the YDIP lists could not be found, owners were to be

180 · HOMECOMING

financially compensated based on the items' current market value. Moreover, the people who had "Aryanized" Jewish property (as its "trustees") were now supposed to pay rent for the use of that real estate since the time of its forced transfer into their hands during the war. But in practice things were quite different. If Jews in Athens were at least able to collect back rent, the more Jews returned to Thessaloniki, the more their claims were ignored or backfired: the YDIP warehouses were found empty, and a wave of public indignation rose against restitution. The trustees in Thessaloniki united in the newly created Association of Tenants of Jewish Property in Northern Greece (SMIAVE) to try and legalize their ownership with the help of slanderous media campaigns, physical threats to both Jewish and Greek representatives, lobbying, and court trials.[22] Under the circumstances, anti-Jewish sentiment escalated, and Jews were repeatedly vilified as "profiteers."[23]

For heirless property, legal measures favoring the Jewish Community in Greece were passed in January 1946, thanks to the work of Jacobson and JDC headquarters, an achievement of which they felt particularly proud. The provisions, nevertheless, presupposed the existence of an organization that would administer this property.[24] The Jewish Communities had to wait another three years before a decree was issued, which created the Organization for the Relief and Rehabilitation of the Jews of Greece (OPAIE).[25] The full operation of the OPAIE was then hampered by problems connected to the issuing of death certificates without evidence of death, especially of people murdered en masse in the camps. As late as 1959, the Central Board of Jewish Communities (KIS) was still trying to resolve this question, thus becoming self-sufficient only in the mid-1960s when relief from the JDC could gradually be phased out.[26] At that very moment, the Jews of Greece received the first—and in most cases only—compensation for physical damage from the Federal Republic of Germany.[27]

Over time, the Jewish Communities of Greece succeeded in having most of their property returned. Yet only by selling what they reacquired did they slowly manage to restore their financial stability.[28] Greece's decision to transfer all heirless property to the Jewish Community, coupled with national and international publicity highlighting Greek generosity in this regard, laid the foundation for the country's positive media image concerning its treatment of Holocaust survivors.[29] The following two anecdotes, one about negotiations with the Metropolitan Bishop of the Greek Orthodox Church and the other about the Greek administration's perception of the "Jewish element," may shed some light on this supposedly altruistic Greek attitude to the rebuilding of Jewish life.

Even if rarely stated publicly, the reconstruction of Community life and the restitution of Community property led to considerable anti-Jewish outcries and thus challenged the untarnished image enjoyed by key Greek institutions like the Greek Orthodox Church. The return of the Jewish temple chandelier is a good example. From the perspective of a young survivor in Greece, recorded by Bea Lewkowicz, this may at first appear to be a shining example of solidarity: "The only remaining synagogue during the German occupation was the Monastirioton Synagogue [...]. Before leaving Salonika, the Germans wanted to destroy whatever had remained in the synagogue. When one priest realised what was about to happen, he asked the Germans whether he could have the chandelier for his church. The Germans gave it to him, and, after, he returned it to the Jews, who put it back in place, where it is still today."[30]

Jacobson, however, describes the situation rather differently in his report to JDC Headquarters. According to him, the JDC had to get personally involved and use a good deal of ingenuity and a considerable amount of money to help the Jewish Community in Thessaloniki retrieve one of the last Judaica artefacts remaining in the country:

> The Monastir-Synagogue, on the Syngrou-street is in need of repairs. The large chandelier of the Synagogue has disappeared during the occupation. We learned however that a Greek Orthodox church, Analypsis, had taken a large beautiful chandelier from one of the other Synagogues. The Board of the Jewish Community had requested its return from the Priest in charge of the church. He refused, saying that he had saved the chandelier from destruction and it was originally purchased to serve God and it was now doing so in his church. [...] He explained that he loved the chandelier and has spent 50,000 drachmas to have it moved and installed. I returned the 50,000 drachmas to him, got his receipt and agreement that the next day electricians and movers would come and return it to the Synagogue.[31]

In his 1988 interview, in which the chandelier story reappears, Jacobson identifies the priest as Gennadios (1868–1951), the Metropolitan of

182 · HOMECOMING

Thessaloniki, who remained in office until his death and was posthumously awarded the title of Righteous Among the Nations.[32]

The left-leaning Jewish newspaper *Echo of Orient* published a long article on the impact of the event. This was, however, dismissed as "exaggerated" by the Central Board in a letter addressed to the international World Jewish Congress.[33] Compiled by Leon Saki in mid-January 1946, the article suggested that even the JDC intervention did not bring much reconciliation:

> Some weeks ago, a pogrom could not have been prevented had it not been for the prompt intervention of the authorities upon the advice of the British Consul and of the Greek Metropolit. Here is the story: During the German occupation, the Nazis had stolen the big silver candlesticks of the synagogue "Beth-Saul" and handed it [*sic*] over to the Orthodox Greek church "Analipsis" as a present. [...] The priests agreed to return them on condition that 75,000 drachmas (several pounds) be paid to them for expenses. This sum was paid and the candlesticks were brought to the synagogue. Next day, the walls of the building were covered with placards saying that the Jews had assaulted the church, beaten the priests and dropped the holy icons, etc. In the evening, the first attack occurred.[34]

In reality, what was probably most at stake for the Greek Orthodox Metropolitan in Thessaloniki in the chandelier affair was money.

Neither legal provisions nor the skills of capable attorneys could, however, guarantee a positive outcome for restitution claims. This is well illustrated by the property claims of Elie Modiano (1881–1968). A son of a famous Thessalonican banker, together with his brothers, Arthur and Charles, Elie, a skilled man and accomplished architect, owned the Modiano Market, the largest food market in Thessaloniki before the war. To protect the family fortune, the Modianos applied for, and were granted, Italian citizenship. Shortly before the first deportations of the Jews of Thessaloniki in 1943, Elie and his family departed for Italy, where they hoped for safety. During the war in Africa, Elie left Italy and fought with the Allies. He intended to return to Greece when the war was over. Thus, after the liberation, but while he and his family were still residing in Italy, he applied for the restitution of the family property. In summer 1951, Elie returned to Greece for good.[35]

Although Elie Modiano had been a prominent member of the Jewish and Italian communities in Thessaloniki before World War II, the Greek authorities claimed that he had showed himself capable of the worst possible behavior toward Greece and the Allies, having allegedly been a member of Fascio, the local Italo-Fascist organization, during the Greco-Italian War.[36] The Greek authorities then accused him of having unlawfully appropriated food rations to the detriment of needy Greeks. But the charges against Elie fail to account for the fact that until Rome signed the armistice in September 1943, the German persecution of Jews with Italian citizenship was fundamentally different from their persecution of Jews with Greek citizenship. However the Greek postwar authorities argued that Elie had been exempt from the anti-Jewish measures because he had been a prominent Jew, not because he was an Italian.[37] When the Modiano family members were arrested in Greece as enemy aliens and pressed to renounce their Italian citizenship during the Greco-Italian War, they refused. By doing so, they had given credence to the postwar accusation of disloyalty to Greece.

Greeks continued publicly to defame Elie Modiano, reporting, for instance, that "in his conversations he was pro-Axis and pro-Italy." He had been, in addition, allegedly involved in anti-Greek espionage and propaganda. He was said to have "insulted Greek national feeling," considered himself "superior" to Greeks, and to have lived for many years with a Greek woman whom he refused to marry because he found her "background unsuitable to a man like himself." None of these accusations was ever proven. Various locals reported to the Greek authorities that he had kept his distance from the Greek community, acted arrogantly, and, despite the war and the persecution of the Jews, still had a great fortune in real estate in the center of Thessaloniki.[38]

An example of Elie's alleged collaboration is the construction of wells in Macedonia and Thrace in late 1941 and early 1942, for which he was commissioned by the Italian Fascists. Finally, an allegation of prewar fraud was made against him in connection with this public procurement project. The Greek government called his attitude venal and said it was typical of the Jews as a whole. More than that, the government argued that the Jews of Greece had never felt at home in the country and were therefore not loyal citizens: "The Jews in general never loved Greece, especially those in Thessaloniki, because, since the liberation of Thessaloniki, they gradually lost their social,

184 · HOMECOMING

economic and political influence."[39] In particular, throughout the process of reviewing the allegations, the Greek authorities accused the Modiano family of showing hatred for Greeks at every opportunity, which made them not only unwanted but also dangerous for Greece.[40] Regardless of all these accusations, Elie Modiano did not give up and, together with his wife, Beatrice Frances, spent the rest of his life in Greece fighting for his family property.[41] With actions like these, however, Greek state institutions suffered a significant loss of credibility in the eyes of many Holocaust survivors.

Instead of returning the Holocaust survivors in Greece to prewar normality, the end of the war put them at the beginning of a new stage in their lives, painfully marked by another war of destruction, suffering, and struggle. The trauma resurfacing through long-lasting nightmares, anxiety, and intense grief caused by the death of loved ones and fellow Jews in the Holocaust is reflected in the accounts of virtually all survivors. It became a crucial element of individual, family, and community memory, irrespective of how one had experienced the war. In this framework of mourning and uncertainty, while trying to hold on to what was left, many returnees decided to devote themselves fully to their families. Socializing resulting in marriages and baby boom, education, work, and family life were essential components of the postwar reality that kept their spirits up.[42] Starting anew was, however, obstructed not only by the absence of finances and by the constant presence of grief for those who were gone forever but also by poor health, physical and mental, as well as a lack of traditional Jewish rituals or rather of trained people to perform them.

Spiritual comfort was hardly available since of the roughly sixty prewar synagogues in Greece, only two in Athens, two in Thessaloniki, and one each in Chalcis, Trikala, Ioannina, Patras, and elsewhere were still standing, but in a pitiful state. Moreover, hardly any rabbis remained in the country. The *bet din* (rabbinical court) was paralyzed, and under Greek law no other institution could decide on matters related to Jewish families. In many towns, there were no *mohels* to perform the ritual circumcision of newborn Jewish boys, nor were there *shohets* for the ritual slaughter of animals as prescribed by Jewish law. Only one Jewish school existed in all of Greece, and that was in Athens. Nevertheless, several dozen Holocaust survivors decided to start a new life by marrying, many of them for the second time, having lost their spouses and children during the war. This, however, was not a straightfor-

AFTER HOMECOMING · 185

ward process, since according to Jewish law they could only enter a new bond after proving the death of the former spouse. For those murdered in the gas chambers, there was rarely, if ever, anyone to deliver a valid testimony. More often than not, therefore, camp survivors did not marry until twelve months after liberation, regardless of supposed adultery and the birth of the first child.[43]

Overall, the Greek rule of law was malfunctioning, and the Greek regime was unable to provide for the religious or personal rehabilitation of the Holocaust survivors. As a result of all the difficulties, many of them chose to leave the country for good. Already by the end of 1945, about 450 Jews of Greece had emigrated to Palestine.[44] Their decision to leave Greece was shaped mostly by their unfulfilled expectations and was therefore more part of personal restoration than of survival and return. When the World Jewish Congress called on all Jewish communities in the once German-occupied countries to prepare suitable memorials to the people lost in the Holocaust, the Council of the Central Board, after a lengthy debate, offered an odd response. The Central Board aimed to transfer from Poland as much of the ashes as possible of those "Greek Jews" who had been cremated in Auschwitz and to build a monument in Palestine. This decision was taken only two days before the third memorial service, which by 1946 the Central Board was already promoting as Pan-Hellenic, in memory of the murdered Jewish brethren of the Greeks. For the Greek parliament to legislate for an official Day of Remembrance, the Jews of Greece had to wait until 2004.[45]

Since refugees were, yet again, not embraced by most target countries, migration was hardly a straightforward process. Because of British government restraints on Jewish migration to Palestine, many migrants were redirected to refugee camps in Cyprus.[46] Some, aided by the JDC, chose Latin America for a new place of residence, while others emigrated to Canada or the United States.[47] Once the State of Israel was established on May 14, 1948, and the Knesset passed the Law of Return on July 5, 1950, which granted every Jew in the world the right to settle in Israel, a legal way was open for Holocaust survivors to come to Israel. In the United States, the 1948 Act on Displaced Persons and especially the 1953 Refugee Relief Act enabled the migration of many Jews to that country.[48] Though it is probably impossible to determine from statistical data, it is quite evident in personal accounts that the main impetus to migration was the experience not of the

186 · HOMECOMING

Holocaust but of the Greek Civil War. Twenty years later, in summer 1967, at the beginning of the new military dictatorship in Greece, there were only 5,190 Jews living in Greece.[49]

As the last World War II witnesses die of old age, the sense of the depth and extent of the suffering in once war-stricken Europe is fading away. Despite something of a competition to prove who truly suffered, all survivors in one way or another shared the traumatizing memory of wartime deprivation and a tacit collective agreement on social silence as a way to start their formal and informal reconstruction. For many Holocaust survivors in Greece, the Jewish Community as such ceased to be the one and only institution taking care of their lives and thus no longer played a prominent role in their narrations. Instead, the void was, and continues to be, filled by recollections of one's interaction with the majority population. Though often exaggerated, especially when compared to the situation described in the JDC records, the extent of the Greeks' altruistic assistance during the war has remained highly important for the Holocaust survivors themselves. Once a new system of institutions was established in the aftermath, Jews were registered with their Communities, which surely helped in the reintegration of those who returned but provided only nominal community support without full material and psychological restitution.

Made destitute even before the war and with little Greek education, Jews returning from the camps in the aftermath had typically lost all family bonds and hence also lost their main reason for remaining in Greece. Others joined the leftist resistance and were therefore soon silenced, exposed to structural violence within the state of Greece or pushed out of the country when right-wing Greeks won the Civil War. The Jews of Greece were thus deprived both of their traditionally pious fellow Jews, murdered in the concentration camps, and the progressive capacity of the leftists, excluded from postwar Greek society. Most of the Holocaust survivors with some assets outside Greece or with well-established transnational ties or with both, which they had thanks to a university education and business dealings, had no intention of remaining in Greece or, sometimes, of even returning to a country that was politically and economically torn apart. So it happened that the majority of the Jews who remained in Greece after the war, hoping to reacquire, bit by bit, what they could of their property there, were those who had survived in hiding, often as a family, with at least some assistance from their non-Jewish compatriots. Family reunification was largely the survivors' main motivation in returning to what had once been home, and family cohesion was perhaps their most important reason for remaining in Greece and getting involved in the reconstruction of the local Jewish Community.

CONCLUSION

Each moment of history is a junction of tracks leading toward a number of futures.
Being at the crossroads is the way human society exists.

ZYGMUNT BAUMAN[1]

ON JUNE 24, 2022, my grandmother, a Jewish child survivor, left us for good. Death came at the blessed age of ninety without robbing her too soon of sharp wit and critical judgment. When the Russian invasion in Ukraine began in February 2022, my grandmother was still fit enough to share her thoughts on unexpected refugees her townspeople let into their homes, providing a time-lapse recollection of the eve of World War II. She spoke of the indulgent yet uncanny understanding or appreciation of the new kind of cohabitation that emerged from the war and the seeming inadequate gratitude of newcomers fleeing the unforeseen. She feared both the war and its aftermath, finally finding the missing words to reflect on a previously indescribable and unexamined part of her early life. So much had changed since 1939 in terms of technology, mobility, relief, and civil rights, but woefully little in terms of the everyday lives of those affected by the war.

Considering her age, my grandmother was one of the last still alive who had experienced the horrors of World War II and among the last who could compare that time with what is happening today. In this respect, she was like Paulette Nehama or Astro Beti-Hatzi, the youngest of the narrators we followed on the previous pages. It was only in her last months that dementia clouded her mind, as it did to many survivors her age, regardless of their wartime experiences and postwar whereabouts. These days, it is hard for an extended period of time to pass without word reaching me that one of them is no longer with us. In a few years, there will be nobody to share vital memories of the Holocaust. A whole long century will no longer be sustained by the living, but by the dead. We are moving from communicative

190 · CONCLUSION

toward cultural memory, in which World War II may assume a place like any previous war, history only documented, not negotiated based on lived experiences that have opened up a whole new era of Holocaust research.

This book emerged out of a genuine concern for affectively rooted visions of who we are and how what we remember informs and is informed by our will to remember. Despite their specificities, the histories and memories of the survival and return of Holocaust survivors offer significant opportunities to engage with questions of hope, despair, and mnemonic imagination. At the same time, the memories of survival and the spectrum of hope, expectations, and despair involved in any mnemonic process that deals with painful pasts inform the ways in which we act toward each other, within or outside national borders. The future we hope for is not disengaged from our past, and as temporal beings, we build on our memories and post-memories' coherent narratives, to paraphrase Marianne Hirsch,[2] about who we are. If we believe in the possibility of a future, we will continue to have hopes which are backed up by our memories and imagination, and even by nostalgia for a future that might not ever happen. McGeer made it clear that "our hope provides a scaffold for others."[3]

Although hope is central to our identity construction, it does not exclusively concern individuals and their being in the world. The initial, highly personal motivation for writing these pages was my belief that Holocaust returnees and their narrations of survival and return can no longer be neglected or merged with terms, such as "victimhood," that invoke passivity and lack of agency. Each survivor had some scope and space to act, even if limited, for their own decisions, actions, and hopes and took their own course.[4] By providing insights into micro-histories of the daily struggles of Jewish homecoming plagued by the Holocaust, I expanded a new avenue: those who survived and returned home had to have an extraordinary lust for life, resilience, determination, a good portion of luck, and expectations of a new, better life within their own communities.

Yet beyond the fortunes of the Holocaust survivors, their life stories allow us to come closer to understanding how the war and its immediate aftermath destabilized their very notion of home. Returning home was also supposed to be a return to the prewar past that would restore their stability. This nostalgic instantiation of hope for homecoming is inscribed in the accounts of the feeling of longing for the "good" past, in which home has restorative

CONCLUSION · 191

undertones. The survivors, however, mostly ended up confused, tormented, and disappointed. In the fluid timespace between rescue, liberation, and restoration, where today does not match tomorrow or yesterday, they often felt an existential and material emptiness and anger that the most intimate place had become eerily unfamiliar and inaccessible. They were forced to realize that their dreams had been shattered in a bygone era.[5]

In offering important lessons for postwar reconstruction of precarious lives, Holocaust survivorship and homecoming also have wider implications for post-conflict studies in general. For example, the prioritization of property return after the war in Bosnia and Herzegovina shows that the struggles of property return that Jewish returnees underwent have provided some historical lessons.[6] In any violent conflict, from Rwanda in 1994 to Myanmar today, as far as the target groups are concerned, it is inconceivable to imagine the devastating scale of the atrocities, let alone genocide, even though the evil transformation had long been creeping into daily life. One may think of the present-day war in Ukraine and look back to 2014, when Russia annexed Donbas. How painfully reminiscent this episode may feel of 1938, the Sudetenland's annexation as German territory in central Europe, almost five years before the deportations of Jews in Greece began. For locals determined to survive but unable to imagine the fatal consequences or comprehend what they might experience tomorrow, as for Jews in wartime Europe, making informed decisions is close to impossible.[7]

While exploring the full spectrum of existential unease between hope and despair, this book takes homecoming as a reference point. In doing so, it reveals the complexity of the traumatic consequences of the past that affected the Jews of Greece, but which resonate remarkably with other persecuted communities. By zooming in on the micro-(hi)stories and memories of return, the book unveils the individual and collective sequelae that have been obliterated, misinterpreted, or alleviated by the hegemonic narratives. The physical and symbolical return from a traumatic past to an uncertain present and future happens—as in other aftermaths of violence—in an "intertemporal aspect of justice as a struggle against the ongoing effects of bad history."[8] This intertemporal aspect is seldom addressed in the studies dedicated to the daunting return of the Jews surviving the Holocaust, as well as in other explorations of other survivors of mass violence. The memories and histories of the survivors' hopes and despair should be rendered both

192 · CONCLUSION

accessible and visible to repudiate the ongoing patterns of exclusion, naturalized practices of silencing, and violence in the present.

Linking the memories and histories of survival and return of the Holocaust survivors across Europe can facilitate a more nuanced understanding of our ethical and political imagination and, at the same time, create the space for understanding the struggle of others who did not experience firsthand violence and injustice in the same temporal and geographical frame. This space of hermeneutical care for the struggle of others (closer or more distant inheritors of trauma) can be instituted through facilitating the grounds for these histories of survival to be heard. The undoing of the "victimhood" paradigm—to make space for histories and memories of resistance, survival, and return—requires a great deal of mnemonic imagination but also more awareness in dealing with history and political temporalities.

After the liberation of Greece in 1944, which had seen the war and subsequent occupation by three Axis powers at the same time, the first Jews to return and reestablish the Jewish Communities were internally displaced refugees with strong ties to the non-Jewish population. With constantly changing conditions on the ground, they often watched the end of the German occupation in Greece in hiding. Most of them found refuge in the Greek capital, which provided them with the anonymity of a crowd and protected them from the undesired attention a newcomer in a small and close community often provokes. About half of the eight thousand Jews who hid in Athens came from Thessaloniki, closing an era of this cosmopolitan, multilingual, multiethnic, and multireligious city once and for all.[9]

More than the other Jews of Greece, those in hiding were significantly integrated (or at least one of the adult family members was) and had well-developed social ties to Greek townspeople, which had been built through their occupations or education. From this cohort, the leading figures of the postwar Central Board of Jewish Communities emerged, such as Asher Moissis and Kanaris Konstantinis, who spearheaded the institutional reestablishment of the Jewish Community in Greece. For the first time, they made Athens the postwar Jewish center of Greece. For the first time, they negotiated their positions with Greek government institutions in close proximity. And although these Jews had not been particularly preoccupied with their acculturation to Greek society between the two World Wars, their identities and loyalties shifted in favor of Greece and its authorities in the aftermath.

CONCLUSION · 193

Under the supervision of the German officers and their collaborators, only a handful of Jews, stripped of nearly everything, found the courage and means to flee and hide. Several hundreds of others, mostly young men with connections to local non-Jews (like Isaac Nehama), and thanks to their work, studies, or military service, dared to join the emerging armed resistance.[10] Some had gained their combat experience as soldiers in the Greco-Italian War of 1940–41 and were not ready to simply give up to the Germans. This is true not only of the partisans but also those who joined the Greek Armed Forces in the Middle East and Africa, including Alfred Cohen and Elie Modiano, representatives of the Jewish upper milieu in Greece. Other Jews, both men and women, were smuggled into partisan-controlled territories and were efficiently recruited by the partisans.

Unlike elsewhere in Europe, such as in Belgium, France, Poland, and Ukraine,[11] Jews in Greece never formed their own (para)military unit but were integrated into the Greek-dominated resistance army. After the war, with the disarmament of the resistance and the unsettling atmosphere of a country on the brink of civil war, many of these Jews felt threatened. They justifiably feared persecution by the ruling authorities, which denounced the partisans as Communists or fellow travelers. As in Eastern Europe, this political context and the fear of being stigmatized silenced Jewish survivors and their memories, forcing them to reconsider and redefine their identities for many decades to come. Afraid of othering and political implications, they chose to follow the safe hegemonic narrative of Greek national struggle and victimhood and to rebuild their lives by concentrating on their families and careers.

For Jews displaced internally in Greece, the ultimate impetus to return home came with the German withdrawal in October 1944, before the Allies even set foot on Greek soil. Yet for those outside, the decision was generally made only at the end of World War II, about six months later. In spring 1945, when the internal forced displacement had essentially reached its end, Jewish survivors in Greece were emotionally preparing for the worst. An eerie sensation engulfed them, namely, that they had lost not only their possessions but possibly and probably also their loved ones who had been among the deportees. In those days, when letters took weeks to arrive or simply got lost along the way, waiting at the most logical place to be reunited—at home—was a natural part of reconsidering temporal horizons of present.

194 · CONCLUSION

At that point, it was not the economically and politically troubled Greek state that provided them comfort, but the transnational Jewish networks, in particular the American Jewish Joint Distribution Committee.[12] The bold JDC country director Gaynor I. Jacobson, who served in Greece from March 1945 to January 1946 only to be sent to Czechoslovakia and Hungary at the onset of the Cold War, became a genuine facilitator of relief and recovery in the country. At the onset of the internal Greek conflict, the JDC offices in Greece (driven by nonpartisan policy, although their personal views may have differed from institutional practice) facilitated the reception as well as the financial, material, and spiritual provision of all Jewish survivors. The cooperation of the JDC as an external and effective aid giver with the Greek government probably created a sense of urgency in the Jewish community to keep a low profile and accept the Greek political reality, albeit with gnashing of teeth or perhaps deep inner revulsion.

Though utterly personal and therefore unique trajectories often shifted, merged, or overlapped during World War II, by the end of the war, we can clearly distinguish between the homecoming of Jews in hiding, combatants, deportees, and refugees, that is, between the internally and externally displaced. This typology also yields a universal chronology of return and its narrative structure. During the war, all Jews were faced with the painful choice of abandoning hard-earned property as well as friends and family. They had to find the best possible hiding place and then find means to pay for it, join the resistance at home or armed forces abroad, stay behind in Greece waiting for better days, be deported, or board a ship to go overseas. After the war, they were sidelined or even excluded from society in their home countries, to which they belonged and adhered and which they dully accepted as they were. Still, by the non-Jewish majority, they were considered second-class citizens and feared for their possible disloyalties, or worse, as enemies from within. They were deprived of the support of strong communities, which had been dashed by the war, but were ready to show gratitude although there was little to be thankful for.

Out of approximately 58,500 Jewish deportees from Greece who arrived at Auschwitz-Birkenau, about 85 percent were almost immediately separated from the others and, without knowing what awaited them, murdered in the gas chambers.[13] Nobody returned from the Treblinka death camp. Those who survived the selection process at Auschwitz-Birkenau, generally only those under forty and older than fourteen, regardless of gender, had visions of returning home with hopes, expectations, and memories. The approximately two thousand deportees who were lucky enough to survive, mostly Jews from Thessaloniki, saw homecoming as a chance to reunite with at least some of their loved ones, brothers or sisters, husbands or wives, parents or children. In this way, the postwar Jewish Community of Thessaloniki became a community of camp survivors. And so did Corfu, Ioannina, and Kastoria.

Only several railroad cars from Athens and Thessaloniki did not head to occupied Poland but were detached and sent instead to Bergen-Belsen. Most of the "privileged" passengers, as they are often called by the Auschwitz survivors, were identified as citizens of Spain and Portugal (neutral to Nazi Germany) or were leading representatives of the Thessaloniki Jewish Community and their immediate families or both. Their resilience enabled them to withstand the privations of internment and eventually brought them back home along perplexing paths in different zones of liberation all over Europe. In Allied policy during the liberation and in its aftermath, however, it was not religious affiliation but nationality on which the authorities based their treatment of survivors, generally disregarding their anguish.

While young people survived the extermination camps largely on their own, occasionally being able to form pacts of solidarity with a fellow inmate or family member of the same sex, sometimes entire families returned from the Bergen-Belsen concentration camp. If they had endured the hardships of incarceration, the Nazi decision not to send them to the extermination camps but to Bergen-Belsen stigmatized those Jews as unjustified "prominents" in the postwar period. That was the case with the family of Thessaloniki Chief Rabbi Koretz, whose family only narrowly escaped death. In the camps and on their way home, the deportees maintained personal friendships and family ties. Upon their return, though, the general disbelief and bitterness of what they could have encountered or had to encounter in the camps cast a long dark spell over the Jewish survivors' communities in Europe. After experiencing extreme physical violence, including hunger, torture, and continuous deprivation, they were confronted with structural violence that surpassed all expectations. Ironically, it became their only gateway to the future. With shattered dreams of the past and broken social reference points, they only began to realize the true extent of the Holocaust

196 · CONCLUSION

as a biographical and historical rupture that would leave an indelible mark on them and on future generations.

And then there were those who, during and after the Thessaloniki deportations in the spring of 1943, at considerable cost, succeeded in fleeing from Greece to go overseas. Several thousand Jews escaped to neighboring countries, such as Albania, Bulgaria, Turkey, and, most commonly, British-controlled areas of the Middle East. This complex picture has relevance for the precarious migration situation today when country representatives worldwide make the decision to accept or reject war refugees. Given the political climate back in the 1940s, it was rare that an escape route for Jewish refugees would open, even to Mandatory Palestine. For the British government, the often ill-fated return of Jewish survivors to their home countries, as told by Rachel Saporta and Lili-Nina Revah, became a priority immediately after the war. Regardless of the financial implications or the later political context of the Civil War and the Cold War, the supportive efforts of the leftist resistance in Greece were not forgotten.[14] Again, as in Eastern Europe, Jewish survivors in Greece chose either to remain silent about these experiences or were subjected to silencing by Greek institutions.

February 1946, a year and a half after the liberation of Greece, marked not only the symbolic end of the physical return of Holocaust survivors but also a massive power shift that sparked what has gone down in history as the Greek Civil War. In March 1946, Churchill delivered the famous Fulton speech, in which he used the term "Iron Curtain" to divide Europe into two camps for the first time. The next three years brought Greece new hardships and forced more people to leave their homes for political and economic reasons.[15] Questioning their own belonging led to new, personally unforeseen decisions. From then on, the reasons for emigration, for both Jews and non-Jews in Greece, significantly differed from the previous period. Even though for about 50 percent of the Jewish survivors postwar return was only temporary, it profoundly impacted them when they reached the end of their Holocaust trajectory. The Greek-Jewish community and the narrative identity of Jews in Greece changed dramatically and irrevocably, affecting their language, ideology, and property; these changes were symptomatic of the early stage of reconstruction and in stark contrast to the expectations of Jewish returnees.

Today, when European memory policy is more united on its past and future than ever before and accepts the Holocaust as its negative founding myth, three phenomena coexist: the "rise of Holocaust consciousness," as Dan Stone coined it; the proliferation of "human rights discourse"; and revisionist tendencies in which the past is again exploited for political opportunism and new armed conflicts.[16] This last worrying development provides more reason to remind ourselves of the Jews who survived the Holocaust and their daunting return. With their hopes dashed and expectations shattered, they became vulnerable within the hostile and authoritarian environment of postwar Greece, permeated by long-fueled antisemitism, which continued to shape their personal attitudes for decades to come.

When World War II ended, my grandmother was thirteen, and life was just beginning to unfold before her. My daughter is the same age now as I close the book, and another war rages nearby in Ukraine. A war that provides us with documentation of crimes, atrocities, and suffering in a new millennium that is still largely ahead of us. A documentation so rich and varied that it will undoubtedly occupy scholars for many years. They will uncover stories of struggle, anguish, and despair, but also of courage, resilience, departures full of expectation, and homecomings full of hopes, perhaps similar to the experiences of the survivors in this book. They will hold up a mirror to humanity and ask which of the available paths to the future we will take this time, paths unique to each person but painfully universal in their essence.

Acknowledgments

MUCH OF THE INSPIRATION for this book stems from my long-standing professional and personal interest in modern Greek history and memory and in the fate of the Jews of Europe during the direst series of events of the twentieth century. For a long time, I toyed with the idea of treating these topics together, and I am very happy to say that the book you hold in your hands is the materialization of that desire fulfilled. I could not have completed my work, however, without the dedicated support of numerous colleagues and friends who have stood by me, encouraged me, and shared valuable suggestions with me over the years.

First, colleagues from my alma mater, Charles University, Prague, and its Institute of International Studies at the Faculty of Social Sciences, have had an undeniable impact on my continuous academic development and have generously let me consult them on this project and many others. Jiří Pešek, Jaroslav Kučera, Maria Alina Asavei, Kostas Tsivos, and Jiří Vykoukal were all highly supportive of my research, encouraging me all along the way. Besides them, other colleagues from my own institution and others, both Czech and Slovak, were advisers and commentators on the subject; among them are Hana Kubátová (Charles University), Monika Vrzgulová (Slovak Academy of Science), Martin Šmok, Michal Frankl, and Kateřina Čapková (Czech Academy of Sciences). I have always been pleasantly challenged by their research and intriguing questions, and our discussions made me aware of how different, yet similar, the case studies are that we have chosen for our research. Their insightful, critical scholarship has deeply influenced my own approach.

It was a happy coincidence that I asked about historical maps in an informal conversation during the Prague workshop, and Chad Bryant (University of North Carolina at Chapel Hill) astutely introduced me to Philip Schwartzberg, the creator of all the visual materials in this book. The cover design,

200 · ACKNOWLEDGMENTS

by contrast, has been in my mind ever since I first saw the work of Artemis Alcalay. From then on, I urged Artemis to let me see her new creations, which for years she generously did, and she helped me choose the most suitable piece for this publication. I am deeply indebted to her.

Since my research path on the topic of Greece and on the country itself started some twenty years ago, I must mention my Greek colleagues who guided my first steps into the field, the archives, and academia in Greece in general. Many of them have always showed a keen interest in my work, and our conversations evolved into long-lasting academic collaboration. It was, however, Maria Kavala and Giorgos Antoniou (Aristotle University, Thessaloniki), who pointed me in the right directions in search of archival materials, potential interviewees, and academic contacts, as well as in the direction of the research itself. Many more people should be named here because of the fruitful collaboration and inspiration they provided to me, but of all those dear to me, Nikos Marantzidis (University of Macedonia), who has been my insightful and witty guardian through Greek academia since 2004, stands out.

Of the many colleagues who provided invaluable feedback and assistance at the various stages of my research, I must name four brilliant women who have travelled highly diverse trajectories and who left their imprint on me. They are Tasoula Vervenioti, Rena Molho, Rika Benveniste, and Riki van Boeschoten, who invited me to become part of the Greek Oral History Association, from which I benefited tremendously. I am also indebted to Ioannis Armakolas and Stratos Dordanas, who encouraged my writing and invited me to publish some of my preliminary ideas with them. And to Leon Saltiel, perhaps the most skilled networker I have ever met in Greece; to Philip Carabott, Vasilis Ritzaleos, Vasilis Gounaris, and Karina Lampsa for their constant encouragement; and to Spyros Kakouriotis and his family for their support, friendship, kindness, and even occasional lodging in their home when my finances were scarce.

My research trips to Greece in 2012–2013 and 2016–2018 were largely funded by the Research Program THALIS: Operational Program "Education and Lifelong Learning" and the Grant Agency of the Czech Republic for the project entitled "'We Had to Live, We Had to Survive Somehow...': Jews in Greece, 1944–2012," specifically designed for this book. It was the latter that allowed me to enlist two PhD students, constant companions and dear friends, Nikola Tohma and Jiří Kocián, to assist in the research. They provided me with endless inspiration, assistance, and technical as well as moral support in these otherwise often solitary years of writing. They are setting off on their own independent research paths, and I am certain that Nikola's work on Greece and Jiří's on the digital humanities will make considerable contributions to the social sciences and beyond.

I consider my one-year stay as a Sosland Family Fellow at the Jack, Joseph and Morton Mandel Center for Advanced Holocaust Studies of the United States Holocaust Memorial Museum, Washington, DC (2015–2016) to be a major breakthrough in the course of my work. The immense archival material and other resources available to researchers on site further defined and narrowed the field and the direction in which I was heading. During my stay in the United States and ever after, I have been supported by excellent scholars, including John Iatrides, Mark Mazower, Sarah Abrevaya Stein, Gonda Van Steen, Mirna Zakic, Irene Kacandes, Robert Austin, Ken Walzer, André Gerolymatos, Devin Naar, Michael Brenner, Katerina Lagos, Atina Grossmann, Katherine Fleming, Debórah Dwork, Marion Kaplan, Steven Sage, Benjamin Frommer, and many other colleagues and fellows in Washington, DC, particularly Paul Shapiro, Suzanne Brown-Fleming, Steve Feldman, Martin Dean, Natalya Lazar, Emil Kerenji, Jürgen Matthäus, and Vadim Altskan (all affiliated with the United States Holocaust Memorial Museum) and Margit Meissner (a survivor at the USHMM), Andrew Apostolou (an independent scholar), Ildikó Barna (Eötvös Loránd University), Pedro Correa Martín-Arroyo (London School of Economics), Fabien Theofilakis (the Sorbonne), and Zoltán Tibori-Szabó (Babeş-Bolyai University, Cluj-Napoca). Struggling time and again with anything related to numbers and tables, I am always relieved to have Ildikó as an excellent quantitative researcher by my side.

The academic support was not, however, limited to Greece and the United States; more often than not, it was given around the clock and over the continents. For a better understanding of the logic of violence and Nazi Germany, I could always turn to excellent colleagues, such as Stathis Kalyvas, Dieter Steinert, Gerald Steinacher, Helga Steinbacher, Tanja Petrovic, Boaz Cohen, Natalia Aleksiun, Amikam Nachmani, Robert Gerwarth, A. Dirk Moses, Barbara Törnquist-Plewa, and Andrea Petö. They helped me articulate the fundamental thread of my book. I greatly benefited from working with

202 · ACKNOWLEDGMENTS

Christian Voss, who brought me to the CENTRAL project on the institution-alization of memory and knowledge in post-conflict societies, which soon developed into my own five-year PRIMUS project on hegemonic narratives. To Christian, my wonderful mentor during the polishing period while on a Humboldt fellowship in Berlin, and to his former doctoral student Snežana Stanković and to the inspiring teams of both projects, I am greatly indebted.

Being awarded research fellowships from the University of Regensburg and the Institut für Ost- und Südosteuropa Forschung in Regensburg, I was able to get a peaceful haven as a visiting research fellow at the Graduate School for East and Southeast European Studies. That gave me the necessary impulse to conclude the writing process. For their long-lasting support, I must, first and foremost, thank Ulf Brunnbauer (director of the Institut für Ost- und Südosteuropa Forschung) and Rainer Liedtke (head of the Department of European History of the Nineteenth and Twentieth Centuries, University of Regensburg). In 2020–2021, I had the chance to take a fresh look at my manuscript thanks to a research fellowship at the Vienna Wiesenthal Institute for Holocaust Studies and also to stimulating exchanges with Eva Kovács, Rita Horváth, and Kinga Frojimovics, which took place against all odds in the pandemic.

Other institutions were instrumental in providing me with key sources. Important archival material was made accessible to me by the staff at the Greek State Archive in Thessaloniki, Historical Archive of Macedonia (Areti Makri), the International Tracing Service experts at the USHMM, the Wiener Library, and the Arolsen Archives—especially Elisabeth Anthony, Jo-Ellyn Decker, Christine Smidt, and Nicole Tödtli—the American Jewish Distribution Committee Archives (Misha Mitsel). Alexios Menexiadis provided his detailed knowledge as he helped in preparing the digital collections of the Central Board of Jewish Communities (Athens) and the Jewish Community of Thessaloniki for the USHMM. Vadim Altskan, as project director of the International Archival Programs at the USHMM Center for Advanced Holo-caust Studies, where he supervises these collections, was equally helpful in steering my work. Elizabeth Anthony, who was at that time the International Tracing Service and partnerships program manager at the USHMM, and Nicole Tödtli, head of the Arolsen Archives reference services team, gave me necessary training on the ITS collection. The JDC senior archivist Misha Mitsel, introduced me in 2008 to his archive in New York, which has lately

ACKNOWLEDGMENTS · 203

become searchable online. Without the tireless devotion of these people and many others, this book would hardly have materialized.

For the excellent library services at the USHMM, I am deeply indebted to Peter Black, Ronald Coleman, Vincent Slatt, Liviu Carare, Megan Lewis, and Michlean Amir. For personal accounts, I delved deep into the USHMM Survivor Reflections and Testimonies collection, the USC Shoah Foundation Institute's Visual History Archive, and the Fortunoff Video Archive for Holocaust Testimonies at Yale University under the direction of Steven Nahon, the last two of which I accessed primarily at the Malach Center for Visual History at Charles University (Prague) with the helpful assistance of its staff members Jakub Mlynář, Jiří Kocián, Karin Hofmeisterová, and Petra Hoffmannová.

I was also privileged to have had the chance to record some personal accounts with survivors themselves, and I will never forget the special moments spent with Paulette Nehama, Michael Matsas and Ninette Matsas-Feldman, Iosif Venturas, Heinz Kounio and Erika Kounio-Amariglio, Miko and Mari Alvo, Berry Nachmias, Fratelis Nahmias, Esdra Moissis, Rafail Frezis, Moisis Konstantinis, Esther Franko, Ester Florentin, Rina and Paulina Cohen, and Laura Simon and her nephew Harry Zinn, who not only introduced me to his aunt but also went through my writing with care and gave constructive criticism. Especially in Greece, I would hardly have had a chance to reach the survivors had it not been again for my dear friend Alexios Menexiadis, who introduced me to many of them twelve years ago. He also introduced me to the Jewish Museum of Greece in Athens, which became the most welcoming place for my research in Greece. And Alexios carefully read my manuscript. In a similar vein, my professional path has been shaped by friendship and academic exchange with Jessie Barton-Hronešová, Tobias Blümel, and Alexios Ntetorakis. It was their great contribution which enabled this book to see the light of day. Finally, I thank my junior colleagues, Maria-Paschalina Dimopoulou and Tereza Juhászová, who were immensely helpful with organizing the technical aspects of this book; Jacob Maze and Megan Nagel, who as native speakers helped me shape the language of the manuscript; and ultimately Derek Paton, a patient guide to English and language editor for a non-native speaker like me.

At Brandeis University Press, I am deeply grateful to Sylvia Fuks Fried for her exceptional guidance, support, and enthusiasm as my editor. Her

204 · ACKNOWLEDGMENTS

thoughtful and collaborative approach shepherded my project from inception to completion. I also wish to extend my heartfelt thanks to Sue Berger Ramin, Beth Fong, and Ashley Burns for their invaluable support throughout the production process. Special appreciation goes to production editor Jim Schley and copyeditor Benjamin Woollard for their careful work in polishing the text.

Last but not least, I owe a debt of gratitude to my family, who cheered me and put up with me during this long period of being isolated from most company while researching. I thank my parents and especially my daughter, Hermína, and my husband, Jindřich, for their immeasurable patience, understanding, and support through all these years, since they practically shaped their lives around the course of this book. With Jindřich by my side, and in our never-ending conversations, I began to see the personalized Holocaust trajectories in a more global perspective of justice and injustice, the way he, as a lawyer, is far more inclined to do than I. With his deep interest in history, Jindřich also became my strictest and most critical reader. Above all, I am grateful to my grandmother, who has been there for me all my life and in her kind way, ever since my childhood, has shared with me her insights of a child's experience of war and its aftermath. This book is dedicated to you, Grandma. You will remain in my heart forever.

Notes

Preface

1. Quoted from Gordon Parks, "The Cycle of Despair," *Life*, March 8, 1968, 48.

2. Ute Frevert, "Defining Emotions: Concepts and Debates over Three Centuries," Ute Frevert et al., eds., *Emotional Lexicons: Continuity and Change in the Vocabulary of Feeling, 1700–2000* (Oxford, UK: Oxford University Press, 2014), 2.

3. Steven Brown and Paula Reavey, *Vital Memory and Affect: Living with a Difficult Past* (London: Routledge, 2015).

4. Ute Frevert, "Piggy's Shame," in Uffa Jensen et al., eds., *Learning How to Feel: Children's Literature and Emotional Socialization, 1870–1970* (Oxford: Oxford University Press, 2014), 134–36. Concerning personal involvement based on one's background, see Saul Friedländer, "Trauma and Transference," in *Memory, History, and the Extermination of the Jews of Europe* (Bloomington: Indiana University Press, 1993), 117–37; Saul Friedländer, *Nazi Germany and the Jews, 1933–1945* (New York: Harper Perennial, 2009), 1.

5. Carol A. Kidron, "Sensorial Memory: Embodied Legacies of Genocide," in Frances E. Mascia-Lees, ed., *A Companion to the Anthropology of the Body and Embodiment* (Chichester, UK: Blackwell, 2011), 462–63.

6. Jiří Hanuš and Stanislav Balík, *Katolická církev v Československu 1945–1989* (Brno: Centrum pro studium demokracie a kultury CDK, 2007), 9; Karel Kaplan, *Stát a církev v Československu v letech 1948–1953* (Brno: Doplněk, 1993), 23.

7. Milan Kundera, "The Kidnapped West. The Tragedy of Central Europe," *Le Débat* 27, no. 5 (1983): 3–23.

Introduction

1. Quoted from Isaac Matarasso, Pauline Maud Matarasso, Robert Matarasso, and François Matarasso, *Talking until Nightfall: Remembering Jewish Salonica, 1941–44* (London: Bloomsbury, 2020), 128. After the war, the prewar center of Jewish life in mainland Greece, Salonica, ceased to exist and soon disappeared from the dominant Greek narrative. Instead, it became Thessaloniki, the toponym used by Holocaust survivors in Greece and in this book.

206 · NOTES TO INTRODUCTION

2. Isaac Aron Matarasso, *Ki omos oli tous den pethanan* [*And Yet Not All of Them Died*] (Athens: A. Bezes, 1948).

3. See Michael Brenner, *Nach dem Holocaust: Juden in Deutschland 1945–1950* (Munich: C. H. Beck, 1995). For comparisons with other countries, see also Atina Grossmann and Tamar Lewinsky, "1945–1949: Zwischenstation," in Michael Brenner et al., eds., *Geschichte der Juden in Deutschland von 1945 bis zur Gegenwart: Politik, Kultur und Gesellschaft* (Munich: C. H. Beck, 2012), 67–152; Eva Kolinsky, *After the Holocaust: Jewish Survivors in Germany after 1945* (London: Pimlico, 2004); Guri Schwarz, *After Mussolini: Jewish Life and Jewish Memories in Post-Fascist Italy*, translated by Noor Giovani Mazhar (Portland, OR: Vallentine Mitchell, 2012); and Anna Cichopek-Gajraj, *Beyond Violence: Jewish Survivors in Poland and Slovakia, 1944–48* (New York: Cambridge University Press, 2014).

4. To respect the conditionalities of identity, citizenship, and religious affiliation in Greece, as explained in later in the introduction, I use in this book the term "Jews of Greece" rather than "Greek Jews."

5. William Styron, *Sophie's Choice* (New York: Random House, 1979).

6. John J. Sigal and Morton Weinfeld, *Trauma and Rebirth: Intergenerational Effects of the Holocaust* (New York: Praeger, 1989), 13.

7. David Bankier, ed., *The Jews Are Coming Back: The Return of the Jews to Their Countries of Origin after WW II* (New York: Berghahn, 2005).

8. Yad Vashem, "Names and Numbers of Righteous among the Nations - per Country & Ethnic Origin, as of January 1, 2021," www.yadvashem.org/righteous/statistics.html.

9. Hagen Fleischer, "Griechenland," in Wolfgang Benz, ed., *Dimension des Völkermords: Die Zahl der Jüdischen Opfer des Nationalsozialismus* (Munich: Oldenbourg, 1991), 272. Fleischer includes in the total number his estimate of Jews who were not registered or did not repatriate.

10. Cichopek-Gajraj, *Beyond Violence*, 30.

11. Roberta Rubin Greene et al., "Conceptualizing a Holocaust Survivorship Model," *Journal of Human Behavior in the Social Environment* 20, no. 4 (2010): 423–39.

12. Yael Danieli, "On the Achievement of Integration in Aging Survivors of the Nazi Holocaust," *Journal of Geriatric Psychiatry* 14 (1981): 191–210.

13. In feminist scholarship this is a debate going back to the 1970s; see Jennifer L. Dunn, *Judging Victims: Why We Stigmatize Survivors, and How They Reclaim Respect* (Boulder, CO: Lynne Rienner Publishers, 2009).

14. Shira Hantman, Zahava Solomon, and Yoav Horn, "Long-Term Coping of Holocaust Survivors: A Typology," *Israel Journal of Psychiatry and Related Sciences* 40, no. 2 (2003): 126–34.

NOTES TO INTRODUCTION · 207

15. Reinhart Koselleck, *Futures Past: On the Semantics of Historical Times* (Cambridge, MA: MIT Press, 1985), 255–75.

16. After World War II, Jewish Communities, established by Greek law in 1920, were renewed by Law 367/1945 (4 June 1945)—"Peri anasygkrotiseos Israilitikon Koinotiton," FEK A'143/1945.

17. Haim Avni, "Spanish Nationals in Greece and Their Fate during the Holocaust," *Yad Vashem Studies* 8 (1970): 36.

18. PAAA, B 26/65—Vermerk. Betr.: Deutsch-griechische Wiedergutmachungsverhandlungen, hier: In Griechenland lebende Juden nichtgriechischer Staatsangehörigkeit (29 March 1960).

19. Avni, "Spanish Nationals in Greece," 37.

20. Devin E. Naar, *Jewish Salonica: Between the Ottoman Empire and Modern Greece* (Stanford, CA: Stanford University Press, 2016), 54–55; Sidoni Antzel, 37990, VHA, USC Shoah Foundation.

21. Julia P. Cohen and Sarah A. Stein, "Sephardic Scholarly Worlds: Toward a Novel Geography of Modern Jewish History," *Jewish Quarterly Review* 100, no. 3 (2010): 352.

22. Mark Mazower, *Salonica, City of Ghosts: Christians, Muslims and Jews, 1430–1950* (London: HarperCollins, 2004), 305–70; Rena Molho, *I Evrei tis Thessalonikis: Mia idieteri kinotita* (Athens: Pataki, 2014); Naar, *Jewish Salonica*, 5.

23. Zvi Y. Gitelman, "Reconstructing Jewish Communities and Jewish Identities in Post-Communist East Central Europe," in András Kovács and Eszter Andor, eds., *Jewish Studies at the Central European University* (Budapest: CEU Press, 2000), 1–8. On *millet* see, Sarah Stein, *Family Papers: A Sephardic Journey through the Twentieth Century* (New York: Farrar, Straus and Giroux, 2019), 54.

24. Sakis Gekas, "The Port Jews of Corfu and the 'Blood Libel' of 1891: A Tale of Many Centuries and of One Event," *Jewish Culture and History* 7, nos. 1–2 (2004): 171–96; Maria Margaroni, "Antisemitic Rumours and Violence in Corfu at the End of 19th Century," *Quest. Issues in Contemporary Jewish History* 3 (July 2012), 267–88. See also Eutychia D. Liata, *I Kerkyra ke i Zakynthos ston kyklona tou antisimitismou: i "sykofantia gia to aima" tou 1891* [*Corfu and Zante in the Vortex of Antisemitism: the Blood Libel of 1891*] (Athens: INEEIE, 2006), 122.

25. Several scholars have examined blood libel in other places of contemporary Greece. For Rhodes, see Jonathan Frankel, *The Damascus Affair: "Ritual Murder," Politics, and the Jews in 1840* (Cambridge: Cambridge University Press, 1997); Yitzchak Kerem, "The 1840 Blood Libel in Rhodes," *World Congress of Jewish Studies* 12, no. B (1997): 137–46; Maria Margaroni, "The Blood Libel on Greek Islands in the Nineteenth Century," in Robert Nemes and Daniel Unowsky, eds., *Sites of European Antisemitism in the Age of Mass Politics, 1880–1918* (Hanover, NH: University Press of New England, 2014), 185–89. For Thessaloniki, see

208 · NOTES TO INTRODUCTION

Rena Molho, "The Close Ties between Nationalism and Antisemitism: The Helleniza-
tion of Salonika, 1917–1948," *Jahrbuch für Antisemitismusforschung* 24 (2015): 217–28. For
Ioannina and Pogoni, see Annette B. Fromm, "A Ritual Blood Libel in Northwestern
Greece," in Yedida K. Stillman and Norman A. Stillman, eds., *From Iberia to Diaspora:
Studies in Sephardic History and Culture* (Leiden: Brill, 1999), 49–57.

26. In this vein, some Jewish authors to this day refer to the Greek conquest of Ottoman
territories, including those of the Jewish Communities in Greece, as the "liberation from
Ottoman/Turkish yoke." See Paul Isaac Hagouel, "The Annihilation of Jewish Greeks in
Eastern Macedonia and Thrace during WWII: Balkan Particularities, Facts, Memory,"
eSefard, https://esefarad.com/?p=52726 (accessed 12 March 2021); Rae Dalven, *The Jews of
Ioannina* (Athens: Lykavittos, 2011), 35.

27. Jews and other groups who did not belong to the Greek Orthodox Church were des-
ignated citizens of non-Greek descent and assigned a second-class status, making them
vulnerable to being stripped of their citizenship. This definition of Greek citizenship
long outlived World War II, and the spirit of Greek homogeneity based on nationhood
predefined by Greek Orthodoxy has become an indispensable part of Greek political
discourse. Lambros Baltsiotis, "I ithagenia ston Psychro Polemo" ["Citizenship in the
Cold War"], in Michael Tsapogas, Dimitris Christopoulos, and Nikos Alivizatos, eds., *Ta
dikeomata stin Ellada 1953–2003: apo to telos tou emphyliou sto telos tis metapoliteusis [Rights in
Greece, 1953–2003: From the End of the Civil War to the End of the Metapolitefsi]* (Athens: Kastaniotis Editions, 2004), 81–82.

28. Nikos Alivizatos, *Oi politikoi thesmoi se krisi 1922–1974: Opseis tis ellinikis empirias [Politi-
cal Institutions in Crisis, 1922–1974: Greek Aspects]* (Athens: Themelio, 1983), 360–74; Tobias
Blümel, "Der Teufel, die Juden, die Protokolle der Weisen von Zion und die zionistische
Weltverschwörung. Grundlinien des Antisemitismus in Griechenland," in *Historische
Interventionen: Festschrift für Wolfgang Wippermann zum 70. Geburtstag*, ed. Axel Weipert,
Jakob Müller, and Tobias Blümel (Berlin: Trafo, 2015), 121–28; see also Rena Molho,
"I antievraiki nomothesia tou Venizelou ston Mesopolemo kai pos i Dimokratia borei
na ginei arogos tou antisimitismou" ["The Anti-Jewish Legislation of Venizelos in the
Interwar Period and How Democracy Can Be a Succourer of Antisemitism"], *Sychrona
Themata* 82 (June 2003): 53–59.

29. AJDC, NY AR 1919-21/4/21/146.1, Greece, 1918, 1919, "Letter from Hetty Goldman Joint
Distribution Committee" (27 February 1919); regarding schooling, see Bernard Pierron,
*Evrei ke Christiani sti Neoteri Ellada, Istoria ton diakinotikon scheseon apo to 1821 os to 1945 [Jews
and Christians in Contemporary Greece: History of Intercommunal Relations from 1821 to 1945]*
(Athens: Polis, 2004). For Thessaloniki, see Naar, *Jewish Salonica*, 139–88.

30. Leon Saltiel, "Voices from the Ghetto of Thessaloniki: Mother–Son Correspondence
as a Source of Jewish Everyday Life under Persecution," *Southeast European and Black Sea
Studies* 17, no. 2 (2017): 203–22. For details of letter exchanges and a unique collection of

NOTES TO INTRODUCTION · 209

ego-documents, see Leon Saltiel, *Mi me ksechasete* [*Do Not Forget Me*] (Athens: Alexandria, 2018), 189. Mylonas claims that the ultimate aim of Greek state policy toward the Jews was not their acculturation but assimilation. Harris Mylonas, *The Politics of Nation-Building* (Cambridge, UK: Cambridge University Press, 2012), 105–9.

31. For an explanation of the problem of minorities in Greece, see the introduction to Richard Clogg, ed., *Minorities in Greece: Aspects of a Plural Society* (London: Hurst, 2003), ix–xix.

32. USHMM, RG-45.010, Selected records of the Central Board of Jewish Communities (KIS) Athens, Greece, KIS0127—KIS to the Central British Fund for Jewish Relief and Rehabilitation (24 February 1946).

33. Bea Lewkowicz, "'After the War We Were All Together': Jewish Memories of Postwar Thessalonica," in *After the War Was Over: Reconstructing the Family, Nation, and State in Greece, 1943–1960*, ed. Mark Mazower (Princeton: Princeton University Press, 2000), 247–72; Bea Lewkowicz, *The Jewish Community of Salonika: History, Memory, Identity* (London: Vallentine Mitchell, 2006); Rika Benveniste, *Auti pou epezisan: antistasi, ektopisi, epistrophi: Thessalonikis Evrei sti dekaetia tou 1940* [*Those Who Survived: Resistance, Deportation, Return: The Jews of Thessaloniki in the 1940s*] (Athens: Polis, 2014); published in German as *Die Überlebenden: Widerstand, Deportation, Rückkehr. Juden aus Thessaloniki in den 1940er Jahren* (Berlin: Edition Romiosini, 2016). For a recent publication in a similar vein, see Rika Benveniste, *Louna* (Athens: Polis, 2017).

34. Katherine E. Fleming, *Greece: A Jewish History* (Princeton, NJ: Princeton University Press, 2008); Paris Papamichos Chronakis, "'We Lived as Greeks and We Died as Greeks': Thessalonican Jews in Auschwitz and the Meanings of Nationhood," in *The Holocaust in Greece*, ed. Giorgos Antoniou and A. Dirk Moses (Cambridge, UK: Cambridge University Press, 2018), 157–80.

35. Andrew Apostolou, "Greek Collaboration in the Holocaust and the Course of the War," in Antoniou and Moses, *Holocaust in Greece*, 90.

36. Pieter Lagrou, "Return to a Vanished World: European Societies and the Remnants of Their Jewish Communities, 1945–1947," in *The Jews Are Coming Back: The Return of the Jews to Their Countries of Origin after WW II*, ed. David Bankier (New York: Berghahn, 2005), 13–24.

37. See Hanna Yablonka and Ora Cummings, *The State of Israel vs. Adolf Eichmann* (New York: Schocken, 2004). In Greece, the trial was largely overshadowed by an escalating affair concerning Greek politicians accused of collaboration with the Germans. See Kateřina Králová, "In the Shadow of the Nazi Past: Post-War Reconstruction and the Claims of the Jewish Community in Salonika," *European History Quarterly* 46, no. 2 (2016): 275–78.

38. Aron Rodrigue, *Sephardim and the Holocaust* (Washington, DC: United States Holocaust Memorial Museum, 2005), 2–6.

210 · NOTES TO INTRODUCTION

39. Fleming, *Greece*, 202–4. The prosecution also admitted as evidence the sworn deposition of Asher Moissis, the ex-president of the Jewish Community in Thessaloniki, who was at the time of the Eichmann trial a lawyer at the Court of Appeal in Athens. Moissis, however, only submitted a written account together with the wartime diary of the late Yomtov Yacoel, which was in his possession. The Nizkor Project, *The Trial of Eichmann: Record of Proceedings in the District Court of Jerusalem*, session 47 (Jerusalem: Ministry of Justice, 1992), www.nizkor.org/the-trial-of-adolf-eichmann/.

40. Irith Dublon-Knebel, *German Foreign Office Documents on the Holocaust in Greece (1937–1944)* (Tel Aviv: Tel Aviv University, 2007), 41–42.

41. Tad Szulc, *The Secret Alliance: The Extraordinary Story of the Rescue of the Jews since World War II* (1991; repr., London: Pan, 1993); USHMM, RG-50.968.0032—Oral history interview with Gaynor I. Jacobson, conducted by Tad Szulc (1988).

42. On the ITS and its uses, see Suzanne Brown-Fleming, *Nazi Persecution and Postwar Repercussions: The International Tracing Service Archive and Holocaust Research* (Lanham, MD: Rowman & Littlefield, 2015); and on JDC operation and records, see Avinoam Patt, Atina Grossmann, Linda G. Levi, and Maud S. Mandel, introduction to *The JDC at 100: A Century of Humanitarianism* (Detroit: Wayne State University Press, 2019), 1–39.

43. Tim Cole, "(Re)Placing the Past: Spatial Strategies of Retelling Difficult Stories," *The Oral History Review* 42, no. 1 (2015): 30–49.

44. Charlotte McIvor, Emilie Pine, Stef Craps, Astrid Erll, Paula McFetridge, Ann Rigney, and Dominic Thorpe, "Roundtable: Moving Memory," *Irish University Review* 47, no. 1 (2017): 165–96.

45. I am avoiding the term "testimony" not only because of its use as a legal term but also because, unlike in English, in many other languages, including Greek, other terms, such as "interview" (*synenteuxi*), seem to be better established for this format. Concerning terminology, see Rebecca Clifford, *Survivors: Children's Lives after the Holocaust* (New Haven: Yale University Press, 2020), 219.

46. The Visual History Archive of the USC Shoah Foundation, http://vhaonline.usc.edu. Currently, the VHA collection contains interviews, each more than two hours long on average, in forty-one languages, amounting to about 115,000 hours of video material. To facilitate working with such a vast quantity of material, the search engines are equipped with a list of over sixty-five thousand thematic keywords.

47. The oldest narrator from Greece, Lea-Lily Siaki (b. 1903), was in her early forties at the end of the war. Lea-Lily Siaki, 7796, VHA USC Shoah Foundation. See also the Database of Greek-Jewish Holocaust Survivors' Testimonies (in Greek and English): http://gjst.ha.uth.gr.

48. On the ITS and Holocaust survivors more specifically, see Kenneth Waltzer, "Moving Together, Moving Alone: The Story of Boys on a Transport from Auschwitz to Buch-

enwald," in *Jewish Families in Europe, 1939–Present: History, Representation and Memory*, ed. Joanna B. Michlic (Waltham, MA: Brandeis University Press, 2017), 86; Ildikó Barna, "Hungarian Jewish Holocaust Survivors Registered in Displaced Persons Camps in Apulia: An Analysis Based on the Holdings of the Arolsen (International Tracing Service) Digital Archive," in *Beyond Camps and Forced Labour: Proceedings of the Sixth International Conference*, ed. Suzanne Bardgett, Christine Schmidt, and Dan Stone (Cham: Springer Nature Switzerland, a Palgrave Macmillan imprint, 2021), 173–74.

49. Clifford, *Survivors*, 218–19.

50. See François Azouvi, *Le mythe du grand silence: Auschwitz, les Français, la mémoire* (Paris: Le Grand livre du mois, 2012); Christopher R. Browning, *Remembering Survival: Inside a Nazi Slave-Labor Camp* (New York: W. W. Norton, 2011); Dalia Ofer, "The Community and the Individual: The Different Narratives of Early and Late Testimonies and Their Significance for Historians," in *Holocaust Historiography in Context: Emergence, Challenges, Polemics and Achievements*, ed. David Bankier and Dan Michman (Jerusalem: Yad Vashem, 2008), 519–37.

51. Voices of the Holocaust, http://voices.iit.edu (accessed on 1 May 2019), includes seven interviews with Jews of Greece. Concerning the particular value of early interviews and especially the David Boder Collection, see Rachel Deblinger, "David P. Boder: Holocaust Memory and Displaced Persons Camps," in *After the Holocaust: Challenging the Myth of Silence*, ed. D. Cesarani and E. J. Sundquist (London: Routledge), 2003, 115–26.

52. On narration as a reciprocal activity, see Jane Elliot, *Using Narrative in Social Science Research: Qualitative and Quantitative Approaches* (London: Sage, 2009), 10–11.

53. The greatest number of Holocaust survivors in all the interview collections come from Thessaloniki, perhaps because they constituted the largest number of camp returnees. But the most striking collection is Centropa, especially since it seeks to represent the plurality of survival strategies. Of its thirteen interviews conducted in Greece, including with camp survivors, resistance fighters, Jews in hiding, and exiles (but also, for example, a soldier in the Greek army-in-exile and a non-Jewish wife of a Holocaust survivor), all the narrators come from Thessaloniki. Centropa, Database of Jewish Memory, http://www.centropa.org (accessed on 20 November 2020).

54. Hannah Pollin-Galay, *Ecologies of Witnessing: Language, Place, and Holocaust Testimony* (New Haven: Yale University Press, 2018).

Chapter One: Coming out of Hiding in Greece

1. Throughout, brackets with ellipses are used to indicate omissions, whereas long pauses are indicated by ellipses alone. Interview with Maria Curtis (neé Rachel Serror), 34110.

212 · NOTES TO CHAPTER ONE

2. Katherine E. Fleming, *Greece: A Jewish History* (Princeton: Princeton University Press, 2008); Steven B. Bowman, *The Agony of Greek Jews, 1940–1945* (Stanford: Stanford University Press, 2009), 163–65; Steven B. Bowman, *Jewish Resistance in Wartime Greece* (London: Vallentine Mitchell, 2006).

3. For a general picture of the procedure in a Thessaloniki orphanage, see Aigli Brouskou, "Opoia petra ke an sikosis: To dimotiko vrefokomio Thessalonikis 'Agios Stylianos' ke i schesis tou me tin evraiki kinotita tis polis" ["Whichever Rock You Pick Up: The 'Agios Stylianos' Municipal Nursery of Thessaloniki and Its Relations with the Jewish Community of the City"], in *O Ellinikos Evraismos* [*Greek Jewry*], ed. Maria Stefanopoulou (Athens: Eteria Spoudon Scholis Moraiti, 1999), 205–24; Aigli Brouskou, "Evrees trofi sto Christianiko vrefokomio 'Agios Stylianos' stis arches tou aiona" ["Jewish Nurses in the Christian Nursery 'Agios Stylianos' in the Beginning of the Century"], in *Oi evreoi ston elliniko choro, zitimata istorias sti makra diarkeia* [*The Jews in Greece: Historical Questions in the Long Term*], ed. Eutychia Avdela and Odette Varon-Vassard (Athens: Gavriilidis, 1995); Leon Saltiel, "Prospathies diasosis Evraiopedon Thessalonikis kata tin Katochi: ena agnosto kykloma paranomon yiothesion" ["Attempts to Rescue the Jewish Children of Thessaloniki during the Occupation: An Unknown Illegal Adoption Network"], *Sychrona Themata* 127, no. B (2014): 75–78. For personal stories of Jewish children, see Nina Nachmia, *Reina Zilberta: ena pedi sto geto tis Thessalonikis* [*Reina Zilberta: A Child in the Thessaloniki Ghetto*] (Athens: Okeanidis, 1996); Esther Franko, *To pechnidi ton rolon ke i defteri genia tou Olokautomatos* [*Role-Playing and the Second Generation of the Holocaust*] (Athens: Odos Panos, 2012).

4. For comparisons with other countries, see Frank Caestecker, "The Reintegration of Jewish Survivors into Belgian Society," in *The Jews Are Coming Back: The Return of the Jews to Their Countries of Origin after WWII*, ed David Bankier (New York: Berghahn, 2005), 80.

5. Erkanas Tsezanas, 39196, VHA, USC Shoah Foundation.

6. Centropa, Database of Jewish Memory, Lily [*sic*] Arouch (née Pardo), interviewed by Annita Mordechai, November 2005, www.centropa.org/biography/lily-arouch (accessed on 20 November 2018); USHMM, RG-50.030.0475, Oral history interview with Paulette Nehama (neé Mourtzoukou), conducted by Margaret West (24 June 2003).

7. Greek Office of Information, *Greece: Basic Statistics* (London: Greek Office of Information, 1949), 24–25.

8. USHMM, RG-50.968.0032—Oral history interview with Gaynor I. Jacobson, conducted by Tad Szulc (1988).

9. Keith Lowe, *Savage Continent: Europe in the Aftermath of World War II* (New York: Viking Press, 2012), 24.

10. Nelli Nachmias (neé Tampach), 40116, VHA, USC Shoah Foundation.

11. Michael Matsas, *The Illusion of Safety: The Story of the Greek Jews during World War II* (New

NOTES TO CHAPTER ONE · 213

York: Pella, 1997). Matsas's book comprises hundreds of personal accounts by the Jews of Greece, which the author collected throughout his life from all over the world.

12. Lowe, *Savage Continent*; Tim Cole, *Holocaust Landscapes* (London: Bloomsbury Continuum, 2016), loc. 222–24 (Kindle).

13. Tasoula Vervenioti, "12 October 1944, Liberation Trauma and Memorialization in Greece," *Journal of Modern Greek Studies Occasional Papers* 2 (2014): 1–12.

14. NA, T 311/196—Beobachtungen in Athen am 12.10.44 (4 November 1944); and T 311/196—Lage in Athen (21 October 1944). For the circumstances relating to the Bulgarian withdrawal, see Marietta Stankova, *Bulgaria in British Foreign Policy, 1943–1949* (London: Anthem Press, 2014); or Dimitris Livanios, *The Macedonian Question: Britain and the Southern Balkans: 1939–1949* (Oxford, UK: Oxford University Press, 2008).

15. John O. Iatrides, *Revolt in Athens: The Greek Communist "Second Round," 1944–1945* (Princeton, NJ: Princeton University Press, 1972), 3, 90; Flora Tsigala, "UNRRA's Relief Efforts in Post-War Greece: Political Impartiality versus Military Exigencies," in *Bearing Gifts to Greeks: Humanitarian Aid to Greece in the 1940s*, ed. Richard Clogg (Basingstoke, UK: Palgrave Macmillan, 2008), 195. For more information on the December events, see Paris K. Diamantouros, *Ta Dekemvriana [The Dekemvriana]* (Athens: Archeio, 2014).

16. Rika Benveniste, *Die Überlebenden: Widerstand, Deportation, Rückkehr: Juden aus Thessaloniki in den 1940er Jahren* (Berlin: Edition Romiosini, 2016), 129.

17. USHMM, RG-50.030.0475, Paulette Nehama (24 June 2003); Interview with Paulette Nehama (26 July 2015).

18. Rudolf Amariglio [*sic*], 23446, VHA, USC Shoah Foundation, and interview with Erika and Roli Amarilio in Thessaloniki, conducted by Kateřina Králová (9 June 2008); Maria Curtis, 34110, VHA, USC Shoah Foundation.

19. Dan Stone, *The Liberation of the Camps: The End of the Holocaust and Its Aftermath* (New Haven: Yale University Press, 2015), 3.

20. Philip Carabott, "State, Society and the Religious 'Other' in Nineteenth-Century Greece," *Kampos: Cambridge Papers in Modern Greek* 18 (November 2011): 13.

21. Samuel Kline Cohn, "The Black Death and the Burning of Jews," *Past & Present* 196, no. 1 (1 August 2007): 3–36. See also Kateřina Králová, "Řecko [Greece]," in *Návraty [Returns]*, ed. Kateřina Králová and Hana Kubátová (Prague: Karolinum, 2016), 208; Fleming, *Greece*; Derek August Taylor, *Don Pacifico: The Acceptable Face of Gunboat Diplomacy* (London: Vallentine Mitchell, 2008), 141–42.

22. For the invasion, see Heinz Richter, *Griechenland zwischen Revolution und Konterrevolution (1936–1946)* (Frankfurt am Main: Europäische Verlagsanstalt, 1973), 131–34. For the sex, age, social, and national composition of the Jews hiding in Athens, Michael Molho and Joseph Nehama, *In Memoriam: Gewidmet dem Andenken an die jüdischen Opfer*

214 · NOTES TO CHAPTER ONE

der Naziherrschaft in Griechenland, trans. Peter Katzung (1948; repr., Essen: Peter Katzung, 1981), 341. A Greek translation was published by the Jewish Community in Thessaloniki only after the fall of the Greek junta in 1974, ten years after Molho had died in Buenos Aires, where he had emigrated in 1950. "Rabbi Michael Molho, Noted Sephardic Rabbi, Dies in Argentina, Aged 73," *Jewish Telegraphic Agency*, July 27, 1964, www.jta.org/1964/07/27/archive/.

23. Asher Moissis, *Greek-Jewish Patrimony* (North Charleston, SC: CreateSpace, 2012), 11, 89–96. AJDC, NY AR 1945-54/4/33/402, Greece, Survivors, 1945–1946, "Letter from Central Location Index, Inc., to American Jewish Joint Distribution Community" (24 May 1945).

24. Moissis, *Greek-Jewish Patrimony*, 13.

25. Moissis, 11.

26. Rafail Frezis, *O Evraikos typos stin Ellada* [*The Jewish Press in Greece*] (Volos: Ekdosi Israilitikis Kinotitas Volou, 1999), 438–39.

27. Moissis, *Greek-Jewish Patrimony*, 65–68; "Prosecution document 351, Evidence T/1134," in the Nizkor Project, *The Trial of Eichmann: Record of Proceedings in the District Court of Jerusalem* (Jerusalem: Ministry of Justice, 1992).

28. For the most recent information on the EAM, see Giannis Skalidakis, *I exousia tou EAM sta chronia tis Katochis 1943–1944* [*The Power of the EAM during the Occupation*] (Athens: Asini, 2014).

29. Leften Stavros Stavrianos, "The Jews of Greece," *Journal of Central European Affairs* 8, no. 3 (1948): 262. See also Kateřina Králová, "Hachsharot in Greece, 1945–1949: Camps or Vocational Centers?," *Quest: Issues in Contemporary Jewish History* 21, no. 1 (2022): 75–101.

30. AJDC, NY AR 1945/54-4/33/2/387, Greece, General, I.–VII. 1945, "The American Joint Distribution Committee's Program Greece" (1 August 1945); Michael Matsas, *The Illusion of Safety: The Story of the Greek Jews during World War II* (New York: Pella, 1997), 109; Moissis, *Greek-Jewish Patrimony*, 70–71; Karina Lampsa and Iakov Sibi, *I diasosi: i siopi tou kosmou, i antistasi sta geto ke ta stratopeda, i Ellines Evrei sta chronia tis Katochis* [*The Rescue: The Silence of the People, the Resistance in the Ghettos and the Camps, and the Greek Jews during the Occupation*] (Athens: Ekdosis Kapon, 2012), 289–96; Leon Saltiel, "Two Friends in Axis-Occupied Greece: The Rescue Efforts of Yomtov Yacoel and Asher Moisis," *Journal of Genocide Research* 21, no. 3 (2019): 342–58.

31. NA, RG 226/G190/Box 73/File 27—Statement on the Jews in Greece and their Present Situation (14 June 1944); TNA, FO 371/42900, WR 1896—Jews in Greece (5 December 1944).

32. AJDC, IST 1937-49/4/9/IS.217, "Greece 1944–1946," "Letter from Charles Passman to Mr. Ch. Barlas" (15 March 1945).

NOTES TO CHAPTER ONE · 215

33. Centropa, Database of Jewish Memory, Mario Modiano, interviewed by Milena Molho, November 2005, http://www.centropa.org/biography/mario-modiano (accessed on 20 November 2018); AJDC, NY AR 1945/54-4/33/2/387, Greece, General, I.–VII. 1945, "The American Joint Distribution Committee's Program Greece" (1 August 1945). Concerning skepticism about the possibility of returning home and getting back to normal, see Patricia Heberer, *Children during the Holocaust* (Lanham, MD: Rowman & Littlefield, 2015), 376.

34. Interview with Moisis Konstantinis in Athens, conducted by Kateřina Králová (22 April 2015).

35. N. 367/1945 (4 June 1945)—"Peri anasygkrotiseos Israilitikon Kinotiton," FEK A' 143/1945; see also Kateřina Králová, "In the Shadow of the Nazi Past: Post-War Reconstruction and the Claims of the Jewish Community in Salonika," *European History Quarterly* 46, no. 2 (2016): 262–90.

36. Moisis K. Konstantinis, *I Israilitikes kinotites tis Ellados meta to Olokautoma, apo tis ekthesis tou Kanari D. Konstantini* [*The Jewish Communities of Greece after the Holocaust, in the Essays of Kanaris D. Konstantinis*] (Athens: self-published, 2015); for the Thessalonican faction and Jacobson, see AJDC, NY AR 1945-54/4/33/2/387, Greece, General, I.–VII. 1945, "The American Joint Distribution Committee's Program Greece" (1 August 1945).

37. Molho and Nehama, *In Memoriam*, 341.

38. AJDC, IST 1937-49/4/9/IS.217, Greece 1944–1946, "Untitled Typewritten Memorandum" (19 July 1944).

39. AJDC, NY AR 1945-54/4/33/402, Greece, Survivors, 1945–1946, "For Immediate Release First List of 3,300 Greek Jews received by J. D. C." (31 May 1945).

40. AJDC, NY AR 1945-54/4/33/402, Greece, Survivors, 1945–1946, "Letter from Central Location Index, Inc to American Jewish Joint Distribution Community" (24 May 1945); AJDC, NY AR 1945-54/4/33/2/387, Greece, General, I.–VII. 1945, "The American Joint Distribution Committee's Program Greece" (1 August 1945); AJDC, NY AR 1945-54/4/33/402, Greece, Survivors, 1945–1946, "For Immediate Release First list of 3,300 Greek Jews received by J. D. C." (31 May 1945).

41. Kateřina Králová, *Das Vermächtnis der Besatzung: Deutsch-griechische Beziehungen seit 1940* (Cologne: Böhlau, 2016), 77–78. For more testimonies on Chaidari, see Anna Maria Droumpouki, *Mnimia tis Lithis – Ichni tou V' Pagosmiou Polemou stin Ellada ke tin Evropi* [*Monuments of Oblivion: Traces of World War II in Greece and Europe*] (Athens: Polis, 2014), 151–70.

42. Claiming 400 in AJDC, NY AR1945-54/4/76/2/970, Spain, General, 1945, 1948–1954, "With the Compliments of D. de sola Pool" (24 June 1949). Avni, by contrast, indicates it was several dozen of Jews at most; Haim Avni, "Spanish Nationals in Greece and Their Fate During the Holocaust," *Yad Vashem Studies* 8 (1970): 31–68. For Radigales, see Yad Vashem, Collection of the Righteous Among the Nations Department, M.31.2/12740—

216 · NOTES TO CHAPTER ONE

Sebastián de Romero (1882–1970), date of registration: 26 February 2014, at https://righteous.yadvashem.org/.

43. Yvonni Molcho Kapoyano, 41963, VHA, USC Shoah Foundation.

44. For more information on Jews who were citizens of Turkey, Portugal, Italy, and Spain, see Corry Guttstadt, *Turkey, the Jews, and the Holocaust* (Cambridge: Cambridge University Press, 2013); Avraham Milgram, "Portugal, the Consuls, and the Jewish Refugees, 1938–1941," *Yad Vashem Studies* 27 (1999): 123–56; Leon Poliakov and Jacques Sabille, *Jews under the Italian Occupation*, foreword by Justin Godart (Vichy: Éditions du Centre, 1955); Guri Schwarz, *After Mussolini: Jewish Life and Jewish Memories in Post-Fascist Italy* (London: Valentine Mitchell, 2012), 97–107; Avni, "Spanish Nationals in Greece."

45. See Isaac Aron Matarasso, "Greek Jews of Salonika under German Occupation," in Steven B. Bowman, ed., *The Holocaust in Salonika: Eyewitness Accounts*, introduction by Steven Bowman, translation and notes by Isaac Benmayor (New York: Sephardic House, 2002), 153; Mark Mazower, *Salonica, City of Ghosts: Christians, Muslims and Jews, 1430–1950* (London: HarperCollins, 2004), 411.

46. USHMM, RG-11.001M, reel B 1—Abschlussbericht über die Tätigkeit des Sonderkommandos Rosenberg in Griechenland (15 November 1941).

47. Molho and Nehama, *In Memoriam*, 403.

48. Mark Mazower, *Inside Hitler's Greece: The Experience of Occupation, 1941–44* (New Haven: Yale University Press, 2001).

49. Kostis Kornetis, "Expropriating the Space of the Other: Property Spoliations of Thessalonican Jews in the 1940s," in Giorgos Antoniou and A. Dirk Moses, eds., *The Holocaust in Greece* (Cambridge: Cambridge University Press, 2018), 241; Salomon Uziel, "They Encircled and Encompassed Me," in Steven B. Bowman, ed., *The Holocaust in Salonika: Eyewitness Accounts*, trans. with an introduction by Issac Benmayor (New York: Sephardic House, 2002), 243.

50. Pothiti Hantzaroula, *Child Survivors of the Holocaust in Greece. Memory, Testimony and Subjectivity* (Andover: Routledge, 2020), 57–60.

51. Mentes M. Molho, "Asset of Jewish Salonica," in *The Holocaust in Salonika: Eyewitness Accounts*, ed. Steven B. Bowman and Isaac Benmayor (New York: Sephardic House, 2002); Stratos N. Dordanas, "I Yperesia Diachiriseos Israilitikon Periouson (YDIP)" ["The Office for the Disposal of Jewish Property"], in Giorgos Antoniou et al., eds., *To Olokautoma sta Balkania [The Holocaust in the Balkans]* (Thessaloniki: Epikentro, 2011), 332–36. On the contestation of the term "Aryanization," see Constantin Goschler and Philipp Ther, "A History Without Boundaries: The Robbery and Restitution of Jewish Property in Europe," in Martin Dean, Constantin Goschler, and Philipp Ther, eds., *Robbery and Restitution: The Conflict over Jewish Property in Europe* (New York: Berghahn; United States Holocaust Memorial Museum, 2007), 4.

NOTES TO CHAPTER ONE · 217

52. Benveniste, *Die Überlebenden*, 271–74.

53. Maria Kavala, "I ektelesis Evreon sti Thessaloniki sta chronia tis Katochis – Politiki antipinon ke fyletismos" ["The Execution of Jews in Thessaloniki during the Occupation: Retaliation Policy and Tribalism"], in *Evraikes Kinotites anamesa se Anatoli ke Dysi, 15os – 20os eonas: Ikonomia, Kinonia, Politiki, Politismos [Jewish Communities between East and West, the Fifteenth to the Twentieth Century: Economics, Society, Politics, Culture]* (Athens: Isnafi, 2016), 256–62.

54. Andreas Sephiha [*sic*], 48935, VHA, USC Shoah Foundation. See also, Kateřina Králová, "Silenced Memories and Network Dynamics in Holocaust Testimonies: The Matalon Family and Case of Greece," *S: I. M. O. N. Shoah: Intervention. Methods. Documentation. 9*, no. 2 (2022): 51–66.

55. Rozina Asser Pardo, *548 Days with Another Name: Salonika 1943: A Child's Diary, an Adult's Memories of War* (New York: Bloch, 2005), 72–74. For more on this, see the following interviews with the three daughters: Lili Aroych, 44441; Rozina Pardo, 44631; Nteniz Mperacha, 44212, VHA, USC Shoah Foundation.

56. Maria Curtis, 34110, VHA, USC Shoah Foundation.

57. Loykia Antzel, 42070, VHA, USC Shoah Foundation. More on EDES in Vangelis Tzoukas, *O EDES 1941–1945 [The National Republican Greek League, 1941–45]* (Athens: Alexandria, 2017).

58. Stathis N. Kalyvas, "Armed Collaboration in Greece, 1941–1944," *European Review of History: Revue Européenne d'histoire* 15, no. 2 (1 April 2008): 131–32; Králová, *Das Vermächtnis der Besatzung*, 39–41.

59. Loykia Antzel, 42070, VHA, USC Shoah Foundation.

60. Moris Leon, 43190, VHA, USC Shoah Foundation.

61. Piatra Neamţ was called the "Jerusalem of Romania"; see Jean Ancel et al., *Pinkas ha-kehilot: Romanyah [Encyclopedia of Jewish Communities: Romania]* (Jerusalem: Yad Vashem, 1969), 210. Czernowitz was called the Jerusalem of Bukovina; see Daniel Hrenciuc, "Czernowitz: The Jerusalem of Bukovina," *Codrul Cosminului* 18, no. 2 (2012): 361–80. And Sarajevo is called "Little Jerusalem" in Francine Friedman, "Contemporary Responses to the Holocaust in Bosnia and Herzegovina," in John-Paul Himka and Joanna B. Michlic, eds., *Bringing the Dark Past to Light: The Reception of the Holocaust in Postcommunist Europe* (Lincoln: University of Nebraska Press, 2013), 88. For Thessaloniki as the "Jerusalem of the Balkans," see Naar, *Jewish Salonica*, 34.

62. Naar, *Jewish Salonica*, 61–67.

63. Isaac Matarasso, Pauline Maud Matarasso, Robert Matarasso, and François Matarasso, *Talking until Nightfall: Remembering Jewish Salonica, 1941–44* (London: Bloomsbury Continuum, 2020); Uzicl, "They Encircled Me and Encompassed Me," 276.

218 · NOTES TO CHAPTER ONE

64. Rudolf Amariglio [*sic*], 23446, VHA, USC Shoah Foundation.

65. Isaac Aron Matarasso, "And Yet Not All of Them Died," in Bowman, *Holocaust in Salonika*, 123–233.

66. Matsas, *Illusion of Safety*, 48.

67. Bea Lewkowicz, *The Jewish Community of Salonika: History, Memory, Identity* (London: Vallentine Mitchell, 2006), 48; Andreas L. Seficha, *Remembering a Life and a World* (Thessaloniki: Ianos, 2015), 89.

68. See Yad Vashem, Collection of the Righteous Among the Nations Department, M.31.2/4465, Stratos Paraskevaidis, November 16, 1989; M.31.2/9007, Ioannis Iatrou (1897–1978), July 30, 2000; M.31.2/3731, Panayotis Tsirigakis, January 1, 1980, at https://righteous.yadvashem.org/. The romance of those couples, however, makes one wonder by how much the grand title of the Righteous Among the Nations, which the husbands later received, adheres to its definition of truly selfless, impartial help.

69. Naar, *Jewish Salonica*, 209–35; Julia P. Cohen and Sarah A. Stein, "Sephardic Scholarly Worlds: Toward a Novel Geography of Modern Jewish History," *Jewish Quarterly Review* 100, no. 3 (2010): 349–84; Alisa Meyuḥas Ginio, *Between Sepharad and Jerusalem: History, Identity and Memory of the Sephardim* (Leiden: Brill, 2015); Yosef Hayim Yerushalmi, "Response to Rosemary Ruether," in Eva Fleischner, ed., *Auschwitz: Beginning of a New Era? Reflections on the Holocaust* (New York: KTAV, 1977), 103.

70. Molho and Nehama, *In Memoriam*, 335–36.

71. USHMM, RG-45.011, Archives of the Jewish Community of Thessaloniki, I K TH-02701, Chaim, Flor, and David Saltiel, no. 7, in the registration books of the Jewish Community of Thessaloniki (August 1945); Molho and Nehama, *In Memoriam*, 403; concerning the postwar Community, see also Leon A. Nar, "Israilitiki Kinotita Thessalonikis (1945–1950)" ["The Jewish Community of Thessaloniki (1945–1950)"] (master's thesis, Thessaloniki: University of Macedonia, 2017).

72. Fratelis Nahmias [*sic*], 22138, VHA, USC Shoah Foundation.

73. Hans-Joachim Hoppe, "Bulgarien," in Wolfgang Benz, ed., *Dimension des Völkermords: Die Zahl der jüdischen Opfer des Nationalsozialismus* (Munich: Oldenbourg, 1991), 292–93.

74. Hans-Joachim Hoppe, "Bulgarien," 291–95. More recently, for example, Rumyana Marinova-Christidi, "From Salvation to Alya: The Bulgarian Jews and Bulgarian-Israeli Relations (1948–1990)," *Southeast European and Black Sea Studies* 17, no. 2 (2017): 223–44; and especially Nadège Ragaru, *"Et les Juifs bulgares furent sauvés…": une histoire des savoirs sur la Shoah en Bulgarie* (Paris: Sciences Po, 2020).

75. Molho and Nehama, *In Memoriam*, 413.

76. Aleksandros Simcha, *Ta chamena chronia* [*Lost Years*] (Athens: self-published, 2003).

77. Aleksandros [*sic*] Simcha, 39862, VHA, USC Shoah Foundation.

NOTES TO CHAPTER ONE · 219

78. Violetta Hionidou, *Famine and Death in Occupied Greece, 1941–1944* (Cambridge: Cambridge University Press, 2006), 25–26.

79. Interview with Laura Simon (neé Haim) in Woodland Hills, CA, conducted by Kateřina Králová, Woodland Hills, CA (3 January 2016).

80. Kateřina Králová, "From Kavala to California: Sarah Haim and Her Family," in *100 Years of Sephardic Los Angeles*, ed. Sarah Abrevaya Stein and Caroline Luce (Los Angeles: UCLA Leve Center for Jewish Studies, 2020), https://sephardiclosangeles.org/portfolios /from-kavala-to-california/. For more on KKE history, see Nikos Marantzidis, *Under Stalin's Shadow: A Global History of Greek Communism* (Ithaca: Cornell University Press, 2023).

81. Interview with Laura Simon (3 January 2016).

82. Nelli Nachmias (neé Tampach), 40116, VHA, USC Shoah Foundation.

83. Gentille Notrica (neé Koen), 37988, VHA, USC Shoah Foundation.

84. Gentille Notrica (neé Koen), 37988, VHA, USC Shoah Foundation.

85. Molho and Nehama, *In Memoriam*, 83. See also Isaac Kapuano, 1439, Sam Nissim, 1471, and Jacob Coumeri, 47768, VHA, USC Shoah Foundation.

86. Iosif Venturas, *Tanais* (Athens: Gavriilidis, 2001). Interview with Iosif Venturas in Athens, conducted by Kateřina Králová (7 June 2016); Matsas, *Illusion of Safety*, 152–58. See also Adam J. Goldwyn, "An Exile from the Sea with the Desert in His Mouth: A Conversation with Iossif Ventura," *World Literature Today*, January 2016.

87. AJDC, IST 1937-49/4/9/IS.217, Greece 1944–1946, "Untitled Typewritten Memorandum" (19 July 1944).

88. Yad Vashem, Collection of the Righteous Among the Nations Department, M.31.2/3731, Panayotis Tsirigakis, 1 January 1980, https://righteous.yadvashem.org/.

89. "O epilogos mias tragodias: I spira Rekanati-Michailidi klp. Enopion tis Dikeosynis. Anatrichiastike leptomerie tis eglimatikis draseos ton katadoton ton Israiliton Athinon. Pos organothi i exonthosis ton Evreon Kerkyras ke Rodou" ["Epilogue to a Tragedy: The Gang of Rekanati-Michailidis et al. before the Courts. Gruesome Details of the Criminal Actions of the Betrayers of the Athenian Israilites. How the Extermination of the Jews of Corfu and Rhodes Was Organized"], *Evraiki Estia*, 18 July 1947; Molho and Nehama, *In Memoriam*, 380–81. See also Dimitris Kousouris, *Dikes ton dosilogon, 1944–1949: Dikeosyni, synechia tou kratous ke ethniki mnimi* [*The Traitor on Trial, 1944–49: Justice, Continuity of the State and National Memory*] (Athens: Polis, 2014), 548–51.

90. In this vein, some Jewish authors today still refer to the Greek conquest of Ottoman territories, including Jewish Communities in Greece, as "liberation from the Ottoman/Turkish yoke." See Frezis, *O Evraikos typos stin Ellada*, 15. KIS: Kentriko Israilitiko Symvoulio (Central Board of the Jewish [Communities]), Kinotites (Communities) Arta and Volos at https://kis.gr (accessed on 17 October 2018); Paul Isaac Hagouel, "The

220 · NOTES TO CHAPTER ONE

Annihilation of Jewish Greeks in Eastern Macedonia and Thrace during WWII," *eSefard*, https://esefarad.com/?p=52726 (accessed 12 March 2021). Dalven also considers Ioannina in February 1913 to have been "finally liberated." Rae Dalven. *The Jews of Ioannina* (Athens: Lykavittos, 2011).

91. Concerning Katerini, see Maria Vassilikou, "Griechenland," in Sara Berger et al., eds., *Die Verfolgung und Ermordung der europäischen Juden durch das nationalsozialistische Deutschland, 1933–1945*, vol. 14 (Berlin: de Gruyter Oldenbourg, 2017). For more about Veria, see Giorgos Antoniou, "Bystanders, Rescuers, and Collaborators: A Microhistory of Christian-Jewish Relations, 1943–1944," in Giorgos Antoniou and A. Dirk Moses, eds., *The Holocaust in Greece* (Cambridge, UK: Cambridge University Press, 2018), 135–56.

92. Miriam Novitch, *The Passage of the Barbarians: Contribution to the History of the Deportation and Resistance of Greek Jews*, trans. from the French by P. Senior (Hull: Hyperion Books, 1989), 89–94; Matsas, *Illusion of Safety*, 63–64. For the oral testimonies of the sons of Menachem Stroumza, see USHMM, VHA Interview Code: 4137 and 39864, USC Shoah Foundation Institute testimony of Isaac Stroumza and Roympen Stroymsa, respectively. By contrast, the narrative of Veria in Giorgos Liolios, *Skies tis polis: anaparastasi tou diogmou ton Evreon tis Verias* [*Shadows of the City: A Reenactment of the Pogrom against the Jews of Veria*] (Athens: Ekdosis Eurasia, 2008), is structured far more around Greek solidarity with the Jews of Veria. See also Antoniou, "Bystanders, Rescuers, and Collaborators," 135–56.

93. Matsas, *Illusion of Safety*, 62–63; see also Vassilikou, "Griechenland," 75. Matthew Yosafat, 10295, VHA, USC Shoah Foundation. Like Stroumpsa, Matthew never mentions his father's position in the Katerini Community.

94. Matsas, *Illusion of Safety*, 333–400; USHMM, RG-50.030.0403, Oral history interview with Michael Naoum Matsas, conducted by Joan Ringelheim (4 October 1999). See also USHMM, A.N. 2008.253.1, Leon Matsas memoirs.

95. USHMM, RG-50.030.0586, Oral history interview with Ninetta Matsas Feldman, conducted by Joan Ringelheim (14 September 2010). See also her mother's memoir, USHMM, 2008.256.1, Esther Cohen Matsas memoirs.

96. Konstantinis, *I Israilitikes kinotites*, 57–58.

97. AJDC, NY AR 1945-54/4/33/2/387, Greece, General, I.–VII. 1945, "The American Joint Distribution Committee's Program Greece" (1 August 1945); USHMM, RG-50.030.0475, Paulette Nehama (24 June 2003); Interview with Paulette Nehama in Bethesda, MD, conducted by Kateřina Králová (29 July 2015); Rafail Frezis, *I Israilitiki Kinotita Volou* [*The Jewish Community of Volos*] (Volos: Ores, 1994), 180–85.

98. Frezis, *I Israiltiki Kinotita Volou*, 177–79.

99. Rachil Papadrianou (neé Barouch), 46032, VHA, USC Shoah Foundation.

100. Eleftherios M. Ioanidis, *Tekmiria gia tin istoria tis Israilitikis Kinotitos Chalkidos kata tin periodo tis katochis. Apo ta archia tou dimou Chalkideon* [*Documents about the History of the Jewish*

NOTES TO CHAPTER TWO · 221

Community of Chalcis during the Occupation. From the Archives of the Municipality of Chalcis] (Chalcis: Manifesto, 2013), 13–16; Matsas, *Illusion of Safety*, 218–20.

101. The Jewish Museum of Greece Archive, the Database of Greek-Jewish Holocaust Survivors' Testimonies, EME 21, Esdra Moisi [*sic*], b. 1923, Larissa (interviewed in 2007, Greece); Esdra Moissis, 48271, VHA, USC Shoah Foundation. See also his documentation in USHMM, RG-45.009, Personal archives of Esdras Moissis related to the history of the Jewish Community of Larissa in Greece (1931–1970).

102. Deno Seder, *Miracle at Zakynthos: The Only Greek Jewish Community Saved in Its Entirety from Annihilation* (Washington, DC: Philos Press, LLC, 2014). See also Erkanas Tsezanas, 39196, VHA, USC Shoah Foundation.

103. Erkanas Tsezanas, 39196, VHA, USC Shoah Foundation.

104. AJDC, NY AR 1945-54/4/33/389, Greece, Disasters, 1953–1954, "They were to be permitted to stay until their final emigration, while any returnee arriving after this transfer was to be deported from Germany..." (29 September 1953).

105. Stavrianos, "Jews of Greece," 264. Matsas argues that "the Jews of Zakinthos remained free and the Germans left Greece before they could arrest them." See Matsas, *Illusion of Safety*, with additions and corrections from September 2006 at http://www.theopavlidis.com/reprints/matsas_2/IllusionSafetyAddendum.htm. See also Hertsel Matsas, 16634, VHA, USC Shoah Foundation, a survivor from Zakynthos, who made Aliyah illegally from Greece in November 1945.

CHAPTER TWO: DEMOBILIZATION AND ITS AFTERMATH

1. Quoted from Kostas Gazis, ed., *Antartika Tragoudia* [*Partisan Songs*] (Athens: Damianou, 1986), 13.

2. AJDC, NY AR 1945-54/4/33/2/386, Greece, General, VIII.–XII. 1945, "The Jews and the Liberation Struggle" (12 September 1945).

3. Philip Friedman, *Martyrs and Fighters: The Epic of the Warsaw Ghetto* (London: Routledge & Kegan Paul, 1954); Philip Friedman, *Preliminary and Methodological Problems of the Research on the Jewish Catastrophe in the Nazi Period* (Jerusalem: Yad Vashem Remembrance Authority, 1958). A detailed discussion about what constitutes resistance, like those one finds in Hilberg or Bauer, is beyond the scope of this book. See Raul Hilberg, *Perpetrators, Victims, Bystanders: The Jewish Catastrophe, 1933–1945* (New York: Aaron Asher, 1992); Yehuda Bauer, *Rethinking the Holocaust* (New Haven: Yale University Press, 2001).

4. Boaz Cohen, *Israeli Holocaust Research: Birth and Evolution* (London: Routledge, 2017), 208–35.

5. Asher Moissis, *Greek-Jewish Patrimony* (North Charleston, SC: CreateSpace, 2012).

6. Katherine E. Fleming, *Greece: A Jewish History* (Princeton: Princeton University Press,

222 · NOTES TO CHAPTER TWO

2008), 107; Steven B. Bowman, *The Agony of Greek Jews, 1940–1945* (Stanford: Stanford University Press, 2009), 253; Evdoxios Doxiadis, *State, Nationalism, and the Jewish Communities of Modern Greece* (London: Bloomsbury Academic, 2018), 130; Irith Dublon-Knebel, *German Foreign Office Documents on the Holocaust in Greece (1937–1944)* (Tel Aviv: Tel Aviv University, 2007), 20; Rafail Frezis, *I Israilitiki Kinotita Volou* [*The Jewish Community of Volos*] (Volos: Ores, 1994), 227; Photini Constantopoulou and Thanos Veremis, eds., *Documents on the History of the Greek Jews: Records from Historical Archives of the Ministry of Foreign Affairs* (Athens: Kastaniotis Editions, 1998), 34. On Jews under Metaxas, see Katerina Lagos, *The Fourth of August Regime and Greek Jewry, 1936–1941* (Cham: Palgrave Macmillan, 2023).

7. Maria Kavala, "I Thessaloniki sti Germaniki Katochi (1941–1944): Kinonia, Ikonomia, diogmos Evreon" ["Thessaloniki under German occupation, 1941–1944: Society, Economy, and the Persecution of the Jews"] (Voutes-Heraklion: University of Crete, 2009), 305; Rika Benveniste, *Die Überlebenden: Widerstand, Deportation, Rückkehr: Juden aus Thessaloniki in den 1940er Jahren* (Berlin: Edition Romiosini, 2016), 128–29, 271–76..

8. Maria Kavala, "I ektelesis Evreon sti Thessaloniki sta chronia tis Katochis – Politiki antipinon ke fyletismos" ["The Execution of Jews in Thessaloniki during the Occupation: Retaliation Policy and Tribalism"], in *Evraikes Kinotites anamesa se Anatoli ke Dysi, 150s – 200s eonas: Ikonomia, Kinonia, Politiki, Politismos* [*Jewish Communities between East and West, the Fifteenth to the Twentieth Century: Economics, Society, Politics, Culture*] (Athens: Isnafi, 2016), 261. According to one of the KKE cadres, Markos Vafiadis, only 150 Jews in Thessaloniki were members of the Communist Party in 1942. See also Markos Vafiadis, *Apomnimonevmata 1940–1944* [*Memoirs, 1940–1944*], vol. 2 (Athens: Livanis, 1985), 88–89.

9. Evgeny Finkel, *Ordinary Jews: Choice and Survival during the Holocaust* (Princeton, NJ: Princeton University Press, 2018), 162–63.

10. Steven B. Bowman, *Jewish Resistance in Wartime Greece* (London: Vallentine Mitchell, 2006), 7.

11. For more information on the EAM, see Giannis Skalidakis, *I exousia tou EAM sta chronia tis Katochis 1943–1944* [*The Power of the EAM during the Occupation*] (Athens: Asini, 2014). On the strongest anti-Communist resistance organization, the EDES, which nonetheless did not really include Jews in its ranks, see Vangelis Tzoukas, *O EDES 1941–1945* [*The National Republican Greek League, 1941–1945*] (Athens: Alexandria, 2017).

12. According to Matsas's findings in Joseph Matsas, "The Participation of the Greek Jews in the National Resistance, 1940–1944," *Journal of the Hellenic Diaspora* 17, no. 1 (1991), 49–53, it was 650 people. Bowman, on the other hand, claims that "estimates ranging from 1,000 to 2,000 are not necessarily exaggerated." Bowman, *Agony of Greek Jews*, 162.

13. Aleksandra Milićević, "Joining the War: Masculinity, Nationalism and War Participation in the Balkans War of Secession, 1991–1995," *Nationalities Papers* 34, no. 3 (2006): 277.

14. Rae Dalven, *The Jews of Ioannina* (Athens: Lykavittos, 2011), 40.

15. Michael Molho and Joseph Nehama, *In Memoriam: Gewidmet dem Andenken an die jüdischen Opfer der Naziherrschaft in Griechenland* (Essen: Peter Katzung, 1981), 278.

16. André Gerrits, "Antisemitism and Anti-Communism: The Myth of 'Judeo-Communism' in Eastern Europe," *East European Jewish Affairs* 25, no. 1 (1995): 49–72; Paul Benjamin Gordiejew, *Voices of Yugoslav Jewry* (Albany: State University of New York Press, 1999); Ivo Goldstein, "Restoring Jewish Life in Communist Yugoslavia, 1945–1967," *East European Jewish Affairs* 34, no. 1 (2004): 58–71; Ari Kerkkänen, *Yugoslav Jewry: Aspects of Post-World War II and Post-Yugoslav Developments* (Helsinki: Societas Orientalis Fennica, 2001); Albert Koen and Anri Assa, *Saving of the Jews in Bulgaria, 1941–1944*, trans. Ljudmila Dimova (Sofia: Setemvri, 1977); Ĭosif Ilel and Stella T. Ilel-Vatcheva, *The Rescue and Survival of the Bulgarian Jews in World War II and the Jewish Participation in the Wars of Bulgaria: Short Essays* (n.p.: self-published, 2003). For later debates, see also John-Paul Himka and Joanna B. Michlic, *Bringing the Dark Past to Light: The Reception of the Holocaust in Postcommunist Europe* (Lincoln: University of Nebraska Press, 2013).

17. See my pilot study to this chapter, Kateřina Králová, "'Being Traitors': Post-War Greece in the Experience of Jewish Partisans," *Southeast European and Black Sea Studies* 17, no. 2 (2017): 263–80; followed by Eleni Beze, "Being Leftist and Jewish in Greece during the Civil War and Its Aftermath: Constraints and Choices," *Historein* 18, no. 2 (2019), http://dx.doi.org/10.12681/historein.14601.

18. In 1978, *Chronika*, the monthly of the Central Board in Athens, published the article "The Participation of Jews in the Wars of Greece, 1821–1949," prefaced by the words: "The following manuscript was found in the late Joseph Nehama's papers. It discusses the participation of the Jews in the various wars of the Greeks. Anonymous (though perhaps by Nehama), it is printed here on the occasion of the 28th October anniversary [the celebration of the Greeks' declaration of war against Fascist Italy in 1940]. Dimitrios N. Dimitriou, "I symmetochi ton Evreon stin Ethniki Antistasi" ["The Jews' Participation in the National Resistance"], *Chronika* 12, no. 104 (February 1989): 5–9.

19. In 1991, Matsas published a speech he gave at the cultural center of the Jewish Community in Athens on October 2, 1982, and then at the Jewish Community in Thessaloniki two months later. Joseph Matsas, "The Participation of the Greek Jews in the National Resistance, 1940–1944," *Journal of the Hellenic Diaspora* 17, no. 1 (1991): 55.

20. Philip Carabott and Maria Vassilikou, "'New Men vs Old Jews': Greek Jewry in the Wake of the Shoah, 1945–1947," in Giorgos Antoniou and A. Dirk Moses, eds., *The Holocaust in Greece* (Cambridge, UK: Cambridge University Press, 2018), 256.

21. Bowman, *Jewish Resistance in Wartime Greece*; Iasonas Chandrinos, *Synagonistes: To EAM ke i Evrei tis Elladas* [*Comrades-in-Arms: The EAM and the Jews of Greece*] (Athens: Psifydes, 2020); Nikos Tzafleris, "Persecution and Rescue of the Jews of Volos during the Holocaust in Greece 1943–1944," in Dan Michman, ed., *Hiding, Sheltering, and Borrowing Identities:*

224 · NOTES TO CHAPTER TWO

Avenues of Rescue during the Holocaust (Jerusalem: Yad Vashem, 2017), 125–43; Fleming, *Greece*, 113–142; Mark Mazower, *Inside Hitler's Greece: The Experience of Occupation, 1941–44* (New Haven: Yale University Press, 2001), 265–321.

22. Kalyvas, Stathis, and Nikos Marantzidis, "Nees taseis sti meleti tou Emfyliou Polemou" ["New Approaches to Researching the Civil War"], *Ta Nea*, 20 March 2004; Nikos Marantzidis and Giorgos Antoniou, "The Axis Occupation and Civil War: Changing Trends in Greek Historiography, 1941–2002," *Journal of Peace Research* 41, no. 2 (2004): 223–31; Stathis Kalyvas, *The Logic of Violence in Civil War* (New York: Cambridge University Press, 2006); Stathis Kalyvas and Nikos Marantzidis, *Emfylia pathi: 23+2 nees erotisis ke apantisis gia ton Emfylio* [*Civil Passions: 23+2 New Questions and Answers about the Civil War*] (Athens: Metehmio, 2016); Polymeris Voglis and Ioannis Nioutsikos, "The Greek Historiography of the 1940s: A Reassessment," *Südosteuropa* 65, no. 2 (2017), https://doi .org/10.1515/soeu-2017-0020.

23. Tzafleris, "Persecution and Rescue," 142–43.

24. George M. Alexander, "The Demobilization Crisis of November 1944," in John O. Iatrides, ed., *Greece in the 1940s: A Nation in Crisis* (Hanover, NH: University Press of New England, 1981), 157–66.

25. Of the many publications, see Tasoula Vervenioti, "12 October 1944, Liberation Trauma and Memorialization in Greece," *Journal of Modern Greek Studies*, Occasional Papers, no. 2 (2014): 1–12; Tasoula Vervenioti, *Anaparastasis tis Istorias* [*Representations of History*] (Athens: Melissa, 2009); Dimitris Kousouris, "Liberation 1944: Not a Moment. A Time in History," *Journal of Modern Greek Studies*, Occasional Papers, no. 3 (2014); Neni Panourgia, *Dangerous Citizens: The Greek Left and the Terror of the State* (New York: Fordham University Press, 2009); Javier Rodrigo, "Under the Sign of Mars: Violence in European Civil Wars, 1917–1949," *Contemporary European History* 26, no. 3 (2017): 487–506; Mazower, *Inside Hitler's Greece*; Mark Mazower, ed., *After the War Was Over: Reconstructing the Family, Nation, and State in Greece, 1943–1960* (Princeton, NJ: Princeton University Press, 2000); Stratos N. Dordanas and Eleni Paschaloudi, "Enas akirychtos polemos: I 'Eamokratia' sti Thessaloniki" ["An Undeclared War: The 'Eamokratia' in Thessaloniki"], in Polymeris Voglis, Ioanna Papathanasiou, and Tasos Sakellaropoulos, eds., *Dekemvris 1944: To parelthon ke i hrisis tou* [*December 1944: The Past and Its Use*] (Athens: Alexandria, 2017), 173–92.

26. André Gerolymatos, *An International Civil War: Greece 1943–1949* (New Haven: Yale University Press, 2016), 98; Heinz Richter, "The Varkiza Agreement and the Origins of the Civil War," in John O. Iatrides, ed., *Greece in the 1940s: A Nation in Crisis*, preface by A. Lily Macrakis (Hanover, NH: University Press of New England, 1981), 173–75.

27. Panourgia, *Dangerous Citizens*, 69–70; Mazower, *Inside Hitler's Greece*, 368–72. See also Gerolymatos, *International Civil War*, 99–142; or the pioneering John O. Iatrides, *Revolt in Athens: The Greek Communist "Second Round," 1944–1945* (Princeton, NJ: Princeton University Press, 1972).

NOTES TO CHAPTER TWO · 225

28. Interview with Shlomo Cohen [*sic*], 6883, VHA, USC Shoah Foundation.

29. Shlomo Cohen, 6883, VHA, USC Shoah Foundation. See also Salvator Mpakolas, 41842, VHA, USC Shoah Foundation; and "List of Members of the Hachsharaoth 'Patissia' and 'Frankoklissia' on the 15.1.46," in Registration of Liberated Former Persecutees at Various Locations 3.1.1.3/0015_78779800 1, ITS Digital Archive, USHMM. Karina Lampsa and Iakov Sibi, *I zoi ap' tin archi: i metanasteusi ton Ellinon Evreon stin Palestini (1945–1948)* [*Life from the Beginning: The Emigration of Greek Jews to Palestine, 1945–1948*] (Athens: Alexandria, 2010), 367–77.

30. Karina Lampsa and Iakov Sibi, *I diasosi: i siopi tou kosmou, i antistasi sta geto ke ta stratopeda, i Ellines Evrei sta chronia tis Katochis* [*The Rescue: The Silence of the People, the Resistance in the Ghettos and the Camps, and the Greek Jews during the Occupation*] (Athens: Ekdosis Kapon, 2012), 275.

31. Nelli Nachmias (neé Tampach), 40116, VHA, USC Shoah Foundation.

32. Andreas L. Seficha, *Remembering a Life and a World* (Thessaloniki: Ianos, 2015), 83; Andreas Sephiha [*sic*], 48935, VHA, USC Shoah Foundation.

33. Richard Clogg, *Parties and Elections in Greece: The Search for Legitimacy* (Durham, NC: Duke University Press, 1987), 13–14; Flora Tsigala, "UNRRA's Relief Efforts in Post-War Greece: Political Impartiality versus Military Exigencies," in *Bearing Gifts to Greeks: Humanitarian Aid to Greece in the 1940s*, ed. Richard Clogg (Basingstoke: Palgrave Macmillan, 2008), 109. TNA, FO 371/48295, R 2214/52/19—Reports of the Anglo-American Military Headquarters for relief and rehabilitation in Greece (30 January 1945).

34. AJDC, NY AR 1945-54/4/33/2/387, Greece, General, I.–VII. 1945, "Letter from Committee of Supply and Relief to Mr. Harry Greenstein" (2 February 1945); TNA, FO 371/48295, R 2214/52/19—Reports of the Anglo-American Military Headquarters for relief and rehabilitation in Greece (30 January 1945). See also Kateřina Králová, *Das Vermächtnis der Besatzung: deutsch-griechische Beziehungen seit 1940* (Cologne: Böhlau, 2016).

35. AJDC, NY AR 1945-54/4/33/2/387, Greece, General, I.–VII. 1945, "Letter from the President to the Honorary Jewish Agency" (29 January 1945).

36. TNA, FO 371/48295, R 2214/52/19—Allied Force Headquarters Reports on relief and rehabilitation in Greece (30 January 1945); AJDC, NY AR 1945-54/4/33/2/386, Greece, General, VIII.–XII. 1945, "Letter from Israel G. Jacobson to Mr. Leavitt" (17 December 1945); Tsigala, "UNRRA's Relief Efforts," 190–91.

37. AJDC, NY AR 1945-54/4/33/2/386, Greece, General, VIII.–XII. 1945, "Letter from Morris Laub to Dr. J. Schwartz, Re: Greece," (23 August 1945).

38. AJDC, NY AR 1945-54/4/33/5/399, Greece, Medical, 1945–1953, "Supplementary Medical and Public Health Survey AJDC Greece" (28 September 1948); NY AR 1945-54/4/33/2/386, Greece, General, VIII.–XII. 1945, "Project No. 1" (26 October 1945); NY AR 1945-54/4/33/2/387, Greece, General, I.–VII. 1945, "Letter from the American Joint

226 · NOTES TO CHAPTER TWO

Distribution Committee, Rome, to the American Joint Distribution Committee, New York [and] Lisbon, Subject: Memorandum on the Present Situation of Jewish Communities in Greece" (14 January 1945). See also Avinoam Patt, Atina Grossmann, Linda G. Levi, and Maud S. Mandel, eds., *The JDC at 100: A Century of Humanitarianism* (Detroit: Wayne State University Press, 2019).

39. For more about Varkiza Agreement, see Heinz A. Richter, *British Intervention in Greece: From Varkiza to Civil War, February 1945 to August 1946* (London: Merlin, 1985), 39.

40. Moise Eskaloni, 28007, VHA, USC Shoah Foundation. Dick Benveniste, a partisan, is not to be confused with Rika Benveniste, a respected Greek historian. Nevertheless, they are relatives, and Rika insists that part of her desire to do research is to understand her family history. See Rika Benveniste, *Auti pou epezisan: Antistasi, ektopisi, epistrophi: Thessalonikis Evrei sti dekaetia tou 1940 [Those Who Survived: Resistance, Deportation, Return: The Jews of Thessaloniki in the 1940s]* (Athens: Polis, 2014), 363.

41. Raphail Sampetai, 44379, VHA, USC Shoah Foundation.

42. Leften Stavros Stavrianos, "The Jews of Greece," *Journal of Central European Affairs* 8, no. 3 (1948): 263–67; Lampsa and Sibi, *I diasosi*, 289–96; Moissis, *Greek-Jewish Patrimony*, 70–71.

43. AJDC, NY AR 1945-54/4/33/402, Greece, Survivors, 1945–1946, "Letter from Central Location Index, Inc, to American Jewish Joint Distribution Com" (24 May 1945). See also Moissis, *Greek-Jewish Patrimony*, 70–71; Iasonas Chandrinos, *Synagonistis: Ellines Evrei stin Ethniki Antistasi [Synagonistis: Greek Jews in the National Resistance]* (Athens: Evraiko Mousio Ellados, 2013), 6; Dimitriou, "I symmetochi ton Evreon stin Ethniki Antistasi," 6.

44. Rafail Frezis, *I Israilitiki Kinotita Volou [The Jewish Community of Volos]* (Volos: Ores, 1994), 32–36; Devin E. Naar, *Jewish Salonica: Between the Ottoman Empire and Modern Greece* (Stanford, CA: Stanford University Press, 2016), 85.

45. Quoted in Stavrianos, "Jews of Greece," 266–67. Stavrianos adds that the letter was published on 6 January 1945 in the EAM newspaper *Anagennisis [Rebirth]* and reprinted in English in *The Nation* on 28 May 1945.

46. AJDC, IST 1937-49/4/9/IS.217, Greece 1944–1946, "Letter from Reuben B. Resnik to Mr. Robert Pilpel" (19 July 1944); NY AR 1945-54/4/33/2/386, Greece, General, VIII.–XII. 1945, "Letter from Israel G. Jacobson to Moses A. Leavitt, Subject: UNRRA Displaced Persons Division" (18 November 1945).

47. AJDC, NY AR 1945-54/4/33/2/387, Greece, General, I.–VII. 1945, Letter from the American Joint Distribution Committee, Rome, to the American Joint Distribution Committee, New York [and] Lisbon, "Memorandum on the Present Situation of Jewish Communities in Greece" (14 January 1945).

48. Iatrides, *Revolt in Athens*, 22–27. For Jewish resistance fighters who died in combat, see Chandrinos, *Synagonistis*, 22–27.

NOTES TO CHAPTER TWO · 227

49. AJDC, IST 1937-49/4/9/IS.217, Greece 1944–1946, "Untitled Typewritten Memorandum [Memorandum: The Rescue of Jews Remaining in Greece]" (19 July 1944).

50. Yad Vashem, Collection of the Righteous Among the Nations Department, M.31.2/5643, Dimosthenis Pouris, 11 March 1993; M.31.2/5643, Princess Alice (1885–1969), 11 March 1993, at https://righteous.yadvashem.org/.

51. AJDC, NY AR 1945-54/1/1/5/2295, General, 1945–1946, "J. D. C. Key Personnel Overseas" (10 December 1946); NY AR 1965-74/4/25/100, Greece: Loan Kassas, 1970–1974, "Letter to Kohane" (10 April 1974); G 1945-54/4/9/11/GR.64, Greece: Various 1948–1952, "Memorandum from Daniel Lack, Re: Visit of Mr. Alfred Cohen" (1 December 1973); USHMM, RG-50.968.0032—Oral history interview with Gaynor I. Jacobson, conducted by Tad Szulc (1988).

52. *Chronika* 113 (December 1990): 5–7.

53. Bowman, *Agony of Greek Jews*, 42; Gerolymatos, *International Civil War*, 58. See also Gavriil Gavriilidis, 41612, VHA, USC Shoah Foundation; David Frances, 7792, VHA, USC Shoah Foundation. See also Yitzchak Kerem, "The Greek Government-in-Exile and the Rescue of Jews from Greece," in Jan Láníček and James Jordan, eds., *Governments-in-Exile and the Jews during the Second World War* (London: Vallentine Mitchell, 2012), 189–212.

54. Centropa, Database of Jewish Memory, Mico [*sic*] Alvo, interviewed by Paris Papamichos Chronakis, November 2005, http://www.centropa.org/biography/mico-alvo (accessed 20 November 2018). Mico [*sic*] Alvo, 12990, and Daniel Alvo, 21276, VHA, USC Shoah Foundation.

55. Edmund C. W. Myers, *Greek Entanglement* (Gloucester: Sutton, 1985), 243.

56. AJDC, IST 1937-49/2/2/5/ IS.96, "Jewish Agency Accounts 1943–1945" (November 1943–December 1945); Lampsa and Sibi, *I diasosi*, 312–15; Tuvia Friling, "Between Friendly and Hostiel Neutrality: Turkey and the Jews during World War II," in Minna Rozen, ed., *The Last Ottoman Century and Beyond: The Jews in Turkey and the Balkans, 1808–1945* (Tel Aviv: TAU Press, 2002), 309–406.

57. Mico [*sic*] Alvo, Centropa. See also Mico [*sic*] Alvo, 12990, Daniel Alvo, 21276, and David Konis, 731, VHA, USC Shoah Foundation.

58. David Konis, 731, VHA, USC Shoah Foundation.

59. Tzakos Aroych [*sic*], 39871, VHA, USC Shoah Foundation.

60. Solomon Saltiel, 39393, VHA, USC Shoah Foundation; USHMM, Permanent Collection, 2003.144.1, Levy-Saltiel family papers; USHMM, RG-45.011, Archives of the Jewish Community of Thessaloniki, I K TH-02707, Solomon Saltiel, no. 1028, in the survivors register at the Jewish Community of Thessaloniki (October 1945).

61. Hagen Fleischer, *The "Anomalies" in the Greek Middle East Forces: 1941–1944* (Indianapolis: Hellenic American Society, 1978), 5–36.

228 · NOTES TO CHAPTER TWO

62. Close and Veremis, "The Military Struggle, 1945–9," in David H. Close, ed., *The Greek Civil War: Studies of Polarization* (London: Routledge, 1993), 97–128; Panourgia, *Dangerous Citizens*, 62; Leften Stavros Stavrianos, "The Mutiny in the Greek Armed Forces, April 1944." *The American Slavic and East European Review* 9, no. 4 (December 1950): 302–11; Gerolymatos, *International Civil War*, 90; Haris Vlavianos, *Greece, 1941–49: From Resistance to Civil War: The Strategy of the Greek Communist Party* (New York: St. Martin's Press, 1992), 39. See also John Sakkas, "Greece and the British Factor," in J. Sakkas, *Britain and the Greek Civil War: British Imperialism, Public Opinion and the Coming of the Cold War* (Berlin: Franz Philipp Rutzen, 2013), 17–27.

63. Gavriil Gavriilidis, 41612, VHA, USC Shoah Foundation.

64. USHMM, RG-45.011, Archives of the Jewish Community of Thessaloniki, I K TH-02703, Mois Kamchi, no. 235, Samouil Beza, no. 240, Albertos and Samouil Nissim, no. 265, in the survivors register at the Jewish Community of Thessaloniki (August 1945).

65. Mico [*sic*] Alvo, Centropa.

66. The gravestone of Edgar Allalouf, the Jewish cemetery in Athens, visited by the author on 7 June 2016.

67. Benveniste, *Auti pou epezisan*, 44. USHMM, RG-45.011, Archives of the Jewish Community of Thessaloniki, I K TH-02703, the survivors register at the Jewish Community of Thessaloniki (August 1945).

68. Bowman, *Jewish Resistance*, 54–60.

69. Benveniste, *Auti pou epezisan*, 44–46.

70. Benveniste, *Auti pou epezisan*, 363; Dordanas and Paschaloudi, "Enas akirychtos polemos," 173–92.

71. Benvenisste, *Auti pou epezisan*, 103.

72. Benveniste, 110.

73. TNA, GFM 33/2518—Behandlung der Judenfrage im Ausland, Griechenland (18 August 1942).

74. Yad Vashem, Testimony of Yitzhak Moshe (03/4542), interviewed by Yitzhak Alperowitch, Tel Aviv, April 1988; for more about Isaac Moissis and his comrade in arms, see Bowman, *Jewish Resistance*, 30. Bowman built his research on the resistance experience and the personal accounts of Moissis.

75. Rika Benveniste states that the number of Greek collaborators leaving together with the Germans was as high as twelve thousand. Benveniste, *Die Überlebenden*, 364, n. 119.

76. Stratos N. Dordanas, *Ellines enantion Ellinon: o kosmos ton Tagmaton asphalias stin katochiki Thessaloniki 1941–1944* [*Greeks against Greeks: The World of the Security Battalions in Occupied Thessaloniki, 1941–1944*] (Athens: Epikentro, 2006), 498–514.

NOTES TO CHAPTER TWO · 229

77. Matsas, "Participation of the Greek Jews," 273.

78. See Yad Vashem, Transports to Extinction, Ioannina: Shoah Deportation Database at https://collections.yadvashem.org/en/deportations; see also the Jewish Museum of Greece Archive, the Database of Greek-Jewish Holocaust Survivors' Testimonies, EME 47, Avraam Svolis, born in Ioannina, in 1923 (interviewed in Greece, in 2007).

79. Leon Idas-Gabrielides [*sic*], 22884, VHA, USC Shoah Foundation.

80. Loring M. Danforth and Riki Van Boeschoten, *Children of the Greek Civil War: Refugees and the Politics of Memory* (Chicago: University of Chicago Press, 2011), 37–38. On KKE, see Nikos Marantzidis, *Under Stalin's Shadow: A Global History of Greek Communism* (Ithaca: Cornell University Press, 2023).

81. Richard Clogg, *Greece, 1940–1949: Occupation, Resistance, Civil War. A Documentary History* (Basingstoke, UK: Palgrave Macmillan, 2002), 188.

82. Leon Idas-Gabrielides [*sic*], 22884, VHA, USC Shoah Foundation; AJDC, NY AR 194554/4/33/4/391, Greece, Emigration, 1945–1954, "Incoming Cable from Communaute Israelite to Jointdisco New York" (28 February 1951); Jacques Kelly, "Leon S. Idas," *Baltimore Sun*, 22 April 2013, www.baltimoresun.com.

83. EME 47, Avraam Svolis.

84. Matsas, "Participation of the Greek Jews," 316.

85. Tasoula Vervenioti, *Diplo Vivlio; I afigisi tis Stamatias Mparmpatsi – I istoriki anagnosi* [*Double Book: The Narrative of Stamatia Barbatsi. A Historical Reading*] (Athens: Koykkida, 2017). For more on women in the EAM, see Janet Hart, *New Voices in the Nation: Women and the Greek Resistance, 1941–1964* (Ithaca: Cornell University Press, 2018).

86. USHMM, RG-45.011, Archives of the Jewish Community of Thessaloniki, I K TH-02702, the Carasso Family, no. 187, in the survivors register at the Jewish Community of Thessaloniki (24 August 1945).

87. USHMMC, RG-45.011, Archives of the Jewish Community of Thessaloniki, I K TH-02702, the Carasso Family, no. 187, in the survivors register at the Jewish Community of Thessaloniki (24 August 1945); Bowman, *Agony of Greek Jews*, 166, 171, 220; Yad Vashem, Collection of the Righteous Among the Nations Department, M.31.2/4465, Dimitrios Zannas (16 November 1989), at https://righteous.yadvashem.org/.

88. Benveniste, *Auti pou epezisan*, 101. Also see, USHMM, RG-45.011, Archives of the Jewish Community of Thessaloniki, I K TH-02701, Matalon Leon and Fanny, no. 91, in the survivors register of the Jewish Community of Thessaloniki (22 August 1945); Yad Vashem, Collection of the Righteous Among the Nations Department, M.31.2/4465, Dimitrios Zannas (16 November 1989), at https://righteous.yadvashem.org/; the National Archives at Seattle (Seattle, Washington), RG 21 United States District Courts, Volume: Petitions for Naturalization—P. N. 50759, Juda Matalon and P. N. 50758, Fanny Gracia Matalon

230 · NOTES TO CHAPTER TWO

(2 July 1957); Fanny Gracia (Florentin) Matalon's obituary in *Seattle Times*, 13 June 2010, www.legacy.com/obituaries/seattletimes.

89. Bouena [*sic*] Garfinkle (neé Sarfati), 54525, and Rozita Arditti (neé Koen), 47848, VHA, USC Shoah Foundation; Database of Greek-Jewish Holocaust Survivors' Testimonies, EME 55, Elli Siakki-Decastro (interviewed in Greece, in 2005), and EME 50, Sara Forti (neé Yesoua) (interviewed in Israel, in 2010).

90. See Tasoula Vervenioti, *I Gyneka tis Antistasis. I isodos ton gynekon stin politiki* [*The Resistance Woman: Women's Entry into Politics*] (Athens: Odysseas, 1994); Hart, *New Voices*.

91. For Bouena Sarfati, see Lampsa and Sibi, *I diasosi*, 383–84; Renée Levine Melammed, "The Memoirs of a Partisan from Salonika," *Nashim: A Journal of Jewish Women's Studies & Gender Issues* no. 7 (2004): 151–73. For Sara Yesoua, see EME 50, Sara Forti (neé Yesoua); and Chandrinos, *Synagonistis*, 20.

92. Dora Bourla-Handeli, Interview mog088, 17 November 2017, Interview-Archiv "Erinnerungen an die Okkupation in Griechenland," archive.occupation-memories.org. See also the accounts of her brother, Moise Bourla, 9368, VHA, USC Shoah Foundation; Moshe [*sic*] Bourla, Centropa; Moisis Bourlas, *Ellinas, Evreos ke Aristeros* [*Greek, Jew, and Leftist*] (Skopelos: Nisides, 2000), 79–80.

93. Dora Bourla-Handeli, Interview mog088, 17 November 2017, Interview-Archiv "Erinnerungen an die Okkupation in Griechenland," archive.occupation-memories.org.

94. Dora Bourla-Handeli, Interview mog088, 17 November 2017.

95. Allegra Skifti (neé Felous), two interviews: one from 21 June 1995 (three ninety-minute cassettes), the other from 20 November 1995 (two ninety-minute cassettes) in Athens, conducted by Tasoula Vervenioti, 1995. Skifti is the name she adopted later in life; for historical accuracy, I use her name after her first marriage.

96. Giorgos Petropoulos, "To 70 Synedrio tou KKE" ["The 7th Congress of the Greek Communist Party"], *Rizospastis*, 9 January 2005.

97. USHMM, RG-50.968.0032—Oral history interview with Gaynor I. Jacobson, conducted by Tad Szulc (1988).

98. Concerning postwar violence in the two political camps, see Mark Mazower, "Three Forms of Political Justice: Greece, 1944–1945," in Mazower, *After the War*, 3–12; Stathis N. Kalyvas, "Red Terror: Leftist Violence during the Occupation," in Mazower, *After the War*, 142–83. For state-organized persecution, see Polymeris Voglis, *Becoming a Subject: Political Prisoners in the Greek Civil War* (New York: Berghahn, 2002).

99. Moisis Sakkis, "Saranta peripou chronia apo tote" ["Almost Forty Years On"], *Chronika* 9, no. 86 (April 1986): 13; "Greek Military Court Condemns Two Jews on Charges of Being in Contact with Rebel Forces," *Jewish Telegraphic Agency*, 1 August 1949; "Two More Greek Jews Given Life Terms by Military Court for Contact with Rebels," *Jewish Telegraphic*

NOTES TO CHAPTER TWO · 231

Agency, 2 August 1949. For the general framework of postwar justice in Greece, see Voglis, *Becoming a Subject*; and also Gabriella Etmektsoglu, "Collaborators and Partisans on Trial: Political Justice in Postwar Greece," in Claudia Kuretsidis-Haider and Winfried R Garscha, eds., *Keine "Abrechnung": NS-Verbrechen, Justiz und Gesellschaft in Europa nach 1945* (Leipzig: Akademische Verlagsanstalt, 1998), 231–57.

100. USHMM, RG-50.030.0472, Oral history interview with Isaac Nehama, conducted by Joan Ringelheim (22 October 2002).

101. For Kolonomos's experience, see Jamila Andjela Kolonomos, *Monastir without Jews: Recollections of a Jewish Partisan in Macedonia* (New York: Foundation for the Advancement of Sephardic Studies and Culture, 2008). Also, Zamila Sadikario, 47542, VHA, USC Shoah Foundation. For Nehama, see the description in the USHMM, photograph number 92903, Portrait of Solomon Nehama at http://collections.ushmm.org/search/ (accessed 10 November 2018). For more information on Nehama, see Solomon Nehama Family of Monastir at www.cassorla.net/ (accessed 3 January 2019); and USHMM, RG-50.030.0472, an oral history interview with Isaac Nehama, conducted by Joan Ringelheim (22 October 2002); USHMM, RG-50.030.0475, Oral history interview with Paulette Nehama, conducted by Margaret West (24 June 2003).

102. USHMM, RG-50.030.0472, Isaac Nehama (22 October 2002). For transports to Auschwitz, see Danuta Czech, *The Auschwitz Chronicle, 1939–1945* (New York: Henry Holt, 1990), 5–37. See also Hagen Fleischer, "Griechenland," in *Dimension des Völkermords: Die Zahl der jüdischen Opfer des Nationalsozialismus*, ed. Wolfgang Benz (Munich: Oldenbourg, 1991), 273.

103. See the work by the former ELAS commander-in-chief, Stephanos G. Saraphis, *ELAS: Greek Resistance Army* (London: Merlin, 1980), 156, 166–17.

104. Moise Eskaloni, 28007, VHA, USC Shoah Foundation.

105. USHMM, RG-50.030.0472, Isaac Nehama (22 October 2002).

106. USHMM, RG-50.030.0472. Gestapo headquarters, which became notorious for the torture used during interrogations, were at 6 Merlin St., Athens. This gruesome period was commemorated in 1983 with a memorial to its victims, which was erected at the entrance to the building. For a discussion of the Gestapo headquarters in Athens, see Richter, *British Intervention in Greece*, 159; and Anna Maria Droumpouki, *Mnimia tis Lithis – Ichni tou V' Pagosmiou Polemou stin Ellada ke tin Evropi* [*Monuments of Oblivion: Traces of World War II in Greece and Europe*] (Athens: Polis, 2014), 173–76.

107. AJDC, NY AR 1945-54/4/33/2/386, Greece, General, VIII.–XII. 1945, "The Jews and the Liberation Struggle" (12 September 1945).

108. USHMM, RG-50.030.0472, Isaac Nehama (22 October 2002).

109. Another inmate in Goudi and later in El-Daba was Barouch Shiby, who, in 1959,

232 · NOTES TO CHAPTER TWO

became the president of the Jewish Community in Thessaloniki. In his interview with Miriam Novitch, he mentioned that the internment lasted three months, and he did not get back to Athens until April 1945. Miriam Novitch, *The Passage of the Barbarians: Contribution to the History of the Deportation and Resistance of Greek Jews* (Hull: Hyperion Books, 1989), 49–55.

110. USHMM, RG-50.030.0472, Isaac Nehama (22 October 2002). See also Rafail Filosof, 48557, VHA, USC Shoah Foundation; EME 47, Avraam Svolis; EME 28, Louis Koen, born in Xanthi, 1912 (interviewed in Greece, in 2006); EME 33, Mois Giousouroum, born Athens in 1920 (interviewed in Greece, in 2010); Panourgia, *Dangerous Citizens*, 70; Neni Panourgia and George Marcus, eds., *Ethnographica Moralia: Experiments in Interpretive Anthropology* (New York: Fordham University Press, 2008), 246.

111. Gentile Notrica (née Koen),, 37988, VHA, USC Shoah Foundation.

112. EME 28, Louis Koen.

113. David Brudo [*sic*], 4466, VHA, USC Shoah Foundation; and EME 20, David Broudo, born in Thessaloniki in 1924 (interviewed in Israel in 2019); Dimitriou, "I symmetochi ton Evreon stin Ethniki Antistasi," 1–3.

114. Moise Bourla [*sic*], 9368, VHA, USC Shoah Foundation; Bourlas, *Ellinas, Evreos ke Aristeros*, 79–80.

115. USHMM, RG-45.011, Archives of the Jewish Community of Thessaloniki, I K TH-02701, the Mpourlas Family, no. 80, in the survivors register of the Jewish Community of Thessaloniki (22 August 1945).

116. Moise Bourla [*sic*], 9368, VHA, USC Shoah Foundation; Bourlas, *Ellinas, Evreos ke Aristeros*, 90–109. For the "detention" of Jews on Greek islands, see USHMM, RG-45.010, KIS 247—Fakelos kratoumenon [Files of the detainees]; and RG-45.01, KIS 240—Allilografia me kratoumenous [Correspondence of the detainees] (1948–1953); Moisis Sakkis, "Saranta peripou chronia apo tote" ["Almost Forty Years On"], *Chronika* 9, no. 86 (April 1986): 13.

117. USHMM, RG-68.045—Jewish Prisoners in Greece (13 June 1951); Amikam Nachmani, *Israel, Turkey, and Greece: Uneasy Relations in the East Mediterranean* (London: F. Cass, 1987), 88; Králová, "'Being Traitors,'" 272.

118. Bourlas, *Ellinas, Evreos ke Aristeros*. The Jewish Partisan Education Foundation features an article on David Broudo, where it is stated that he wrote an article entitled "Saloniki Memories" about his experiences in the war, but I have been unable to find this. Recently, a hidden manuscript by a Jewish partisan was discovered and published in Greece. See Samouil Mizan, *Itan pio poly to ksipnima tou anthropou. I prosopiki martyria tou Ellinoevreou Samouil Mizan apo to Antartiko ke tin Katochi* [*It Was More the Awakening of Man: The Personal Account of the Greek Jew Samuel Mizan on the Resistance during the Occupation*] (Athens: Diethnes Vima, 2018).

NOTES TO CHAPTER THREE · 233

119. Philip Mendes, *Jews and the Left: The Rise and Fall of a Political Alliance* (London: Palgrave Macmillan, 2014), 219–34.

120. AJDC, NY AR 1945-54/4/33/2/384, Greece, General, 1949–1954, "Letter from Herbert Katzki to AJDC New York, Re: Report on Greece" (23 October 1950).

121. AJDC, NY AR 1945-54/4/33/2/387, Greece, General, I.–VII. 1945, "Letter from the American Joint Distribution Committee, Rome, to the American Joint Distribution Committee, New York [and] Lisbon, Subject: Memorandum on the Present Situation of Jewish Communities in Greece" (14 January 1945).

122. USHMM, RG-50.030.0404, Oral history interview with Marguerite Glicksman, conducted by Joan Ringelheim (17 December 1999).

123. Recently, some historians have introduced the resistance as a topic strictly in the context of Jewish history. See Bowman, *Jewish Resistance in Wartime Greece*; Chandrinos, *Synagonistis*; Benveniste, *Auti pou epezisan*. In his latest book, Chandrinos has turned his attention to an ideological framing of Jewish resistance. Chandrinos, *Synagonistes* (2020).

124. Voglis and Nioutsikos, "Greek Historiography of the 1940s"; Panourgia, *Dangerous Citizens*; Katherine Stefatos, "Engendering the Nation: Women, State Oppression and Political Violence in Post-war Greece (1946–1974)" (PhD diss., Goldsmiths, University of London, 2012).

125. The sole exception to this is Bowman mentioning Mico [*sic*] Alvo. See Bowman, *Agony of Greek Jews*, 153, 176.

126. Constantopoulou and Veremis, *Documents on the History*, 17.

127. Moris Leon, 43190, VHA, USC Shoah Foundation.

CHAPTER THREE: RETURNING FROM THE CAMPS

1. Quoted from Moshé Bechar, "You Will Have to Look for Me on Every Corner...," trans. Anna Crowe, in Jean Boase-Beier and Marian de Voogh, eds., *Poetry of the Holocaust: An Anthology* (Todmorden, UK: Arc Publications, 2019), 180.

2. For details of the evacuation of Auschwitz, see Danuta Czech, *Auschwitz Chronicle, 1939–1945* (New York: Henry Holt, 1990), 782–805. For Batis's trajectories, see "Batis, Leon," 11 February 1949, in the Repository of T/D Cases, 6.3.3.2/14124453#01, ITS Digital Archive, USHMM.

3. Quoted from Isaac Aron Matarasso, "And Yet Not All of Them Died," in *The Holocaust in Salonika: Eyewitness Accounts*, ed. Steven B. Bowman (New York: Sephardic House, 2002), 180.

4. Interview with Astro-Beki Hatzi (neé Batis), 44596, VHA, USC Shoah Foundation; "Ta Hitlerika Krematoria" ["Hitler's Crematoria"], *Eleftheria*, April 6, 1945.

234 · NOTES TO CHAPTER THREE

5. The VHA alone has more than twenty interviews with Jews who recall Batis's story. See 47723, 44441, 44430, 47852, 40860, 44595, 43033, 38940, 42651, 45321, 43190, 41424, 48018, 45163, 38380, 35270, 37303, 52592, 45308, 41854, including the interview with Batis's daughter, Astro-Beki Hatzi, 44596, VHA, USC Shoah Foundation.

6. David Bankier, introduction to *The Jews Are Coming Back: The Return of the Jews to Their Countries of Origin after WW II*, ed. David Bankier (New York: Berghahn, 2005), vii–xi; Eva Kolinsky, *After the Holocaust: Jewish Survivors in Germany after 1945* (London: Pimlico, 2004); Laura Hammond, "Examining the Discourse of Repatriation: Towards a More Proactive Theory of Return Migration," in Richard Black and Khalid Koser, eds., *The End of the Refugee Cycle? Refugee Repatriation and Reconstruction* (New York: Berghahn, 1999), 230.

7. Whereas Bell Mazur, a JDC and UNRRA representative, when depicting the desperate situation in Thessaloniki, provided the number of 700 in her letter of 20 March 1945, table 3.1 (using data from the United States Mission in Athens, 2 April 1945) gives the number of 800, estimating that another 1,500 Thessalonican Jews in Athens were considering the possibility of returning. See AJDC, NY AR 1945-54/4/33/2/387, Greece, General, I.–VII. 1945, "Letter from Louis H. Sobel to Dr. Isaac Alcalay" (18 April 1945).

8. AJDC, NY AR 1945-54/4/33/2/386-387, Greece, General, I.–VII., VIII.–XII. 1945, "Letter from Florence Hodel to Mr. Leavitt" (6 April 1945) and "Letter from Morris Laub to Dr. J. Schwartz, Re: Greece" (23 August 1945) and KIS reports in USHMM, RG 45.011, KIS 0096 (9 April 1946) and KIS 0214 (18 August 1967).

9. Concerning exchange Jews, see Eberhard Kolb, *Bergen-Belsen: Geschichte des "Aufenthaltslagers" 1943–1945*, vol. 6 of *Geschichte des Holocaust* (1962; repr., Berlin: Lit, 2011), 44–62. For more on the liberation of Bergen-Belsen, see Ben Shephard, *After Daybreak: The Liberation of Belsen, 1945* (London: Jonathan Cape, 2005). On concentration camps in general, see David Cesarani et al., eds., *Belsen in History and Memory* (1997; repr., Hoboken, NJ: Taylor & Francis, 2013), 583–764; or Nikolaus Wachsmann, *KL: A History of the Nazi Concentration Camps* (London: Little, Brown, 2016).

10. PA AA, B81/353—Deutsch-griechische Wiedergutmachungsverhandlungen (2 February 1960).

11. TNA, FO 371/48295, R 2214/52/19—Allied Force Headquarters Report No. 11 (6–12 January 1945).

12. AJDC, NY AR 1945-54/4/33/2/386, Greece, General, VIII.–XII. 1945, "Letter from Israel G. Jacobson to Mr. Barger" (7 August 1945).

13. AJDC, NY AR 1945-54/4/33/2/386, Greece, General, VIII.–XII. 1945, "Letter from Israel G. Jacobson to Mr. Leavitt" (17 December 1945).

14. TNA, FO 371/48295, R 2214/52/19—Allied Force Headquarters Report No. 4 (18–24 November 1944). According to the International Committee of the Red Cross estimates, at least 2.5 million people in Greece were suffering from malaria in 1944. See Katerina

NOTES TO CHAPTER THREE · 235

Gardikas, "Relief Work and Malaria in Greece, 1943–1947," *Journal of Contemporary History* 43, no. 3 (2008): 497.

15. Concerning Varvaressos and his economic reforms, see Athanasios Lykogiannis, *Britain and the Greek Economic Crisis, 1944–1947: From Liberation to the Truman Doctrine* (Columbia, MO: University of Missouri Press, 2002), 112–39. Concerning the plight of the Holocaust survivors, see AJDC, NY AR 1945-54/4/33/2/387, Greece, General, I.–VII. 1945, "The American Joint Distribution Committee's Program Greece" (1 August 1945).

16. AJDC, NY AR 1945-54/4/33/2/386, Greece, General, VIII.–XII. 1945, "Letter from D. Bitran and L. Allalouf to Central Committee American Joint Distribution Committee New York" (17 November 1945).

17. AJDC, NY AR 1945-54/4/33/2/387, Greece, General, I.–VII. 1945, "The American Joint Distribution Committee's Program Greece" (1 August 1945).

18. Quoted from Matarasso, "And Yet Not All of Them Died," 178.

19. Dan Stone, *Concentration Camps: A Short History* (Oxford: Oxford University Press, 2017), 6–8; see also David Cesarani, *Final Solution: The Fate of the Jews 1933–49* (London: Pan Books, 2017), 268–69; Eva Kolinsky, *After the Holocaust: Jewish Survivors in Germany after 1945* (London: Pimlico, 2004), 37–70.

20. AJDC, NY AR 1945-54/4/33/2/386, Greece, General, VIII.–XII. 1945, "Letter from Israel [*sic*] G. Jacobson to Moses Leavitt, Subject: General Report on Greece" (24 December 1945).

21. USHMM, RG-34.001, Gaynor I. Jacobson Papers, Accession No. 1991.A.0102.

22. Kolinsky, *After the Holocaust*, 2004, 71.

23. John J. Sigal and Morton Weinfeld, *Trauma and Rebirth: Intergenerational Effects of the Holocaust* (New York: Praeger, 1989), 13.

24. AJDC, NY AR 1945-54/4/33/2/387, Greece, General, I.–VII. 1945, "Letter from Committee of Supply and Relief to Mr. Harry Greenstein" (February 02, 1945); NY AR1945-54/4/33/2/387, Greece, General, I.–VII. 1945, "Letter from the President to Honorary Jewish Agency" (29 January 1945).

25. Hans Günter Hockerts, Claudia Moisel, and Tobias Winstel, *Grenzen der Wiedergutmachung: Die Entschädigung für NS-Verfolgte in West- und Osteuropa, 1945–2000* (Göttingen: Wallstein, 2006).

26. See Katherine E. Fleming, *Greece: A Jewish History* (Princeton: Princeton University Press, 2008), 170–71.

27. AJDC, NY AR 1945-54/4/33/2/386, Greece, General, VIII.–XII. 1945, "Letter from J. C. Hyman to Rabbi Philip Bernstein" (6 December 1945).

28. For more on the term "hostages" and its application and impact in Greece, see Rika Benveniste, *Die Überlebenden: Widerstand, Deportation, Rückkehr: Juden aus Thessaloniki in den 1940er Jahren* (Berlin: Edition Romiosini, 2016), 316–21.

236 · NOTES TO CHAPTER THREE

29. David P. Boder, *Die Toten habe ich nicht befragt* (Heidelberg: Universitätsverlag Winter, 2011).

30. See AJDC, NY AR 1945-54/4/33/2/386, "Letter from Israel [*sic*] G. Jacobson to Moses Leavitt, Subject: General Report on Greece" (24 December 1945); or AJDC NY AR 1945-54/4/33/2/386, "Letter from Israel G. Jacobson to Mr. Leavitt" (17 December 1945). See also Erika Kounio-Amarilio, *From Thessaloniki to Auschwitz and Back: Memories of a Survivor from Thessaloniki* (London: Vallentine Mitchell, 2000), 142; and the testimony of Palomba A., in Bea Lewkowicz, *The Jewish Community of Salonika: History, Memory, Identity* (London: Vallentine Mitchell, 2006), 196. For further information on the return of survivors, see Tullia Santin, *Der Holocaust in den Zeugnissen griechischer Jüdinnen und Juden* (Berlin: Duncker & Humblot, 2003), 118–23.

31. The Holocaust Memorial, unveiled in 2015 in a public space in the center of Kavala, has already been vandalized several times. See "Controversial Greek Holocaust Memorial Is Vandalized," *Forward*, June 22, 2015, https://forward.com/; "Vandals Attack Holocaust Memorial in Northern Greece," *World Jewish Congress*, March 31, 2017, www.worldjewishcongress.org/.

32. "Testimony of M. Benveniste," in Miriam Novitch, *The Passage of the Barbarians: Contribution to the History of the Deportation and Resistance of Greek Jews* (Hull: Hyperion Books, 1989), 95.

33. Novitch, 94–105. See also Vasilis Ritzaleos, "I evraiki kinotita Kavalas ton elegcho ton Voulgarikon Archon Katochis: organosi, ekmetalleysi, dialysi (1942–1944)" ["The Jewish Community of Kavala under the Bulgarian Occupying Forces: Organization, Exploitation, Dissolution"], in Vasilis Dalkavoukis et al., eds., *Afigisis gia ti dekaetia tou 1940* [*Narrations about the 1940s*] (Thessaloniki: Epikentro, 2012), 72–76; Hans-Joachim Hoppe, "Bulgarian Nationalities Policy in Occupied Thrace and Aegean Macedonia," *Nationalities Papers* 14, no. 1–2 (March 1, 1986): 97. See also Nadège Ragaru, *"Et les Juifs bulgares furent sauvés…": une histoire des savoirs sur la Shoah en Bulgarie* (Paris: Science Po, 2020).

34. The numbers are based on the data provided by the Deportations of Jews Project of the International Institute for Holocaust Research, Transports to Extinction: Holocaust (Shoah) Deportation Database, at Yad Vashem, the World Holocaust Remembrance Center: https://deportation.yadvashem.org/.

35. Ibid. See also Hoppe, "Bulgarian Nationalities Policy," 97; Fleischer, "Griechenland," 256.

36. Six of them (all from Xanthi) were deported from Belitsa to Vratsa on 16 March 1943 and later to Treblinka, where they were murdered like other Jews from Belomorie. See Natan Grinberg, *Dokumenti: Izdireni i subrani iz arhiva na Komisarstvoto za evreiskite vuprosi* [*Documents: Searched and Collected from the Archive of the Commissariat for Jewish Affairs*] (Sofia: Tsentralna Konsistoria na Evreite v Bulgaria, 1945), 123–24. For information about the

NOTES TO CHAPTER THREE · 237

transport route, including the stopover in Simitli, see Transports to Extinction: Holocaust (Shoah) Deportation Database, Yad Vashem, https://deportation.yadvashem.org/.

37. Sampetai Tsimino, 45117, VHA, USC Shoah Foundation; see "Testimony of M. Benveniste," in Novitch, *Passage of the Barbarians*, 96.

38. Yad Vashem Archives, TR.6—Documentation of the People's Court in Bulgaria, 1944–1945: Minutes of Session No. 9 of the People's Court in Sofia (16 March 1945) at https://collections.yadvashem.org/en/documents/4440080.

39. USHMM, RG-45.010, Archives of the Jewish Community of Thessaloniki, KIS 0096—Report to the Central British Fund for Jewish Relief and Rehabilitation (9 April 1946). By contrast, earlier publications claim that it was the Bulgarians who sunk the Jews in the Danube. See Michael Molho and Joseph Nehama, *In Memoriam: Gewidmet dem Andenken an die jüdischen Opfer der Naziherrschaft in Griechenland* (Essen: Peter Katzung, 1981), 153.

40. Jankiel Wiernik, *A Year in Treblinka: An Inmate Who Escaped Tells the Day-to-Day Facts of One Year of His Torturous Experience* (New York: American Representation of the General Jewish Workers' Union of Poland, 1944), 30.

41. Moisis K. Konstantinis, *I Israilitikes kinotites tis Ellados meta to Olokautoma, apo tis ekthesis tou Kanari D. Konstantini* [*The Jewish Communities of Greece after the Holocaust, in the Essays of Kanaris D. Konstantinis*] (Athens: self-published, 2015).

42. USHMM, RG-34.001, Gaynor I. Jacobson Papers, Accession No. 1991.A.0102.

43. Novitch, *Passage of the Barbarians*, 94–105. Concerning confiscated and stolen Jewish property in Kavala, see Ritzaleos, "I evraiki kinotita Kavalas," 81–90. Concerning Jewish records and objects returned to Greece in the late 1970s, see Nicholas Stavroulakis, "The Fate of the Material Evidence of the Jews of Greece," *Journal of Modern Hellenism* 23–24 (2006–2007): 118–20; and also mentioned in USHMM, RG-50.968.0032—Oral history interview with Gaynor I. Jacobson, conducted by Tad Szulc (1988).

44. Danuta Czech, "Deportation und Vernichtung der griechischen Juden im KL Auschwitz (im Lichte der sogenannten 'Endlösung der Judenfrage')," *Hefte von Auschwitz* 11 (1970): 24.

45. David Cesarani, *Final Solution: The Fate of the Jews 1933–49* (London: Pan, 2017), 655–61. See also Robert Jan van Pelt and Debórah Dwork, *Auschwitz: von 1270 bis heute*, trans. Klaus Rupprecht (1996; repr., Zurich: Pendo, 1998), 365–67; or Sybille Steinbacher, *Auschwitz: Geschichte und Nachgeschichte* (2004; repr., Munich: C. H. Beck, 2007), 84–87.

46. Ellen Ben-Sefer, "Forced Sterilization and Abortion as Sexual Abuse," in Sonja M. Hedgepeth and Rochelle G. Saidel, eds., *Sexual Violence against Jewish Women during the Holocaust* (Hanover, NH: University Press of New England, 2010), 162–64.

47. Kerem Yitzchak, "Greek Jews in Auschwitz: Doctors and Victims," in Michael A.

238 · NOTES TO CHAPTER THREE

Grodin, ed., *Jewish Medical Resistance in the Holocaust* (New York: Berghahn, 2016), 197. See also Saul S. Friedman, *A History of the Holocaust* (London: Vallentine Mitchell, 2004), 264.

48. Massarano (née Tchemino), 5868, VHA, USC Shoah Foundation. See also Erika Kounio-Amariglio, *From Thessaloniki to Auschwitz and Back: Memories of a Survivor from Thessaloniki*, Library of Holocaust Testimonies (London: Vallentine Mitchell, 2000), 64. For life writing not written in Greek, for example, from Romania, see Elly Gross, *Elly: My True Story of the Holocaust* (New York: Scholastic, 2007), 74.

49. Steven B. Bowman, *The Agony of Greek Jews, 1940–1945* (Stanford: Stanford University Press, 2009), 93.

50. Kolinsky, *After the Holocaust*, 40–69.

51. AJDC, NY AR 1945-54/4/33/2/386, Greece, General, VIII.–XII. 1945, "Letter from Israel [*sic*] G. Jacobson to Phillip Bernstein" (12 November 1945). For estimations of the number of Jewish DPs who did not return to Greece, see Fleischer, "Griechenland," 272; and Benveniste, *Die Überlebenden*, 150–51.

52. Arieh J. Kochavi, *Post-Holocaust Politics: Britain, the United States, and Jewish Refugees, 1945–1948* (Chapel Hill: University of North Carolina Press, 2001), 13–15.

53. Leften Stavros Stavrianos, "The Jews of Greece," *Journal of Central European Affairs* 8, no. 3 (1948): 267.

54. AJDC, NY AR 1945-54/4/33/2/386, Letter from Israel [*sic*] G. Jacobson to Moses A. Leavitt (17 December 1945).

55. Novitch, *Passage of the Barbarians*, 34. See also photographs from the permanent exhibition at the Memorial and Museum Auschwitz-Birkenau, section "Physical evidence of crime," in Block 5, Auschwitz I, www.auschwitz.org/en/gallery/exhibits/evidence-of-crimes,1.html.

56. Rudolf Vrba, *Utekl jsem z Osvětimi* (Praha: Sefer, 2007), 275. See also Ruth Linn, *Escaping Auschwitz: A Culture of Forgetting* (Ithaca, NY: Cornell University Press, 2004), 275.

57. More on Jewish solidarity during the Holocaust in Dan Michman and Robert Rozett, eds., *Jewish Solidarity: The Ideal and the Reality in the Turmoil of the Shoah* (Jerusalem: Yad Vashem, The International Institute for Holocaust Research, 2022) as a result of the Yad Vashem Biennial Conference, Jerusalem (15–18 December 2014).

58. Database of Greek-Jewish Holocaust Survivors' Testimonies, http://gjst.ha.uth.gr. For social networks in Auschwitz among the Holocaust deportees from Thessaloniki, see Paris Papamichos Chronakis, "From the Lone Survivor to the Networked Self: Social Networks Meet the Digital Holocaust Archive," *Quest: Issues in Contemporary Jewish History* 13 (2018): 52–84. Concerning young survivors, see Kenneth Waltzer, "Moving Together, Moving Alone: The Story of Boys on a Transport from Auschwitz to Buchenwald," in Joanna B. Michlic, ed., *Jewish Families in Europe, 1939–Present: History, Representation and Memory* (Waltham, MA: Brandeis University Press, 2017), 85–109.

NOTES TO CHAPTER THREE · 239

59. See Berry Nachmia, *Kraugi gia to aurio, 76859 . . . [Scream for Tomorrow, 76859 . . .]* (Athens: Kaktos, 1989), 145–47. Odette Varon-Vassard has pointed out the high level of sociability among female prisoners. The same is expressed—only differently—in the accounts of male prisoners. Odette Varon-Vassard, "Voix de femmes: Témoignages de jeunes filles juives grecques survivantes de la Shoah," *Cahiers Balkaniques* 43 (December 2015), https://doi.org/10.4000/ceb.8528. The company of Greek girlfriends, which Berry repeatedly brings up in her memoirs and Varon-Vassard emphasizes as essential seems to diminish in importance in Berry's later accounts.

60. Nachmia, *Kraugi gia to aurio*, 82. Mperry [*sic*] Nachmia (née Cassouto), 35270, VHA, USC Shoah Foundation and notes from an interview with Berry Nachmia in Kifissia, conducted by Kateřina Králová on 15 June 2008. For similar examples of solidarity, see Waltzer, "Moving Together, Moving Alone," 85–109.

61. Nachmia, *Kraugi gia to aurio*, 190.

62. Nachmia, 192–97.

63. Nachmia, 212.

64. Mperry [*sic*] Nachmia, 35270, Stella Massarano (née Tchemino), 5868, and Suzanne Nissim (née Tchemino), 5867, VHA, USC Shoah Foundation. Also, AJDC, NY AR 1945-54/4/19/4/163, Belgium, Aide aux Israelites Victimes de la Guerre (A.I.V.G.), Printed Matter, 1945–1948, "Unknown" (17 April 1946); "List of members of Jew. Comm. Salonika already back in Salonica, who have been in CCs. in Germany." 14 February 1946, no. 70, Polina Alcheh [*sic*] and no. 545, Buena Cassouto [maiden name of Berry Nachmia], in Registration of Liberated Former Persecutees at Various Locations (F-18-310), 3.1.1.3/0055_78780214#1 and 0071_78780231#1, "Anfragekarte: Altcheh, Paula Paulina," 27 February 1967, in Repository of T/D Cases, 6.3.3.2/ 0198636, ITS Digital Archive, USHMM.

65. AJDC, NY AR194554/4/33/2/386, Report from Israel G. Jacobson to Moses A. Leavitt, Subject: Athens Relief Report from August 1st to November 30th, 1945 (28 December 1945).

66. "List of members of Jew. Comm. Salonika already back in Salonica, who have been in CCs. in Germany," no. 70, Polina Alcheh [*sic*] and no. 545, Buena Cassouto [maiden name], in 3.1.1.3/0055_78780214#1 and 0071_78780231#1; "Anfragekarte: Altcheh, Paula Paulina," in 6.3.3.2/0198636, ITS Digital Archive, USHMM.

67. Nachmia, *Kraugi gia to aurio*, 180–81. For the psychological impact of Auschwitz on Holocaust survivors in Greece, see Santin, *Der Holocaust*, 121; USHMM, RG-45.011, Archives of the Jewish Community of Thessaloniki, I K TH-02702, the Nachmias Family, no. 174, in the survivor register of the Jewish Community of Thessaloniki (23 August 1945).

68. Nata Gattegno [*sic*], 30258, VHA, USC Shoah Foundation; EME 10, Nata Gategnio [*sic*], born in 1923, Kerkyra (interviewed in Israel, in 2010,). See also Nata Gattegno-Osmo

240 · NOTES TO CHAPTER THREE

[sic], *Apo tin Kerkyra sto Birkenaou ke stin Ierousalim, I istoria mias kerkyreas* [*From Corfu to Birkenau and Jerusalem: The Story of a Corfu Woman*] (Athens: Gavriilidis, 2005), 106–27; Karina Lampsa and Iakov Sibi, *I zoi ap' tin archi: i metanasteusi ton ellinon Evreon stin Palestini (1945–1948)* [*Life from the Beginning: The Emigration of Greek Jews to Palestine, 1945–1948*] (Athens: Alexandria, 2010), 319–22.

69. Gattegno-Osmo [sic], *Apo tin Kerkyra sto Mpirkenaou*, 84–98. See also EME 10, Nata Gategnio [sic]; and Transports to Extinction: Shoah Deportation Database, Yad Vashem, at https://deportation.yadvashem.org/.

70. "Osmo, Eftichia," [sic] in Repository of T/D Cases, 6.3.3.2/99157571#1, ITS Digital Archive, USHMM; EME 10, Nata Gategnio [sic].

71. AJDC, NY AR 1945-54/3/2/5/1051, General 1944–1945, "Israel J. Jacobson to Moses A. Leavitt, Subject: Deportees returned to Corfu" (1 October 1945), Registration of Liberated Former Persecutees at Various Locations (F-18-541), 3.1.1.3/0241_78780136#1, ITS Digital Archive, USHMM.

72. Lampsa and Sibi, *I zoi ap' tin archi*, 321. Similarly in EME 10, Nata Gategnio [sic]; and Gattegno-Osmo [sic], *Apo tin Kerkyra sto Mpirkenaou*, 130–31.

73. Gattegno-Osmo [sic], *Apo tin Kerkyra sto Mpirkenaou*, 134–35. For more information about the *Huviva Raik*, including the list of passengers by name, age, and nationality, see Lampsa and Sibi, *I zoi ap' tin archi*, 230–33, 367–78. See also Kateřina Králová, "Hachsharot in Greece, 1945–1949: Camps or Vocational Centers?," *Quest: Issues in Contemporary Jewish History* 21, no. 1 (2022): 75–101.

74. Quotation of Minos Moisis in Dimitris Vlachopanos, *Isaak Mizan: Arithmos vrachiona 182641* [*Isaak Mizan; Arm Number 182641*] (Athens: Apiros Hora, 2016), 12.

75. Isaak Mizan, 44916, VHA, USC Shoah Foundation; see also Vlachopanos, *Isaak Mizan*, 146–67; Moisis K. Konstantinis, *I Israilitikes kinotites*, 61–67.

76. Transports to Extinction: Shoah Deportation Database, Yad Vashem, at https://deportation.yadvashem.org/; Isaak Mizan, 44916, VHA, USC Shoah Foundation.

77. Isaak Mizan, 44916, VHA, USC Shoah Foundation.

78. The Bergen-Belsen scholar Christine Lattek simply calls the last months of the Bergen-Belsen camp an "inferno." See Christine Lattek, "Bergen-Belsen: From 'Privileged' Camp to Death Camp," in David Cesarani et al., eds., *Belsen in History and Memory* (Hoboken, NJ: Taylor & Francis, 2013). On Bergen-Belsen see also the work she coauthored nearly three decades earlier with Eberhard Kolb, Gregory Claeys, and Christine Lattek, *Bergen-Belsen: From "Detention Camp" to Concentration Camp, 1943–1945* (Göttingen: Vandenhoeck & Ruprecht, 1986).

79. "Mizan Isaac" [sic], in Central Name Index, 0.1/42000104, ITS, Digital Archive, USHMM; Isaak Mizan, 44916, VHA, USC Shoah Foundation; Vlachopanos, *Isaak Mizan*, 140–41.

NOTES TO CHAPTER THREE · 241

80. See the recollections in Vlachopanos, *Isaak Mizan*, which reflects in some detail on what Mizan suggests when interviewed (in Isaak Mizan, 44916, VHA, USC Shoah Foundation).

81. "Mizan Isaac" [*sic*], in Central Name Index, 0.1/42000104, ITS, Digital Archive, USHMM; Isaak Mizan, 44916, VHA, USC Shoah Foundation; see also Vlachopanos, *Isaak Mizan*, 161. The solitude may be an explanation of what Sofsky calls the "collapse of their personal and moral integrity." Wolfgang Sofsky, *The Order of Terror* (Princeton: Princeton University Press, 1997), 82.

82. Samuel Nehama, 687, VHA, USC Shoah Foundation.

83. Ibid.; "Samuel Nehama," in Individual Documents Mail Buchenwald/6696554#1, ITS, Digital Archive, USHMM; "Nehama Samuel," in Repository of T/D Cases 6.6.3.2/41660095, ITS, Digital Archive, USHMM.

84. "Samuel Nehama," in Individual Documents Mail Buchenwald/6696554#1, ITS, Digital Archive, USHMM.

85. EME 1, Nehama Samouil (Sam), born in Athens, in 1930 (interviewed in Greece, in 2005).

86. Samuel Nehama, 687, VHA, USC Shoah Foundation.

87. USHMM, RG-50.030.0472, Oral history interview with Isaac Nehama, conducted by Joan Ringelheim, USHMM Collections, 22 October 2002.

88. See Stella Massarano (née Tchemino), 5868, and Suzanne Nissim (née Tchemino), 5867, VHA, USC Shoah Foundation; and Shmuel Refael, *Bi-netiveyshe'ol: yehudey yavan ba-sho'ah-pirqey edut* [*The Road to Hell: Greek Jews in the Shoah. Testimonies*] (Tel Aviv: ha-Makhon le-heqer yahadut Saloniki, 1988), 261–77; Shlomo Venezia, *Inside the Gas Chambers: Eight Months in the Sonderkommando of Auschwitz* (Oxford: Polity, 2009); see also Dario Gabbai, "To Zonterkomanto [The *Sonderkommando*] – From an Interview in the Newspaper 'Aggelioforos', 23 April 2004," *Chronika* 29, no. 201 (February 2006): 78–79. On the Refael documentation project see Alisa M. Ginio, *Between Sepharad and Jerusalem: History, Identity and Memory of the Sephardim* (Leiden: Brill, 2015), 304.

89. Refael, *Bi-netiveyshe'ol*, 259–76.

90. Refael, 261–73. For information about the transport from Thessaloniki to Auschwitz-Birkenau, see Transports to Extinction: Shoah Deportation Database, Yad Vashem, at https://deportation.yadvashem.org/.

91. Refael, *Bi-netiveyshe'ol*, 264–73. See also Transports to Extinction: Shoah Deportation Database, Yad Vashem, https://deportation.yadvashem.org/. The nationalization and heroization of the "Greek" role in the uprising seems to be overestimated by some scholars, including Steven B. Bowman, *Jewish Resistance in Wartime Greece* (London: Vallentine Mitchell, 2006), 85; Bowman, *Agony of Greek Jews*, 109–10.

242 · NOTES TO CHAPTER THREE

92. Refael, *Bi-netivey she'ol*, 276. Concerning repatriation, I compared the data from Raphael with the personal account of Leon Perachia, who had traveled with the Levi brothers from Chernivtsi to Thessaloniki. See Leon Perahia, 17390, VHA, USC Shoah Foundation; and Leon Perachia, *Mazal: Anamnisis apo ta stratopeda tou thanatou (1943–1945)* [*Mazal: Memories of the Death Camps, 1943–1945*] (Thessaloniki: Self-published, 1990).

93. Concerning Sidirokastro, see AJDC, NY AR 1945-54/4/33/2/386, Greece, General, VIII–XII 1945, "Many Jewish skulls and bones are visible all over the cemetery…" (21 August 1945). On the screenings, see Bea Lewkowicz, "'After the War We Were All Together': Jewish Memories of Postwar Thessalonica," in *After the War Was Over: Reconstructing the Family, Nation, and State in Greece, 1943–1960*, ed. Mark Mazower (Princeton, NJ: Princeton University Press, 2000), 267.

94. Refael, *Bi-netiveyshe'ol*, 276. See also Lampsa and Sibi, *I zoi ap' tin archi*, 372.

95. The number of Jews in Greece with non-Greek citizenship as of 15 March 1943 in PA AA, B 26/65—Vermerk. Betr.: Deutsch-griechische Wiedergutmachungsverhandlungen, hier: In Griechenland lebende Juden nicht griechischer Staatsangehörigkeit (29 March 1960). Fleischer, "Griechenland," 255.

96. Maria Vassilikou, "Griechenland," in Sara Berger et al., eds., *Die Verfolgung und Ermordung der europäischen Juden durch das nationalsozialistische Deutschland, 1933–1945*, vol. 14 (Berlin: de Gruyter Oldenbourg, 2017), 62.

97. Joseph Rochlitz, "Excerpts from the Salonika Diary of Lucillo Merci February-August 1943," *Yad Vashem Studies* 18, no. 18 (1987): 319–20.

98. Shlomo Venezia, 36179, and Morris Venezia, 20405, VHA, USC Shoah Foundation.

99. See Transports to Extinction: Shoah Deportation Database, Yad Vashem, at https://deportation.yadvashem.org/; Czech, "Deportation und Vernichtung," 273–74.

100. Quotation from the account of Jacob Gabbai in Refael, *Bi-netiveyshe'ol*, 127. When inmates from Greece refer to the revolt as an "uprising," it is merely an incorrect translation of the German word *Aufstand* into Greek. For this misinterpretation see, e.g., "Joseph Varouh," in Bowman, *Jewish Resistance*, 84–90; and "Greek Uprising," in Photini Tomai, *Greeks in Auschwitz-Birkenau* (Athens: Papazisis, 2009), 148–57. Furthermore, attributing this predominantly to the "Greeks" may be because the Jews of Greece who did not know any German or Yiddish could barely communicate with Hungarian, Polish, Slovak, and Russian prisoners and therefore remained considerably isolated. Most research on Birkenau, however, does not highlight a particular nationality; rather, it focuses on the special conditions under which the *Sonderkommando* members had to work. See Steinbacher, *Auschwitz*, 94–97; Cesarani, *Final Solution*, 746–47; Sofsky, *Order of Terror*, 268–71, 273–74.

101. Dario Gabbai, 142, and Morris Venezia, 20405, VHA, USC Shoah Foundation. See also USHMM, RG-50.477.0661, Oral history interview with Dany Bennahmias, USHMM Collections, 12 November 1991.

NOTES TO CHAPTER THREE · 243

102. Florian Freud, "Ebensee," in *Der Ort des Terrors: Geschichte der nationalsozialistischen Konzentrationslager*, ed. Wolfgang Benz and Barbara Distel, Flossenbürg, Mauthausen, Ravensbrück 4 (Munich: C. H. Beck, 2006), 354–56.

103. Shlomo Venezia, 36179, VHA, USC Shoah Foundation; Venezia, *Inside the Gas Chambers*, 152; and Eric Friedler, Andreas Kilian, and Barbara Siebert, *Zeugen aus der Todeszone: Das jüdische Sonderkommando in Auschwitz* (Munich: dtv, 2008), 306–7. Eva Kolinsky confirms the desperate situation caused by starvation, pointing out that in Dachau, after its liberation, survivors devoured raw meat (also mentioned in the VHA testimony of Morris Venezia, 20405, VHA, USC Shoah Foundation), egg shells, and, in some instances causing death, even consumed DDT and rat poison. Kolinsky, *After the Holocaust*, 65–66.

104. Venezia, *Inside the Gas Chambers*, 143–45.

105. Dario Gabbai, 142, VHA, USC Shoah Foundation.

106. Testimony of Jacob Gabbai in Refael, *Bi-netiveyshe'ol*, 128–29. Dario Gabbai, 142, and Shlomo Venezia, 36179, VHA, USC Shoah Foundation. Quotation from Friedler, Kilian, and Siebert, *Zeugen aus der Todeszone*, 315.

107. Stella Massarano (née Tchemino), 5868, and Suzanne Nissim (née Tchemino), 5867, VHA, USC Shoah Foundation.

108. USHMM, RG-50.822.0004, Oral history interview with Agi Geva, conducted by Hannes Ravic, USHMM, 14 October 2014. Also Massarano, 5868, VHA, USC Shoah Foundation; see also Danuta Czech, *Auschwitz Chronicle*, 356; Gross, *Elly*, 59.

109. Czech, *Auschwitz Chronicle*, 791. See also Massarano, 5868, and Nissim, 5867, VHA, USC Shoah Foundation.

110. Massarano, 5868, and Nissim, 5867, VHA, USC Shoah Foundation; AJDC, NY AR 1945-54/4/19/4/163, Belgium, Aide aux Israelites Victimes de la Guerre (A.I.V.G.), Printed Matter, 1945–1948, "Unknown" (17 April 1946).

111. Massarano, 5868, and Nissim, 5867, VHA, USC Shoah Foundation.

112. For a useful discussion of the death marches, see Tim Cole, *Holocaust Landscapes* (London: Bloomsbury Continuum, 2016), 185; concerning Greek identity in camps, see Katherine E. Fleming, *Greece: A Jewish History* (Princeton: Princeton University Press, 2008), 162; and, most recently, Paris Papamichos Chronakis, "'We Lived as Greeks and We Died as Greeks': Thessalonican Jews in Auschwitz and the Meanings of Nationhood," in *The Holocaust in Greece*, eds. Giorgos Antoniou and A. Dirk Moses (Cambridge, UK: Cambridge University Press, 2018), 157–80, though, surprisingly, only male inmates of Auschwitz are discussed.

113. Quotation from USHMM, RG-50.233.0014, Oral history interview with Renee Carasso [née Gani], conducted by Sharon Tash, USHMM Collections, 13 May 1992. On the trajectory from Auschwitz to liberation, see "Carasso Rene [*sic*]," in Repository of T/D Cases, 6.3.3.2/98440577#1, ITS Digital Archive, USHMM.

244 · NOTES TO CHAPTER THREE

114. USHMM, RG-50.233.0014, Renee Carasso (13 May 1992). For the numbers of deportees, see Transports to Extinction: Shoah Deportation Database, Yad Vashem, at https://deportation.yadvashem.org/; for the survivors of Preveza on 20 May 1945, see Moisis K. Konstantinis, "Evraiki Kinotita Prevezis" ["The Jewish Community of Preveza"], *Chronika* 19, no. 142 (April 1996): 29–30.

115. Lucia Capelluto, *Testimony: My Life in Auschwitz and Bergen Belsen* (Marseille: Levant, 1997), 17. See also Lucia Habib, 8310, VHA, USC Shoah Foundation.

116. Santin, *Der Holocaust*, 137–52. For Greece, see Phragkiski Abatzopoulou, "I genoktonia ke i gynekia foni" ["The Genocide and the Voice of Women"], *Dini: Feministiko Periodiko* 9 (1997): 11–50; and Gabriella Etmektsoglou, "Reading Lisa Pinhas in the 21st Century," in *A Narrative of Evil: Lisa Pinhas Confronts the Holocaust*, ed. Zanet Battinou, introduction by Gabriella Etmektsoglou (Athens: Jewish Museum, 2014), 43–50. Etmektsoglou stresses, however, that Holocaust accounts should be understood first and foremost from the perspective of survivor identity rather than religion and gender.

117. Marco Nahon, *Birkenau: The Camp of Death* (Tuscaloosa: University of Alabama Press, 1989), 38, 51.

118. Nahon, *Birkenau*, 109–18. Also "Nahon Marco," in Repository of T/D Cases, 6.3.3.2/89467221#1, ITS Digital Archive, USHMM; Geoffrey P. Megargee, ed., *The United States Holocaust Memorial Museum Encyclopedia of Camps and Ghettos, 1933–1945*, vol. 1, foreword by Elie Wiesel (Indianapolis: Indiana University Press, 2009), 1027–28.

119. AJDC, NY AR 1945-54/4/33/2/386, Greece, General, VIII.–XII. 1945, "Letter from Dr. Nahon to Mr. Israel Djivre" (1 October 1945).

120. AJDC, NY AR 1945-54/4/33/2/385, Greece, General, 1946–1948, "Conference of Jewish Communities Greece" (4 January 1946); Rafail Frezis, "I palia Evraiki kinotita Didymotichou" ["The Old Jewish Community of Didymoteicho"], *Chronika* 21, no. 158 (November 1998): 9–16.

121. Quotation from AJDC, NY AR 1945-54/4/33/2/386, "Letter from Dr. Nahon to Mr. Israel Djivre" (1 October 1945).

122. Nahon, *Birkenau*; "Nahon, Dr. Marco," in Repository of T/D Cases, 6.3.3.2/89467221#1, ITS Digital Archive, USHMM.

123. Michael Matsas, *The Illusion of Safety: The Story of the Greek Jews during World War II* (New York: Pella, 1997), 283–86; USHMM, RG-50.030.0313, Oral history interview with Henry Levis, conducted by Radu Ioanid, USHMM Collections, 28 October 1993.

124. Errikos Levis, 49887, VHA, USC Shoah Foundation; Megargee, *United States Holocaust Memorial*, 1:796–98; "Obóz Koncentracyjny Gross-Rosen w latach 1943–1944 Czesc II," in Records of Gross-Rosen, 1.1.11.1/143227; "Levis Erics," in Central Name Index, 0.1/31853017#1, ITS Digital Archive, USHMM; Matsas, *Illusion of Safety*, 283–86.

NOTES TO CHAPTER THREE · 245

125. Quote from Errikos Sevillias, *Athens–Auschwitz* (Athens: Lykavittos, 1983), 48.

126. Sevillias, 76–82.

127. Sevillias, 82–87. Concerning Jewish assets, see Kateřina Králová, "In the Shadow of the Nazi Past: Post-War Reconstruction and the Claims of the Jewish Community in Salonika," *European History Quarterly* 46, no. 2 (2016): 268–71; Philip Carabott and Maria Vassilikou, "'New Men vs Old Jews': Greek Jewry in the Wake of the Shoah, 1945–1947," in *The Holocaust in Greece*, eds. Giorgos Antoniou and A. Dirk Moses (Cambridge, UK: Cambridge University Press, 2018), 255–72; and regarding Thessaloniki, see the following three chapters in Giorgos Antoniou and A. Dirk Moses, *The Holocaust in Greece* (Cambridge: Cambridge University Press, 2018); Maria Kavala, "The Scale of Jewish Property Theft in Nazi-Occupied Thessaloniki," 183–207; Stratos N. Dordanas, "The Jewish Community of Thessaloniki and the Christian Collaborators: 'Those That Are Leaving and What They Are Leaving Behind,'" 208–27; Kostis Kornetis, "Expropriating the Space of the Other," 228–51.

128. Chella Koynio [*sic*] (née Löwy), 40822, VHA, USC Shoah Foundation.

129. Heinz Salvator Kounio, *A Liter of Soup and Sixty Grams of Bread: The Diary of Prisoner Number 109565*, trans. Marcia Haddad Ikonomopolous (New York: Bloch, 2003) 81.

130. Venezia, *Inside the Gas Chambers*, 147–48.

131. AJDC, NY AR 1945-54/4/33/2/387, Greece, General, I.–VII. 1945, "Letter from Israel [*sic*] G. Jacobson to Moses Leavitt, Subject: Address Delivered by Salvator Kunio – Returned Deportee" (20 August 1945); Heinz Kounio, 41892, VHA, USC Shoah Foundation.

132. Quotation from AJDC, NY AR 1945-54/4/33/2/387, Greece, General, I.–VII. 1945, "Letter from Israel [*sic*] G. Jacobson to Moses Leavitt, Subject: Address Delivered by Salvator Kunio – Returned Deportee" (20 August 1945).

133. Chella Koynio [*sic*] (née Löwy), 40822, and Erika Amariglio (née Kounio), 21678, VHA, USC Shoah Foundation. For a memoir in which several details about the return deviate from other sources, see Kounio-Amariglio, *From Thessaloniki to Auschwitz*, 132–42. For the distinctiveness of Hella's narrative, even though some information was apparently adopted from the memoir, see Lewkowicz, *Jewish Community of Salonika*, 147–49, 155–57.

134. Letter from Hella [Kounio] to Gretl [Grete Reichl], 18 February, and 8 May 1946, in Jan Láníček, Kate Ottevanger, and Marie Bader, *Life and Love in Nazi Prague: Letters from an Occupied City* (London: Bloomsbury Publishing, 2019), 302–3.

135. Odette Beser, 29118, and Mazeltov Angel, 29541, VHA, USC Shoah Foundation. Concerning Allegra Hassid, see the Records of Dachau (female), 1.1.8.4./11055688–11055690; 1.1.8.4./11067245–11067247; Repository of T/D Cases, 6.3.3.2/99901892, 99901893, 9901895–99901897; 6.3.3.2/99901900, 99901900#1, 99901900#2, ITS Digital Archive, USHMM.

246 · NOTES TO CHAPTER THREE

136. Albert Menasche, *Birkenau (Auschwitz II), Memoirs of an Eye-Witness: How 72,000 Greek Jews Perished* (New York: I. Saltiel, 1947).

137. Kateřina Králová, "What Is True and What Is Right? An Infant Jewish Orphan's Identity," in *Beyond Camps and Forced Labour: Proceedings of the Sixth International Conference*, ed. Suzanne Bardgett, Christine Schmidt, and Dan Stone (London: Palgrave Macmillan, 2020), 105–23.

138. Zermain [*sic*] Koen (née Matalon), 48674, and Claire Beza (née Matalon, Altcheh from her first marriage), 43697, VHA, USC Shoah Foundation; USHMM C, HVT-3011, "Palomba M., Riketta C., and Vida C. (née Koen) Holocaust Testimony," interviewed by Jaša Almuli; USHMM, HVT-3009, "Germain C. [*sic*] Holocaust Testimony," interviewed by Jaša Almuli; "Altzek Klara [*sic*]," in Central Name Index, 0.1/13282551; "Altcheh Clara [*sic*]," in Central Name Index, 0.1/13241150, ITS Digital Archive, USHMM. Also, Kateřina Králová, "Silenced Memories and Network Dynamics in Holocaust Testimonies: The Matalon Family and Case of Greece," *S: I.M.O.N. Shoah: Intervention. Methods. Documentation* 9, no. 2 (2022): 51–66.

139. Claire Beza (née Matalon, Altcheh from her first marriage), 43697, VHA, USC Shoah Foundation. For a similar observation, but regarding Jews from Lodz, see van Pelt and Dwork, *Auschwitz*, 386.

140. Quotation from Rozina Asser Pardo, *548 Days with Another Name: Salonika 1943: A Child's Diary, an Adult's Memories of War*, trans. Demetrios Argyriades (New York: Bloch, 2005), 94–95. For Claire's narration, see Claire Beza, 43697, VHA, USC Shoah Foundation. Compare this with Ida Angel's story in Novitch, *Passage of the Barbarians*, 121–23.

141. Zermain [*sic*] Koen (née Matalon), 48674, VHA, USC Shoah Foundation; "Cohen [*sic*] Germaine," in Central Name Index, 0.1/27938875, 27938878; "Ústřední kartotéka – transporty," in Central Name Index, 0.1/4966252, ITS Digital Archive, USHMM.

142. AJDC, NY AR 1945-54/4/33/2/386, Greece, General, VIII.–XII. 1945, "Letter from Morris Laub to Dr. J. Schwartz, Re: Greece." (23 August 1945).

143. Claire Beza, 43697, and Zermain [*sic*] Koen, 48674, VHA, USC Shoah Foundation; Ester Florentin (née Altcheh), 43029, VHA, USC Shoah Foundation; "Jews who left Greece for Palestine on 8/4/45" (30 August 1945), in Registration of Liberated Former Persecutees at Various Locations, 3.1.1.3.(F 18-56 Griechenland, 045)/0060_78779776_1– 0067_78779789_1, ITS Digital Archive, USHMM. Concerning Germaine's daughters, Vetta Mioni (née Koen), Paylina Matathia (née Koen), and Riketta Koen, see Zermain [*sic*] Koen (née Matalon), 48674, VHA, USC Shoah Foundation; USHMM, HVT-3011, "Palomba M., Riketta C., and Vida C. (née Koen) Holocaust Testimony"; USHMM, HVT-3009, "Germain C. [*sic*] Holocaust Testimony." See also AJDC, NY AR1945-54/4/33/2/386, Greece, General, VIII.–XII. 1945, "Letter from American Joint Distribution Committee Jewish Relief Office to Israel G. Jacobson, Subject: General Report" (December 7, 1945);

NOTES TO CHAPTER THREE · 247

NY AR194554/4/33/2/387, Greece, General, I.–VII. 1945, "The American Joint Distribution Committee's Program Greece" (1 August 1945).

144. Primo Levi, *If This Is a Man* and *The Truce*, trans. Stuart Woolf (1947 and 1963; repr., London: Abacus, 2013).

145. AJDC, NY AR 1945-54/4/33/2/386, Letter from Israel [*sic*] G. Jacobson to Moses A. Leavitt (17 December 1945).

146. Lattek, "Bergen-Belsen," 46–52.

147. Nina Nachmia, *Reina Zilberta: Ena pedi sto geto tis Thessalonikis* [*Reina Zilberta: A Child in the Thessaloniki Ghetto*] (Athens: Okeanidis, 1996), 35–37. See the Voices of the Holocaust David Boder Archive, Interview with Eda Button (5 August 1946) at http://voices.iit .edu/ (accessed 5 May 2019).

148. Eberhard Kolb, Gregory Claeys, and Christine Lattek, *Bergen-Belsen: From "Detention Camp" to Concentration Camp, 1943–1945* (Göttingen: Vandenhoeck & Ruprecht, 1986), 33–54. See also Haim Avni, "Spanish Nationals in Greece and Their Fate During the Holocaust," *Yad Vashem Studies* 8 (1970): 55–64. Concerning the transport of 2 August 1943 from Thessaloniki to Bergen Belsen, see Transports to Extinction: Shoah Deportation Database, Yad Vashem, at http://db.yadvashem.org/deportation/.

149. Cesarani et al., *Belsen in History and Memory*, 22.

150. Lattek, "Bergen-Belsen," 45–51; Hans-Dieter Arntz, *Der letzte Judenälteste von Bergen-Belsen: Josef Weiss – würdig in einer unwürdigen Umgebung* (Aachen: Helios, 2012); Rolf Keller, ed., *Konzentrationslager Bergen-Belsen: Berichte und Dokumente* (Hannover: Niedersächs. Landeszentrale für Politische Bildung, 1995).

151. USHMM, RG-45.011, Archives of the Jewish Community of Thessaloniki, I K TH 00159—Petition to the Commissioner of the Special Court for Judging Persons Guilty of Collaboration with the Germans (12 September 1945).

152. Devin E. Naar, *Jewish Salonica: Between the Ottoman Empire and Modern Greece* (Stanford, CA: Stanford University Press, 2016), 122–33.

153. Lattek, "Bergen-Belsen," 46; Kolb, *Bergen-Belsen*, 53–54, 63.

154. See also "Albala, Lorie," in Repository of T/D Cases, 6.3.3.2/88197436#1, ITS Digital Archive, USHMM; Interview with Zermain [*sic*] Koen, 48674, VHA, USC Shoah Foundation.

155. Lattek, "Bergen-Belsen," 45–51; Arntz, *Der letzte Judenälteste*, 214–31; Shlomo Samson, *Zwischen Finsternis und Licht: 50 Jahre nach Bergen-Belsen* (Jerusalem: Verlag Rubin Mass, 1995), 246.

156. Molho and Nehama, *In Memoriam*, 376–78.

157. Arntz, *Der letzte Judenälteste*, 220. See also Edgar Kounio, 42145, VHA, USC Shoah Foundation.

248 · NOTES TO CHAPTER THREE

158. Compare this with Benveniste, *Die Überlebenden*, 279–302.

159. "Alfred Garwood," in David Cesarani et al., *Belsen in History and Memory*, 221.

160. Against Koretz, see USHMM, VHA Interview Code: 4137, USC Shoah Foundation Institute testimony of Isaac Stroumza. See also Raul Hilberg, *Die Vernichtung der europäischen Juden*, vol. 2 (1961; repr., Frankfurt am Main: Fischer-Taschenbuch-Verlag, 1990), 740; and Hannah Arendt, *Eichmann in Jerusalem: A Report on the Banality of Evil* (1963; repr., New York: Penguin, 2006), 186.

161. FDR Library, War Refugees Abroad—Hitachduth Oley Yavan to World Jewish Congress (4 August 1944), available at http://www.fdrlibrary.marist.edu; "Koretz, Zvi," in Repository of T/D Cases, 6.3.3.2/100427258#1, ITS Digital Archive, USHMM, and also in Benveniste, *Die Überlebenden*. See also Molho and Nehama, *In Memoriam*, 101–23; or, recently, Iasonas Chandrinos and Anna Maria Droumpouki, "The German Occupation and the Holocaust in Greece: A Survey," in *The Holocaust in Greece*, eds. Giorgos Antoniou and A. Dirk Moses (Cambridge, UK: Cambridge University Press, 2018), 22, n. 33, "The German Occupation and the Holocaust in Greece," 22, n. 33.

162. Arieh Koretz, *Bergen-Belsen Tagebuch eines Jugendlichen; 11.7.1944–30.3.1945*, trans. Gerda Steinfeld (Göttingen: Wallstein, 2011), 165–67. See also USHMM, HVT-3513, Arieh K. Holocaust Testimony, interviewed by Rachel Jadaio and Anita Tarsi (3 May 1993). Since Leo Koretz did not change his name to Arieh till he moved to Israel, I use his given name, Leo.

163. Thomas Rahe, "Bergen-Belsen Stammlager," in Wolfgang Benz, Barbara Distel, and Angelika Königseder, eds., *Der Ort des Terrors 7: Geschichte der nationalsozialistischen Konzentrationslager* (Munich: Beck, 2008), 212; Kolb, *Bergen-Belsen*, 72.

164. "List of Persons in Soviet Zone, Namensliste," in German Democratic Republic—New, 2.1.4.2/70992598#1; "Albala, Sigurd," in Repository of T/D Cases, 6.3.3.2/84606789#1, ITS Digital Archive, USHMM; USHMM, HVT-3513, Arieh K. Holocaust Testimony, interviewed by Rachel Jadaio and Anita Tarsi (May 3, 1993). See also Arntz, *Der letzte Judenälteste von Bergen-Belsen*.

165. Bella Barzilai (née Uziel), 41749, VHA, USC Shoah Foundation.

166. Benveniste, *Die Überlebenden*, 309–12; also, "Benveniste, Leon," in Repository of T/D Cases, 6.3.3.2/108843509#1, ITS Digital Archive, USHMM.

167. Salomon Uziel, "They Encircled Me and Encompassed Me," in *The Holocaust in Salonika: Eyewitness Accounts*, ed. Steven B. Bowman, trans. Isaac Benmayor (New York: Sephardic House, 2002), 237–80.

168. USHMM, RG-50.968.0032—Oral history interview with Gaynor I. Jacobson, conducted by Tad Szulc (1988).

169. AJDC, NY AR 1945-54/4/33/2/386, Greece, General, 1946–1948: "Incoming cable from [Arthur] Greenleigh Jointdisco New York" (28 June 1946).

NOTES TO CHAPTER THREE · 249

170. "Albala, Lorie," in Repository of T/D Cases, 6.3.3.2/88197436#1, ITS Digital Archive, USHMM. See also the interview with Laura Albala, where she avoids any reference to the position of her husband during the war, at USHMM, HVT-905, Lori B. Holocaust Testimony, interviewed by James W. Pennebaker and Sarah Mendel (January 24, 1987); USHMM, HVT-3513, Arieh K. Holocaust Testimony, interviewed by Rachel Jadaio and Anita Tarsi (3 May 1993); "Koretz, Zvi," in Repository of T/D Cases, 6.3.3.2/100427258#1, ITS Digital Archive, USHMM. Of the many newspaper articles, see those in *Ellinikos Vorras*, *Makedonia*, and *Laiki Foni* for 30 June 1946; *Makedonia*, *Laiki Foni*, *Eleftheria*, and *Fos* for 3 July 1946; and *Machi* for 11 July 1946.

171. Avni, "Spanish Nationals in Greece," 61–66.

172. "Das Neutralen-Lager Bergen-Belsen (23 July 1945)," in General Information on Bergen Belsen concentration Camp, 1.1.3.0/82351043#01–82351054#01, ITS Digital Archive, USHMM; Flora Benveniste, 47902, and Flora Carasso Michael, 1885, VHA, USC Shoah Foundation.

173. Molho and Nehama, *In Memoriam*, 145.

174. Levy in "Das Neutralen-Lager Bergen-Belsen (23 July 1945)," ITS Digital Archive, USHMM. See also Kolb, *Bergen-Belsen*, 69.

175. Levy in "Das Neutralen-Lager Bergen-Belsen (23 July 1945)," ITS Digital Archive, USHMM. Concerning the Star Camp, see Arntz, *Der letzte Judenälteste*, 214.

176. For gender questions, see Marion A. Kaplan, *Hitler's Jewish Refugees: Hope and Anxiety in Portugal* (New Haven: Yale University Press, 2020), 18–20.

177. Alberto Benadón Saporta, *Live…* (Madrid: Cultiva, 2009), 39; Flora Benveniste, 47902, VHA, USC Shoah Foundation; Lista de los Sepharditas Espanioles Residentes en Atenas que Fueror Deportados el dia 2 de Avril de 1944," in General Information on Bergen Belsen Concentration Camp, 1.1.3.0/ 3394011#01–3394014#01; "Nehama (Ezralty), Maria," in Repository of T/D Cases, 6.3.3.2/41660171#01; "Nehama, Jose," in Repository of T/D Cases, 6.3.3.2/41660217#01; "Saporta, Nora," in Repository of T/D Cases, 6.3.3.2/108840446#1, ITS Digital Archive, USHMM.

178. USHMM, Holocaust Survivors and Victims Database, Dr. David Benadon, at www.ushmm.org/online/hsv/person_advance_search.php (accessed on 10 May 2019).

179. Flora Benveniste, 47902, VHA, USC Shoah Foundation.

180. Aron Rodrigue, *French Jews, Turkish Jews: The Alliance Israélite Universelle and the Politics of Jewish Schooling in Turkey, 1860–1925* (Bloomington: Indiana University Press, 1990).

181. "Lista de los Sepharditas Espanioles […]," in General Information on Bergen Belsen Concentration Camp, 1.1.3.0/3394011#01–3394014#01; "Nehama (Ezralty), Maria," in Repository of T/D Cases, 6.3.3.2/41660171#01; "Nehama, Jose," in Repository of T/D Cases, 6.3.3.2/41660217#01; "Saporta, Nora," in Repository of T/D Cases, 6.3.3.2/108840446#1, ITS Digital Archive, USHMM. Levy in "Das Neutralen-Lager

250 · NOTES TO CHAPTER THREE

Bergen-Belsen (23 July 1945)," in General Information on Bergen Belsen Concentration Camp, 1.1.3.0/82351043#01–82351054#01, ITS Digital Archive, USHMM; AJDC, G 1955-64/4/28/16/GR.75, "Letter from E. Katzenstein to Mr. Saul Kagan" (23 March 1961). See also Naar, *Jewish Salonica*, 210–19.

182. Flora Carasso Michael, 1885, VHA, USC Shoah Foundation.

183. Molho and Nehama, *In Memoriam*, 579.

184. "Nehama (Ezralty), Maria," in Repository of T/D Cases, 6.3.3.2/41660171#01; "Saporta, Nora," in Repository of T/D Cases, 6.3.3.2/108840446#1, ITS Digital Archive, USHMM; USHMM, HVT-926, Ketty L. Holocaust Testimony, interviewed by Toby Blum-Dobkin (November 27, 1991); Maria Saporta, "50th Anniversary of Alliance Francaise School, a Time to Honor My Mother," *Saporta Report* (8 September 2013), https://saportareport.com/50th-anniversary-of-alliance-francaise-school-a-time-to-honor-my-mother/ (accessed on 10 May 2019).

185. Avni, "Spanish Nationals in Greece," 66; Molho and Nehama, *In Memoriam*, 145; Kolb, *Bergen-Belsen*, 317.

186. Matthew A. Rozell, *A Train near Magdeburg: A Teacher's Journey into the Holocaust, and the Reuniting of the Survivors and Liberators, 70 Years On* (Hartford, NY: Woodchuck Hollow Press, 2016), 8. See also the memoir of Uri Orlev, *The Sandgame* (Kibbutz Dalia: Ghetto Fighters House, 1999). Compare this with the fear expressed in Flora Benveniste, 47902, VHA, USC Shoah Foundation; and Molho and Nehama, *In Memoriam*, 145.

187. See the following sources in ITS Digital Archive, USHMM: "List of Spanish Jews arrested by the SS in Athens on March 25, 1944 and deported on April 2, 1944," 5. Benadon y Matalon David, 6. Benadon de Hambourger Esther and 7. Benadon y Hambourger Elias, in General Information on Bergen-Belsen Concentration Camp, 1.1.3.0 /3394229#01; "List of Deportees who returned to Greece, September 1945, 92. Benadon Esther Rodolphe and 93. Benadon Eliot David," in Registration of Liberated Former Persecutees at Various Locations, 3.1.1.3/78779827#01.

188. Frank W. Towers, "30th Division Medical Detachment, Diary & Log (105th Medical Battalion) By T/4 Wilson Rice, April 13, 1945," *JewishGen* (blog), n.d., www.jewishgen.org/databases/holocaust/.

189. Flora Carasso Michael, 1885, VHA, USC Shoah Foundation.

190. USHMM, HVT-926, "Ketty L. Holocaust Testimony," interviewed by Ted Zinnreich and Phyllis Braverman (22 March 1987); Esther Hassid, *Reflets de ma vie* (Paris: Pensée Universelle, 1979). See also Flora Carasso Michael, 1885, VHA, USC Shoah Foundation. "Nehama, Jose," in Repository of T/D Cases, 6.3.3.2/41660217#01, ITS Digital Archive, USHMM.

191. USHMM, HVT-926, "Ketty L. Holocaust Testimony" (22 March 1987).

NOTES TO CHAPTER FOUR · 251

192. AJDC, NY AR 1945-54/4/33/2/386, Greece, General, VIII.–XII. 1945, "Translated Letter from Jos. Nehama and Jessua Perahia to American Joint Distribution Committee Inc." (30 October 1945).

193. AJDC, G 1955-64/4/28/16/GR.75, "Letter from E. Katzenstein to Mr. Saul Kagan," (23 March 1961).

194. Bella Barzilai, 41749, VHA, USC Shoah Foundation.

195. Flora Carasso Michael, 1885, VHA, USC Shoah Foundation.

196. Molho and Nehama, *In Memoriam*; Uziel, "They Encircled Me and Encompassed Me," 237–80; Benveniste, *Die Überlebenden*, 317–18; Flora Carasso in Erika Kounio-Amarilio, Almpertos Nar, and Phragkiski Abatzopoulou, *Prophorikes martyries Evreon tis Thessalonikis gia to Olokaytoma* [*Oral Testimonies of Thessaloniki Jews on the Holocaust*] (Thessaloniki: Paratiritis, 1998). For more about Nehama's and Molho's work together, see Naar, *Jewish Salonica*, 210, 214.

CHAPTER FOUR: RETURNING FROM ABROAD

1. Quoted from Nina Kokkalidou Nahmia, "Them and Us," trans. David Connoly, in *Poetry of the Holocaust: An Anthology*, ed. Jean Boase-Beier and Marian de Voogh (Todmorden, UK: Arc Publications, 2019), 207.

2. Interview with Matilda Benroubi (née Pisante), 41794, VHA, USC Shoah Foundation. Concerning the Crete campaign, see the two classic works Antony Beevor, *Crete: The Battle and the Resistance* (London: Penguin, 1991); and Peter Antill, *Crete 1941: Germany's Lightning Airborne Assault* (Oxford, UK: Osprey, 2005).

3. Dimitrios Psarras, *To best seller tou misous. Ta "protokolla ton sofon tis Sion" stin Ellada, 1920–2013* [*The Bestseller of Hatred: The "Protocols of the Elders of Zion" in Greece, 1920–2013*] (Athens: Polis, 2013); see Tobias Blümel, "Der Teufel, die Juden, die Protokolle der Weisen von Zion und die zionistische Weltverschwörung: Grundlinien des Antisemitismus in Griechenland," in Wolfgang Wippermann and Axel Weipert, eds., *Historische Interventionen: Festschrift für Wolfgang Wippermann zum 70. Geburtstag* (Amsterdam: Trafo, 2015), 121–28.

4. Moses Moskowitz, "Review of the Year 5699 – Bulgaria," in *The American Jewish Year Book*, vol. 41 (Philadelphia, PA: The Jewish Publication Society of America, 1939), 323–25, http://ajcarchives.org/main.php.

5. Eugene Hevesi, "Review of the Year 5702 – Greece," in *The American Jewish Year Book*, vol. 44 (Philadelphia: The Jewish Publication Society of America, 1942), 275; "Spain Permits Return of 12 Jewish Refugee Families from Greece," *Jewish Telegraphic Agency*, April 15, 1940, www.jta.org/1940/04/15/archive/.

252 · NOTES TO CHAPTER FOUR

6. Renée Poznanski, *Jews in France during World War II*, trans. Nathan Bracher (Waltham, MA: Brandeis University Press, USHMM, and University Press of New England, 2001), 304; Rebecca Clifford, *Commemorating the Holocaust: The Dilemmas of Remembrance in France and Italy* (Oxford, UK: Oxford University Press, 2013), 76, n. 18; Jens Hoppe, "Ferramonti Di Tarsia," in *The United States Holocaust Memorial Museum Encyclopedia of Camps and Ghettos, 1933–1945*, vol. 3, *Camps and Ghettos under European Regimes Aligned with Nazi Germany* (Indianapolis: Indiana University Press, 2018), 424–26; Sarah Abrevaya Stein, *Family Papers: A Sephardic Journey through the Twentieth Century* (New York: Farrar, Straus and Giroux, 2019), 153–56; Serge Klarsfeld, *Memorial to the Jews Deported from France, 1942–1944: Documentation of the Deportation of the Victims of the Final Solution in France* (New York: Beate Klarsfeld Foundation, 1983), 344–47.

7. Odette Beser (née Hassid), 29118, and Mazeltov Angel (née Hassid), 29541, VHA, USC Shoah Foundation.

8. Kristina Birri-Tomovska, *Jews of Yugoslavia, 1918–1941: A History of Macedonian Sephards* (Berne: Peter Lang, 2012), 285–91.

9. USHMM, Portrait of Solomon Nehama, Photograph No. 92903, United States Holocaust Memorial Museum Collections, http://collections.ushmm.org/search/catalog /pa1132623.

10. For more information on the Nehama family tree, see "Solomon Nehama Family of Monastir," *Sefaradim of Monastir*, http://www.cassorla.net/Solomon_Nehama.html, and in USHMM, RG-50.030.0472, Oral history interview with Isaac Nehama, conducted by Joan Ringelheim, 22 October 2002; USHMM, RG-50.030.0475, Oral history interview with Paulette Nehama, conducted by Margaret West, 24 June 2003. For Jamila and Monastir, see Jamila Andjela Kolonomos, *Monastir without Jews: Recollections of a Jewish Partisan in Macedonia* (New York: Foundation for the Advancement of Sephardic Studies and Culture, 2008). For more information about Isak Kamhi, see the Kamhi Family Portrait, Encyclopedia of Holocaust Archive, USHMM, https://encyclopedia.ushmm.org/en.

11. Vicki Tamir, *Bulgaria and Her Jews: The History of a Dubious Symbiosis* (New York: Sepher-Hermon Press for Yeshiva University Press, 1979), 193; for more on Bulgarian policy toward the Jews, see Tamir, *Bulgaria and Her Jews*, 159–218; and Hans-Joachim Hoppe, "Bulgarien," in Wolfgang Benz, ed., *Dimension des Völkermords: Die Zahl der Jüdischen Opfer des Nationalsozialismus* (Munich: Oldenbourg, 1991), 279–306.

12. "Muschon Kamhi Family of Monastir," *Sefaradim of Monastir*, www.cassorla.net /Kamhi.html; "Jews who left Greece for Palestine on 8/4/45" (30 August 1945), in Registration of Liberated Former Persecutees at Various Locations, 3.1.1.3.(F 18-56 Griechenland, 045)/0060_78779776_1–0067_78779789_1, ITS Digital Archive; and AJDC, NY AR 1945-54/4/33/2/386, Greece, General, VIII.–XII. 1945, "Letter from Morris Laub to Dr. J. Schwartz, Re: Greece" (23 August 1945). On postwar migration of Bulgarian Jews

NOTES TO CHAPTER FOUR · 253

to Palestine, see Rumyana Marinova-Christidi, "From Salvation to Alya: The Bulgarian Jews and Bulgarian-Israeli Relations (1948–1990)," *Southeast European and Black Sea Studies* 17, no. 2 (2017): 229–31. See also Nadège Ragaru, *"Et les Juifs bulgares furent sauvés…": une histoire des savoirs sur la Shoah en Bulgarie* (Paris: Science Po, 2020).

13. Natan Grinberg, *Dokumenti; izdireni i subrani iz arhiva na Komisarstvoto za evreiskite vuprosi* [*Documents, Searched and Collected from the Archive of the Commission for Jewish Affairs*] (Sofia: Tsentralna Konsistoria na Evreite v Bulgaria, 1945), 123–24.

14. Sampetai Tsimino, 45117, VHA, USC Shoah Foundation.

15. Sampetai Tsimino, 45117, VHA, USC Shoah Foundation; Iasonas Chandrinos, *Synagonistis: Ellines Evrei stin Ethniki Antistasi* [*Synagonistis: Greek Jews in the National Resistance*] (Athens: Evraiko Mousio Ellados, 2013), 18.

16. Sampetai Tsimino, 45117, VHA, USC Shoah Foundation.

17. For more about Buljkes, see Kateřina Králová, "Die Griechen," in Kamil Pikal, Kateřina Králová, and Jiří Kocian, eds., *Minderheiten im sozialistischen Jugoslawien: Brüderlichkeit und Eigenheit* (Frankfurt am Main: Peter Lang, 2015), 233–37. See also Milan D. Ristović, *To pirama Boulkes: I elliniki dimokratia sti Giougoslavia 1945–1949* [*The Buljkes Experiment: Greek Democracy in Yugoslavia, 1945–1949*] (Thessaloniki: Ekdot. Oikos Adelphon Kyriakidi, 2006). On the expulsion of Germans from Yugoslavia, see e.g., Jiří Kocián, "Die Deutschen," in Pikal, Králová, and Kocian, *Minderheiten im sozialistischen Jugoslawien*, 161–63.

18. Markos Mpotton [*sic*], 43906, VHA, USC Shoah Foundation.

19. After liberation, Abraham Benaroya returned via Italy to Athens. He resettled in Israel in the 1950s, but Marios moved to the United States. See the T/D file of Abraham Benaroya, 17 February 1955, in Repository of T/D Cases, 6.3.3.2/ 99461450-51#1, ITS Digital Archive, USHMM.

20. Mpotton [*sic*] Anry, 42858, VHA, USC Shoah Foundation. Concerning Tiso and the declaration of the Slovak State, see James Mace Ward, *Priest, Politician, Collaborator: Jozef Tiso and the Making of Fascist Slovakia* (Ithaca, NY: Cornell University Press, 2013), 158. Also, David Cymet, *History vs. Apologetics: The Holocaust, the Third Reich, and the Catholic Church* (Lanham, MD: Lexington Books, 2011), 324. For more information on Slovak complicity in the Holocaust, see Hana Kubátová, *Nepokradeš! Nálady a postojeslovenské společnosti k židovské otázce, 1938–1945* [*Thou Shalt Not Steal!: The Moods and Attitudes of Slovak Society to the Jewish Question, 1938–1945*] (Prague: Academia, 2013), 178–231.

21. Mpotton [*sic*] Anry, 42858, VHA, USC Shoah Foundation; Ruth Linn, *Escaping Auschwitz: A Culture of Forgetting* (Ithaca, NY: Cornell University Press, 2004), 21.

22. AJDC, IST 1937-49/4/15/IS.227, Lisbon 1944–1945 (2 of 2), "Telegram, Resnik to Schwarz" (24 April 1944).

23. One should also take into account that the Turkish authorities were not averse to

254 · NOTES TO CHAPTER FOUR

anti-Jewish policies, as confirmed by the violent expulsion of Jews from Turkish Thrace in 1934. See Corry Guttstadt, *Turkey, the Jews, and the Holocaust* (Cambridge: Cambridge University Press, 2013), 61–69.

24. AJDC, NY AR 1945-54/4/81/2/990, Turkey, General, "Letter from Arthur Fishzohn to Mr. Donald Hurwitz" (26 May 1945).

25. AJDC, IST 1937-49/4/9/IS.217, Greece 1944–1946, "Untitled Typewritten Memorandum" (19 July 1944).

26. Renée Hirschon, "The Jews of Rhodes: The Decline and Extinction of an Ancient Community," in Minna Rozen, ed., *The Last Ottoman Century and Beyond: The Jews in Turkey and the Balkans, 1808–1945* (Tel Aviv: TAU Press, 2002), 291–309. Concerning the Rhodian Jews before the Holocaust, see also Andreas Guidi, "Defining Inter-Communality between Documents, Tradition and Collective Memory: Jewish and Non-Jewish Capital and Labor in Early Twentieth Century Rhodes," *Southeast European and Black Sea Studies* 17, no. 2 (April 3, 2017): 165–80; Tuvia Friling, "Between Friendly and Hostile Neutrality: Turkey and the Jews during World War II," in *The Last Ottoman Century and Beyond: The Jews in Turkey and the Balkans, 1808–1945*, ed. Minna Rozen (Tel Aviv: TAU Press, 2002). 378. Concerning Rhodian refugees to Cyprus, see AJDC, G 1945-54/4/9/13/GR.84, Greece: Greek Islands—Survivors 1945, "Translation of Letter from Michel Menasce to [the] Honorable President of Hebrew Community of Los Angeles, California" (29 December 1944).

27. Maurice Sorriano, 45045, VHA, USC Shoah Foundation.

28. See the work of an Oxford-based anthropologist of Rhodian origin, Hirschon, "The Jews of Rhodes," 306. See also Lina Kantor (née Amato), 33706, VHA, USC Shoah Foundation.

29. "Gesetz zu dem Vertrag vom 18. März 1960 zwischen der Bundesrepublik Deutschland und dem Königreich Griechenland über Leistungen zugunsten griechischer Staatsangehöriger, die von nationalsozialistischen Verfolgungsmaßnahmen betroffen worden sind," *Bundesgesetzblatt Jahrgang* 1961, pt. 2, no. 49 (21 September 1961), 1596.

30. PAAA, B 81/203—Correspondence with Maurice Soriano (June 1959).

31. Turiel account in Franziska Ehricht and Elke Gryglewski, *Geschichten teilen: Dokumentenkoffer für eine interkulturelle Pädagogik zum Nationalsozialismus* (Berlin: Haus der Wannseekonferenz, 2009).

32. Isaac Benatar, *Rhodes and the Holocaust: The Story of the Jewish Community from the Mediterranean Island of Rhodes* (New York: iUniverse, 2010), 82–84.

33. Lina Kantor (née Amato), 33706, VHA, USC Shoah Foundation. For more information about the Rhodian emigration to Africa and the Sephardic Hebrew Congregation of Rhodesia established in 1931, see the special edition published to mark the seventy-fifth anniversary of the Hebrew Sephardic Society of Rhodesia, on the Zimbabwe Jewish Community website, www.zjc.org.il/.

NOTES TO CHAPTER FOUR · 255

34. Michael Matsas, *The Illusion of Safety: The Story of the Greek Jews during World War II* (New York: Pella, 1997), 398.

35. Nina Kohen, 23299, and David Kohen, 23300, VHA, USC Shoah Foundation.

36. AJDC, NY AR 1945-54/4/14/2/88, Albania, Relief Supplies: Matzot, 1950–1954, "Letter from H. Benrubi to Mrs. Henrietta K. Buchman, Re: J. R. F." (14 March 1953); Nina Kohen, 23299, and David Kohen, 23300, VHA, USC Shoah Foundation.

37. AJDC, G 1945-54/4/18/13/YU.49, Jews in Need of Relief 1947–1953, "Letter from Fred. C. White to Melvin S. Goldstein, Re: Jews in Albania" (25 September 1947). The document mentions eight Jewish families in Vlorë and one family in Gjirokastër as well as two or three families in Tirana. According to the report, however, the Tirana families were sufficiently looked after thanks to their direct contacts to the Albanian Communist Party. See also AJDC, NY AR 1945-54/4/14/2/88, Albania, Relief Supplies: Matzot, 1950–1954, "Letter from H. Benrubi to Mrs. Henrietta K. Buchman, Re: J. R. F." (14 March 1953). For more about Greek prisoners in Albania, see Nikolaos Stavrou, "The Little Country with the Big Gulag," *Washington Post*, December 9, 1984.

38. Yad Vashem, Collection of the Righteous among the Nations Department, M.31.2/12915—Isuf Panariti (?–1980), date of registration: 21 October 2014 at https://righteous.yadvashem.org/ (accessed on 1 May 2019).

39. Frida Matalon (née Kounne), 32950, VHA, USC Shoah Foundation; Yad Vashem, Collection of the Righteous among the Nations Department, Isuf Panariti; "Son of Albanian Righteous Among the Nations and Albanian Minister of Agriculture Visits Yad Vashem," Yad Vashem, April 30, 2015, www.yadvashem.org/about/events.html.

40. Levis Errikos, 49887, VHA, USC Shoah Foundation; see also Matsas, *The Illusion of Safety*, 285–86.

41. Shaban Sinani, *Hebrenjtë në Shqipëri: Prania dhe shpëtimi [Jews in Albania: Presence and Rescue]* (Tirana: Naimi, 2009), 142–44. For the postwar trials, see the entries on Jozef Levi and Mateo Matathia in the Online Archives of the Victims of Communism, KUJTO.al, https://kujto.al/personat/jozef-levi/ and https://kujto.al/personat/mateo-matathia-2/. Concerning Erricos Levis and Epirus Jews, see AJDC, G 1945-54/4/18/13/YU.49, Yugoslavia: Jews in Need of Relief 1947–1953, "Letter from Fred. C. White to Melvin S. Goldstein, Re: Jews in Albania" (25 September 1947); NY AR 1945-54/3/5/8/1300, Passover, 1952–1954, "Letter from H. Benrubi to Mrs. Henrietta K. Buchman, Re: J. R. F." (14 March 1953). See also the interview with Michael Matsas in Potomac, conducted by Kateřina Králová (3 August 2015), deposited at the USHMM (though not yet accessible).

42. Michael Molho and Joseph Nehama, *In Memoriam: Gewidmet dem Andenken an die jüdischen Opfer der Naziherrschaft in Griechenland* (Essen: Peter Katzung, 1981), 375–78; USHMM, RG-45.010, KIS 0152—Trial with Chasson—testimony of Emilios Neri (2 June 1946). See also Renée Carpi, "Salonika during the Holocaust," in Rozen, *Last Ottoman Century*, 275–79. Concerning his whereabouts after Albania, see also FDR Library, War

256 · NOTES TO CHAPTER FOUR

Refugees Abroad—Hitachduth Oley Yavan to World Jewish Congress (4 August 1944), www.fdrlibrary.marist.edu/_resources/images/wrb/wrb0922.pdf; and the newspapers *Kathimerini* (5 July 1946) and *Empros* (5 July 1946). See also Sarah Abrevaya Stein, *Family Papers: A Sephardic Journey through the Twentieth Century* (New York: Farrar, Straus and Giroux, 2019), 170–79, 204–5.

43. For more about Merten, see Kateřina Králová, *Das Vermächtnis der Besatzung: deutsch-griechische Beziehungen seit 1940* (Cologne: Böhlau, 2016), 64–71, 151–72; Kateřina Králová and Katerina Lagos, "Nazi Crimes, Max Merten and His Prosecution as Reflected in Greece and Beyond," *Journal of Modern European History* 22, no. 2 (May 1, 2024): 169–87; and Susanne-Sophia Spiliotis, "'An Affair of Politics, Not Justice': The Merten Trial (1957–1959) and Greek-German Relations," in M. Mazower, ed., *After the War Was Over: Reconstructing the Family, Nation, and State in Greece, 1943–1960* (Princeton, NJ: Princeton University Press, 2000), 293–301.

44. Králová, *Das Vermächtnis der Besatzung*, 128–129; Tobias Blümel, "The Case of Alois Brunner and the Divided Consciousness in Processing the Holocaust in Greece," *Südosteuropa Mitteilungen* 2–3 (2021): 93–106; for a more extensive version in German, Tobias Blümel, "(K)eine Frage ethischer Natur. Der Fall Alois Brunner und das gespaltene Bewusstsein im Umgang mit der Shoah in Griechenland," in Nikolas Pissis and Dimitris Karydas, *Die "neue Ordnung" in Griechenland 1941 1944* (Berlin: Edition Romiosini, 2020), 125–96.

45. Yvet Leon (née Beza), 43188, and Almperto [*sic*] Nachmias, 41256, VHA, USC Shoah Foundation; USHMM, RG-50.426.0001, Oral history interview with Albert Nahmias, USHMM Collections, 17 June 1996.

46. Yvet Leon (née Beza), 43188, VHA, USC Shoah Foundation; USHMM, HVT-3014, Fortunoff Video Archive for Holocaust Testimonies, "Sabetai B. and Yvette L. Holocaust testimony," interviewed by Jaša Almuli.

47. Yvet Leon (née Beza), 43188, VHA, USC Shoah Foundation; USHMM, RG-50.426.001, Albert Nahmias (17 June 1996).

48. Olga Borovaya, *Modern Ladino Culture: Press, Belles Lettres, and Theater in the Late Ottoman Empire* (Bloomington: Indiana University Press, 2011), 100.

49. Jacob Norris, *Land of Progress: Palestine in the Age of Colonial Development, 1905–1948* (Oxford, UK: Oxford University Press, 2013), 76–77, 123–34.

50. Thurston Clarke, *By Blood and Fire: The Attack on the King David Hotel* (New York: Putnam, 1981), 255–64; Friling, "Turkey and the Jews," 376, 407–16; Karina Lampsa and Iakov Sibi, *I diasosi: i siopi tou kosmou, i antistasi sta geto ke ta stratopeda, i Ellines Evrei sta chronia tis Katochis* [*The Rescue: The Silence of the People, the Resistance in the Ghettos and the Camps, and the Greek Jews during the Occupation*] (Athens: Ekdosis Kapon, 2012), 190–206. For a personal account, see "Leon Recanati and I," in Asher Moissis, *Greek-Jewish Patrimony* (North Charleston, SC: CreateSpace, 2012), 148–51.

NOTES TO CHAPTER FOUR · 257

51. The Union of Jews from Greece in Palestine reported that about 1,000 Jews of Greece had arrived in Palestine in August 1944 with about 2,000 more expected to come. FDR Library, War Refugees Abroad—Hitachduth Oley Yavan to World Jewish Congress (4 August 1944), www.fdrlibrary.marist.edu. In December 1944, however, the British Foreign Office stated that at least 1,500 Jews from Greece had escaped to Turkey and elsewhere in the Middle East. TNA, FO 371/42900—I. L. Henderson to Intergovernmental Committee on Refugees (5 December 1944). According to the EAM figures referred to by Stavrianos, there were about 3,000 Jews in all. Leften Stavros Stavrianos, "The Jews of Greece," *Journal of Central European Affairs* 8, no. 3 (1948): 265.

52. Steven B. Bowman, *The Agony of Greek Jews, 1940–1945* (Stanford: Stanford University Press, 2009), 187–91; and Friling, "Turkey and the Jews," 407–16.

53. Concerning repatriation policies, see Arieh J. Kochavi, *Post-Holocaust Politics: Britain, the United States, and Jewish Refugees, 1945–1948* (Chapel Hill: University of North Carolina Press, 2001), 13–15. On the cooperation between the Jewish Agency, Yishuv, and the Greek resistance, see TNA, HS 5-351—Correspondence between Major G. H. Packer and Steel, H.Q., M.E.F. (27 July, 10 and 17 August 1944). Compare that with Stavrianos, "Jews of Greece," 265–66; Constantopoulou and Veremis, eds., *Documents on the History of the Greek Jews*, 334–38.

54. FDR Library, War Refugees Abroad—Hitachduth Oley Yavan to World Jewish Congress (4 August 1944). For Lovinger, see Lampsa and Sibi, *I diasosi*, 286.

55. TNA, FO 371/42900—Jews in Greece; Leeper to Eden (3 November 1944), and in the testimony of Mpeki Kovo, 42140, USC Shoah Foundation. See also Friling, "Turkey and the Jews," 408; Bowman, *Agony of Greek Jews*, 200–202; Lampsa and Sibi, *I diasosi*, 312–15.

56. Lampsa and Sibi, *I diasosi*, 336–37. See also Acher Benroubi, 41796, and Eytychia Avdela (née Negris), 43876, VHA, USC Shoah Foundation.

57. Acher Benroubi, 41796, VHA, USC Shoah Foundation.

58. David Frances, 7792, and Albert Marcos, 453, VHA, USC Shoah Foundation.

59. Lampsa and Sibi, *I diasosi*, 379–80. See also Eytychia Avdela (née Negris), 43876, Lora Loyna Sasson, 40304, and David Frances, 7792, VHA, USC Shoah Foundation.

60. Eytychia Avdela (née Negris), 43876, VHA, USC Shoah Foundation. For siblings, see Mico Alvo, 12990, and Daniel Alvo, 21276, or Albert Marcos, 453, VHA, USC Shoah Foundation. Since Eftyhia was unmarried at the time, I use her maiden name for historical accuracy.

61. Neni Panourgia, *Dangerous Citizens: The Greek Left and the Terror of the State* (New York: Fordham University Press, 2009), 62; Leften Stavros Stavrianos, "The Mutiny in the Greek Armed Forces, April 1944," *The American Slavic and East European Review* 9, no. 4 (December 1950): 302–11. See also André Gerolymatos, *An International Civil War: Greece, 1943–1949* (New Haven: Yale University Press, 2016), 58; Haris Vlavianos, *Greece, 1941–49:*

258 · NOTES TO CHAPTER FOUR

From Resistance to Civil War: The Strategy of the Greek Communist Party (New York: St. Martin's Press and Palgrave Macmillan, 1992), 39; John Sakkas, "Greece and the British Factor," in J. Sakkas, *Britain and the Greek Civil War: British Imperialism, Public Opinion and the Coming of the Cold War* (Berlin: Franz Philipp Rutzen, 2013), 21–22.

62. FDR Library, War Refugees Abroad—Hitachduth Oley Yavan to World Jewish Congress (4 August 1944). See also Eytychia Avdela (née Negris), 43876, and Albert Marcos, 453, VHA, USC Shoah Foundation.

63. TNA, FO 371/51171—Refugee Department (March 14, 1945). See also the lists in "UNRRA N.A.R.C, Arivees and Departs [*sic*]. May 12 to Nov. 15 1944," 24.11.44, in DP Registration Lists 3.1.1.2/82050707#01–82050721#01; and "En Encargado de Asuntos Consulares de la Embajada de Espanaen Atenas, certifica: Que los súbditos españoles de origen sefarditas que a continuación se idican, fueron deportados por las autoridades Alemanas de ocupación a Bergen-Belsen el día 2 Agosto 1943," in "Vorgang abgelegt unter File 209/433," 6.6.3.5/105611887#01–105611887#10, ITS Digital Archive, USHMM. The Argentine Jews deported from Poland shared the same fate in Bergen-Belsen for a while but were soon deported to Auschwitz. See Christine Lattek, "Bergen-Belsen: From 'Privileged' Camp to Death Camp," in David Cesarani et al., eds., *Belsen in History and Memory* (Hoboken, NJ: Taylor & Francis, 2013), 45. For German-Spanish negotiations, see Bernd Rother, "Spain and the German Repatriation Ultimatum 1943/44," in Corry Guttstadt et al., eds., *Bystanders, Rescuers or Perpetrators? The Neutral Countries and the Shoah* (Berlin: Metropol, 2016), 169–79.

64. Izi Revah, 40024, VHA, USC Shoah Foundation.

65. Isac Gattegno [*sic*], 12843, VHA, USC Shoah Foundation.

66. Izi Revah, 40024, VHA, USC Shoah Foundation. On the Spanish rescue myth, see Pedro Correa Martín-Arroyo, "'Franco, Savior of the Jews'? Tracing the Genealogy of the Myth and Assessing Its Persistence in Recent Historiography," in Alexandra Garbarini and Paul Jaskot, eds., *Lessons and Legacies*, vol. 13, *New Approaches to an Integrated History of the Holocaust: Social History, Representation, Theory* (Evanston, IL: Northwestern University Press, 2018), 195–218; Bernd Rother, "Myth and Fact: Spain and the Holocaust," in Antonio Gómez López-Quiñones and Susanne Zepp, eds., *The Holocaust in Spanish Memory: Historical Perceptions and Cultural Discourse* (Leipzig: Leipziger Universitätsverlag, 2010), 51–63.

67. Lily-Nina Benroubi (née Revah), 37989, VHA USC Shoah Foundation, FDR Library, War Refugees Abroad—Hitachduth Oley Yavan to World Jewish Congress (4 August 1944).

68. "UNRRA N.A.R.C. Arivees and Departs [*sic*]. May 12 to Nov. 15 1944," 24 November 44, in DP Registration Lists 3.1.1.2/ 82050707#01, ITS Digital Archive, USHMM.

69. Quotation from Rachel Revah (née Saporta), 25197, VHA, USC Shoah Foundation. For conditions in Morocco, see also Nelli Gattegno, 12845, and Isac Gattegno [*sic*], 12843, VHA,

USC Shoah Foundation. Concerning his bar mitzvah, see Zilmper Nachmias, 40850, VHA, USC Shoah Foundation.

70. "UNRRA N.A.R.C. Arivees and Departs [sic]. May 12 to Nov. 15 1944," 24 November 1944, in DP Registration Lists 3.1.1.2/ 82050709#01, ITS Digital Archive, USHMM; Raymonde Tauber, 2934, VHA, USC Shoah Foundation. None of the Jews of Spanish citizenship in Nuseirat ever mentioned any separation of ex-inmates from Bergen-Belsen. On the contrary, they insisted that they had always stayed together. See Choyan Chassid-Mosseri, 48965, Zilmper Nachmias, 40850, and Lily-Nina Benroubi, 37989, VHA USC Shoah Foundation.

71. "UNRRA N.A.R.C. Arivees and Departs [sic]. May 12 to Nov. 15 1944," ITS Digital Archive, USHMM.

72. Rachel Revah (née Saporta), 25197, VHA, USC Shoah Foundation.

73. Choyan Chassid-Mosseri, 48965, Frenty Ampravanel, 47797, Dan Saporta, 40729, and Zilmper Nachmias, 40850, VHA, USC Shoah Foundation.

74. Izi Revah, 40024, VHA, USC Shoah Foundation.

75. Lily-Nina Benroubi (née Revah), 37989, VHA USC Shoah Foundation.

76. Albert Marcos, 453, VHA, USC Shoah Foundation.

Chapter Five: After Homecoming

1. Quoted from Nina Kokkalidou Nahmia, "After Twenty Years in Auschwitz," trans. David Connoly, in *Poetry of the Holocaust: An Anthology*, ed. Jean Boase-Beier and Marian de Voogh (Todmorden, UK: Arc Publications, 2019), 218.

2. N. 367/1945 (4 June 1945)—Peri anasygkrotiseos Israilitikon Koinotiton, FEK A'143/1945.

3. Dan Stone, *Goodbye to All That?: The Story of Europe Since 1945* (Oxford: Oxford University Press, 2014), 15–43.

4. USHMM, RG-50.968.0032—Oral history interview with Gaynor I. Jacobson, conducted by Tad Szulc (1988).

5. USHMM, RG-45.010, Selected records of the Central Jewish Board (KIS) Athens, Greece, KIS 0127—Memorandum (28 February 1946).

6. Eduard Mark, *Revolution by Degrees: Stalin's National-Front Strategy for Europe, 1941–1947* (Washington, DC: Woodrow Wilson International Center for Scholars 2001), 5–46.

7. USHMM, RG-45.010, KIS 0096—KIS to the American Jewish Committee (22 September 1946), and RG-45.010, KIS 096—"KIS to the Congrès Juif Mondial" (17 January 1946).

8. USHMM, RG-45.010, KIS 0134—KIS Minutes from the Meetings (16 May 1945).

260 · NOTES TO CHAPTER FIVE

9. USHMM, RG-45.010, KIS 096—SALONICA. Echo of the Orient. Leon Saki (18 January 1946). In accordance with the sources, here I use the more recent transliteration of Sciaky into Greek.

10. AJDC, NY AR 1945-54/4/33/2/384, Greece, General, 1949–1954, "Letter from Herbert Katzki to AJDC New York, Re: Report on Greece" (23 October 1950). See also Katherine E. Fleming, *Greece: A Jewish History* (Princeton, NJ: Princeton University Press, 2008), 183.

11. Stone, *Goodbye to All That?*, 63–64.

12. AJDC, NY AR 1945-54/4/33/2/384 and 386, Greece, General, VIII.–XII. 1945, "The Jews and the Liberation Struggle" (12 September 1945) or "Letter from Herbert Katzki to AJDC New York, Re: Report on Greece" (23 October 1950). See also Kateřina Králová, "'Being Traitors': Post-War Greece in the Experience of Jewish Partisans," *Southeast European and Black Sea Studies* 17, no. 2 (2017): 263–80.

13. Stone, *Goodbye to All That?*, 21.

14. Karina Lampsa and Iakov Sibi. *I diasosi: i siopi tou kosmou, i antistasi sta geto ke ta stratopeda, i Ellines Evrei sta chronia tis Katochis* [*The Rescue: The Silence of the People, the Resistance in the Ghettos and the Camps, and the Greek Jews during the Occupation*] (Athens: Ekdosis Kapon, 2012), 118–21.

15. AJDC, NY AR 1945-54/4/33/2/385, Greece, General, 1946–1948, "Need for Combating Manifestations of Anti-Semitism in Greece" (1 April 1947).

16. For example, in Frederic J. Kakis, *Legacy of Courage: A Holocaust Survival Story* (Bloomington, IN: 1st Books Library, 2003), 244. Lewkowicz refers to a testimony according to which the new inhabitants of a house belonging to a former Auschwitz inmate complained to him after his return: "What a pity you were not turned into soap." See Bea Lewkowicz, *The Jewish Community of Salonika: History, Memory, Identity* (London: Vallentine Mitchell, 2006), 197. A similar statement is quoted in Joshua Eli Plaut, *Greek Jewry in the Twentieth Century, 1913–1983: Patterns of Jewish Survival in the Greek Provinces before and after the Holocaust* (Madison, NJ: Fairleigh Dickinson University Press, 1996), 71.

17. USHMM, RG-50.968.0032—Oral history interview with Gaynor I. Jacobson, conducted by Tad Szulc (1988).

18. Erika Kounio-Amariglio, *From Thessaloniki to Auschwitz and Back: Memories of a Survivor from Thessaloniki* (London: Vallentine Mitchell, 2000), 141.

19. Tony Judt, *Postwar: A History of Europe since 1945* (New York: Penguin Books, 2005), 43.

20. N. 2/1944 (26 October 1944)—"Peri katargiseos ton Nomon 1977/1944 kai 1180/1944 kai apodoseos ton Israilitikon periousion," FEK A'6/1944, and A. N. 337 (20 May 1945)— "Peri katargiseos tou Nomou 205/1943," "peri diacheiriseos ton para ton Archon Katochis katechomenon kai egkataleipomenon Israilitikon periousion," FEK A'121/1945. See also Sam Nahmias, "Die Vermögen der deportieren Israiliten Griechenlands," in Michael

NOTES TO CHAPTER FIVE · 261

Molho and Joseph Nehama, eds., *In Memoriam: Gewidmet dem Andenken an die jüdischen Opfer der Naziherrschaft in Griechenland* (Essen: Peter Katzung, 1981), 463.

21. A. N. 808/1945 (31 December 1945)—"Peri sympliroseos ton A. N. 2/1944 kai 337/45," FEK A'324/1945; Nahmias, *Die Vermögen*, 460–63; Kateřina Králová, "In the Shadow of the Nazi Past: Post-War Reconstruction and the Claims of the Jewish Community in Salonika," *European History Quarterly* 46, no. 2 (2016): 262–90. Concerning Jewish property in Greece, see Maria Kavala, "The Scale of Jewish Property Theft in Nazi-Occupied Thessaloniki," in *The Holocaust in Greece*, ed. Giorgos Antoniou and A. Dirk Moses (Cambridge, UK: Cambridge University Press, 2018), 183–207; Stratos N. Dordanas, "The Jewish Community of Thessaloniki and the Christian Collaborators: 'Those That Are Leaving and What They Are Leaving Behind,'" in *The Holocaust in Greece*, ed. Giorgos Antoniou and A. Dirk Moses (Cambridge, UK: Cambridge University Press, 2018), 208–27; Kostis Kornetis, "Expropriating the Space of the Other: Property Spoliations of Thessalonican Jews in the 1940s," in *The Holocaust in Greece*, ed. Giorgos Antoniou and A. Dirk Moses (Cambridge, UK: Cambridge University Press, 2018), 228–51. Concerning Jewish property in general, see Dan Diner and Gotthart Wunberg, eds., *Restitution and Memory: Material Restoration in Europe* (New York: Berghahn, 2007); Martin Dean, *Robbing the Jews: The Confiscation of Jewish Property in the Holocaust, 1933–1945* (Cambridge, UK: Cambridge University Press; United States Holocaust Memorial Museum, 2008); Martin Dean, Constantin Goschler, and Philipp Ther, *Robbery and Restitution: The Conflict over Jewish Property in Europe* (New York: Berghahn Books; United States Holocaust Memorial Museum, 2007).

22. USHMM, RG-50.968.0032—Oral history interview with Gaynor I. Jacobson, conducted by Tad Szulc (1988), AJDC, NY AR 1945-54/4/33/2/386, Greece, General, VIII.–XII. 1945, "Letter from Louis H. Sobel to Dr. John Slawsom" (9 October 1945); Harry Schneiderman and Morris Fine, eds., *The American Jewish Yearbook*, vol. 50 (Philadelphia: The Jewish Publication Society of America, 1948), 372–73.

23. AJDC, NY AR1945-54/4/33/2/385, Greece, General, 1946–1948, "Need for Combating Manifestations of Anti-Semitism in Greece" (1 April 1947); and Mark Mazower, *Salonica, City of Ghosts: Christians, Muslims and Jews, 1430–1950* (London: HarperCollins, 2004), 422–23.

24. N. 846/1946 (18 January 1946)—"Peri katargiseos tou klironomikou dikaiomatos tou Kratous epi ton ekkeimenon Israilitikon periousion," FEK A'17/1946.

25. Diatagma (29 March 1949)—"Peri idryseos Organismou Perithalpseos kai Apokatastaseos Israiliton Ellados," FEK A'79/1949.

26. Lewkowicz, *Jewish Community of Salonika*, 189; Plaut, *Greek Jewry*, 77–79.

27. Kateřina Králová, *Das Vermächtnis der Besatzung: Deutsch-griechische Beziehungen seit 1940* (Cologne: Böhlau, 2016), 196–202; see also Hagen Fleischer and Despina Konstantinakou, "Ad calendas graecas?: Griechenland und die deutsche Wiedergutmachung," in Hans

262 · NOTES TO CHAPTER FIVE

Günter Hockerts, Claudia Moisel, and Tobias Winstel, eds., *Grenzen der Wiedergutmachung: die Entschädigung für NS-Verfolgte in West- und Osteuropa 1945–2000* (Göttingen: Wallstein Verlag, 2006), 439–41.

28. See *Evraiki Estia*, March 14, 1952; *I Ygeia*, September 1989. Concerning the sale of a former Jewish hospital, the Hirsch Hospital, see also Bea Lewkowicz, "'After the War We Were All Together': Jewish Memories of Postwar Thessalonica," in *After the War Was Over: Reconstructing the Family, Nation, and State in Greece, 1943–1960*, ed. Mark Mazower (Princeton, NJ: Princeton University Press, 2000), 249.

29. Photini Constantopoulou and Thanos Veremis, eds., *Documents on the History of the Greek Jews: Records from Historical Archives of the Ministry of Foreign Affairs*, trans. Geoffrey Cox and John Solman (Athens: Kastaniotis Editions, 1998), 36–37.

30. Lewkowicz, *Jewish Community of Salonika*, 192.

31. AJDC, NY AR 1945-54/4/33/2/386, Greece, General, VIII.–XII. 1945, "Many Jewish Skulls and bones are visible all over the Cemetery" (21 August 1945).

32. USHMM, RG-50.968.0032—Oral history interview with Gaynor I. Jacobson, conducted by Tad Szulc (1988); Yad Vashem, M.31.2/546—Gennadios Yiorgios (1868–1951), https://righteous.yadvashem.org/.

33. USHMM, RG-45.010, KIS 096—KIS to WJC (5 May 1946).

34. USHMM, RG-45.010, KIS 096—SALONICA. Echo of the Orient. Leon Saki (18 January 1946).

35. General State Archives—Historical Archives of Macedonia, Collection of Regional Directorate of Aliens; GRGSA-IAM_ADM 281.02. F000505—Italian Citizen MODIANO, 7/191/2d (25 June 1947).

36. GRGSA-IAM_ADM 281.02. F000505—Italian Citizen MODIANO, 7/191/3d (4 September 1947).

37. GRGSA-IAM_ADM 281.02. F000505—Italian Citizen MODIANO, 7/191/4d (27 January 1949).

38. Ibid.

39. GRGSA-IAM_ADM 281.02. F000505—Italian Citizen MODIANO, 7/191/2d (25 June 1947).

40. GRGSA-IAM_ADM 281.02. F000505—Italian Citizen MODIANO, 7/191/4b (3 November 1948) and 7/191/4d (27 January 1949).

41. Mario Modiano, "The Story," The Website of the Modiano Family, www.themodianos.gr/The_Story.pdf.

42. Stone, *Goodbye to All That?*, 6–7.

43. USHMM, RG-45.010, KIS 0096—Report (9 April 1946), KIS 0134—KIS Minutes from the Meetings (19 March 1946), KIS 0250—Ben Sion Meir Ouziel to KIS and Ben Sion Meir

NOTES TO CONCLUSION · 263

Ouziel to Aliaou Pinchas Barzilai (25 February 1945). See also Maria Kavala, "I metapolemiki anasygrotisi tis Evraikis Kinotitas Thessalonikis. O rolos tou gamou sti synochi tis kinotitas (1945–1955)" ["The Postwar Reconstruction of the Jewish Community of Thessaloniki: The Role of Marriage in the Cohesion of the Community (1945–1955)"] (PhD diss., University of Thessaly, 2015), 1–10.

44. USHMM, RG-45.010, KIS 0096—"KIS to the Congrès Juif Mondial" (17 January 1946).

45. USHMM, RG-45.010, KIS 0134—KIS Minutes from the Meetings (26 February and 26 March 1946). Concerning the Holocaust and memory, see also Odette Varon-Vassard, "Der Genozid an den griechischen Juden: Zeugnisse des Überlebens und Geschichtsschreibung seit 1948," in Chryssoula Kambas and Marilisa Mitsou, eds., *Die Okkupation Griechenlands im Zweiten Weltkrieg: Griechische und deutsche Erinnerungskultur* (Cologne: Böhlau, 2015), 85–114; and Rena Molho, "Problems of Incorporating the Holocaust into the Greek Collective Memory: The Case of Thessaloniki," *Journal of Turkish Studies* 40 (2013): 301–13.

46. Vasiliki Selioti, *Vretanika stratopeda Evreon prosfygon stin Kypro (1946–1949)* [*British Camps for Jewish Refugees in Cyprus (1946–1949)*] (Thessaloniki: Epikentro, 2016), 140–53. For excellent research on this topic, see also Eliana Hadjisavvas, "Population Displacement and Transnational Trajectories: Immigration, Internment and Empire in the Case of Jewish Refugees and the Cyprus Camps, 1946–1949" (PhD diss., University of Birmingham, 2018); and Eliana Hadjisavvas, "'From Dachau to Cyprus': Jewish Refugees and the Cyprus Internment Camps – Relief and Rehabilitation, 1946–1949," in Suzanne Bardgett, Christine Schmidt, and Dan Stone, eds., *Beyond Camps and Forced Labour: Proceedings of the Sixth International Conference* (Cham, Switzerland: Palgrave Macmillan, 2021).

47. See AJDC, G 45-54/4/9/6/GR.30, Greece: ICEM-IRO 1949–1953, "Letter from Mr. James P. Rice to Mr. Louis Horwitz, Re: Emigration from Greece" (4 August 1953).

48. Knesset, The Law of Return 5710 (1950); US Constitution, 67 Stat. 400—Act to authorize the issuance of 240,000 special note immigrant visas, and for other purposes (7 August 1953); and 62 Stat. 1009, Chapter 647—Act to authorize for a limited period of time the admission into the United States of certain European displaced persons for permanent residence, and for other purposes (25 June 1948). See also Plaut, *Greek Jewry*, 90.

49. USHMM, RG-45.010, KIS 0214—To Kentriko Israilitiko Symvoulion syntonismuo ke gnomateuseos (18 August 1967).

CONCLUSION

1. Zygmunt Bauman, *Freedom* (Minneapolis: University of Minnesota Press, 1988), 89.

2. Marianne Hirsch, *Family Frames: Photography, Narrative, and Postmemory* (Cambridge: Harvard University Press, 1997).

264 · NOTES TO CONCLUSION

3. Victoria McGeer, "Trust, Hope and Empowerment," *Australasian Journal of Philosophy* 86, no. 2 (2008): 237–54.

4. See Atina Grossmann, *Jews, Germans, and Allies: Close Encounters in Occupied Germany* (Princeton, NJ: Princeton University Press, 2007).

5. Daniel M. Knight, *Vertiginous Life: An Anthropology of Time and the Unforeseen* (New York: Berghahn, 2021).

6. See, e.g., Jessie Barton-Hronešová, *The Struggle for Redress: Victim Capital in Bosnia and Herzegovina* (Cham, Switzerland: Palgrave, 2020).

7. Lawrence Langer, "The Dilemma of Choice in the Deathcamps," *Centerpoint: A Journal of Interdisciplinary Studies* 4, no. 1 (1980): 53–58. It is highly disputable, however, whether choosing between seemingly choiceless options starts, as Langer put it, only in death camps.

8. Robert Meister, *After Evil: A Politics of Human Rights*, Columbia Studies in Political Thought/Political History (New York: Columbia University Press, 2010), 1.

9. Mark Mazower, *Salonica, City of Ghosts: Christians, Muslims and Jews, 1430–1950* (London: HarperCollins, 2004).

10. Matarasso and Mazower argue that the partisan movement in Macedonia was not yet sufficiently developed to provide greater support to members of the Jewish minority. Isaac Aron Matarasso, "And Yet Not All of Them Died," in *The Holocaust in Salonika: Eyewitness Accounts*, ed. Steven B. Bowman, trans. Isaac Benmayor (New York: Sephardic House, 2002), 153; and Mazower, *Salonica*, 411. See also Rika Benveniste, *Auti pou epezisan: antistasi, ektopisi, epistrophi: Thessalonikis Evrei sti dekaetia tou 1940* [*Those Who Survived: Resistance, Deportation, Return: The Jews of Thessaloniki in the 1940s*] (Athens: Polis, 2014), 41–57.

11. José Gotovich, "Resistance Movements and the Jewish Question," in Dan Michman, ed., *Belgium and the Holocaust: Jews, Belgians, Germans* (Jerusalem: Yad Vashem, 1998), 281–82; Lucien Lazare, *Rescue As Resistance: How Jewish Organizations Fought the Holocaust in France* (New York: Columbia University Press, 1996); Evgeny Finkel, *Ordinary Jews: Choice and Survival during the Holocaust* (Princeton: Princeton University Press, 2018), 159–90; Michael R. Marrus, "Jewish Resistance to the Holocaust," *Journal of Contemporary History* 30, no. 1 (1995): 83–110.

12. Nikos Tzafleris, "Rebuilding Jewish Communities after the Holocaust: The American Jewish Joint Distribution Committee's Relief Programme in Postwar Greece," *Historein* 18, no. 2: 2019, https://doi.org/10.12681/historein.14583. On the JDC in general, Avinoam Patt, Atina Grossmann, Linda G. Levi, and Maud S. Mandel, *The JDC at 100: A Century of Humanitarianism* (Detroit: Wayne State University Press, 2019).

13. Hagen Fleischer, "Griechenland," in *Dimension des Völkermords: Die Zahl der jüdischen Opfer des Nationalsozialismus*, ed. Wolfgang Benz (Munich: Oldenbourg, 1991), 272–73.

NOTES TO CONCLUSION · 265

14. For documentation, particularly for Thessaloniki, Corfu, and Ioannina, see Stratos N. Dordanas, "I Yperesia Diachiriseos Israilitikon Periousion (YDIP)" ["The Office for the Disposal of Jewish Property"], in *To Olokautoma sta Balkania* [*The Holocaust in the Balkans*], ed. Giorgos Antoniou, Stratos N. Dordanas, Nikos Zaikos, and Nikos Marantzidis (Thessaloniki: Epikentro, 2011), 351–52; Fleming, *Greece*, 140; Michael Molho and Joseph Nehama, *In Memoriam: Gewidmet dem Andenken an die jüdischen Opfer der Naziherrschaft in Griechenland* (Essen: Peter Katzung, 1981), 231.

15. Concerning repatriation in general, see Richard Black and Khalid Koser, *The End of the Refugee Cycle? Refugee Repatriation and Reconstruction* (New York: Berghahn, 1999). For displacement during the Greek Civil War, see Loring M. Danforth and Riki Van Boeschoten, *Children of the Greek Civil War: Refugees and the Politics of Memory* (Chicago: University of Chicago Press, 2011); and Katerina Tsekou, *Ellines politiki prosfyges stin Anatoliki Europi, 1945–1989* [*Greek Civilian Refugees in Eastern Europe, 1945–1989*] (Athens: Alexandria, 2013).

16. Dan Stone, *Goodbye to All That?: The Story of Europe Since 1945* (Oxford: Oxford University Press, 2014), 294.

Bibliography

Holocaust survivors' testimonies, USC Shoah Foundation Visual History Archive

Accessed at the Malach Centre for Visual History, Charles University, with the support of the LM2015071 LINDAT/Clarin infrastructure.

Alvo, Daniel, #21276 (Oct. 24, 1996, Pylea, Central Macedonia, Greece).

Alvo, Mico, #12990 (Mar. 29, 1996, Panorama, Thessaloniki, Central Macedonia, Greece).

Amariglio, Erika, #21678 (Nov. 11, 1996, Panorama, Thessaloniki).

Amariglio, Rudolf, #23446 (Nov. 18, 1996, Panorama, Thessaloniki).

Ampravanel, Frenty, #47797 (Nov. 3, 1998, Athens, Attica, Greece).

Angel, Mazeltov, #29541 (Mar. 20, 1997, Brussels).

Antzel, Loykia, #42070 (Mar. 15, 1998, Thessaloniki, Central Macedonia, Greece).

Antzel, Sidoni, #37990 (Feb. 5, 1998, Athens).

Arditti, Rozita, #47848 (Nov. 19, 1998, Athens).

Aroych, Lili, #44441 (June 10, 1998, Athens).

Aroych, Tzakos, #39871 (Mar. 29, 1998, Thessaloniki).

Asser, Rozina, #44631 (May 21, 1998, Psychiko Athens).

Avdela, Eftyhia, #43876 (May 5, 1998, Athens).

Barzilai, Bella, #41749 (Mar. 22, 1998, Thessaloniki).

Benroubi, Acher, #41796 (Mar. 12, 1998, Athens).

Benroubi, Lily-Nina, #37989 (Feb. 12, 1998, Athens).

Benveniste, Flora, #47902 (Nov. 12, 1998, Charlotte, North Carolina).

Beser, Odette, #29118 (Mar. 12, 1997, Brussels).

Beza, Claire, #43697 (Apr. 30, 1998, Athens).

Bourla, Moise, #9368 (Feb. 11, 1996, Thessaloniki).

Brudo, David, #4466 (Aug. 16, 1995, Kiryat Moshe, Jerusalem).

Carasso Mihael, Flora, #1885 (Apr. 5, 1995, New York City).

Chassid-Mosseri, Choyan, #48965 (Oct. 29, 1998, Maroussi Attiki, Greece).

Cohen, Shlomo, #6883 (Aug. 14, 1995, Haifa, Israel).

Coumeri, Jacob, #47768 (Oct. 21, 1998, St. Dimitrios-Brahami, Athens).

Curtis, Maria, #34110 (July 9, 1997, Ormond, Victoria, Australia).

Eskaloni, Moise, #28007 (Feb. 22, 1997, Thessaloniki).

268 · BIBLIOGRAPHY

Filosof, Rafail, #48557 (Nov. 24, 1998, Larissa, Greece).

Florentin, Ester, #43029 (Apr. 7, 1998, Athens, Greece).

Frances, David, #7792 (Jan. 14, 1996, Athens, Greece).

Gabbai, Dario, #142 (Nov. 7, 1996, Los Angeles).

Garfinkle, Bouena, #54525 (Feb. 13, 1996, Montreal, Quebec).

Gatenio, Nata, #30258 (June 19, 1997, Tel Aviv).

Gattegno, Isac, #12843 (Mar. 5, 1996, Burbank, California).

Gattegno, Nelli, #12845 (Mar. 5, 1996, Burbank, California).

Gavriilidis, Gavriil, #41612 (Mar. 10, 1998, Athens).

Gkatenio, Ester, #44912 (June 19, 1998, Thessaloniki).

Habib, Lucia, #8310 (Jan. 22, 1996, Cape Town, Western Cape, South Africa).

Hatzi, Astro-Beki, #44596 (May 20, 1998, Kifisia-Athens, Greece).

Idas-Gabrielides, Leon, #22884 (Nov. 17, 1996, Baltimore, Maryland).

Kantor, Lina, #33706 (July 12, 1997, Harare, Zimbabwe).

Kapouano, Isaac, #1439 (Mar. 21, 1995, Marina del Rey, California).

Koen, Zermain, #48674 (Nov. 27, 1998, Athens, Greece).

Kohen, David, #23300 (Nov. 24, 1996, New York City).

Kohen, Nina, #23299 (Nov. 24, 1996, Brooklyn, New York).

Konis, David, #731 (Dec. 23, 1994, Beverly Hills, California).

Kounio, Edgar, #42145 (June 17, 1998, Thessaloniki).

Kounio, Heinz, #41892 (May 29, 1998, Thessaloniki).

Kovo, Mpeki, #42140 (Mar. 17, 1998, Athens).

Koynio, Chella, #40822 (Apr. 11, 1998, Thessaloniki).

Leon, Moris, #43190 (Apr. 14, 1998, Athens).

Leon, Yvet, #43188 (Apr. 14, 1998, Athens).

Levis, Errikos, #49887 (Mar. 5, 1999, Athens).

Marcos, Albert, #453 (Dec. 22, 1994, N. Hollywood, California).

Massarano, Stella, #5868 (Aug. 21, 1995, Woodland Hills, California).

Matalon, Frida, #32950 (June 14, 1997, Thessaloniki).

Matsa, Hertsel, #16634 (June 19, 1996, Tel Aviv).

Mizan, Isaak, #44916 (June 18, 1998, Vrillesia Attikes, Greece).

Molcho Kapoyano, Yvonni, #41963 (Mar. 17, 1998, Athens).

Mpakolas, Salvator, #41842 (May 12, 1998, Athens).

Mpenroympi, Matthildi, #41794 (Mar. 12, 1998, Athens).

Mperacha, Nteniz, #44212 (May 13, 1998, Athens).

Mpotton, Anry, #42858 (Apr. 1, 1998, Kifisia, Greece).

Mpotton, Markos, #43906 (May 5, 1998, Athens).

Nachmia, Mperry, #35270 (Oct. 25, 1997, Kifisia, Greece).

Nachmias, Almperto, #41256 (Feb. 28, 1998, Thessaloniki).

Nachmias, Nelli, #40116 (Jan. 25, 1998, Athens).

Nachmias, Zilmper, #40850 (Mar. 31, 1998, Athens).

Nahmias, Fratelis, #22138 (Nov. 1, 1996, Thessaloniki).

Nehama, Samuel, #687 (Jan. 25, 1995, New York City).

Nissim, Sam, #1471 (Mar. 13, 1995, Rego Park, New York).

Nissim, Suzanne, #5867 (Aug. 21, 1995, Woodland Hills, California).

Notrica, Gentile, #37988 (Feb. 5, 1998, Ambelokepos, Athens).

Papadrianou, Rachil, #46032 (May 22, 1998, Athens).

Perahia, Leon, #17390 (July 31, 1996, Thessaloniki).

Revah, Izi, #40024 (Jan. 18, 1998, Thessaloniki).

Revah, Rachel, #25197 (Dec. 20, 1996, Thessaloniki).

Sadikario, Zamila, #47542 (June 18, 1998, Skopje).

Saltiel, Solomon, #39393 (Feb. 22, 1998, Flint, Michigan).

Sampetai, Raphail, #44379 (May 13, 1998, Kifesia, Greece).

Saporta, Dan, #40729 (Feb. 15, 1998, Thessaloniki).

Sasson, Lora Loyna, #40304 (Apr. 3, 1998, Athens).

Sephiha, Andreas, #48935 (Dec. 13, 1998, Thessaloniki).

Siaki, Lili, #7796 (Jan. 6, 1996, Thessaloniki).

Simcha, Aleksandros, #39862 (Mar. 19, 1998, Athens).

Sorriano, Maurice, #45045 (June 6, 1998, Rhodes, Greece).

Stroumza, Isaac, #4137 (July 20, 1995, St.-Germain-en-Laye, Yvelines, France).

Stroymsa, Roympen, #39864 (Mar. 22, 1998, Thessaloniki, Greece).

Tauber, Raymonde, #2934 (June 1, 1995, Darling Point, Sydney, New South Wales, Australia).

Tsezanas, Erkanas, #39196 (Mar. 11, 1998, Athens).

Tsimino, Sampetai, #45117 (June 7, 1998, Kavala, Greece).

Venezia, Morris, #20405 (Oct. 27, 1996, Inglewood, California).

Venezia, Shlomo, #36179 (Dec. 13, 1997, Rome, Italy).

Yosafat, Matthew, #10295 (Dec. 17, 1995, Cincinnati, Ohio).

The Jewish Museum of Greece Archive (EME)

Categorized based on the Database of Greek-Jewish Holocaust Survivors' Testimonies, http://gjst .ha.uth.gr/en/search.php/.

Broudo, David, born in 1924, Thessaloniki, EME 20 (interviewed in 2019, Israel).

Forti, Sara, born in 1927, Chalkis, EME 50 (interviewed in 2010, Israel).

Gategnio, Nata, born in 1923, Kerkyra, EME 10 (interviewed in 2010, Israel).

Giousouroum, Mois, born in 1920, Athens, EME 33 (interviewed in 2010, Greece).

Koen, Louis, born in 1912, Xanthi, EME 28 (interviewed in 2006, Greece).

Moisi, Esdra, born in 1923, Larissa, EME 21 (interviewed in 2007, Greece).

270 · BIBLIOGRAPHY

Nehama, Samouil (Sam), born in 1930, Athens, EME 1 (interviewed in 2005, Greece).
Siakki-Decastro, Elli, born in Volos, EME 55 (interviewed in 2002, Greece).
Svolis, Avraam, born in 1923, Ioannina, EME 47 (interviewed in 2007, Greece).

INTERVIEWS RECORDED BY THE AUTHOR (PRIVATE ARCHIVE)

Amariglio, Erica. Interviewed in Thessaloniki (June 9, 2008).
Konstantinis, Moisis. Interviewed in Athens (Apr. 22, 2015).
Kounio, Heinz. Interviewed in Thessaloniki (June 4, 2016).
Matsas, Michael, and Ninneta Matsa-Feldman. Interviewed in Potomac (Aug. 3, 2015).
Nachmias, Berry. Interviewed in Kifisia. (June 15, 2008).
Nehama, Paulette. Interviewed in Bethesda, MD (July 29, 2015).
Simon, Laura. Interviewed in Woodland Hills, CA (Jan. 3, 2016).
Skifti, Allegra. Interview courtesy of Tasoula Vervenioti. Two interviews: June 21, 1995
 (three cassettes) and Nov. 20, 1995 (two cassettes) in Athens.
Venturas, Iosif. Interviewed in Athens (June 7, 2016).

CENTROPA, JEWISH WITNESS OF A EUROPEAN CENTURY, DATABASE OF JEWISH MEMORY

Alvo, Mico, interviewed by Paris Papamichos Chronakis, Centropa (Nov. 2005), www.
 centropa.org/biography/mico-alvo/.
Arouch (née Pardo), Lilly, interviewed by Annita Mordechai (Nov. 2005), www.centropa
 .org/biography/lily-arouch/.
Bourla, Moshe, interviewed by Stratos Dordanas (Oct. 2005), www.centropa.org
 /biography/moshe-burla/.
Modiano, Mario, interviewed by Milena Molho, Centropa (Nov. 2005), www.centropa
 .org/biography/mario-modiano/.

FORTUNOFF VIDEO ARCHIVE FOR HOLOCAUST TESTIMONIES, YALE UNIVERSITY

Accessed at the Malach Centre for Visual History, Charles University, and the United States Holocaust Memorial Museum Collection.

Arieh K. Holocaust Testimony, HVT-3513, interviewed by Rachel Jadaio and Anita Tarsi
 (May 3, 1993).
Germain C. Holocaust testimony, HVT-3009, interviewed by Jaša Almuli (Dec. 5, 1994).
Ketty L. Holocaust testimony, HVT-926, interviewed by Ted Zinnreich and Phyllis
 Braverman (March 22, 1987).

Ketty L. Holocaust testimony, HVT-1920, interviewed by Toby Blum-Dobkin (Nov. 27, 1991).

Lori B. Holocaust testimony, HVT-905, interviewed by James W. Pennebaker and Sarah Mendel (Jan. 24, 1987).

Palomba M., Riketta C., and Vida C. Holocaust testimony, HVT-3011, interviewed by Jaša Almuli (Dec. 9, 1994).

Sabetai B. and Yvette L. Holocaust testimony, HVT-3014, interviewed by Jaša Almuli (Dec. 13, 1994).

The Jeff and Toby Herr Oral History Archive, United States Holocaust Memorial Museum Collection

Bennahmias, Daniel, interviewed by Anne Feibelman, RG-50.477.0661 (Nov. 12, 1991).

Carasso, Renne, interviewed by Sharon Tash, RG-50.233.0014 (May 13, 1992).

Geva, Agi, interviewed by Hannes Ravic, RG-50.822.0004 (Oct. 14, 2014).

Glicksman, Marguerite, interviewed by Joan Ringelheim, RG-50.030.0404 (Dec. 17, 1999).

Jacobson, Gaynor I., interviewed by Tad Szulc, RG-50.968.0032 (1988).

Levis, Henry, interviewed by Radu Ioanid, RG-50.030.0313 (Oct. 28, 1993).

Matsas Feldman, Ninetta, interviewed by Joan Ringelheim, RG-50.030.0586 (Scpt. 14, 2010).

Matsas, Michael Naoum, interviewed by Joan Ringelheim, RG-50.030.0403 (Oct. 4, 1999).

Nahmias, Albert, interviewed by Peter Ryan, RG-50.426.0001 (June 17, 1996).

Nehama, Isaac, interviewed by Joan Ringelheim, RG-50.030.0472 (Oct. 22, 2002).

Nehama, Paulette, interviewed by Margaret West, RG-50.030.0475 (June 24, 2003).

Voices of the Holocaust, David Boder Archive

Button, Eda (Aug. 5, 1946), http://voices.iit.edu.

Yad Vashem: Center for the Shoah and Heroism, Department for the Collection of Testimonies

Moshe, Yitzhak #3558586, interviewed by Yitzhak Alperowitch, Tel Aviv (Apr. 11, 1988).

Interview Archive "Erinnerungen an die Okkupation in Griechenland"

Dora Bourla-Handeli, interview m0g088 (Nov. 17, 2017)

272 · BIBLIOGRAPHY

ARCHIVAL SOURCES

Arolsen Archives, International Tracing Service (ITS) (accessed at the USHMM Collection)
Central Name Index, 0.1.
DP Registration Lists, 3.1.1.2.
General Information on Bergen Belsen concentration camp, 1.1.3.0.
German Democratic Republic, New, 2.1.4.2.
Individual Documents Male Buchenwald, 1.1.5.3.
List Material Auschwitz, 1.1.2.1.
Records of Dachau (female), 1.1.8.4.
Records of Gross Rosen, 1.1.11.1.
Registration of Liberated Former Persecutees at Various Locations, 3.1.1.3.
Repository of T/D Cases, 6.3.3.2.

AMERICAN JOINT DISTRIBUTION COMMITTEE ARCHIVE (AJDC)

G 45-54/4/9/6/GR.30, Greece: ICEM-IRO 1949–53.
G 45-54/4/9/11/GR.64, Greece: Various 1948–52.
G 45-54/4/18/13/YU.49, Jews in Need of Relief 1947–53.
G 55-64/4/28/16/GR.75, Greece: Twelve-Power Demarche March 1961.
IST 1937/49-4/9/IS.217, Greece 1944–46.
IST 37-49/2/2/5/IS.96, Jewish Agency Accounts 1943–45.
IST 37-49/3/10/IS.191, Lists of Survivors from Greece 1945.
IST 37-49/4/15/IS.227, Lisbon 1944–45 (2 of 2).
NY AR 1914-18/2/3/68, Sephardic Relief Committee of America, 1917–18.
NY AR 1919-21/4/21/146.1, Greece, 1918, 1919.
NY AR 1945/54-4/33/2/387, Greece, General, I.–VII. 1945.
NY AR 1945/54-4/33/402, Greece, Survivors, 1945–46.
NY AR 1945-54/1/1/5/2295, General, 1945–46.
NY AR 1945-54/3/5/8/1300, Passover, 1952–54.
NY AR 1945-54/4/14/2/88, Albania, Relief Supplies: Matzot, 1950–54.
NY AR 1945-54/4/19/4/163, Belgium, Aide aux Israelites Victimes de la Guerre (AIVG),
    Printed Matter, 1945–48.
NY AR 1945-54/4/33/2/384, Greece, General, 1949–54.
NY AR 1945-54/4/33/2/385, Greece, General, 1946–48.
NY AR 1945-54/4/33/2/386, Greece, General, VIII.–XII. 1945.
NY AR 1945-54/4/33/389, Greece, Disasters, 1953–54.
NY AR 1945-54/4/33/4/391, Greece, Emigration, 1945–54.
NY AR 1945-54/4/33/5/399, Greece, Medical, 1945–53.
NY AR 1945-54/4/76/2/970, Spain, General, 1945, 1948–54.

NY AR 1945-54/4/81/2/990, Turkey, General, 1944, 1945–50, 1953–54.
NY AR 1965-74/4/25/100, Greece: Loan Kassas, 1970–74.

THE NATIONAL ARCHIVES (TNA), LONDON:

TNA, FO 371—Foreign Office: Political Departments: General Correspondence.
TNA, GFM 33—German Foreign Ministry Archives.
TNA, HS 5/351—Jewish Escape Organisation.
TNA, RG 226—OSS.
TNA, T 311—Records on German Field Commands: Heeresgruppe E/F.

THE UNITED STATES HOLOCAUST MEMORIAL MUSEUM COLLECTION

RG-11.001M, Osobyi Archive (Moscow) records.
RG-34.001, Gaynor I. Jacobson Papers, Accession No. 1991.A.0102.
RG-45.009, Personal archives related to the history of the Jewish community of Larissa in Greece.
RG-45.010, Selected records of the Central Jewish Board (KIS) Athens, Greece.
RG-45.011, Archives of the Jewish Community of Thessaloniki.

GENERAL STATE ARCHIVES: HISTORICAL ARCHIVES OF MACEDONIA: COLLECTION OF REGIONAL DIRECTORATE OF ALIENS

GRGSA-IAM_ADM281.02. F000505—Italian Citizen MODIANO.

YAD VASHEM ARCHIVES (ONLINE): THE WORLD HOLOCAUST REMEMBRANCE CENTER, THE INTERNATIONAL INSTITUTE FOR HOLOCAUST RESEARCH

Righteous Among the Nations Database, http://righteous.yadvashem.org/.
Transports to Extinction: Shoah Deportation Database, http://deportation.yadvashem .org/.

POLITISCHES ARCHIV DES AUSWÄRTIGEN AMTES, BERLIN (PA AA)

B 26/65—Griechenland: Offizielle Besuche.
B 81/353—Wiedergutmachung—Deportierte Juden.

274 · BIBLIOGRAPHY

VARIOUS ARCHIVES AND DATABASES ACCESSED ONLINE

Bundesgesetzblatt, https://www.bgbl.de/.

Database of Greek-Jewish Holocaust Survivors' Testimonies, http://gjst.ha.uth.gr/.

Efimeris tis Kyverniseos (FEK), https://www.et.gr/SearchFek.

Franklin D. Roosevelt Library (FDR), https://www.fdrlibrary.org/archives/.

Greek Literary and History Archive, http://www.elia.org.gr/.

KIS: Kentriko Israilitiko Symvoulio (Central Jewish Board), https://kis.gr/.

The Nizkor Project. The Trial of Eichmann: Record of Proceedings in the District Court of Jerusalem. State of Israel: Ministry of Justice, 1992. https://www.nizkor .org/the-trial-of-adolf-eichmann/.

Online Archives of the Victims of Communism, https://kujto.al/.

NEWSPAPERS

Newspapers from Greece

Anagennisis, Eleftheria, Ellinikos Vorras, Empros, Evraiki Estia, Fos, I Ygeia, Kathimerini, Laiki Foni, Machi, Makedonia, Nea Evropi, Rizospastis.

Newspapers from the United States of America

Jewish Telegraphic Agency, Daily News Bulletin, The Baltimore Sun, The Nation, The Washington Post.

MEMOIRS, COLLECTIONS OF INTERVIEWS, AND OTHER PUBLISHED PRIMARY SOURCES

Asser Pardo, Rozina. *548 Days with Another Name: Salonika 1943: A Child's Diary, an Adult's Memories of War*. Translated by Demetrios Argyriades. New York: Bloch, 2005.

Bader, Marie. *Life and Love in Nazi Prague: Letters from an Occupied City*. Edited by Kate Ottevanger with Jan Láníček. Translated by Kate Ottevanger. London: Bloomsbury, 2019.

Bourlas, Moisis. *Ellinas, Evreos ke Aristeros [Greek, Jew, and Leftist]*. Skopelos: Nisides, 2000.

Capelluto, Lucia. *Testimony: My Life in Auschwitz Bergen Belsen*. Marseille: Levant, 1997.

Constantopoulou, Photini, and Thanos Veremis, eds. *Documents on the History of the Greek Jews: Records from Historical Archives of the Ministry of Foreign Affairs*. Translated by Geoffrey Cox and John Solman. Athens: Kastaniotis Editions, 1998.

Dublon-Knebel, Irith. *German Foreign Office Documents on the Holocaust in Greece (1937–1944)*. Tel Aviv: Tel Aviv University, 2007.

Franko, Esther. *To pechnidi ton rolon ke i defteri genia tou Olokautomatos [Role-Playing and the Second Generation of the Holocaust]*. Athens: Odos Panos, 2012.

BIBLIOGRAPHY · 275

Gabbai, Dario. "To Zonterkomanto" ["The Sonderkommando"]. *Chronika* 29, no. 201 (February 2006): 78–79.

Gattegno-Osmo, Nata. *Apo tin Kerkyra sto Mpirkenaou ke stin Ierousalim, I istoria mias kerkyreas* [*From Corfu to Birkenau and Jerusalem: The Story of a Corfu Woman*]. Athens: Gavriilidis, 2005.

Greek Office of Information. *Greece: Basic Statistics*. London: Greek Office of Information, 1949.

Grinberg, Natan. *Dokumenti; izdireni i subrani iz arhiva na Komisarstvoto za evreiskite vuprosi* [*Documents: Searched and Collected from the Archive of the Commissariat for Jewish Affairs*]. Sofia: Tsentralna Konsistoria na Evreite v Bulgaria, 1945.

Gross, Elly. *Elly: My True Story of the Holocaust*. New York: Scholastic, 2007.

Hassid, Esther. *Reflets de ma vie*. Paris: Pensée Universelle, 1979.

Kakis, Frederic J. *Legacy of Courage: A Holocaust Survival Story*. Bloomington, IN: 1st Books Library, 2003.

Kolonomos, Jamila Andjela. *Monastir without Jews: Recollections of a Jewish Partisan in Macedonia*. New York: Foundation for the Advancement of Sephardic Studies and Culture, 2008.

Konstantinis, Moisis K. "Evraiki Kinotita Prevezis" ["The Jewish Community of Preveza"]. *Chronika* 19, no. 142 (April 1996): 29–30.

———. *I Israilitikes kinotites tis Ellados meta to Olokautoma, apo tis ekthesis tou Kanari D. Konstantini* [*The Jewish Communities of Greece after the Holocaust, in the Essays of Kanaris D. Konstantinis*]. Athens: self-published, 2015.

Koretz, Arieh. *Bergen-Belsen Tagebuch eines Jugendlichen; 11.7.1944–30.3.1945*. Göttingen: Wallstein, 2011.

Kounio, Heinz Salvator. *A Liter of Soup and Sixty Grams of Bread: The Diary of Prisoner Number 109565*. Translated by Marcia Haddad Ikonomopolous. New York: Bloch, 2003.

Kounio-Amariglio, Erika. *From Thessaloniki to Auschwitz and Back: Memories of a Survivor from Thessaloniki*. London: Vallentine Mitchell, 2000.

Erika Kounio-Amarilio, Almpertos Nar, and Phragkiski Abatzopoulou. *Prophorikes martyries Evreon tis Thessalonikis gia to Olokaytoma* [*Oral Testimonies of Thessaloniki Jews on the Holocaust*] (Thessaloniki: Paratiritis, 1998).

Levi, Primo. *If This Is a Man* and *The Truce*. Translated by Stuart Woolf. London: Abacus, 2013.

Matarasso, Isaac Aron. "And Yet Not All of Them Died." In *The Holocaust in Salonika: Eyewitness Accounts*, edited by Steven B. Bowman, translated by Isaac Benmayor, 123–235. New York: Sephardic House, 2002.

———. *Ki omos oli tous den pethanan* [*And Yet Not All of Them Died*]. Athens: A. Bezes, 1948.

Matarasso, Isaac Aron, Pauline Maud Matarasso, Robert Matarasso, and François Matarasso. *Talking until Nightfall: Remembering Jewish Salonica, 1941–44*. London: Bloomsbury 2020.

276 · BIBLIOGRAPHY

Matsas, Michael. *The Illusion of Safety: The Story of the Greek Jews during World War II*. New York: Pella, 1997.

Menasche, Albert. *Birkenau (Auschwitz II), Memoirs of an Eye-Witness: How 72,000 Greek Jews Perished*. New York: I. Saltiel, 1947.

Mizan, Samouil. *Itan pio poly to ksipnima tou anthropou; I prosopiki martyria tou Ellinoevreou Samouil Mizan apo to Antartiko ke tin Katochi* [Was It More of a Human Awakening? The Personal Account of the Greek Jew Samuel Mizan on Resistance during the Occupation]. Athens: Diethnes Vima, 2018.

Modiano, Mario. "The Story." The Website of the Modiano Family. http://www.themo dianos.gr.

Moissis, Asher. *Greek-Jewish Patrimony*. Edited by Raphael Moissis. North Charleston, SC: CreateSpace, 2012.

Molho, Michael, and Joseph Nehama. *In Memoriam: Gewidmet dem Andenken an die jüdischen Opfer der Naziherrschaft in Griechenland*. Essen: Peter Katzung, 1981.

Moskowitz, Moses. "Review of the Year 5699 – Bulgaria." In *The American Jewish Year Book*, vol. 41, edited by Harry Schneidermann, 323–24. Philadelphia: The Jewish Publication Society of America, 1939.

Nachmia, Berry. *Kraugi gia to aurio, 76859...* [Scream for Tomorrow, 76859...]. Athens: Kaktos, 1989.

Nachmia, Nina. *Reina Zilberta: Ena pedi sto geto tis Thessalonikis* [Reina Zilberta: A Child in the Thessaloniki Ghetto]. Athens: Okeanidis, 1996.

Nahmias, Sam. "Die Vermögen der deportieren Israeliten Griechenlands." In *In Memoriam: Gewidmet dem Andenken an die jüdischen Opfer der Naziherrschaft in Griechenland*, by Michael Molho and Joseph Nehama, 454–68. Essen: Peter Katzung, 1981.

Nahon, Marco. *Birkenau: The Camp of Death*. Tuscaloosa, AL: University of Alabama Press, 1989.

Novitch, Miriam. *The Passage of the Barbarians: Contribution to the History of the Deportation and Resistance of Greek Jews*. Hull, UK: Hyperion Books, 1989.

Orlev, Uri. *The Sandgame*. Kibbutz Dalia: Ghetto Fighters House, 1999.

Perachia, Leon. *Mazal: Anamnisis apo ta stratopeda tou thanatou (1943–1945)* [Mazal: Memories of the Death Camps, (1943–1945)]. Thessaloniki: self-published, 1990.

Pinhas, Lisa, Zanet Battinou, and Gabriella Etmektsoglou, eds. *A Narrative of Evil: Lisa Pinhas Confronts the Holocaust*. Athens: Jewish Museum of Greece, 2014.

Refael, Shmuel. *Bi-netivey she'ol: yehudey yavan ba-sho'ah-pirqey edut* [The Road to Hell: Greek Jews in the Shoah. Testimonies]. Tel Aviv: ha-Makhon le-heqer yahadut Saloniki, 1988.

Sakkis, Moisis. "Saranta peripou chronia apo tote" ["Almost Forty Years On"]. *Chronika* 9, no. 86 (April 1986): 13.

Seficha, Andreas L. *Remembering a Life and a World*. Thessaloniki: Ianos, 2015.

Sevillias, Errikos. *Athina–Auschwitz*. Athens: Lykavittos, 1983.

Towers, Frank W. "30th Division Medical Detachment, Diary & Log (105th Medical Bat-

talion) by T/4 Wilson Rice, 13 April 1945." JewishGen. www.jewishgen.org/databases
/holocaust/.

Uziel, Salomon. "They Encircled Me and Encompassed Me." In *The Holocaust in Salonika: Eyewitness Accounts*, edited by Steven B. Bowman, translated by Isaac Benmayor, 237–80. New York: Sephardic House, 2002.

Vafiadis, Markos. *Apomnimonevmata 1940–1944* [*Memoirs, 1940–1944*]. Vol. 2. Athens: Livanis, 1985.

Venezia, Shlomo. *Inside the Gas Chambers: Eight Months in the Sonderkommando of Auschwitz.* Oxford, UK: Polity, 2009.

Venturas, Iosif. *Tanais.* Athens: Gavriilidis, 2001.

Vlachopanos, Dimitris. *Isaak Mizan: Arithmos vrachiona 182641* [*Isaac Mizan: Arm Number 182641*]. Athens: Apiros Hora, 2016.

Wiernik, Jankiel. *A Year in Treblinka: An Inmate Who Escaped Tells the Day-to-Day Facts of One Year of His Torturous Experience.* New York: American Representation of the General Jewish Workers' Union of Poland, 1944.

SECONDARY SOURCES

Abatzopoulou, Phragkiski. "I genoktonia ke i gynekia foni" ["The Genocide and the Voice of Women"]. *Dini: Feministiko Periodiko* 9 (1997): 11–50.

Abrevaya Stein, Sarah. *Family Papers: A Sephardic Journey through the Twentieth Century.* New York: Farrar, Straus and Giroux, 2019.

Alexander, George M. "The Demobilization Crisis of November 1944." In *Greece in the 1940s: A Nation in Crisis*, edited by John O. Iatrides, 156–66. Hanover, NH: University Press of New England, 1981.

Alivizatos, Nikos. *Oi politikoi thesmoi se krisi 1922–1974: Opseis tis Ellinikis empirias* [*Political Institutions in Crisis, 1922–1974: Greek Aspects*]. Athens: Themelio, 1983.

Ancel, Jean, Aviva Brushi, Theodor Levi, and Zvi Shal, eds. *Pinkas ha-kehilot: Romanyah* [*Encyclopedia of Jewish Communities: Romania*]. Jerusalem: Yad Vashem, 1969.

Anthony, Elizabeth. *The Compromise of Return: Viennese Jews after the Holocaust.* Detroit: Wayne State University Press, 2021.

Antill, Peter. *Crete 1941: Germany's Lightning Airborne Assault.* Oxford, UK: Osprey, 2005.

Antoniou, Giorgos. "Bystanders, Rescuers, and Collaborators: A Microhistory of Christian-Jewish Relations, 1943–1944." In *The Holocaust in Greece*, edited by Giorgos Antoniou and A. Dirk Moses, 135–56. Cambridge: Cambridge University Press, 2018.

Antoniou, Giorgos, and A. Dirk Moses, eds. *The Holocaust in Greece.* Cambridge, UK: Cambridge University Press, 2018.

Apostolou, Andrew. "Greek Collaboration in the Holocaust and the Course of the War." In *The Holocaust in Greece*, edited by Giorgos Antoniou and A. Dirk Moses, 89–112. Cambridge, UK: Cambridge University Press, 2018.

278 · BIBLIOGRAPHY

Arendt, Hannah. *Eichmann in Jerusalem: A Report on the Banality of Evil*. 1963. Reprint, New York: Penguin, 2006.

Arntz, H.-Dieter. *Der letzte Judenälteste von Bergen-Belsen: Josef Weiss – würdig in einer unwürdigen Umgebung*. Aachen: Helios, 2012.

Avni, Haim. "Spanish Nationals in Greece and Their Fate During the Holocaust." *Yad Vashem Studies* 8 (1970): 31–68.

Azouvi, François. *Le mythe du grand silence: Auschwitz, les Français, la mémoire*. Paris: Le Grand livre du mois, 2012.

Baltsiotis, Lambros. "I ithagenia ston Psychro Polemo" ["Citizenship in the Cold War"]. In *Ta dikeomata stin Ellada 1953–2003: apo to telos tou emphyliou sto telos tis metapoliteusis* [*Rights in Greece, 1953–2003: From the End of the Civil War to the End of the Metapolitefsi*], edited by Michael Tsapogas, Dimitris Christopoulos, and Nikos Alivizatos, 81–98. Athens: Kastaniotis Editions, 2004.

Bankier, David, ed. *The Jews Are Coming Back: The Return of the Jews to Their Countries of Origin after WW II*. New York: Berghahn, 2005.

Barna, Ildikó. "Hungarian Jewish Holocaust Survivors Registered in Displaced Persons Camps in Apulia: An Analysis Based on the Holdings of the Arolsen (International Tracing Service) Digital Archive." In *Beyond Camps and Forced Labour: Proceedings of the Sixth International Conference*, edited by Suzanne Bardgett, Christine Schmidt, and Dan Stone, 165–84. Cham: Palgrave Macmillan, 2021.

Barton-Hronešová, Jessie. *The Struggle for Redress: Victim Capital in Bosnia and Herzegovina*. Cham: Pelgrave, 2020.

Bauer, Yehuda. *Rethinking the Holocaust*. New Haven: Yale University Press, 2001.

Bauman, Zygmunt. *Freedom*. Minneapolis: University of Minnesota Press, 1988.

Beevor, Antony. *Crete: The Battle and the Resistance*. London: Penguin, 1991.

Ben-Sefer, Ellen. "Forced Sterilization and Abortion As Sexual Abuse." In *Sexual Violence against Jewish Women during the Holocaust*, edited by Sonja Maria Hedgepeth and Rochelle G. Saidel, 156–70. Hanover, NH: University Press of New England, 2010.

Benadón Saporta, Alberto. *Live . . .* Madrid: Cultiva, 2009.

Benatar, Isaac. *Rhodes and the Holocaust: The Story of the Jewish Community from the Mediterranean Island of Rhodes*. New York: iUniverse, 2010.

Benveniste, Rika. *Auti pou epezisan: antistasi, ektopisi, epistrophi: Thessalonikis Evrei sti dekaetia tou 1940* [*Those Who Survived: Resistance, Deportation, Return: The Jews of Thessaloniki in the 1940s*]. Athens: Polis, 2014.

―――. *Die Überlebenden: Widerstand, Deportation, Rückkehr: Juden aus Thessaloniki in den 1940er Jahren*. Berlin: Edition Romiosini, 2016.

―――. *Louna*. Athens: Polis, 2017.

Beze, Eleni. "Being Leftist and Jewish in Greece during the Civil War and Its Aftermath: Constraints and Choices." *Historein* 18, no. 2 (2019).

Birri-Tomovska, Kristina. *Jews of Yugoslavia, 1918–1941: A History of Macedonian Sephards*. Bern: Peter Lang, 2012.

Blümel, Tobias. "Antisemitism as Political Theology in Greece and Its Impact on Greek Jewry, 1967–1979." *Southeast European and Black Sea Studies* 17, no. 2 (April 2017): 181–202.

———. "The Case of Alois Brunner and the Divided Consciousness in Processing the Holocaust in Greece." *Südosteuropa Mitteilungen* 2–3 (2021): 93–106.

———. "Der Teufel, die Juden, die Protokolle der Weisen von Zion und die zionistische Weltverschwörung: Grundlinien des Antisemitismus in Griechenland." In *Historische Interventionen: Festschrift für Wolfgang Wippermann zum 70. Geburtstag*, edited by Axel Weipert, Dietmar Lange, Friederike Voermanek, Jakob Müller, Johanna Pumb, Johannes Fülberth, Manfred Wichmann, Martin Holler, Oxana Kosenko, and Tobias Blümel, 121–72. Amsterdam: Trafo, 2015.

———. "(K)eine Frage ethischer Natur. Der Fall Alois Brunner und das gespaltene Bewusstsein im Umgang mit der Shoah in Griechenland." In *Die "neue Ordnung" in Griechenland 1941–1944*, edited by Nikolas Pissis and Dimitris Karydas, 125–96. Berlin: Edition Romiosini, 2020.

Boase-Beier, Jean, and Marian de Voogh, eds. *Poetry of the Holocaust: An Anthology*. Todmorden, UK: Arc Publications, 2019.

Boder, David P. *Die Toten habe ich nicht befragt*. Heidelberg: Universitätsverlag Winter, 2011.

Borovaya, Olga. *Modern Ladino Culture: Press, Belles Lettres, and Theater in the Late Ottoman Empire*. Bloomington: Indiana University Press, 2011.

Bowman, Steven B. *The Agony of Greek Jews, 1940–1945*. Stanford: Stanford University Press, 2009.

———. *Jewish Resistance in Wartime Greece*. London: Vallentine Mitchell, 2006.

Brenner, Michael. *Nach dem Holocaust: Juden in Deutschland 1945–1950*. Munich: C. H. Beck, 1995.

Brouskou, Aigli. "Evrees trofi sto Christianiko vrefokomio 'Agios Stylianos' stis arches tou eona" ["Jewish Nurses in the Christian Nursery 'Agios Stylianos' at the Beginning of the Century"]. In *I Evrei ston Elliniko choro, Zitimata istorias sti makra diarkeia* [*The Jews in Greece: Historical Questions in the Long Term*], edited by Eutychia Avdela and Odette Varon-Vassard, 33–42. Athens: Gavriilidis, 1995.

———. "Opoia petra ke an sikosis: To dimotiko vrefokomio Thessalonikis 'Agios Stylianos' ke i schesis tou me tin evraiki kinotita tis polis" ["Whichever Rock You Pick Up: The 'Agios Stylianos' Municipal Nursery of Thessaloniki and Its Relations with the Jewish Community of the City"]. In *O Ellinikos Evraismos* [*Greek Jewry*], edited by Maria Stefanopoulou, 205–24. Athens: Etairia Spoudon Scholis Moraiti, 1999.

Brown, Steven, and Paula Reavey. *Vital Memory and Affect: Living with a Difficult Past*. London: Routledge, 2015.

Brown-Fleming, Suzanne. *Nazi Persecution and Postwar Repercussions: The International Tracing Service Archive and Holocaust Research*. Lanham, MD: Rowman & Littlefield, 2015.

Browning, Christopher R. *Remembering Survival: Inside a Nazi Slave-Labor Camp*. New York: W. W. Norton, 2011.

280 · BIBLIOGRAPHY

Caestecker, Frank. "Reintegration of Jewish Survivors into Belgian Society." In *The Jews Are Coming Back: The Return of the Jews to Their Countries of Origin after WW II*, edited by David Bankier, 72–107. New York: Berghahn, 2005.

Carabott, Philip. "State, Society and the Religious 'Other' in Nineteenth-Century Greece." *Kampos: Cambridge Papers in Modern Greek* 18 (November 2011): 1–33.

Carabott, Philip, and Maria Vassilikou. "'New Men vs Old Jews': Greek Jewry in the Wake of the Shoah, 1945–1947." In *The Holocaust in Greece*, edited by Giorgos Antoniou and A. Dirk Moses, 255–72. Cambridge, UK: Cambridge University Press, 2018.

Carpi, Daniel. "A New Approach for Some Episodes in the History of Jews in Salonika during the Holocaust: Memory, Myth and Documentation." In *The Last Ottoman Century and Beyond: The Jews in Turkey and in the Balkans, 1808–1945*, edited by Minna Rozen, 259–89. Tel Aviv: TAU Press, 2002.

Cesarani, David. *Final Solution: The Fate of the Jews 1933–49*. London: Pan Books, 2017.

Cesarani, David, Tony Kushner, Jo Reilly, and Colin Richmond. *Belsen in History and Memory*. 1997. Reprint, Hoboken, NJ: Taylor & Francis, 2013.

Chandrinos, Iasonas. *Synagonistis: Ellines Evrei stin Ethniki Antistasi [Synagonistis: Greek Jews in the National Resistance]*. Athens: Evraiko Mousio Ellados, 2013.

———. *Synagonistes. To EAM ke i evrei tis Elladas [Comrades-in-Arms: The EAM and the Jews in Greece]*. Athens: Psifydes, 2020.

Chandrinos, Iasonas, and Anna Maria Droumpouki. "The German Occupation and the Holocaust in Greece: A Survey." In *The Holocaust in Greece*, edited by Giorgos Antoniou and A. Dirk Moses, 15–35. Cambridge, UK: Cambridge University Press, 2018.

Cichopek-Gajraj, Anna. *Beyond Violence: Jewish Survivors in Poland and Slovakia, 1944–48*. New York: Cambridge University Press, 2014.

Clarke, Thurston. "Epilogue, August 1, 1946–1980." In *By Blood and Fire: The Attack on the King David Hotel*, 274–84. New York: Putnam, 1981.

Clifford, Rebecca. *Commemorating the Holocaust: The Dilemmas of Remembrance in France and Italy*. Oxford, UK: Oxford University Press, 2013.

———. *Survivors: Children's Lives after the Holocaust*. New Haven: Yale University Press, 2020.

Clogg, Richard, ed. *Bearing Gifts to Greeks: Humanitarian Aid to Greece in the 1940s*. Basingstoke, UK: Palgrave Macmillan, 2008.

———. *Greece, 1940–1949. Occupation, Resistance, Civil War: A Documentary History*. Basingstoke, UK: Palgrave Macmillan, 2002.

———. *Minorities in Greece: Aspects of a Plural Society*. London: Hurst, 2003.

———. *Parties and Elections in Greece: The Search for Legitimacy*. Durham, NC: Duke University Press, 1987.

Close, David H., and Thanos Veremis, "The Military Struggle, 1945–9." In *The Greek Civil War: Studies of Polarization*, edited by David H. Close, 136–38. London: Routledge, 1993.

Cohen, Boaz. *Israeli Holocaust Research: Birth and Evolution*. London: Routledge, 2017.

Cohen, Julia P., and Sarah A. Stein. "Sephardic Scholarly Worlds: Toward a Novel Geography of Modern Jewish History." *Jewish Quarterly Review* 100, no. 3 (2010): 349–84.

Cohn, Samuel Kline. "The Black Death and the Burning of Jews." *Past & Present* 196, no. 1 (August 2007): 3–36.

Cole, Tim. *Holocaust Landscapes*. London: Bloomsbury Continuum, 2016.

———. "(Re)Placing the Past: Spatial Strategies of Retelling Difficult Stories." *The Oral History Review* 42, no. 1 (2015): 30–49.

Correa Martín-Arroyo, Pedro. "Franco, Savior of the Jews? Tracing the Genealogy of the Myth and Assessing Its Persistence in Recent Historiography." In *Lessons and Legacies. New Approaches to an Integrated History of the Holocaust: Social History, Representation, Theory*, edited by Alexandra Garbarini and Paul Jaskot, 195–218. Evanston, IL: Northwestern University Press, 2018.

Cymet, David. *History vs. Apologetics: The Holocaust, the Third Reich, and the Catholic Church*. Lanham, MD: Lexington Books, 2011.

Czech, Danuta. *Auschwitz Chronicle, 1939–1945*. New York: Henry Holt, 1990.

———. "Deportation und Vernichtung der griechischen Juden im KL Auschwitz: im Lichte der sogannanten 'Endlösung der Judenfrage.'" *Hefte von Auschwitz* 11 (1970): 5–37.

Dalven, Rae. *The Jews of Ioannina*. Athens: Lykavittos, 2011.

Danforth, Loring M., and Riki Van Boeschoten. *Children of the Greek Civil War: Refugees and the Politics of Memory*. Chicago: University of Chicago Press, 2011.

Danieli, Yael. "On the Achievement of Integration in Aging Survivors of the Nazi Holocaust." *Journal of Geriatric Psychiatry* 14 (1981): 191–210.

Dean, Martin. *Robbing the Jews: The Confiscation of Jewish Property in the Holocaust, 1933–1945*. Cambridge, UK: Cambridge University Press; United States Holocaust Memorial Museum, 2008.

Dean, Martin, Constantin Goschler, and Philipp Ther, eds. *Robbery and Restitution: The Conflict over Jewish Property in Europe*. New York: Berghahn Books; United States Holocaust Memorial Museum, 2007.

Deblinger, Rachel. "David P. Boder: Holocaust Memory and Displaced Persons Camps." In *After the Holocaust: Challenging the Myth of Silence*, edited by David Cesarani and Eric J. Sundquist, 115–26. London: Routledge, 2003.

Diamantouros, Paris K. *Ta Dekemvriana* [*The Dekemvriana*]. Athens: Archeio, 2014.

Dimitriou, Dimitrios N. "I symmetochi ton Evreon stin Ethniki Antistasi" ["The Jews' Participation in the National Resistance"]. *Chronika* 12, no. 104 (February 1989): 1–3.

Diner, Dan, and Gotthart Wunberg, eds. *Restitution and Memory: Material Restoration in Europe*. New York: Berghahn, 2007.

Dordanas, Stratos N. *Ellines enantion Ellinon: O kosmos ton Tagmaton asphalias stin katochiki Thessaloniki 1941–1944* [*Greeks against Greeks: The World of the Security Battalions in Occupied Thessaloniki, 1941–1944*]. Athens: Epikentro, 2006.

282 · BIBLIOGRAPHY

———. "I Yperesia Diachiriseos Israilitikon Periousion (YDIP)" ["The Office for the Disposal of Jewish Property"]. In *To Olokautoma sta Balkania* [*The Holocaust in the Balkans*], edited by Giorgos Antoniou, Stratos N. Dordanas, Nikos Zaikos, and Nikos Marantzidis, 331–52. Thessaloniki: Epikentro, 2011.

———. "The Jewish Community of Thessaloniki and the Christian Collaborators: 'Those That Are Leaving and What They Are Leaving Behind.'" In *The Holocaust in Greece*, edited by Giorgos Antoniou and A. Dirk Moses, 208–27. Cambridge, UK: Cambridge University Press, 2018.

Dordanas, Stratos N., and Eleni Paschaloudi. "Enas akirychtos polemos: I 'Eamokratia' sti Thessaloniki" ["An Undeclared War: The 'Eamokratia' in Thessaloniki"]. In *Dekemvris 1944: To parelthon ke i chrisis tou* [*December 1944: The Past and Its Use*], edited by Polymeris Voglis, Ioanna Papathanasiou, and Tasos Sakellaropoulos, 173–92. Athens: Alexandria, 2017.

Doxiadis, Evdoxios. *State, Nationalism, and the Jewish Communities of Modern Greece*. London: Bloomsbury Academic, 2018.

Droumpouki, Anna Maria. *Mnimia tis Lithis – Ichni tou V' Pagosmiou Polemou stin Ellada ke tin Evropi* [*Monuments of Oblivion: Traces of World War II in Greece and Europe*]. Athens: Polis, 2014.

Dunn, Jennifer L. *Judging Victims: Why We Stigmatize Survivors, and How They Reclaim Respect*. Boulder, CO: Lynne Rienner Publishers, 2009.

Ehricht, Franziska, and Elke Gryglewski. *Geschichten teilen: Dokumentenkoffer für eine interkulturelle Pädagogik zum Nationalsozialismus*. Berlin: Haus der Wannseekonferenz, 2009.

Elliot, Jane. *Using Narrative in Social Science Research: Qualitative and Quantitative Approaches*. London: Sage, 2009.

Etmektsoglou, Gabriella. "Collaborators and Partisans on Trial: Political Justice in Postwar Greece." In *Keine "Abrechnung": NS-Verbrechen, Justiz und Gesellschaft in Europa nach 1945*, edited by Claudia Kuretsidis-Haider and Winfried R Garscha, 231–56. Leipzig: Akademische Verlagsanstalt, 1998.

Finkel, Evgeny. *Ordinary Jews: Choice and Survival during the Holocaust*. Princeton, NJ: Princeton University Press, 2018.

Fleischer, Hagen. *The "Anomalies" in the Greek Middle East Forces: 1941–1944*. Indianapolis: Hellenic American Society, 1978.

———. "Griechenland." In *Dimension des Völkermords: Die Zahl der jüdischen Opfer des Nationalsozialismus*, edited by Wolfgang Benz, 241–74. Munich: Oldenbourg, 1991.

Fleischer, Hagen, John O. Iatrides, and Steven Bowman. *Greece in the 1940s: A Bibliographic Companion*. Hanover, NH: University Press of New England, 1981.

Fleischer, Hagen, and Despina Konstantinakou. "Ad calendas graecas?: Griechenland und die deutsche Wiedergutmachung." In *Grenzen der Wiedergutmachung: die Entschädigung für NS-Verfolgte in West- und Osteuropa 1945–2000*, edited by Hans Günter Hockerts, Claudia Moisel, and Tobias Winstel, 375–457. Göttingen: Wallstein Verlag, 2006.

BIBLIOGRAPHY · 283

Fleming, Katherine E. *Greece: A Jewish History*. Princeton: Princeton University Press, 2008.

Frankel, Jonathan. *The Damascus Affair: 'Ritual Murder,' Politics, and the Jews in 1840*. Cambridge, UK: University Press, 1997.

Freud, Florian. "Ebensee." In *Der Ort des Terrors 4: Geschichte der nationalsozialistischen Konzentrationslager Flossenbürg, Mauthausen, Ravensbrück*, edited by Wolfgang Benz and Barbara Distel. Munich: C. H. Beck, 2006.

Frevert, Ute. "Defining Emotions: Concepts and Debates over Three Centuries." In *Emotional Lexicons: Continuity and Change in the Vocabulary of Feeling, 1700–2000*, edited by Ute Frevert, Christian Bailey, Pascal Eitler, Benno Gammerl, Bettina Hitzer, Margrit Pernau, Monique Scheer, Anne Schmidt, and Nina Verheyen, 1–31. Oxford, UK: Oxford University Press, 2014.

———. "Piggy's Shame." In *Learning How to Feel: Children's Literature and Emotional Socialization, 1870–1970*, edited by Ute Frevert, Pascal Eitler, Stephanie Olsen, Uffa Jensen, Margrit Pernau, Daniel Brückenhaus, Magdalena Beljan, Benno Gammerl, Anja Laukötter, Bettina Hitzer, Jan Plamper, Juliane Brauer, and Joachim C. Häberlen, 134–54. Oxford, UK: Oxford University Press, 2014.

Frezis, Rafail, ed. "I palia Evraiki kinotita Didymotichou" ["The Old Jewish Community of Didymoticho"]. *Chronika* 21, no. 158 (November 1998): 9–16.

———. *I Israilitiki Kinotita Volou* [*The Jewish Community of Volos*]. Volos: Ores, 1994.

———. *O Evraikos typos stin Ellada* [*Jewish Press in Greece*]. Volos: Ekdosi Israilitikis Kinotitas Volou, 1999.

Friedländer, Saul. *Nazi Germany and the Jews, 1933–1945*. New York: HarperCollins, 2009.

———. "Trauma and Transference." In *Memory, History, and the Extermination of the Jews of Europe*, 117–37. Bloomington: Indiana University Press, 1993.

Friedler, Eric, Andreas Kilian, and Barbara Siebert. *Zeugen aus der Todeszone: das jüdische Sonderkommando in Auschwitz*. Munich: dtv, 2008.

Friedman, Francine. "Contemporary Responses to the Holocaust in Bosnia and Herzegovina." In *Bringing the Dark Past to Light: The Reception of the Holocaust in Postcommunist Europe*, edited by John-Paul Himka and Joanna B. Michlic, 83–107. Lincoln: University of Nebraska Press, 2013.

Friedman, Philip. *Martyrs and Fighters: The Epic of the Warsaw Ghetto*. London: Routledge & Kegan Paul, 1954.

———. *Preliminary and Methodological Problems of the Research on the Jewish Catastrophe in the Nazi Period*. Jerusalem: Yad Vashem Remembrance Authority, 1958.

Friedman, Saul S. *A History of the Holocaust*. London: Vallentine Mitchell, 2004.

Friling, Tuvia. "Between Friendly and Hostile Neutrality: Turkey and the Jews During World War II." In *The Last Ottoman Century and Beyond: The Jews in Turkey and in the Balkans, 1808–1945*, edited by Minna Rozen, 309–423. Tel Aviv: TAU Press, 2002.

Fromm, Annette B. "A Ritual Blood Libel in Northwestern Greece." In *From Iberia to*

284 · BIBLIOGRAPHY

Diaspora: Studies in Sephardic History and Culture, edited by Yedida K. Stillman and Norman A. Stillman, 49–57. Leiden: Brill, 1999.

Gardikas, Katerina. "Relief Work and Malaria in Greece, 1943–1947." *Journal of Contemporary History* 43, no. 3 (2008): 493–508.

Gazis, Kostas, ed. *Antartika Tragoudia*. Athens: Damianou, 1986.

Gekas, Sakis. "The Port Jews of Corfu and the 'Blood Libel' of 1891: A Tale of Many Centuries and of One Event." *Jewish Culture and History* 7, no. 1–2 (2004): 171–96.

Gerolymatos, André. *An International Civil War: Greece 1943–1949*. New Haven: Yale University Press, 2016.

Gerrits, André. "Antisemitism and Anti-Communism: The Myth of 'Judeo-Communism' in Eastern Europe." *East European Jewish Affairs* 25, no. 1 (1995): 49–72.

Ginio, Alisa M. *Between Sepharad and Jerusalem: History, Identity and Memory of the Sephardim*. Leiden: Brill, 2015.

Gitelman, Zvi Y. "Reconstructing Jewish Communities and Jewish Identities in Post-Communist East Central Europe." In *Jewish Studies at the Central European University*, edited by András Kovács and Eszter Andor, 35–50. Budapest: CEU Press, 2000.

Goldstein, Ivo. "Restoring Jewish Life in Communist Yugoslavia, 1945–1967." *East European Jewish Affairs* 34, no. 1 (2004): 58–71.

Goldwyn, Adam J. "'An Exile from the Sea with the Desert in His Mouth': A Conversation with Iossif Ventura." *World Literature Today* 90, no. 1 (2016): 22–25. https://doi.org/10.1353/wlt.2016.0269.

Gordiejew, Paul Benjamin. *Voices of Yugoslav Jewry*. Albany: State University of New York Press, 1999.

Gotovich, José. "Resistance Movements and the Jewish Question." In *Belgium and the Holocaust: Jews, Belgians, Germans*, edited by Dan Michman, 273–85. Jerusalem: Yad Vashem, 1998.

Grossmann, Atina. *Jews, Germans, and Allies: Close Encounters in Occupied Germany*. Princeton, NJ: Princeton University Press, 2007.

Grossman, Atina, and Tamar Lewinsky, "1945–1949: Zwischenstation." In *Geschichte der Juden in Deutschland von 1945 bis zur Gegenwart: Politik, Kultur und Gesellschaft*, edited by Michael Brenner, 67–152. Munich: C. H. Beck, 2012.

Guidi, Andreas. "Defining Inter-Communality between Documents, Tradition and Collective Memory: Jewish and Non-Jewish Capital and Labor in Early Twentieth Century Rhodes." *Southeast European and Black Sea Studies* 17, no. 2 (April 3, 2017): 165–80.

Guttstadt, Corry. *Turkey, the Jews, and the Holocaust*. Cambridge, UK: Cambridge University Press, 2013.

Hadjisavvas, Eliana. "'From Dachau to Cyprus': Jewish Refugees and the Cyprus Internment Camps – Relief and Rehabilitation, 1946–1949." In *Beyond Camps and Forced Labour: Proceedings of the Sixth International Conference*, edited by Suzanne Bardgett, Christine Schmidt, and Dan Stone. Cham: Palgrave Macmillan, 2021.

———. "Population Displacement and Transnational Trajectories: Immigration, Internment and Empire in the Case of Jewish Refugees and the Cyprus Camps, 1946–1949." PhD diss., University of Birmingham, 2018.

Hagouel, Paul Isaac. "The Annihilation of Jewish Greeks in Eastern Macedonia and Thrace during WWII: Balkan Particularities, Facts, Memory." eSefard, https://esefarad.com/?p=52726.

Hammond, Laura. "Examining the Discourse of Repatriation: Towards a More Proactive Theory of Return Migration." In *The End of the Refugee Cycle? Refugee Repatriation and Reconstruction*, edited by Richard Black and Khalid Koser, 227–44. New York: Berghahn, 1999.

Hantman, Shira, Zahava Solomon, and Yoav Horn. "Long-Term Coping of Holocaust Survivors: A Typology." *Israel Journal of Psychiatry and Related Sciences* 40, no. 2 (2003): 126–34.

Hanuš, Jiří, and Stanislav Balík. *Katolická církev v Československu 1945–1989*. Brno: Centrum pro studium demokracie a kultury CDK, 2007.

Hantzaroula, Pothiti. *Child Survivors of the Holocaust in Greece: Memory, Testimony and Subjectivity*. Andover: Routledge, 2020.

Hart, Janet. *New Voices in the Nation: Women and the Greek Resistance, 1941–1964*. Ithaca, NY: Cornell University Press, 2018.

Heberer, Patricia. *Children during the Holocaust*. Lanham, MD: Rowman & Littlefield, 2015.

Hevesi, Eugene. "Review of the Year 5702 – Greece." In *The American Jewish Year Book*, vol. 44. Philadelphia, PA: The Jewish Publication Society of America, 1942.

Hilberg, Raul. *Die Vernichtung der europäischen Juden*. Vol. 2. 1961. Reprint, Frankfurt am Main: Fischer-Taschenbuch-Verlag, 1990.

———. *Perpetrators, Victims, Bystanders: The Jewish Catastrophe, 1933–1945*. New York: Aaron Asher, 1992.

Himka, John-Paul, and Joanna B. Michlic. *Bringing the Dark Past to Light: The Reception of the Holocaust in Postcommunist Europe*. Lincoln: University of Nebraska Press, 2013.

Hionidou, Violetta. *Famine and Death in Occupied Greece, 1941–1944*. Cambridge: Cambridge University Press, 2006.

Hirsch, Marianne. *Family Frames: Photography, Narrative, and Postmemory*. Cambridge: Harvard University Press, 1997.

Hirschon, Renée. "The Jews of Rhodes: The Decline and Extinction of an Ancient Community." In *The Last Ottoman Century and Beyond: The Jews in Turkey and in the Balkans, 1808–1945*, edited by Minna Rozen, 291–307. Tel Aviv: TAU Press, 2002.

Hockerts, Hans Günter, Claudia Moisel, and Tobias Winstel. *Grenzen Der Wiedergutmachung: Die Entschädigung für NS-Verfolgte in West- Und Osteuropa, 1945–2000*. Göttingen: Wallstein Verlag, 2006.

Hoppe, Hans-Joachim. "Bulgarian Nationalities Policy in Occupied Thrace and Aegean Macedonia." *Nationalities Papers* 14, no. 1–2 (March 1986): 89–100.

286 · BIBLIOGRAPHY

———. "Bulgarien." In *Dimension des Völkermords: Die Zahl der Jüdischen Opfer des National-sozialismus*, edited by Wolfgang Benz, 275–310. Munich: Oldenbourg, 1991.

Hoppe, Jens. "Ferramonti di Tarsia." In *The United States Holocaust Memorial Museum Encyclopedia of Camps and Ghettos, 1933–1945*, vol 3, *Camps and Ghettos under European Regimes Aligned with Nazi Germany*, edited by Geoffrey P. Megargee, Joseph R. White, and Mel Hecker, 1100. Indianapolis: Indiana University Press, 2018.

Hrenciuc, Daniel. "Czernowitz: The Jerusalem of Bukovina." *Codrul Cosminului* 18, no. 2 (2012): 361–80.

Iatrides, John O. *Revolt in Athens: The Greek Communist "Second Round," 1944–1945*. Princeton, NJ: Princeton University Press, 1972.

Ilel, Iosif, and Stella T. Ilel-Vatcheva. *The Rescue and Survival of the Bulgarian Jews in World War II and the Jewish Participation in the Wars of Bulgaria: Short Essays*. n.p.: self-published, 2003.

International Tracing Service. *An Introduction to the International Tracing Service*. Bad Arolsen: International Tracing Service, 2009. https://collections.ushmm.org/search/catalog/bib154833.

Ioanidis, Eleftherios M. *Tekmiria gia tin istoria tis Israilitikis Kinotitos Chalkidos kata tin periodo tis katochis. Apo ta archia tou dimou Chalkideon* [*Documents about the History of the Jewish Community of Chalcis during the Occupation. From the Archives of the Municipality of Chalcis*]. Chalcis: Manifesto, 2013.

Judt, Tony. *Postwar: A History of Europe since 1945*. New York: Penguin Books, 2005.

Kalyvas, Stathis N. "Armed Collaboration in Greece, 1941–1944." *European Review of History: Revue Européenne d'histoire* 15, no. 2 (April 2008): 129–42.

———. *The Logic of Violence in Civil War*. New York: Cambridge University Press, 2006.

———. "Nees taseis sti meleti tou Emfyliou Polemou" ["New Approaches to Researching the Civil War"]. *Ta Nea*, March 20, 2004.

———. "Red Terror: Leftist Violence during the Occupation." In *After the War Was Over: Reconstructing the Family, Nation, and State in Greece, 1943–1960*, edited by Mark Mazower, 142–83. Princeton, NJ: Princeton University Press, 2000.

Kalyvas, Stathis N., and Nikos Marantzidis. *Emfylia pathi: 23+2 nees erotisis ke apantisis gia ton Emfylio* [*Civil Passions: 23+2 New Questions and Answers about the Civil War*]. Athens: Metehmio, 2016.

Kaplan, Karel. *Stát a církev v Československu v letech 1948–1953*. Brno: Doplněk, 1993.

Kaplan, Marion A. *Hitler's Jewish Refugees: Hope and Anxiety in Portugal*. New Haven: Yale University Press, 2020.

Kavala, Maria. "I ektelesis Evreon sti Thessaloniki sta chronia tis Katochis – Politiki antipinon ke fyletismos" ["The Execution of Jews in Thessaloniki during the Occupation: Retaliation Policy and Tribalism"]. In *Evraikes Kinotites anamesa se Anatoli ke Dysi, 15os – 20os eonas: Ikonomia, Kinonia, Politiki, Politismos* [*Jewish Communities between East and West, the Fifteenth to the Twentieth Century: Economics, Society, Politics, Culture*]. Athens: Isnafi, 2016.

———. "I metapolemiki anasygrotisi tis Evraikis Kinotitas Thessalonikis. O rolos tou gamou sti synochi tis kinotitas (1945–1955)" ["The Postwar Reconstruction of the Jewish Community of Thessaloniki: The Role of Marriage in the Cohesion of the Community (1945–1955)"]. PhD diss., University of Thessaly, 2015.

———. "I Thessaloniki sti Germaniki Katochi (1941–1944): Kinonia, Ikonomia, diogmos Evreon" ["Thessaloniki under German Occupation (1941–1944): Society, Economy, and the Persecution of the Jews"]. Voutes-Heraklion: University of Crete, 2009.

———. "The Scale of Jewish Property Theft in Nazi-Occupied Thessaloniki." In *The Holocaust in Greece*, edited by Giorgos Antoniou and A. Dirk Moses, 183–207. Cambridge, UK: Cambridge University Press, 2018.

Keller, Rolf, ed. *Konzentrationslager Bergen-Belsen: Berichte und Dokumente, Bergen-Belsen-Schriften*. Hannover: Niedersächs. Landeszentrale für Politische Bildung, 1995.

Kerem, Yitzchak. "The 1840 Blood Libel in Rhodes." *World Congress of Jewish Studies* 12, no. B (1997): 137–46.

———. "The Greek Government-in-Exile and the Rescue of Jews from Greece." In *Governments-in-Exile and the Jews during the Second World War*, edited by Jan Láníček and James Jordan, 189–212. London: Vallentine Mitchell, 2012.

———. "Greek Jews in Auschwitz: Doctors and Victims." In *Jewish Medical Resistance in the Holocaust*, by Michael A. Grodin, 197–205. New York: Berghahn, 2016.

Kerkkänen, Ari. *Yugoslav Jewry: Aspects of Post-World War II and Post-Yugoslav Developments*. Helsinki: Societas Orientalis Fennica, 2001.

Kidron, Carol A. "Sensorial Memory: Embodied Legacies of Genocide." In *A Companion to the Anthropology of the Body and Embodiment*, edited by Frances E. Mascia-Lees, 451–66. Chichester: Blackwell, 2011.

Klarsfeld, Serge. *Memorial to the Jews Deported from France, 1942–1944: Documentation of the Deportation of the Victims of the Final Solution in France*. New York: Beate Klarsfeld Foundation, 1983.

Knight, Daniel M. *Vertiginous Life: An Anthropology of Time and the Unforeseen*. New York: Berghahn, 2021.

Kochavi, Arieh J. *Post-Holocaust Politics: Britain, the United States, and Jewish Refugees, 1945–1948*. Chapel Hill: University of North Carolina Press, 2001.

Kocián, Jiří. "Die Deutschen." In *Minderheiten im sozialistischen Jugoslawien*, edited by Kamil Pikal, Kateřina Králová, and Jiří Kocian, 151–66. Frankfurt a/M.: P. Lang, 2016.

Koen, Albert, and Anri Assa. *Saving of the Jews in Bulgaria, 1941–1944*. Translated by Ljudmila Dimova. Sofia: Setemvri, 1977.

Kolb, Eberhard. *Bergen-Belsen: Geschichte des "Aufenthaltslagers" 1943–1945*. Vol. 6 of *Geschichte des Holocaust*. Berlin, Münster: Lit, 2011.

Kolb, Eberhard, Gregory Claeys, and Christine Lattek. *Bergen-Belsen: From "Detention Camp" to Concentration Camp, 1943–1945*. Göttingen: Vandenhoeck & Ruprecht, 1986.

288 · BIBLIOGRAPHY

Kolinsky, Eva. *After the Holocaust: Jewish Survivors in Germany after 1945*. London: Pimlico, 2004.

Kornetis, Kostis. "Expropriating the Space of the Other: Property Spoliations of Thessalonican Jews in the 1940s." In *The Holocaust in Greece*, edited by Giorgos Antoniou and A. Dirk Moses, 228–51. Cambridge, UK: Cambridge University Press, 2018.

Koselleck, Reinhart. *Futures Past: On the Semantics of Historical Times*. Cambridge, MA: MIT Press, 1985.

Kousouris, Dimitris. *Dikes ton dosilogon, 1944–1949: Dikaiosyni, synechia tou kratous ke ethniki mnimi* [*The Traitor on Trial, 1944–1949: Justice, Continuity of the State and National Memory*]. Athens: Polis, 2014.

———. "Liberation 1944: Not a Moment. A Time in History." *Journal of Modern Greek Studies Occasional Papers*, no. 3 (2014).

Králová, Kateřina. "'Being Traitors': Post-War Greece in the Experience of Jewish Partisans." *Southeast European and Black Sea Studies* 17, no. 2 (2017): 263–80.

———. *Das Vermächtnis der Besatzung: deutsch-griechische Beziehungen seit 1940*. Cologne: Böhlau, 2016.

———. "Die Griechen." In *Minderheiten im sozialistischen Jugoslawien*, edited by Kamil Pikal, Kateřina Králová, and Jiří Kocian, 223–52. Frankfurt a/M.: P. Lang, 2016.

———. "From Kavala to California: Sarah Haim and Her Family." In *100 Years of Sephardic Los Angeles*, edited by Sarah Abrevaya Stein and Caroline Luce. Los Angeles: UCLA Leve Center for Jewish Studies, 2020. https://sephardiclosangeles.org/portfolios /from-kavala-to-california/.

———. "Hachsharot in Greece, 1945–1949: Camps or Vocational Centers?" *Quest: Issues in Contemporary Jewish History* 21, no. 1 (2022): 75–101.

———. "In the Shadow of the Nazi Past: Post-War Reconstruction and the Claims of the Jewish Community in Salonika." *European History Quarterly* 46, no. 2 (2016): 262–90.

———. "Řecko" ["Greece"]. In *Návraty* [*Returns*], edited by Kateřina Králová and Hana Kubátová, 204–30. Prague: Karolinum, 2016.

———. "Silenced Memories and Network Dynamics in Holocaust Testimonies: The Matalon Family and Case of Greece." *S: I. M. O. N. Shoah: Intervention. Methods. Documentation* 9, no. 2 (2022): 51–66.

———. "What Is True and What Is Right? An Infant Jewish Orphan's Identity." In *Beyond Camps and Forced Labour: Proceedings of the Sixth International Conference*, edited by Suzanne Bardgett, Christine Schmidt, and Dan Stone, 105–23. London: Palgrave Macmillan, 2020, https://doi.org/10.1007/978-3-030-56391-2.

Králová, Kateřina, and Katerina Lagos. "Nazi Crimes, Max Merten and His Prosecution as Reflected in Greece and Beyond." *Journal of Modern European History* 22, no. 2 (2024): 169–87.

Kubátová, Hana. *Nepokradeš!: Nálady a postoje slovenské společnosti k židovské otázce, 1938–1945* [*Thou Shalt Not Steal!: The Moods and Attitudes of Slovak Society to the Jewish question, 1938–1945*]. Prague: Academia, 2013.

BIBLIOGRAPHY · 289

Kundera, Milan. "The Kidnapped West. The Tragedy of Central Europe." *Le Débat* 27, no. 5 (1983): 3–23.

Lagos, Katerina. *The Fourth of August Regime and Greek Jewry, 1936–1941*. Cham: Palgrave Macmillan, 2023.

Lagrou, Pieter. "Return to a Vanished World: European Societies and the Remnants of Their Jewish Communities, 1945–1947." In *The Jews Are Coming Back: The Return of the Jews to Their Countries of Origin after WW II*, edited by David Bankier, 1–24. New York: Berghahn, 2005.

Lampsa, Karina, and Iakov Sibi. *I diasosi: i siopi tou kosmou, i antistasi sta geto ke ta stratopeda, i Ellines Evrei sta chronia tis Katochis* [*The Rescue: The Silence of the People, the Resistance in the Ghettos and the Camps, and the Greek Jews during the Occupation*]. Athens: Ekdosis Kapon, 2012.

———. *I zoi ap' tin archi: i metanasteusi ton ellinon Evreon stin Palaistini (1945–1948)* [*Life from the Beginning: The Emigration of Greek Jews to Palestine (1945–1948)*]. Athens: Alexandria, 2010.

Langer, Lawrence. "The Dilemma of Choice in the Deathcamps." *Centerpoint: A Journal of Interdisciplinary Studies* 4, no. 1 (1980): 53–58.

Lattek, Christine. "Bergen-Belsen: From 'Privileged' Camp to Death Camp." In *Belsen in History and Memory*, edited by David Cesarani, Tony Kushner, Jo Reilly, and Colin Richmond. London: Frank Cass, 1997.

Lazare, Lucien. *Rescue As Resistance: How Jewish Organizations Fought the Holocaust in France*. New York: Columbia University Press, 1996.

Lewkowicz, Bea. "'After the War We Were All Together': Jewish Memories of Postwar Thessalonica." In *After the War Was Over: Reconstructing the Family, Nation, and State in Greece, 1943–1960*, edited by Mark Mazower. Princeton, NJ: Princeton University Press, 2000.

———. *The Jewish Community of Salonika: History, Memory, Identity*. London: Vallentine Mitchell, 2006.

Liata, Eutychia D. *I Kerkyra ke i Zakynthos ston kyklona tou antisimitismou: i "sykofantia gia to aima" tou 1891* [*Corfu and Zante in the Whirlwind of Antisemitism: The Blood Libel of 1891*]. Athens: Institouto Neoellinikon Ereunon Ethnikou Idrymatos Ereunon, 2006.

Linn, Ruth. *Escaping Auschwitz: A Culture of Forgetting*. Ithaca, NY: Cornell University Press, 2004.

Liolios, Giorgos. *Skies tis polis: anaparastasi tou diogmou ton Evreon tis Verias* [*Shadows of the City: A Reenactment of the Pogrom against the Jews of Veria*]. Athens: Ekdosis Eurasia, 2008.

Livanios, Dimitris. *The Macedonian Question: Britain and the Southern Balkans: 1939–1949*. Oxford, UK: Oxford University Press, 2008.

Lowe, Keith. *Savage Continent: Europe in the Aftermath of World War II*. New York: Viking Press, 2012.

Lykogiannis, Athanasios. *Britain and the Greek Economic Crisis, 1944–1947: From Liberation to the Truman Doctrine*. Columbia: University of Missouri Press, 2002.

290 · BIBLIOGRAPHY

Marantzidis, Nikos. *Under Stalin's Shadow: A Global History of Greek Communism*. Ithaca: Cornell University Press, 2023.

Marantzidis, Nikos, and Giorgos Antoniou. "The Axis Occupation and Civil War: Changing Trends in Greek Historiography, 1941–2002." *Journal of Peace Research* 41, no. 2 (2004): 223–31.

Margaroni, Maria. "Antisemitic Rumours and Violence in Corfu at the End of 19th Century." *Quest. Issues in Contemporary Jewish History* 3 (July 2012): 267–88.

———. "The Blood Libel on Greek Islands in the Nineteenth Century." In *Sites of European Antisemitism in the Age of Mass Politics, 1880–1918*, edited by Robert Nemes and Daniel Unowsky. The Tauber Institute Series for the Study of European Jewry. Hanover, NH: University Press of New England, 2014.

Marinova-Christidi, Rumyana. "From Salvation to Alya: The Bulgarian Jews and Bulgarian-Israeli Relations (1948–1990)." *Southeast European and Black Sea Studies* 17, no. 2 (2017): 223–44.

Mark, Eduard. *Revolution by Degrees: Stalin's National-Front Strategy for Europe, 1941–1947*. Washington, DC: Woodrow Wilson International Center for Scholars 2001.

Marrus, Michael R. "Jewish Resistance to the Holocaust." *Journal of Contemporary History* 30, no. 1 (1995): 83–110.

Matsas, Joseph. "The Participation of the Greek Jews in the National Resistance, 1940–1944." *Journal of the Hellenic Diaspora* 17, no. 1 (1991): 55–68.

Mazower, Mark, ed. *After the War Was Over: Reconstructing the Family, Nation, and State in Greece, 1943–1960*. Princeton, NJ: Princeton University Press, 2000.

———. *Inside Hitler's Greece: The Experience of Occupation, 1941–44*. New Haven: Yale University Press, 2001.

———. *Salonica, City of Ghosts: Christians, Muslims and Jews, 1430–1950*. London: HarperCollins, 2004.

———. "Three Forms of Political Justice: Greece, 1944–1945." In *After the War Was Over: Reconstructing the Family, Nation, and State in Greece, 1943–1960*, edited by Mark Mazower. Princeton, NJ: Princeton University Press, 2000.

McGeer, Victoria. "Trust, Hope and Empowerment." *Australasian Journal of Philosophy* 86, no. 2 (2008): 237–54.

McIvor, Charlotte, Emilie Pine, Stef Craps, Astrid Erll, Paula McFetridge, Kabosh Productions, Ann Rigney, and Dominic Thorpe. "Roundtable: Moving Memory." *Irish University Review* 47, no. 1 (2017): 165–96.

Megargee, Geoffrey P., ed. *The United States Holocaust Memorial Museum Encyclopedia of Camps and Ghettos, 1933–1945*. Vol. 1. Foreword by Elie Wiesel. Indianapolis: Indiana University Press, 2009.

Meister, Robert. *After Evil: A Politics of Human Rights*. Columbia Studies in Political Thought/Political History. New York: Columbia University Press, 2010.

Melammed, Renée Levine. "The Memoires of a Partisan from Salonika." *Nashim: A Journal of Jewish Women's Studies & Gender Issues* 7 (2004): 151–73.

BIBLIOGRAPHY · 291

Mendes, Philip. *Jews and the Left: The Rise and Fall of a Political Alliance*. London: Palgrave Macmillan, 2014.

Michman, Dan, and Robert Rozett, eds. *Jewish Solidarity: The Ideal and the Reality in the Turmoil of the Shoah*. Jerusalem: Yad Vashem, The International Institute for Holocaust Research, 2022.

Milgram, Avraham. "Portugal, the Consuls, and the Jewish Refugees, 1938–1941." *Yad Vashem Studies* 27 (1999): 123–56.

Milićević, Aleksandra. "Joining the War: Masculinity, Nationalism and War Participation in the Balkans War of Secession, 1991–1995." *Nationalities Papers* 34, no. 3 (2006): 265–87.

Moissis, Asher. *Greek-Jewish Patrimony*. North Charleston, SC: CreateSpace, 2012.

Molho, Mentes M. "Asset of Jewish Salonica." In *The Holocaust in Salonika: Eyewitness Accounts*, edited by Steven B. Bowman and Isaac Benmayor, 212–32. New York: Sephardic House, 2002.

Molho, Rena. "The Close Ties between Nationalism and Antisemitism: The Hellenization of Salonika, 1917–1948." *Jahrbuch für Antisemitismusforschung* 24 (2015): 217–28.

———. "I antievraiki nomothesia tou Venizelou ston Mesopolemo kai pos i Dimokratia borei na ginei arogos tou antisimitismou" ["The Anti-Jewish Legislation of Venizelos in the Interwar Period and How Democracy Can Support Antisemitism"]. *Sychrona Themata* 82 (June 2003), 53–59.

———. *I Evrei tis Thessalonikis: Mia idieteri kinotita* [*The Jews of Thessaloniki: A Specific Community*]. Athens: Pataki, 2014.

———. "Problems of Incorporating the Holocaust into the Greek Collective Memory: The Case of Thessaloniki." *Journal of Turkish Studies* 40 (2013): 301–13.

Myers, Edmund C. W. *Greek Entanglement*. Gloucester: Sutton, 1985.

Mylonas, Harris. *The Politics of Nation-Building: Making Co-nationals, Refugees, and Minorities*. Cambridge, UK: Cambridge University Press, 2013.

Naar, Devin E. *Jewish Salonica: Between the Ottoman Empire and Modern Greece*. Stanford, CA: Stanford University Press, 2016.

Nachmani, Amikam. *Israel, Turkey, and Greece: Uneasy Relations in the East Mediterranean*. London: F. Cass, 1987.

Nar, Leon A. "Israilitiki Kinotita Thessalonikis (1945–1950)" ["The Jewish Community of Thessaloniki, 1945–1950"]. Master's thesis, Thessaloniki: University of Macedonia, 2017.

Norris, Jacob. *Land of Progress: Palestine in the Age of Colonial Development, 1905–1948*. Oxford, UK: Oxford University Press, 2013.

Ofer, Dalia. "The Community and the Individual: The Different Narratives of Early and Late Testimonies and Their Significance for Historians." In *Holocaust Historiography in Context: Emergence, Challenges, Polemics and Achievements*, edited by David Bankier and Dan Michman, 519–35. Jerusalem: Yad Vashem, 2008.

Panourgia, Neni. *Dangerous Citizens: The Greek Left and the Terror of the State*. New York: Fordham University Press, 2009.

292 · BIBLIOGRAPHY

Panourgia, Neni, and George Marcus, eds. *Ethnographica Moralia: Experiments in Interpretive Anthropology*. New York: Fordham University Press, 2008.

Papamichos Chronakis, Paris. "From the Lone Survivor to the Networked Self: Social Networks Meet the Digital Holocaust Archive." *Quest: Issues in Contemporary Jewish History* 13 (2018): 52–84.

———. "'We Lived as Greeks and We Died as Greeks': Thessalonican Jews in Auschwitz and the Meanings of Nationhood." In *The Holocaust in Greece*, edited by Giorgos Antoniou and A. Dirk Moses, 157–80. Cambridge, UK: Cambridge University Press, 2018.

Patt, Avinoam, Atina Grossmann, Linda G. Levi, and Maud S. Mandel, eds. *The JDC at 100: A Century of Humanitarianism*. Detroit: Wayne State University Press, 2019.

Pelt, Robert Jan van, and Debórah Dwork. *Auschwitz: von 1270 bis heute*. Translated by Klaus Rupprecht. 1996. Reprint, Zurich: Pendo, 1998.

Pierron, Bernard. *Evrei ke Christiani sti Neoteri Ellada: Istoria ton diakinotikon scheseon apo to 1821 os to 1945* [*Jews and Christians in Contemporary Greece: History of Intercommunal Relations from 1821 to 1945*]. Athens: Polis, 2004.

Plaut, Joshua Eli. *Greek Jewry in the Twentieth Century, 1913–1983: Patterns of Jewish Survival in the Greek Provinces before and after the Holocaust*. Madison, NJ: Fairleigh Dickinson University Press, 1996.

Poliakov, Leon, and Jacques Sabille. *Jews under the Italian Occupation*. Foreword by Justin Godart. Vichy: Éditions du Centre, 1955.

Pollin-Galay, Hannah. *Ecologies of Witnessing: Language, Place, and Holocaust Testimony*. New Haven: Yale University Press, 2018.

Poznanski, Renée. *Jews in France during World War II*. Waltham, MA: Brandeis University Press, 2001.

Psarras, Dimitrios. *To best seller tou misous. Ta "protokolla ton sofon tis Sion" stin Ellada, 1920–2013* [*The Bestseller of Hatred: The "Protocols of the Elders of Zion" in Greece, 1920–2013*]. Athens: Polis, 2013.

Ragaru, Nadège. *"Et les Juifs bulgares furent sauvés…": Une histoire des savoirs sur la Shoah en Bulgarie*. Paris: Science Po, 2020.

Rahe, Thomas. "Bergen-Belsen Stammlager." In *Der Ort des Terrors 7: Geschichte der nationalsozialistischen Konzentrationslager*, edited by Wolfgang Benz, Barbara Distel, and Angelika Königseder, 187–220. Munich: Beck, 2008.

Reinisch, Jessica. "Introduction: Relief in the Aftermath of War." *Journal of Contemporary History* 43, no. 3 (2008): 371–404.

Richter, Heinz. *British Intervention in Greece: From Varkiza to Civil War, February 1945 to August 1946*. London: Merlin Press, 1985.

———. *Griechenland zwischen Revolution und Konterrevolution (1936–1946)*. Frankfurt am Main: Europäische Verlagsanstalt, 1973.

———. "The Varkiza Agreement and the Origins of the Civil War." In *Greece in the 1940s: A Nation in Crisis*, 167–80. Hanover, NH: University Press of New England, 1981.

BIBLIOGRAPHY · 293

Ricoeur, Paul. *Time and Narrative*. Chicago: University of Chicago Press, 1984, 1985, 1988.

Ristović, Milan D. *To pirama Boulkes: I elliniki dimokratia sti Giougoslavia 1945–1949 [The Buljkes Experiment: Greek Democracy in Yugoslavia, 1945–1949]*. Thessaloniki: Ekdot. Oikos Adelphon Kyriakidi, 2006.

Ritzaleos, Vasilis. "I evraiki kinotita Kavalas ton elegcho ton Voulgarikon Archon Katochis: organosi, ekmetalleysi, dialysi (1942–1944)" ["The Jewish Community of Kavala under the Bulgarian Occupying Forces: Organization, Exploitation, Dissolution"]. In *Afigisis gia ti dekaetia tou 1940 [Narrations about the 1940s]*, edited by Vasilis Dalkavoukis, Eleni Paschaloudi, and Ilias Skoulidas, 69–90. Thessaloniki: Epikentro, 2012.

Rodrigo, Javier. "Under the Sign of Mars: Violence in European Civil Wars, 1917–1949." *Contemporary European History* 26, no. 3 (2017): 487–506.

Rodrigue, Aron. *Sephardim and the Holocaust*. Washington, DC: United States Holocaust Memorial Museum, 2005.

Rother, Bernd. "Myth and Fact: Spain and the Holocaust." In *The Holocaust in Spanish Memory: Historical Perceptions and Cultural Discourse*, edited by Antonio Gómez López-Quiñones and Susanne Zepp, 51–64. Leipzig: Leipziger Universitätsverlag, 2010.

———. "Spain and the German Repatriation Ultimatum 1943/44." In *Bystanders, Rescuers or Perpetrators? The Neutral Countries and the Shoah*, edited by Corry Guttstadt, Tomas Lutz, Bernd Rother, and Yessica San Ramon, 169–78. Berlin: Metropol-Verlag, 2016.

Rozell, Matthew A. *A Train near Magdeburg: A Teacher's Journey into the Holocaust, and the Reuniting of the Survivors and Liberators, 70 Years On*. Hartford, NY: Woodchuck Hollow Press, 2016.

Rozen, Minna. "Jews and Greeks Remember Their Past: The Political Career of Tzevi Koretz (1933–43)." *Jewish Social Studies* 12, no. 1 (2005): 111–66.

———. *The Last Ottoman Century and Beyond: The Jews in Turkey and the Balkans, 1808–1945*. Tel Aviv: TAU Press, 2002.

Rubin Greene, Roberta, et al. "Conceptualizing a Holocaust Survivorship Model." *Journal of Human Behavior in the Social Environment* 20, no. 4 (2010): 423–39.

Sakkas, John. *Britain and the Greek Civil War: British Imperialism, Public Opinion and the Coming of the Cold War*. Mainz: F. P. Rutzen, 2013.

Saltiel, Leon. *Mi me ksechasete [Do Not Forget Me]*. Athens: Alexandria, 2018.

———. "Prospathies Diasosis Evraiopedon Thessalonikis kata tin Katochi: Ena Agnosto Kykloma Paranomon Yiothesion" ["Attempts to Rescue the Jewish Children of Thessaloniki during the Occupation: An Unknown Illegal Adoption Network"]. *Sychrona Themata* 127, no. B (2014): 75–78.

———. "Two Friends in Axis-Occupied Greece: The Rescue Efforts of Yomtov Yacoel and Asher Moisis." *Journal of Genocide Research* 21, no. 3 (2019): 342–58.

———. "Voices from the Ghetto of Thessaloniki: Mother-Son Correspondence as a Source of Jewish Everyday Life under Persecution." *Southeast European and Black Sea Studies* 17, no. 2 (2017): 203–22.

294 · BIBLIOGRAPHY

Samson, Shlomo. *Zwischen Finsternis und Licht: 50 Jahre nach Bergen-Belsen*. Jerusalem: Verlag Rubin Mass, 1995.

Santin, Tullia. *Der Holocaust in den Zeugnissen griechischer Jüdinnen und Juden*. Berlin: Duncker & Humblot, 2003.

Saporta, Maria. "50th Anniversary of Alliance Francaise School, a Time to Honor My Mother." *Saporta Report* (blog), September 8, 2013. https://saportareport.com/50th-anniversary-of-alliance-francaise-school-a-time-to-honor-my-mother/columnists/mariasmetro/maria_saporta/.

Saraphis, Stephanos G. *ELAS: Greek Resistance Army*. London: Merlin, 1980.

Schneiderman, Harry, and Morris Fine, eds. *The American Jewish Yearbook*. Vol. 50. Philadelphia, PA: The Jewish Publication Society of America, 1948.

Schwarz, Guri. *After Mussolini: Jewish Life and Jewish Memories in Post-Fascist Italy*. London: Vallentine Mitchell, 2012.

Seder, Deno. *Miracle at Zakynthos: The Only Greek Jewish Community Saved in Its Entirety from Annihilation*. Washington, DC: Philos Press, LLC, 2014.

Selioti, Vasiliki. *Vretanika stratopeda Evreon prosfygon stin Kypro (1946–1949) [British Camps for Jewish Refugees in Cyprus, 1946–1949]*. Thessaloniki: Epikentro, 2016.

Shephard, Ben. *After Daybreak: The Liberation of Belsen, 1945*. London: Jonathan Cape, 2005.

Sigal, John J., and Morton Weinfeld. *Trauma and Rebirth: Intergenerational Effects of the Holocaust*. New York: Praeger, 1989.

Sinani, Shaban. *Hebrenjtë në Shqipëri: Prania dhe shpëtimi [Jews in Albania: Presence and Rescue]*. Tirana: Naimi, 2009.

Skalidakis, Giannis. *I exousia tou EAM sta chronia tis Katochis 1943–1944 [The Power of the EAM during the Occupation, 1943–1944]*. Athens: Asini, 2014.

Sofsky, Wolfgang. *The Order of Terror*. Princeton: Princeton University Press, 1997.

Spiliotis, Susanne-Sophia. "An Affair of Politics, Not Justice: The Merten Trial (1957–1959) and Greek-German Relations." In *After the War Was Over: Reconstructing the Family, Nation, and State in Greece, 1943–1960*, edited by Mark Mazower, 293–302. Princeton, NJ: Princeton University Press, 2000.

Stankova, Marietta. *Bulgaria in British Foreign Policy, 1943–1949*. London: Anthem Press, 2014.

Stavrianos, Leften Stavros. "The Jews of Greece." *Journal of Central European Affairs* 8, no. 3 (1948): 256–69.

———. "The Mutiny in the Greek Armed Forces, April 1944." *The American Slavic and East European Review* 9, no. 4 (December 1950): 302–11.

Stavrou, Nikolaos. "The Little Country with the Big Gulag." *The Washington Post*, December 9, 1984.

Stavroulakis, Nicholas. "The Fate of the Material Evidence of the Jews of Greece." *Journal of Modern Hellenism* 23–24 (2006–2007): 113–40.

Stefatos, Katherine. "Engendering the Nation: Women, State Oppression and Political Violence in Post-war Greece (1946–1974)." PhD diss., Goldsmiths, University of London, 2012.

Steinbacher, Sybille. *Auschwitz: Geschichte und Nachgeschichte*. Munich: C.H. Beck, 2007.

Stone, Dan. *Concentration Camps: A Short History*. Oxford: Oxford University Press, 2017.

———. *Goodbye to All That?: The Story of Europe Since 1945*. Oxford, UK: Oxford University Press, 2014.

———. *The Liberation of the Camps: The End of the Holocaust and Its Aftermath*. New Haven: Yale University Press, 2015.

Styron, William. *Sophie's Choice*. New York: Random House, 1979.

Szulc, Tad. *The Secret Alliance: The Extraordinary Story of the Rescue of the Jews since World War II*. London: Pan, 1993.

Tamir, Vicki. *Bulgaria and Her Jews: The History of a Dubious Symbiosis*. New York: Sepher-Hermon Press for Yeshiva University Press, 1979.

Taylor, Derek August. *Don Pacifico: The Acceptable Face of Gunboat Diplomacy*. London: Vallentine Mitchell, 2008.

Tomai, Photini. *Greeks in Auschwitz-Birkenau*. Athens: Papazisis, 2009.

Tsekou, Katerina. *Ellines politiki prosfyges stin Anatoliki Europi, 1945–1989 [Greek Civil Refugees in East Europe, 1945–1989]*. Athens: Alexandria, 2013.

Tsigala, Flora. "UNRRA's Relief Efforts in Post-War Greece: Political Impartiality versus Military Exigencies." In *Bearing Gifts to Greeks: Humanitarian Aid to Greece in the 1940s*, edited by Richard Clogg. Basingstoke, UK: Palgrave Macmillan, 2008.

Tzafleris, Nikos. "Persecution and Rescue of the Jews of Volos during the Holocaust in Greece 1943–1944." In *Hiding, Sheltering, and Borrowing Identities: Avenues of Rescue during the Holocaust*, edited by Dan Michman, 125–43. Jerusalem: Yad Vashem, 2017.

———. "Rebuilding Jewish Communities after the Holocaust: The American Jewish Joint Distribution Committee's Relief Programme in Postwar Greece." *Historein* 18, no. 2 (2019).

Tzoukas, Vangelis. *O EDES 1941–1945 [The National Republican Greek League, 1941–1945]*. Athens: Alexandria, 2017.

Varon-Vassard, Odette. "Der Genozid an den griechischen Juden: Zeugnisse des Überlebens und Geschichtsschreibung seit 1948." In *Die Okkupation Griechenlands im Zweiten Weltkrieg: Griechische und deutsche Erinnerungskultur*, edited by Chryssoula Kambas and Marilisa Mitsou, 85–114. Cologne: Böhlau, 2015.

———. "Voix de femmes: Témoignages de jeunes filles juives grecques survivantes de la Shoah." *Cahiers Balkaniques* 43 (December 2015). http://journals.openedition.org/ceb/8528.

Vassilikou, Maria. "Griechenland." In *Die Verfolgung und Ermordung der europäischen Juden durch das nationalsozialistische Deutschland, 1933–1945*, vol. 14, edited by Sara Berger,

Erwin Lewin, Sanela Schmid, and Maria Vassilikou. Berlin: de Gruyter Oldenbourg, 2017.

Vervenioti, Tasoula. *Anaparastasis tis Istorias [Representations of History]*. Athens: Melissa, 2009.

———. *Diplo Vivlio; I afigisi tis Stamatias Mparmpatsi - I istoriki anagnosi [Double Book: The Narrative of Stamatia Barbatsi. A Historical Reading]*. Athens: Koykkida, 2017.

———. *I Gyneka tis Antistasis. I isodos ton gynekon stin politiki [The Woman of the Resistance: Women's Entry into Politics]*. Athens: Odysseas, 1994.

———. "12 October 1944, Liberation, Trauma, and Memorialization in Greece." *Journal of Modern Greek Studies Occasional Papers*, no. 2 (2014): 1–12.

Vlavianos, Haris. *Greece, 1941–49: From Resistance to Civil War. The Strategy of the Greek Communist Party*. New York: St. Martin's Press, 1992.

Voglis, Polymeris. *Becoming a Subject: Political Prisoners in the Greek Civil War*. New York: Berghahn, 2002.

Voglis, Polymeris, and Ioannis Nioutsikos. "The Greek Historiography of the 1940s: A Reassessment." *Südosteuropa* 65, no. 2 (2017): 316–33.

Wachsmann, Nikolaus. *KL: A History of the Nazi Concentration Camps*. 2015. Reprint, London: Little, Brown, 2016.

Waltzer, Kenneth. "Moving Together, Moving Alone: The Story of Boys on a Transport from Auschwitz to Buchenwald." In *Jewish Families in Europe, 1939–Present: History, Representation and Memory*, edited by Joanna B. Michlic, 85–109. Waltham, MA: Brandeis University Press, 2017.

Ward, James Mace. *Priest, Politician, Collaborator: Jozef Tiso and the Making of Fascist Slovakia*. Ithaca, NY: Cornell University Press, 2013.

Yablonka, Hanna, and Ora Cummings. *The State of Israel vs. Adolf Eichmann*. New York: Schocken, 2004.

Yerushalmi, Yosef Hayim. "Response to Rosemary Ruether." In *Auschwitz: Beginning of a New Era? Reflections on the Holocaust*, edited by Eva Fleischner, 97–107. New York: KTAV, 1977.

Index

NOTE: Page numbers in *italics* indicate tables.

Afghanistan, 11
Africa, 66, 79, 122, 144, 152, 160, 182, 193, 254n33
Aggelochori, 31
Agrinio, 42–43
Aide aux Israélites Victimes de la Guerre (AIVG), 105, 120
Aigio, 38
Akko, 164
Albala, Jacques, 138–42, 162
Albala, Laura, 142
Albania, 160–62, 196, 255n37
Alchanatis, Daniel, 24
Aleppo, 63, 168–69
Alexandria, 162
Alexandroupoli, 35, 94, 96, *117*
Algeria, 171
Alhadeff, Solomon, 151
Alice, Princess of Greece, 62
Aliyah, 55, 71, 108, 163–64
Allalouf, Edgar, 65
Alliance Israélite Universelle, 146
Allied Commission, 108
Altcheh, Ester, 133
Altcheh, Polina, 106
Alvo, Danny, 63–64
Alvo, Haim (Miko), 63–64
Amaratzi, René (née Matalon), 29
Amarilio, Margarette, 33
Amarilio, Rudolf, 21
Amarilio, Salomon, 33
American Jewish Joint Distribution Committee. *See* Joint Distribution Committee (JDC)

Anatolia, 167
And Yet Not All of Them Died (Matarasso), 1
Ankara, 158
anti-communism, xi, 51, 54, 61, 73, 76, 156, 222n11
antisemitism, 6, 22, 151–52, 172, 179, 197
Apulia, 108
Arcadia, 155
Argentina, 6, 164
Arolsen Archives, 11
Arouch, Jackos, 64
Arta, 35, 109
Aryanization, 28, 180, 216n51
Ashkenazi, 6, 9–10, 145
assimilation, 17–18
Association of Jewish Hostages of Greece, 91, 103
Association of Tenants of Jewish Property in Northern Greece (SMIAVE), 180
Athens, 6, 17–27, 35–36, 52, 57, *87*, *177*
Auschwitz, 27, 30–31, 37, 40, 42, 48, 70, 91–92, 158
Auschwitz-Birkenau, 55, 85, 87, 96–135, 194–95
Australia, 31
Austria, 3, 116–117, 129, 138
Avdela, Eftyhia (née Negris), 168–69
Azouvi, François, 12

Bakolas, Salvator, 55
Balasteras, Ilias, 40
Balkans, 5, 32, 153
Balkan Wars, 7, 154
Baltic Sea, 126
Baltimore, 71

Bankier, David, 2
Bank of Greece, 62
Barcelona, 170–71
Bari, 129, 149, 163
Barki, Rafael, 167
Barki, Solomon, 167
Baron Hirsch ghetto, Thessaloniki, 114, 123
Barouch, Isodor, 44
Barouch, Rachil, 44
Barouch-Levis Bank (Universal Bank), 44
Barth, subcamp of Ravensbrück, 126, 130
Barzilai, Bella, 141, 149
Barzilai, Elias (Rabbi of Athens), 22, 24, 59, 61, 81
Batis, Astro, 86
Batis, Leon, 85–86
Batis, Sofia, 85
Battle of Athens, 52–61
Battle of Crete, 39, 62
Bauman, Zygmunt, 189
Beirut, 169
Belgium, 131, 152–53, 193
Belitsa, 155–56, 236n36
Belomorie, 97–98, 155
belonging, 6–7
Benadon, David, 145–47
Benaroya, Abraham, 253n19
Benaroya, Marios, 157, 253n19
Benousiglio, David, 24, 167
Benousiglio, Graciella, 33
Benousiglio, Pepo, 24
Benroubi, Acher, 168
Benroubi, Lili-Nina (née Revah), 171, 173
Benroubi, Matilda (née Pisante), 151
Benvasat, Bella, 155
Benveniste, Adolfo, 172

298 · INDEX

Benveniste, Dick, 59, 68–69, 226n40
Benveniste, Flora, 146
Benveniste, Raymonde, 172
Benveniste, Rika, 8, 68, 141, 226n40, 228n75
Bergen-Belsen, 27, 34–35, 87, 92, 94, 100, 107, 110, 120, 133–50
Berlin, 105, 126, 147, 166
Beth-Saul Synagogue, Thessaloniki, 182
Beti-Hatzi, Astro (née Batis), 189
Beza, Claire (née Matalon, Altcheh from first marriage), 132–34
Beza, Mois, 163
Beza, Yvet, 163–64
Birkenau, 109–10
Bitola, 154, 163
black market, 88
blood libel, 7, 207n25
Bosnia and Herzegovina, 191
Botton, Anry, 157–58
Botton, Markos, 156–57
Bourlas, Dora, 73–74, 81
Bourlas, Moisis, 81–83
Bowman, Steven B., 50, 222n12, 228n74
Bratislava, 142
British Army, 57, 61, 63, 83, 110, 140, 164
British Middle East Forces, 51, 172
Broudo, David, 81–82, 232n118
Browning, Christopher, 12
Brunner, Alois, 162–63
Brussels, 105, 120, 126, 131, 148, 153
Bucharest, 114, 142
Buchenwald, 100, 133
Budapest, 118, 142
Budy, subcamp of Auschwitz-Birkenau, 112
Bukovina, 114
Bulgaria, 2, 6, 20, 35, 92, 94, 96, 236n39; anti-Jewish policy in, 152; escapes to, 196; Jewish Agency and, 64; Jews in, 154–155; liberation

of, 19; Macedonia and, 22, 154; occupation by, 51; in Soviet Bloc, 158
Bulgarian National Bank, 94
Buljkes, 156, 158

Cadiz, 171
Cairo, 61–65, 73, 163
camps, 21, 26–27, 64, 66, 89–90. See also Auschwitz; Bergen-Belsen; Dachau; Echterdingen; Gellenau; Mauthausen; Ravensbrück; Santa Maria di Bagni, Italy (DP camp); Theresienstadt; Treblinka
Carasso, Avraam, 50
Carasso, Flora, 146, 149–50
Carasso, Mordochai, 72
Carbonara di Bari (DP camp), 108
Casablanca, 171
Caserta Agreement, 54
Cassouto, Isaac, 44–45
Cassouto, Israel, 103
cemetery. See Jewish cemetery
Central Board of the Jewish Communities (KIS), 8, 23–25, 44–46, 48, 60–62, 97, 143, 160, 176, 180
Central Relief Committee, 176
Cesarani, David, 136
Çeşme, 63
Chaidari (Haidari) camp, 26–27, 109, 111–12
Chalcis, 41–42, 44, 72, 87, 109, 168, 177, 184
Chalkidiki, 157
Chalkidis, Dimitris, 71
Chania, 40
Chasson (Hasson), Vital, 162
Chernivtsi, 114
children, in camps, 100–13, 132, 147–58
Chronakis, Paris Papamichos, 9
Chrysostomos (Bishop of Zakynthos), 45
Chrysoupoli, 94

Churchill, Winston, 56, 65, 196
citizenship, 7, 81, 135, 138, 153–54, 159
Civil War (Greek, 1946—1949), 9, 42, 51–53, 70–72, 76, 81–84, 111, 178
Cohen, Albertos, 81
Cohen, Alfred, 26, 61–63, 176, 193
Cohen, Chaimaki, 62
Cohen, Daniel, 40
Cohen, Jacques, 62
Cohen, Leon, 160
Cohen, Michel, 62
Cohen, Nina, 160
Cohen, Rachel, 62
Cohen, Tilde, 62
Cold War, 51–52, 54, 136
Cole, Tim, 11
collaboration, 40–41, 142–43, 157, 228n75
collective identity, 5–6
Communist Party of Czechoslovakia, ix, 50–51
Communist Party of Greece (Kommounistiko Komma Ellados, KKE), 8, 42, 50, 54, 75–76
Communist Youth (Omospondia Kommounistikon Neoleon Elladas, OKNE), 75, 81
Confino, Iosif, 96
confiscation, of property, 162, 179
Constantine, King of Greece, 62
Contemporary Social History Archives (ASKI), 47
Corfu, 7, 35, 40, 70, 87, 87, 107–8, 195
Council of Elders, 138, 145, 147
Cracow, 87
Crete, 19, 39–40, 62
Croatia, 77
Curtis, George, 21
Cyprus, 2, 159
Czech, Danuta, 99
Czechoslovakia (Czechia), ix–xi, 3, 142, 175, 194

INDEX · 299

Dachau, 100, 124, 242n103
Dalven, Rae, 51
Damaskinos (Archbishop of
    Athens), 56
Danieli, Yael, 4
Day of Remembrance, 185
December Events, 54–56, 80, 175
Dekemhare (POW camp), 66
denunciation, 23, 25, 31, 71, 132
deportation, 86–87, 93, 103
de Romero Radigales,
    Sebastián (Spanish consul
    in Greece), 27, 153
Didymoticho, 123–24, 177
Dimitriou, Dimitri (alias
    Nikiforos), 59–60
Djivre, Israel, 124
Dodecanese, 2, 6, 22
Dolma, Toula, 55
Drama, Greece, 35, 92, 94, 97, 155
Dupnitsa, 96

Earthquake, 87
Ebensee, 117–18, 125, 128
Echterdingen, 124
Ecole de l'Alliance Française,
    147
Egypt, 2, 6, 54, 61–66, 151,
    162, 168
Eichmann, Adolf, 9–10, 23,
    209n37, 210n39
El-Daba, 79–80, 231n109
Eleftheroupoli, 94, 96
English language, 8, 13, 37, 66,
    123, 128, 178, 210n45
Epirus, 121, 125
Epirus Jews, 160–61
Eskaloni, Moise, 59
Euboea, 63, 167–68
Evert, Angelos, 56
Evros, 124
"exchange Jews," 87–88, 136
executions, 29, 50, 71, 76, 81,
    142, 162–63, 167
Ezratty, Salomon, 171

Falangist Militia, 170
famine, 15, 28, 37, 58

Fascio, 183
Fédala (Fedhala; today,
    Mohammedia), 171–72
Fellous, Chryssoula, 75–76
Felous-Kapeta, Allegra, 75–76
Finkel, Evgeny, 50
Fleming, Katherine E., 9
Florentin, Ester (née Altcheh),
    133
Florentin, Maidy, 33
Florina, 109
Folegandros, 75
forced labor, 28, 35, 69–71,
    87, 95–96, 105, 112–115, 123,
    128, 133–135, 138, 140, 144,
    155, 162
France, 112, 118, 148, 152, 153,
    158, 163, 171, 172, 193
Franco, Allegra, 154
Frank, Anne, 30
Franko, Leon, 132
Frizis, Mordechai, 48
Futures Past (Koselleck), 5

Gabbai, Dario, 115–19, 128
Gabbai, Jacob, 115–19, 128
Gabbai, Victor, 115
Galicia, 6
Gallipoli, 155
Gani, Rachel, 122
Gani, Renee, 121–22
Gara Belitsa, 155
Garfinkle, Bouena (née
    Sarfati), 72–73
Gartner, Frank, 147
Garwood, Alfred, 139
Gatenio, Israel, 109
Gattegnio, Isaac, 170
Gattegnio, Nata (née Eftychia
    Osmo), 106–9, 113, 115
Gavriilidis, Gavriil, 65–66
Gaza, 169
Gellenau, 107
Geni, Sam, 33
Gennadios (Metropolitan
    Bishop in Thessaloniki),
    181–82
Germany, 94, 104, 112, 128,
    161, 221n104; Federal

Republic of Germany,
    91, 125, 162, 180; German
    Democratic Republic, 76;
    Nazi Germany, 2, 10, 19, 20,
    35, 64, 92, 97, 117, 151, 152,
    157, 158, 161, 195, 201; and
    occupation of Greece, 15, 27,
    51, 102, 128
Gjirokastër (Argyrokastro),
    255n37
Glicksman, Marguerite, 82
Glyfada, 79
Gorna Dzhumaya (today,
    Blagoevgrad), 96
Goudi, 231n109
Government of National
    Unity, 19
Grammos, 156
Greco-Italian War, 23, 42, 48–
    50, 69, 80, 115, 151, 183, 193
Greco-Turkish War, 7
Greece: invasion and division
    of, 22; liberation of, 4, 15,
    17–21; map of, 14; overview
    of Jews of, 5–8
Greek Army, 36, 50–51, 64, 66,
    69, 125–26, 158, 211n53
Greek Commune, 156
Greek Constitution, 7
Greek language, 7, 8, 16, 20
Greekness, 7, 41, 109
Greek Orthodox Church, 2,
    7–8, 23, 153, 180–81, 208n27
Greek People's Liberation
    Army (Ellinikos Laikos
    Apeleutherotikos Stratos,
    ELAS), 55, 73; Botton and,
    156–157; collaborators and,
    69; Communists and, 81;
    Gentille and, 39; in German
    withdrawal, 68; hideouts
    and, 26, 33; in liberation, 19,
    41; mutiny and, 65; Nehama
    and, 76–78; number of
    fighters in, 61; partisans,
    57, 62; persecution and, 52;
    Pesach and, 60; in postwar
    scramble, 54–55; resistance
    and, 38, 45, 50, 70; Varon
    in, 155

300 · INDEX

Greek Zionist Club, Tel Aviv, 164
Grinberg, Natan, 155
Gross-Rosen, 125, 127
Gusen, 118

Hachsharah, 55, 107, 109, 115
Haidari camp. *See* Chaidari (Haidari) camp
Haifa, 164, 169, 172
Haim, Allegra, 36–37
Haim, Eliezer, 36–37
Haim, Laura, 36–38
Haim, Sarah, 36–37
Hamburg, 110
Hanover, 87
Hantzaroula, Pothiti, 28
Hassid family, 131, 153
Haviva Reik, 55, 108, 115
Hebrew language, 8, 13, 66, 103, 107, 108, 121, 123, 169, 178
Helleno-Christianity, 153
Hillersleben, 147–48
Hirsch, Marianne, 189
Hitachduth Oley Yavan. *See* Union of Jews from Greece in Palestine
Hitler, Adolf, 151
Hlinka Guards, 157
Hoxha, Enver, 161
Hungary, 6, 116, 179

Idas-Gavrilidis, Leon, 70–71
identity: collective, 5–6; national, 8, 103–4, 153
Illusion of Safety (Matsas), 160
inflation, 58, 88
Institution of Professional Rehabilitation, 176
intermarriage, ix, 21, 32–33
International Committee of the Red Cross. *See* Red Cross
International Tracing Service (ITS), 11–12
interwar period, 32, 154, 164
Ioannina, 6–7, 40, 51–52, 71, 87, 109, 184, 195

Ionian Islands, 6
Iran, 6
Iraq, 11
Israel, 9, 55, 58, 81, 185
Istanbul, 158
Italy, 6, 17, 18, 22, 24, 34, 51, 61, 64, 70, 90, 107, 108, 118, 119, 132, 145, 148–49, 153, 159, 162–63, 182–83, 216n44, 223n18
Izmir, 64, 159, 167–68

Jacobson, Gaynor I., 11, 17, 23, 25, 62, 73, 88, 90–91, 149; on camp conditions, 134; on housing, 179–81, 194; Joint Distribution Committee and, 175; Kavala and, 98; Koretz family and, 142; Kounio and, 129; legacy of, 194; on survivors, 100–102
Jaffa, Israel, 164
Jeanne d'Arc refugee camp, Philippeville, 171
Jerusalem, xi, 24, 32, 58, 60
Jewish Agency, 64, 168
Jewish Brigade, 107
Jewish cemetery: Arta, 109; Athens, 228n66; Thessaloniki, 32; Thrace, 92
Jewish Community, 2, 5, 17, 20, 42. *See also* Central Board of the Jewish Communities (KIS)
Jewish Secret Rescue Committee, 24
Jews and the Liberation Struggle, The, 47
Joint Distribution Committee (JDC), 10–11, 26, 47, 59, 76, 82; Albania and, 160; Central Board and, 143; Cohen and, 61; December Events and, 58; Gabbai and, 119; Jacobson and, 17; Nehama and, 149; Spain and, 170–71; Turkey and, 158; Uziel and, 24–25; Varvaressos and, 88

Judenaktion, 107
Judenrat, 135
Judeo-Spanish (language), 6, 15, 105, 112, 142, 146, 178
junta, in Greece, 51, 60

Kadima, 164
Kalavia-Charathra, 42
Kamchi, Isaac, 77
Kamchi, Miko, 77
Kamchi, Mois, 66
Kamhi, Raphael, 155
Kanada Kommando, 103
Kantor, Lina (née Amato), 159–60
Karditsa, 42, 76
Karia, 69
Karrer, Loukas, 45
Kastoria, 35, 40, 103, 109, 132, 164, 195
Katerini, 41–42
Katowice, 127, 141
Katzki, Herbert, 82
Kavaje camp, Korçë, 162
Kavala, 35, 37, 92, 94–98, 155–56
Kazantzidis, Panagiotis, 31
Kerem, Yitzchak, 13
Kidron, Carol, x
Kielce, 179
Kifissia, 168
Kilkis, 68–69
Kishinev, 6
Koen, Gentille, 38–39, 80
Koen, Germaine (née Matalon), 132
Koen, Louis, 80–81
Koen, Loykia, 31
Koen, Rozita, 72
Koen, Salomon, 55
Kolinsky, Eva, 242n103
Kolonomos, Jamila, 77
Kolonomos, Sarah, 154
Komotini, 35, 38, 94, 96–97, 177
Konis, David, 64
Konstantinis, Kanaris, 25, 192
Konstantinis, Minos, 43
Konstantinis, Mois, 25, 46

INDEX · 301

Korçë, 161
Koretz, Gita, 140–43
Koretz, Leo, 140–43
Koretz, Zvi (Rabbi of
 Salonica), 41, 62, 137–43, 195
Kos, 35, 40
Koselleck, Reinhart, 5
Koula, 110, 131
Kounio, Edgar, 139, 162
Kounio, Erika, 130–31
Kounio, Heinz, 128–29
Kounio, Hella, 128, 130–31
Kounio, Salvator, 128–30
Kounne, Elias, 161
Kounne, Mari, 161
Kunmadaras, 179

Labor, forced, 28, 35, 69–71,
 87, 95–96, 105, 112–15, 123,
 128, 133–35, 138, 140, 144,
 155, 162
Ladino, 6. See also
 Judeo-Spanish
Lagrou, Pieter, 9
Langer, Lawrence, 264n7
language, 6, 8, 13, 16, 20, 176–
 178. See also Judeo-Spanish
Larissa, 41–42, 44–45, 76,
 86; Chaidari and, 109;
 independent operation of,
 177; postwar population of
 Jewish Communities in,
 87; Reception Center for
 Deportees from German
 Concentration Camps at, 88
László, Ágnes, 119
László, Rosalia, 119
Laufen POW camp, 157
Lausanne Treaty, 7
Law of Return, 185
Lebanon, 168
Lecce, 108
Lefkada, 107
Leon, Moris, 32
Levi, Alberto, 113–15
Levi, Allegra, 114–15
Levi, Dario, 113–15
Levi, Dora, 65
Levi, Ketty, 147–48

Levi, Primo, 134
Levis, Errikos, 125–26, 161
Levis, Joseph, 161–62
Levis, Minos, 62–63
Levy, Rudolf, 136, 144–45
Lewkowicz, Bea, 8–9, 33, 181,
 260n16
liberation, 4, 15, 17–21,
 35–36, 90, 110; accounts
 of, 147; deaths after, 122;
 of Neutrals Camp, 147–58;
 starvation and, 242n103
Libya, 65, 79
Lisbon, 158
Lom, 96
looting, 126, 148
Lovinger, Joseph, 167
Löwi, Hella. See Kounio, Hella
Lublin, 97, 114

Macedonia, 19, 77, 119,
 154–55, 158, 179, 264n7
Madrid, 136, 143, 153, 171
Magdeburg, 147
Magen David Adom, 107,
 115, 142
Maisis, Solomon, 44
Makronisos, 71
Malchow, subcamp of
 Ravensbrück, 103–4, 121
Mannheim, 127
Marcos, Albert, 174
Marmaris, 159
marriage, mixed. See
 intermarriage
Massarano, Stella (née
 Tchemino), 100, 119–21
Matalon, Fanny (née
 Florentin), 72
Matalon, Frida, 161
Matalon, Leon, 72
Matalon, Mois, 29–30
Matarasso, Isaac, 1, 32–33,
 85–86, 89
Matathia, Mateo, 161–62
Matathia family, 161–62
Matsas, David, 44, 221n105,
 223n19
Matsas, Joseph, 52

Matsas, Leon, 43
Matsas, Michael, 42–43, 125,
 160, 162
Matsas, Ninetta, 42–43
Mauthausen, 107, 117–18, 128
Mazur, Belle, 233n7
McGeer, Victoria, 190
Mecklenburg, 121
Melk, 125, 128
Menasche, Albert, 131–32
Menasche, Lillian, 131–32
Merten, Max, 162
Metaxas, Ioannis, 27, 48
methodology, 11–13
Mevorach, Benjamin, 155
Mexico, 173
Middle East, 23, 33, 44, 51–52,
 56, 61–66, 108, 158, 166,
 172, 196
Milan, 107, 129
minors, in camps, 100–13
Mizan, Isaak, 109–111, 113
Mizan, Savvas, 43
Mizrachi, Samouil, 108–9
Modena, 107
Modiano, Arthur, 182
Modiano, Charles, 182
Modiano, Elie, 64, 182–84
Modiano, Sam, 24–25
Modiano Market, 182
Moissis, Asher, 22–24, 34, 48,
 51–52, 192, 210n39
Moissis, Daisy (née Carasso),
 71–72
Moissis, Esdra, 44–45
Moissis, Isaac (alias Kitsos),
 69, 228n74
Molcho, Erietti, 27
Molho, Michael, 26, 28, 33–34,
 150, 162, 214n22
Molho, Rena, 13, 139
Molho Kapoyanno, Yvonni, 27
Molotov-Ribbentrop Pact, 50
Monastir (today, Bitola), 154–55
Monastir Synagogue, 28, 181
moral code, 51
Morocco, 171
Moshav Tsur Moshe, 164
Mourtzoukos, Anselmos,
 43–44

302 · INDEX

Mourtzoukos, Paulette. *See*
Nehama, Paulette
Mourtzoukos, Yola, 43
Munich, 105, 127
Myers, Edmund, 63
Mylonas, Harris, 209n30

Nachama, Itzchak, 9
Nachmia, Berry (née Buena
Cassuto), 103–7, 109–10, 113,
238n60
Nahmia, Nina Kokkalidou,
253n19
Nachmias, Albertos, 163–64
Nachmias, Mentes, 106
Nachmias, Nelli (née
Tampach), 38, 56
Nachmias, Samuel, 34–35
Nahon, Chaim, 123–24, 128
Nahon, Marco, 122–25
Naousa, 31, 73–74
National Bank of Greece, 42
Nea Orestias, 124, *177*
Nea Zichni, 94
Negrin, Albertos, 162
Negris, Abraam, 44
Negris family, 168
Nehama, Dario, 154
Nehama, Isaac, 76–80, 84,
231n101
Nehama, Joseph, 24, 144–46,
149–50, 214n22, 223n18
Nehama, Meko (Norman),
77, 111
Nehama, Paulette (née
Mourtzoukou), 16–17, 21,
43–44, 79–80, 189
Nehama, Sam, 77, 111–13
Netanya, 164
Netherlands, 145
Neutrals Camp, 136, 143–50, 170
New York, 82, 100, 124
Nissim, Albertos, 66
Nissim, Samouil, 66
Nissim, Suzanne (née
Tchemino), 119–21
Novitch, Miriam, 231n109
Nuremberg Laws, 152
Nuseirat camp, 172, 259n70

Odessa, 6
Odyssey, The (Homer), 40
Ofer, Dalia, 12
Office for the Disposal of
Jewish Property (Ypiresia
Diachiriseos Israilitikon
Periousion, YDIP), 28–29,
179–80
Office of Military
Government, United States
(OMGUS), 112
Ohrdruf (subcamp of
Buchenwald), 110, 124
Omonia Square, Athens, 57
Operation Barbarossa, 50
Oranienburg, 110
Organization for the Relief
and Rehabilitation of the
Jews of Greece (OPAIE), 180
Osmo, Ika, 108
Osmo, Rina, 108
Ottoman Empire, 5–6, 153,
207n26

Palestine, 2, 10, 58, 64, 92, 103,
164–74
Palestine Discount Bank, 164
Panariti family, 161
Pan-Hellenism, 185
Papandreou, Giorgos, Sr.,
55, 68
Pardo, Haim, 30
Pardo, Lili, 30
Pardo, Rozina, 30
Parks, Gordon, ix
Patras, 6, 41–42, *87*, 108–9,
177, 184
Pavlos Melas camp, 29, 72, 115,
156, 162
Peloponnese, 17, 19, 41, 106–7,
155, *177*
Percentages Agreement, 50
Peres, Yitzhak, 83
Pesah, Allegra, 60
Pesah, David, 60
Pesah, Iosif, 60
Pesah, Moshe (Rabbi of Volos),
59–60
Pesah, Simeon, 60

Philippeville, 171
Pietra Neamţ, 217n61
Piraeus, 149, 172
Pisante, Haim, 151–52
Plovdiv, 155
pogroms, 6, 152, 179, 182
Poland, 16, 41, 48, 50, 87, 89,
127, 179. *See also* Union of
Jewish Deportees of Poland
police, 2, 56, 78, 79, 88, 94, 95,
162, 174
population exchange, 7, 155
Portbou, 170
Portugal, 6, 20, 195
Preveza, 35, 40, 42, 121–22
prisoners of war (POWs), 27,
100, 104, 106, 110, 130, 135
Projekt Riese, 125
property, 28–29, 179–81, 194.
See also restitution
prostitution, 89
*Protocols of the Elders of Zion,
The*, 151–52
Psychiko, 38–39

Raguhn, 133
Raphael, Robert, 24, 26
Ravensbrück, 103, 121, 126, 130
real estate, 179–80
Recanati, Leon, 164
Red Army, 111, 133
Red Cross, 28, 59, 72–73, 104,
106, 108, 118, 127, 132–33
Rekanati family, 40
resistance, 21, 38, 52–53,
68–76
Resnik, Reuben, 158
restitution, 62, 159, 179–82,
186. *See also* property
Retzow, subcamp of
Ravensbrück, 103
Revah, Izi, 170, 173
Rhodes, Greece, 7, 16, 19, 35,
40, 122, 159–60
Rhodesia, 64, 151
Rice, Wilson, 147–58
"Righteous among the
Nations," 2–3, 27, 161, 182,
218n68

Ritzaleos, Vasilis, 13
Romania, 64, 159
Romaniote Jews, 6, 10, 121, 125
Russia, 6, 21, 189, 191. *See also* Soviet Union
Rwanda, 191

Sachsenhausen, 110
Saki, Leon, 178, 182
Salonika, 19, 34, 175, 179, 205n1
Saltiel, Beniko, 141
Saltiel, Chaim, 34
Saltiel, Moise, 29
Saltiel, Olga, 29
Saltiel, Solomon, 64–65
Sampetai, Raphail, 59
Sandbostel (POW camp), 110
Santa Maria di Bagni, Italy (DP camp), 108
Saporta, Nora, 147
Saporta, Rachel, 172
Sarajevo, 217n61
Security Battalions, 31
Seficha, Andreas, 29–30, 56–57
Sephardic Jews, 6, 8–10, 34, 41, 121, 145, 164, 254n33
Serres, 35, 92, 120
Serror, Lola, 31
Serror, Rachel, 15–16, 21, 30–31
Sevillias, Errikos, 126–27
Sharett, Moshe, 164
Shiby, Barouch, 231n109
Shimshi, Ido (alias Makkabaios), 68
Siaki, Lea-Lily, 210n47
Siakki-Decastro, Elli, 72
siblings, in camps, 113–22
Sidirokastro, 95, 156
Simcha, Alvertos, 36
Simcha, Matilda, 36
Sinai, 163
Skifti, Allegra (née Felous), 230n95. *See also* Felous-Kapeta, Allegra
Skopelos, 32
Skopje, 154
Slovakia, 158, 163, 179
Slovak Jewish Council, 157

Slovak National Uprising, 157
Sochnut, 108
socialism, 51–52
Sofia, 142, 155
Sonderkommando, 110, 116–17, 121
Soriano, Maurice, 159
Soufli, 124
Sounio, 108, 115
Soussi, Elpida, 40
Southern Rhodesia, 64
Soviet Union: army of, 21, 127; attack on, 50; authorities of, 105; as front, 104; in liberation, 114, 118, 130, 142; in Percentages Agreement, 53; prisoners of war from, 110, 135; territory of, 110, 115, 158. *See also* Russia
Spain, 6, 20, 135, 138, 143–44, 147, 152–53, 170–71, 195
Special Court on Collaborators, 142
Sponheim, 127
STALAG VII-A, 65
Stalin, Joseph, 176
Star Camp, 136–43
Stavrianos, Leften, 23
Štip, 154
Stomio, 44
Stone, Dan, 21, 89, 175, 197
Stroop, Jürgen, 24
Stroumza, Menachem, 41
Styron, William, 2
Sudetenland, 191
Suez Crisis, 163
suicide, 99–100
Supreme Headquarters Allied Expeditionary Force (SHAEF), 166
Svolis, Avraam, 71
Switzerland, 6
Syntagma Square, 55–56
Syria, x, 11, 63, 163, 168–69
Szulc, Tad, 11

"Tanais" (Venturas), 40
Tchemino, Stella. *See* Massarano, Stella

Tel Aviv, 164, 169, 172
Thasos, 94
Theresienstadt, 133, 140, 143, 147
Thessaloniki, 6–7, 27–35, 86, 156, 205n1, 211n53; Auschwitz-Birkenau and, 102–3; deportations in, 43, 50, 60, 63; liberation of, 15; opposition in, 57; postwar population of Jewish Communities in, 87; resistance in, 68–70; Salonika and, 19; Sephardic Jews in, 16; Spanish Jews in, 136; survivors in, 195; Treblinka and, 96; Visual History Archive and, 12–13
Thessaly, 70
Thrace, 19, 35–36, 155, 158, 253n23
Tirana, 160
Tiso, Jozef, 157
tobacco, 94–95, 98
Tomai-Constantopoulou, Photini, 83
Topolčany, 102
Treblinka, 35, 48, 87, 92, 94–98, 154–155, 194
Treviso, 107
"Trial of the Jews," 143
Trikala, 22–23, 41–42, 59, 61, 86, 87, 109, 177, 184
Tsakei, 168
Tsimino, Jacques, 95–96
Tsimino, Sampetai, 95–96, 155–56
Turiel family, 159
Turkey, 2, 6, 7, 61, 63, 145, 158–59, 168, 196, 253n23
Tzafleris, Nikos, 53
Tzezanas, Erkanas, 16, 45–46

Udine, 118
Ukraine, 11, 189, 191
Union Bank, 146
Union of Jewish Deportees of Poland, 89, 150, 176

304 · INDEX

Union of Jews from Greece in Palestine (Hitachduth Oley Yavan), 58, 140, 167, 169, 257n51
United Greek Youth Organization (Eniea Panelliniki Organosi Neon, EPON), 45, 61, 72–73
United Kingdom, 6, 21, 54, 65, 131.. *See also* British Army
United Nations Relief and Rehabilitation Administration (UNRRA), 58–59, 61, 88, 102, 112, 122, 141, 155, 166, 171–72
United States, 6, 21, 37, 42, 65, 71, 72, 79, 80, 88, 90, 100, 106, 119, 121, 122, 125, 142, 147, 159, 160, 174, 185. *See also* US Army
US Army, 107, 112, 118, 124, 128, 147–58
Uziel, Ben-Zion (Sephardic Chief Rabbi in Jerusalem), 24
Uziel, Salomon, 142

Vardar Macedonia, 35, 154
Varkiza Agreement, 59, 68, 71, 76, 86, 156

Varon, Leon, 155
Varvaressos, Kyriakos, 88
Veľké Topoľčany, 179
Venezia, Mois, 115–17, 128
Venezia, Shlomo, 115–19, 128
Venizelos, Eleftherios, 8
Venturas, Iossif, 40
Venturas family, 39–40
Veria, 41, 87, 220n92
Vienna, 95–96, 118, 136, 138, 143
Vistula River, 114
Visual History Archive (VHA), 10, 12–13, 41, 65, 149, 210n46, 242n103
Vitsi, 156
Vlorë, 160, 255n37
Vlorë Community, 161
Vojvodina, 156
Volos, 6, 41–44, 72, 86, 87, 109, 177
Vratsa, 236n36
Vrba, Rudolf, 102

Warsaw Ghetto Uprising, 24, 48, 114
Wehrmacht, 19, 52, 54, 62, 74
Weimar, 124
Weiss, Joseph, 136, 141, 143
Weiss, Klaus-Albert, 143

Welzer, Alfred, 102
Wiernik, Yankel, 97
Wisliceny, Dieter, 162–63
Wolfsberg, 125
women, 71–76, 89, 99, 132
World Jewish Congress, 140, 182
World War I, 7, 57

Xanthi, 35, 38, 92, 94, 236n36

Yad Vashem, 27, 48
Yakoel, Yomtov, 23–24, 34, 210n39
Yesoua, Sara, 72–73
Yiddish language, 242n100
Yom Kippur, 99
Yosafat, Matthew, 42
Yugoslavia, 94, 154, 160

Zakynthos, 16, 25, 41, 45, 86, 87
Žilina, 157
Zimbabwe, 64
Zionism, 18, 23, 44, 54, 103, 146, 164
Zionist Federation of Greece, 176

ABOUT THE AUTHOR

KATEŘINA KRÁLOVÁ is professor of contemporary history and a memory studies scholar at Charles University in Prague and the Czech Academy of Science. This is her first book in English.